SUPERS

INTERNATIONAL TAXATION

IN A NUTSHELL®

TENTH EDITION

RICHARD L. DOERNBERG
Emeritus Professor of Law
Emory University School of Law

WEST
ACADEMIC
PUBLISHING

COPYRIGHT © 1989, 1993, 1997, 1999 WEST PUBLISHING CO.
© West, a Thomson business, 2001, 2004, 2009
© 2012 Thomson Reuters
© 2016 LEG, Inc. d/b/a West Academic
    444 Cedar Street, Suite 700
    St. Paul, MN 55101
    1-877-888-1330

West, West Academic Publishing, and West Academic are trademarks of West Publishing Corporation, used under license.

Printed in the United States of America

ISBN: 978-1-62810-555-1

To My Family, including Edie and Noa
who may one day like to see
their names in print
(when they learn how to read)

PREFACE

For those who are or will be involved in international business and investment transactions, it is important to have some basic understanding of the relevant tax laws. This book is intended to serve as an introduction to the U.S. law of international taxation. It is primer aimed at law and accounting students, foreign tax practitioners or scholars, U.S. tax practitioners seeking an introduction to the area or a refresher, and others who might benefit from an overview of the U.S. tax laws governing international trade and investment. The book attempts to summarize the law, offering some attention to the purposes of the various legal rules. However, it is beyond the scope of the book to offer a critical evaluation of the provisions summarized or to delve deeply into tax planning structures and techniques. Actually practicing international tax in reliance solely on this primer could be hazardous to your career.

It will come as no revelation that the U.S. income tax laws are wondrously complex. Moreover, the student of U.S. international tax law should have some grounding in U.S. individual, partnership, state, employment and corporate tax principles. U.S. international tax does not exist in a vacuum. Knowledge of foreign tax systems is also useful. But realistically, many practitioners have their hands full trying to understand the U.S. system and collaborate with foreign colleagues on cross-border transactions. Ironically it is because of the complexity that it is important to present a straight-forward conceptual framework of the U.S. international tax provisions. Even with a framework, the intricate rules governing U.S. taxation of international transactions can be mind-numbing. Without an understanding of the structure of the U.S. international tax provisions (and often even with such an understanding), the rules are all but incomprehensible. Unfortunately, that is all too often the case even with an understanding of the structure.

To use this book effectively, it is helpful to have the Internal Revenue Code open at all times. If you are truly ambidextrous, you should have the Income Tax Regulations at hand as well. Frequent references are made to both the Code and the Regulations. There are some citations to caselaw and administrative rulings where they help illustrate the subject matter. However, the book is not a treatise, and so there is no attempt to treat comprehensively the caselaw and rulings.

To consider fully the international tax laws affecting international trade would require the study not only of U.S. international tax laws but also of foreign tax laws. However, such a study is beyond the scope of this book. So too is any consideration of the non-tax legal concerns affecting international transactions, including private international law, European Union law, the WTO, NAFTA, the internal laws of other nations, customs law, tariffs, and non-tax international treaties. The tax laws of the individual states of the United States are not discussed. The focus here is on U.S. international tax laws and U.S. income tax treaties.

The book is divided into three Parts. After an introduction to the fundamentals of U.S. international taxation and the source rules, the second Part addresses the U.S. activities of foreign taxpayers—that is, investment and business activities carried on by nonresident individuals and foreign corporations in the United States. After a consideration of what a nonresident is for U.S. tax purposes, the basic U.S. jurisdictional tax principles are considered in this Part. Special attention is given to the branch profits tax and the provisions affecting foreign investment in U.S. real estate. Also included in this Part is a chapter on U.S. income tax treaties and a chapter on filing withholding and reporting requirements.

The third Part of the book is directed at foreign activities of U.S. citizens and residents—that is, investment and business activities of U.S. citizens and residents, including domestic corporations that generate income outside the United States. The centerpiece of this Part is a consideration of the U.S. foreign tax credit. This Part also discusses intercompany pricing, controlled foreign corporations, the treatment of foreign currency, and international tax-free transactions. There is also a chapter on tax arbitrage—the heart of much international tax planning. Those income tax provisions regulating the "ethics" of U.S. business behavior abroad are also briefly addressed.

Hopefully, this book kindles an interest in international taxation. If it does, the reader must move beyond this primer into the maw of the Internal Revenue Code, Regulations, rulings and caselaw that make up the substance of U.S. international taxation. In addition, there are ample secondary sources that explore the subject more comprehensively.

The material presented is current through October 15, 2015 with occasional attempts to gaze into the tax crystal ball in order to anticipate likely changes to U.S. international tax law.

I would like to thank George Soba and Ivan Gutierrez for their contributions to Chapter 9 dealing with Intercompany Pricing. They have more years of experience in the intercompany pricing areas than they probably care to admit.

Please send any comments, suggestions or corrections to rdoernberg@gmail.com.

RICHARD L. DOERNBERG

Atlanta, Georgia
October 15, 2015

OUTLINE

PART 1. OVERVIEW OF
FUNDAMENTAL CONCEPTS

PART 2. U.S. ACTIVITIES OF FOREIGN TAXPAYERS

TABLE OF CASES

References are to Pages

TABLE OF INTERNAL REVENUE CODE SECTIONS

References are to Pages

TABLE OF REVENUE RULINGS AND TREASURY REGULATIONS

References are to Pages

TABLE OF REVENUE RULINGS AND
TREASURY REGULATIONS

INTERNATIONAL TAXATION

IN A NUTSHELL®

TENTH EDITION

PART 1

OVERVIEW OF
FUNDAMENTAL CONCEPTS

CHAPTER 1

INTRODUCTION

§ 1.01   GROWTH OF INTERNATIONAL TRADE

Technological improvements in communications and transportation continue to make the world smaller and create a climate that is ripe for international trade. Consider the changes during the past 55 years. Commerce Department data show that for all of 1960 the United States exported just under $26 billion and imported approximately $22 billion of goods and services. For the month of March 2015 alone, exports of goods and services were more than $185 billion while imports were more than $225 billion. How things have changed.

§ 1.02   ECONOMICS OF INTERNATIONAL TRADE

Why do foreign taxpayers invest in the United States or U.S. taxpayers invest abroad? The following short excerpt from a venerable first-grade reader is instructive:

Mr. Smith had a horse. He used to ride his horse to work. One day Mr. Smith said, "I want to get a car to go to work."

Mr. Smith went to a place that sells cars. He asked, "Will you give me a car if I give you my horse?" The man who sells the cars wanted a horse. He took the horse and gave Mr. Smith a car. Both men were happy.*

Trade makes both parties better off. In this respect international trade is no different from domestic trade.

§ 1.03   THE CENTRAL PROBLEM OF INTERNATIONAL TAXATION

When there is bilateral trade, the governments of both trading parties may want to collect a tax on any gains from the trade. To change slightly the example above, suppose that Mr. Smith exchanged cash instead of a horse for the car. Suppose further that the seller of the car is a U.S. citizen who resides in the United States, the car is manufactured in Canada, and Mr. Smith lives in Canada. The United States may claim the right to tax any gain on the sale of the car because of the seller's residence or citizenship, and Canada may claim taxing authority because the car was manufactured in Canada and sold in Canada to a Canadian resident. Overlapping claims of taxing authority—sometimes referred to as juridical double taxation—can create coordination difficulties.

To illustrate the necessity for coordination, suppose that Canada imposes a 50 percent tax on any gains occurring in Canada, and the United States imposes a 50 percent tax on any gains

---

wherever they occur if earned by a U.S. resident (or citizen). Under these assumptions, the combined tax rate is 100 percent, the entire gain on the transaction would be taxed away, and it is likely that the transaction would never take place. The loss of the transaction would hurt both parties, others who would benefit from the trade (*e.g.,* employees of, and suppliers to, the manufacturer) as well as the treasuries of Canada and the United States. The study of international tax is the study of coordinating the tax authority of sovereign countries.

In the example just considered, potential double taxation arises because one country claims taxing authority based on the residence (or citizenship) of the taxpayer and another country claims taxing authority based on where the income arises. Juridical double taxation can also arise when each of two countries claims a taxpayer as a resident or where each of two countries claims that income arises in that country. Countries generally attempt to combat juridical double taxation both through unilateral domestic legislation and bilateral tax treaties with other countries. *See infra* Chapters 5 and 8.

§ 1.04 ECONOMICS OF JURIDICAL DOUBLE TAXATION

From an efficiency point of view, the aspirational goal for a tax system in general, or for the U.S. rules governing international transaction specifically, is the implementation of a tax-neutral set of rules that neither discourage nor encourage particular activity. The tax system should remain in the background, and business, investment and consumption decisions should be made for non-tax reasons. In the international tax context, the concept of tax neutrality has several standards.

One standard is capital-export neutrality. A tax system meets the standard of capital-export neutrality if a taxpayer's choice between investing capital at home or abroad is not affected by taxation. For example, if X Corp., a U.S. corporation, is subject to a 35 percent tax rate in the United States on its worldwide income, and the income from its French branch is also subject to a 30 percent French tax, a U.S. tax system with capital-export neutrality would credit the French tax against the potential U.S. tax liability and tax the French profits in the United States at a 5 percent residual tax rate. X Corp.'s tax rate is 35 percent regardless of the location of the investment. If the investment is located in the United States, taxes are paid to the U.S. treasury; if the investment is located in France, the French treasury would collect as tax 30 percent of the income and the United States would collect as tax 5 percent of the income. With perfect competition, capital-export neutrality results in an efficient allocation of capital. X Corp. will make its investment decision based on business factors rather than tax rates.

The second neutrality standard is capital-import neutrality, sometimes referred to as foreign or competitive neutrality. This standard is satisfied when all firms doing business in a market are taxed at the same rate. For example, if the United States exempted X Corp.'s French income from U.S. taxation, there would be capital-import neutrality from a French perspective because X Corp. would be taxed at the same rate as a comparable French corporation doing business in France. Compared with a tax crediting mechanism, this exemption method violates capital-export neutrality. A U.S. taxpayer will pay lower overall taxes if the investment is made in France (30 percent rate) than if the investment is made in the United States (35 percent rate).

A third neutrality standard is national neutrality. Under this standard, the total U.S. returns on capital which are shared between the taxpayer and the U.S. Treasury are the same whether the capital is invested in the United States or abroad. That is, if the U.S. tax rate is 35 percent of a taxpayer's income (with the taxpayer keeping the other 65 percent of the income), the imposition of foreign taxes will not alter that rate. Applying the national neutrality principle to the example above, any taxes paid to France by X Corp. would be deductible and not creditable against U.S. income tax liability; foreign income taxes would be treated in the same manner as any other domestic or international business expense. Notice the effect on the taxpayer is higher overall taxes because the deductibility of French income tax does not reduce U.S. tax dollar-for-dollar.

The U.S. tax system has elements of all three standards of neutrality. The tax credit mechanism, discussed *infra* in Chapter 8, subject to limitation allows U.S. taxpayers operating abroad to reduce U.S. taxes by an amount equal to any income taxes paid to other countries on foreign income. This provision is driven by notions of capital-export neutrality. However, not all foreign taxes are creditable (*e.g.*, foreign property taxes, value added taxes, capital taxes). To the extent that a U.S. taxpayer incurs foreign taxes that are not creditable, those foreign taxes normally can be deducted for U.S. tax purposes. This treatment and other restrictions on the foreign tax credit mechanism are in keeping with the concept of national neutrality. Finally to the extent that the United States generally exempts (at least while the earnings remain abroad) from U.S. taxation the earnings of foreign subsidiaries of U.S. corporations (so that they can compete against local businesses), the capital-import neutrality principle is advanced.

§ 1.05 OVERVIEW OF WORLDWIDE INTERNATIONAL TAX SYSTEMS

Virtually every country has tax rules that govern the tax treatment of its residents operating abroad and foreign taxpayers operating in that country. While international taxing systems differ from country to country, there are some basic similarities and understandings. Sometimes these understandings are set forth in bilateral income tax treaties working in tandem with domestic tax laws; in other cases, it is the domestic tax laws of a country that determine the appropriate tax treatment.

In general, a country exercises jurisdiction for legal purposes based on either *nationality* or *territoriality*. With respect to taxation, a country may claim that all income earned by a citizen or a company incorporated in that country is subject to taxation because of the legal connection to that country. The United States exercises such jurisdiction over its citizens and companies incorporated in the United States regardless of where income is earned. Business profits earned by a U.S. corporation in Italy are subject to tax in the United States (and normally in Italy as well). Salary earned by a U.S. citizen who is a resident of Switzerland from Swiss employment is subject to tax in the United States (and in Switzerland as well).

Basing tax jurisdiction on nationality can be justified by the benefits available to nationals. For example, in a very real sense U.S. citizens have an insurance policy; they can return to the United States whenever they want, and they have the protection of the U.S. government wherever they are abroad. Tax payments contribute to the availability of that "insurance." U.S. corporations, regardless of their physical presence in the United States, enjoy the benefits of U.S. laws that define corporate relationships. However, the United States is somewhat unusual in relying on citizenship or mere place of incorporation as a basis for jurisdiction.

In addition to nationality, countries often exercise jurisdiction based on *territoriality*. A territorial connection justifies the exercise of taxing jurisdiction because a taxpayer can be expected to share the costs of running a country which makes possible the production of income, its maintenance and investment, and its use through consumption. The principle of territoriality applies with respect to *persons* and *objects* (*i.e.*, income). Country A may claim taxing authority over a citizen of country B if that individual is considered a resident of country A. Similarly, a company incorporated in country B may be subject to tax in country A if there are sufficient connections. For example, many countries (not including the United States) find a sufficient territorial connection if the place of effective management of a corporation is situated within their boundaries.

Territorial jurisdiction over a *person* is analytically similar to jurisdiction based on *nationality*. In both cases it is the connection of the person to a country that justifies taxing jurisdiction. In the case of nationality, that connection is a legal one (*e.g.*, citizenship or incorporation). In the case of territorial jurisdiction over a person, the connection is factual (*e.g.*, whether that person is actually resident in a particular country).

Even if a person is not a citizen or resident of a country, that country may assert territorial tax jurisdiction over income deriving from within the territory of that country earned by a citizen or resident of another country. This is sometimes referred to as "source" jurisdiction because the source of the income is within a country. For example, a country may impose a tax on business profits of a nonresident earned within that country. Investment income, including dividends, interest, royalties, and rent, may also be subject to tax in the country in which such income arises. Typically, a country does not attempt to tax income with which it has no connection. For example, the United States normally does not tax income earned by a French corporation in France or in Germany. But even here there are significant exceptions. For example, under the U.S. subpart F rules, that income of the French company may be taxable in the United States if it is deemed to be earned by its U.S. shareholder.

The potential for double taxation occurs when conflicting jurisdictional claims arise. For example, country A may claim the right to tax a person (including a corporation) based on that person's nationality or residence while country B stakes its claim of taxing authority because income is earned in country B. There is a norm of international taxation which the United States generally follows that cedes the primary taxing authority to the country of territorial connection (*i.e.*, where the income is earned) and the residual taxing authority to the country of nationality or residence. Accordingly, the United States normally credits any income taxes paid in India on income earned in India by a U.S. citizen or resident against the income tax otherwise due in the United States, and only the excess, if any, of U.S. income tax on the foreign income over the foreign tax on such income is collected by the U.S. treasury. Similarly, many countries have adopted more of a territorial approach to jurisdiction and relieve any double taxation by exempting certain income (*e.g.*, business profits) earned in another country from the tax base, rather than including such income in the tax base and then granting a credit for foreign taxes paid as the United States does.

The taxation of income based on *territorial* jurisdiction generally takes one of two forms. A country typically asserts full jurisdiction over business profits generated within that country by a nonresident (who in the case of the United States is not a U.S. citizen), taxing those profits in the same manner as if they were earned by a resident of that country. Expenses associated with generating such income are normally deductible. Non-business, investment income, such as passive dividends, interest, royalties and rent, typically is subject to limited jurisdiction. Often such income is taxed by a country in which the income arises on a gross basis (*i.e.*, no deductions permitted) at rates ranging from 0 to 30 percent. The lower rates that often apply to such income when compared with business profits reflect, in part, the fact that the territorial connection for a full-blown business within a jurisdiction is often more significant than the territorial connection for an investment where the only connection may be the payer's residence. Moreover, the lower rate reflects the fact that the tax is on gross income. However, it should also be noted that a low tax rate on gross income may in fact result in a high tax rate on net income. Suppose country A imposes a 30 percent tax on $100 of passive royalty income earned by a resident of country B from a license with a country A licensee. If the country B resident incurs $60 of expenses to produce the $100 of gross income, the effective tax rate in country A is 75 percent (*i.e.*, a $30 tax on $40 of net income).

CHAPTER 2

BASIC U.S. JURISDICTIONAL TAX PRINCIPLES

§ 2.01 INTRODUCTION TO U.S. TAXING PROVISIONS

International transactions can be grouped into two broad categories outbound and inbound transactions. The term "outbound transactions" refers to U.S. residents and citizens doing business and investing abroad. The term "inbound transactions" refers to foreign taxpayers doing business and investing in the United States.

§ 2.02 OUTBOUND TRANSACTIONS

The taxation of outbound transactions is fairly straightforward. U.S. individual residents and citizens wherever residing are taxed on their worldwide income under the rates specified in I.R.C. § 1. Domestic corporations (*i.e.*, those created or organized in the United States, *see* I.R.C. § 7701(a)(4)) are also taxed on worldwide income under the rates specified in I.R.C. § 11. U.S. individuals or corporations that are partners in either a U.S. or foreign partnership are also taxable on worldwide income. U.S. taxpayers engaged in activities abroad generally compute taxable income in the same manner as U.S. taxpayers operating solely within the United States. There are some differences with respect to foreign activities of U.S. taxpayers. For example under I.R.C. § 168(g)(1)(A), there are limits on the method of depreciation available for property used outside the United States.

There are some important rules governing the U.S. taxation of foreign activities that are treated in more detail *infra*. In a domestic context, normally the income of a corporate subsidiary is not imputed to the parent corporation. Instead in the absence of consolidation, the parent corporation is taxed when a dividend is paid by a subsidiary. *But see* I.R.C. § 243. However, the U.S. parent of a foreign subsidiary is sometimes taxed on the earnings of a subsidiary even if those earnings are not distributed. I.R.C. §§ 951–960. *See infra* Chapter 10. The purpose of this treatment is to discourage U.S. corporations from redirecting income outside the United States in order to avoid immediate U.S. taxation. In a domestic context, normally U.S. taxpayers are taxed on all income. However, under I.R.C. § 911 (discussed *infra* at § 7.02), there is an exclusion for certain income earned abroad.

For U.S. citizens and residents, including domestic corporations, among the most important international tax provisions are those dealing with the foreign tax credit. I.R.C. §§ 901–909. *See infra* Chapter 8. If a U.S. taxpayer earns income in Germany, that income is taxable in the United States and may be taxable in Germany as well. In order to alleviate this double tax, the United States allows the taxpayer to offset taxes due in the United

States with the income taxes paid in Germany. This foreign tax mechanism is full of twists and turns that are considered in more detail *infra*. For example, if Germany decides to tax income that the United States considers to be U.S. source income, no credit for German taxes paid is allowed to offset U.S. tax on that income. Also, if the German tax on the income earned in Germany is higher than the U.S. tax on that income, the U.S. taxpayer will not be able to credit the entire German tax against the U.S. tax liability. Essentially, the German tax can be used only to offset the U.S. tax on the German income (and in some cases other foreign source income), not the U.S. tax on U.S. source income. Otherwise the United States would cede to Germany the right to collect taxes on U.S. income.

Because the United States only provides a foreign tax credit for foreign income taxes imposed on what the United States considers to be foreign source income, the U.S. source rules, described *infra* in Chapter 3 play an important role. U.S. taxpayers generally want to plan to maximize their foreign source income to allow a maximum foreign tax credit and thereby minimize any potential U.S. tax on the income. Whether a U.S. taxpayer earns foreign or U.S. source income, it will be taxable in the United States. But with foreign source income, the amount of U.S. tax may be lowered if foreign tax credits are available.

For example, suppose U.S.CO currently earns $100 million of foreign source income from country X, paying income taxes there of $70 million, and

$100 million of U.S. source income. For U.S. tax purposes, USCO declares $200 million of taxable income and faces a potential U.S. tax (assuming a 35% tax rate) of $70 million. However, USCO may be able to take a credit for the foreign taxes paid, but only to the extent of the U.S. tax that would be imposed on the foreign source income. In this example, the credit would be limited to $35 million (*i.e.*, the potential U.S. tax on the foreign source income). In total, USCO would pay $35 million of U.S. tax and $70 million of foreign tax. Now suppose, that USCO were able to change the source of what is now the $100 million of U.S. source income. If USCO can turn that income into foreign source income and not incur any additional foreign tax in doing so, then USCO may be able to use the full $70 million of foreign taxes paid to offset the $70 million potential U.S. tax on the foreign source income. The result would be $0 U.S. tax liability and $70 million of foreign tax. By changing the source, the taxpayer may be able to save $35 million in U.S. tax.

§ 2.03   INBOUND TRANSACTIONS

The taxation of inbound transactions is not as all-encompassing as the taxation of outbound transactions. Nonresident aliens and foreign corporations are not subject to U.S. taxation on their worldwide income. While I.R.C. §§ 1 and 11 appear to apply to all taxpayers, I.R.C. §§ 2(d) and 11(d) apply the rates in a manner set forth in other specified provisions.

(A) INDIVIDUALS

For nonresident alien individuals, the basic taxing provisions are found in I.R.C. § 871. Under I.R.C. § 871(b), a nonresident alien individual engaged in a trade or business in the United States is taxed like a U.S. taxpayer under I.R.C. § 1 on taxable income which is effectively connected with the conduct of the trade or business. Broadly stated, nonresident alien individuals are taxed like U.S. taxpayers on most U.S. business income. Section 871(b) contains two important terms of art that are described in more detail *infra* at §§ 4.02–4.03: "engaged in a trade or business" (hereinafter sometimes referred to as "ETB"), and income "effectively connected" with the conduct of a trade or business within the United States (hereinafter sometimes referred to as "effectively connected income" or "ECI"). For a definition of these terms, *see* I.R.C. §§ 864(b) (engaged in a trade or business) and 864(c)(effectively connected income).

Nonresident alien individuals are also subject to U.S. taxation on some types of recurring investment income. I.R.C. § 871(a) imposes a flat 30 percent tax on amounts received from sources within the United States which are "fixed or determinable annual or periodical gains, profits, and income" (hereinafter sometimes referred to as "FDAP" income). (One unsettled area of U.S. international tax is whether the term is pronounced "FEE´–DAP," "EFF´–DAP," or "FUH–DAP´".) The most important categories of FDAP income are interest, dividends, rents, and royalties. These types of income generally are subject to a 30 percent tax on the gross amount of the distribution unless the distributions are income effectively connected with the conduct of a U.S. trade or business (*e.g.*, receipt of interest by a bank) in which case the income is subject to taxation as business income on the net amount of income. Although FDAP income includes "salaries, wages, . . . compensations, remunerations, [and] emoluments," virtually all income from services performed within the United States results in effectively connected income that is taxed under I.R.C. §§ 871(b) or 882. *See* I.R.C. § 864(c)(2) and Reg. § 1.864–4(c)(6)(ii).

Generally nonresident alien individuals are not taxable on capital gains transactions as such gains are not the recurring type of FDAP income addressed by I.R.C. § 871(a)(1). There are at least three exceptions to this rule. First, capital gains generated by the sale of U.S. real property or the stock of certain U.S. real property holding corporations are treated as effectively connected income under I.R.C. § 897 and are therefore subject to taxation in the same manner as other business income. *See infra* § 4.06.

Second, any capital gains transaction that is effectively connected with the conduct of a trade or business will be taxable under I.R.C. § 871(b) as business income. For example, suppose an Italian resident who is engaged in a paperback publishing business in the United States sells U.S. securities that were purchased with funds generated by the business and are managed by employees of the business who use the income generated by the securities to meet the current needs of the business. Gain from that sale would at first glance be taxable in the same manner as other business income. *See* I.R.C. § 864(c)(2). However, the Regulations take the position that stock of a corporation shall not be treated as an asset held for use in a U.S. trade or business. Reg. § 1.864–4(c)(2)(iii). If the Italian resident sells assets used in the U.S. trade or business at a gain, the gain would probably be § 1231 gain that would be treated as capital gain. That capital gain would be taxable in the United States as income effectively connected with the conduct of the U.S. trade or business.

Under the third exception, which will almost never apply, capital gains for nonresident aliens present in the United States 183 days or more during the taxable year may be taxable in the United States. I.R.C. § 871(a)(2). Generally, a person present in the United States for more than 183 days will be a U.S. resident and will not be taxable under § 871(a)(2). *See* § 4.04(G) for a discussion of when § 871(a)(2) may apply.

(B) CORPORATIONS

The treatment of foreign corporations (*i.e.*, those incorporated abroad) parallels the treatment of nonresident alien individuals. A foreign corporation is taxed under I.R.C. § 11 on its taxable income effectively connected with the conduct of a U.S. trade or business. I.R.C. § 882. That is, a foreign corporation like a domestic corporation is taxed on business profits from the conduct of a trade or business in the United States. The fixed or determinable annual or periodical gains, profits, and income (*i.e.*, investment income) of a foreign corporation from U.S. sources is subject to a flat 30 percent gross basis tax under I.R.C. § 881 to the extent such income is not effectively connected with the conduct of a U.S. trade or business.

There is one other taxing provision affecting foreign corporations that must be considered—the branch profits tax under I.R.C. § 884. *See infra* § 4.05. Suppose a nonresident alien individual does business in the United States through a U.S. corporation. The corporation is taxed on its earnings under I.R.C. § 11 and the shareholder is subject to the 30 percent tax on any dividend paid in accordance with I.R.C. § 871(a). The two taxes comprise the double tax system that is a mainstay of U.S. corporate taxation in general. Suppose instead that the nonresident alien individual operates the U.S. business through a foreign corporation. The corporation's business income (the effectively connected income) is still taxable. I.R.C. § 882. Historically, when the foreign corporation distributed a dividend to its foreign shareholders, it was not difficult for the shareholder to avoid the imposition of the 30 percent tax under I.R.C. § 871(a). In order to equalize the overall taxation of distributed corporate earnings regardless of whether the distributing corporation is a U.S. or foreign corporation, Congress enacted a branch profits tax. Under I.R.C. § 884, a foreign corporation must pay a 30 percent branch profits tax to the extent that its U.S. branch repatriates (or is deemed to repatriate) its earnings from the United States to the home country. The branch profits tax is levied in addition to the tax under I.R.C. § 882 on corporate income. Where the branch profits tax applies, there is no further tax when a foreign corporation makes a dividend distribution to its foreign shareholders.

(C) PARTNERSHIPS

A nonresident alien individual or nonresident corporation that is a partner in either a U.S. or foreign partnership is generally taxed as if the partner had earned the income directly. For example, a nonresident alien individual or foreign corporation is considered to be engaged in a trade or business within the United States if the partnership is so engaged. I.R.C. § 875. *See* also *Donroy, Ltd. v. United States*, 301 F.2d 200 (9th Cir. 1962). Ordinarily, a partnership is not a taxable entity for U.S. tax purposes.

§ 2.04   CITIZENSHIP AND RESIDENCY

(A) INDIVIDUALS

The United States is unusual among nations in taxing its citizens on their worldwide income regardless of their residence. In *Cook v. Tait*, 265 U.S. 47 (1924), plaintiff, a citizen of the United States, was a resident of Mexico. The Supreme Court held that U.S. taxation of the taxpayer's worldwide income violated neither the U.S. Constitution nor international law. The Court justified taxation on the theory that the benefits of citizenship extend beyond territorial boundaries. For example, the United States seeks to protect its citizens anywhere in the world. Also citizens have the right to return to the United States whenever they want and participate in the economic system. In effect, a citizen of the United States has an insurance policy, and taxes are the cost of maintaining that policy.

Every person born or naturalized in the United States and subject to its jurisdiction is a citizen. Reg. § 1.1–1(c). A noncitizen who has filed a declaration of intention of becoming a citizen but who has not yet been granted citizenship by a final order of a naturalization court is an alien.

It is usually not difficult to determine whether a taxpayer is or is not a U.S. citizen for U.S. tax purposes. Determining residency can be more troublesome. Whether an individual is taxed on worldwide income under § 1 or essentially on U.S. business and investment income under I.R.C. § 871 often depends on the definition of residency. Prior to 1984, the definition evolved judicially, resulting in uncertainty in many situations. Now I.R.C. § 7701(b) provides a "bright line" test.

An individual is considered to be a resident of the United States if the individual meets any one of three tests: lawful admission to the United States (*i.e.*, "green card" test); "substantial presence" in the United States, or; a first year election to be treated as a resident. I.R.C. § 7701(b)(1)(A). An individual becomes a lawful permanent resident of the United

States in accordance with the immigration laws. Once permanent residence is obtained, an individual remains a lawful permanent resident until the status is revoked or abandoned.

The heart of I.R.C. § 7701(b) is the "substantial presence" test. An individual meets this test if the individual is present in the United States for at least 31 days during the current year and at least 183 days for the three-year period ending on the last day of the current year using a weighted average. I.R.C. § 7701(b)(3). The weighted average works as follows: days present in the current year are multiplied by 1; days in the immediate preceding year are multiplied by 1/3; days in the next preceding year are multiplied by 1/6 For example, suppose an individual is present in the United States for 120 days in the current year and in each of the two preceding years. The individual does not satisfy the substantial presence test because the weighted average is only 180 days ((120 × 1) + (120 × 1/3) + (120 × 1/6)). If the individual were present in the United States 122 days each year, the individual would exactly meet the 183 day weighted average ((122 × 1) + (122 × 1/3) + (122 × 1/6)) and would be considered a U.S. resident.

An individual is present in the United States on any day the individual is physically present at any time during the day (except for commuters from Mexico and Canada). I.R.C. § 7701(b)(7). For purposes of the residency test, individuals do not count days where the individual was unable to leave the United States because of a medical condition or days where the individual is a foreign government employee, a teacher, a student, or a professional athlete. I.R.C. § 7701(b)(3)(D).

Even if an alien satisfies the substantial presence test, the alien is not a resident if the individual is present in the United States on fewer than 183 days during the current year and has a tax home in a foreign country to which the individual has a closer connection than to the United States. I.R.C. § 7701(b)(3)(B). For this purpose, a tax home is considered to be located at a taxpayer's regular or principal place of business or if the taxpayer has no regular or principal place of business at his regular place of abode. I.R.C. § 911(d)(3); Reg. § 1.911–2(b).

A newly-arrived individual in the United States may be unable to satisfy the substantial presence test but may want to be considered a U.S. resident. For example, an individual present in the United States and earning a salary is fully taxable on the amount of salary income whether the individual is or is not a U.S. resident. However, if the individual is a U.S. resident, the overall tax burden may be less because of various personal deductions (*e.g.*, dependency deductions) that are not available to nonresidents. A special first-year election of residency is available for an alien if the individual is present in the United States for 31 consecutive days and at least 75 percent of the days in the part of the current year that begins with the first of the 31 consecutive days. I.R.C. § 7701(b)(4). In addition, the election may not be made before the individual meets the substantial presence test for the succeeding year (*i.e.,* the taxpayer either obtains a filing extension for the first year or files an amended return). If the election can be made, it is effective for the portion of the year beginning with the first of the 31 days.

(B) CORPORATIONS

The residency test for corporations is much simpler than the test for individuals. A U.S. corporation taxable on its worldwide income is a corporation created or organized in the United States. I.R.C. §§ 7701(a)(3) and (4). A foreign corporation (*i.e.,* a corporation not created or organized in the United States) is taxable under I.R.C. §§ 881 and 882 on income effectively connected with the conduct of a trade or business in the United States or on specified U.S. investment income. I.R.C. § 7701(a)(5).

While the residence of a corporation may be easy to determine under U.S. law, it is not always easy to determine whether an entity is to be treated as a corporation. Suppose entity E is formed in country X by US1 and US2, who are individual residents of the United States. Is the income earned by E, income earned by a nonresident corporation or is the income earned by a transparent partnership in which case individuals US1 and US2, U.S. residents, will be taxable? Historically, this has been a difficult problem compounded by the fact that country X might treat E as a corporation while the United States might treat E as a transparent partnership (or vice versa). The Treasury has issued "check-the-box" Regulations that provide the following basic rules with respect to business entities: (1) a business entity incorporated under U.S. federal or state law is a corporation for U.S. tax purposes; (2) a business entity formed or created under foreign law is a corporation for U.S. tax purposes if that form of entity is specifically listed in the Regulations ("per se" corporations); (3) a business entity that is not treated as a corporation under (1) or (2) can elect its classification (*i.e.,* check a box on Form 8832) as a transparent partnership (or a transparent disregarded entity) or a nontransparent corporation for U.S. tax purposes. *See infra* § 13.02. If an entity has only one owner and elects not to be treated as a corporation, it will be treated as a disregarded entity (*i.e.*, income of this "tax nothing" will be deemed to be earned directly by that owner). Reg. §§ 301.7701–2 and –3. The Regulations provide default rules. As a result, an entity may be treated as disregarded unless an election is made to treat it as a corporation, while another entity may default to corporation status unless an election is made to treat it as a transparent entity.

These "check-the-box" Regulations govern the classification of an entity for U.S. tax purposes; another country may rely on its own domestic provisions in determining how it will treat the same entity for its tax purposes. The ability to have an entity treated one way for U.S. tax purposes and another way for foreign tax purposes is an important part of tax planning and is discussed throughout the book and in particular in § 13.03.

§ 2.05   EXPATRIATES

Suppose a citizen of the United States fearing a high U.S. tax liability renounces citizenship. First note that if the individual is a resident of the United States, the renunciation has no tax effect because U.S. residents are taxed in the same manner as U.S. citizens. If the individual is a nonresident, income from foreign sources (*e.g.*, interest or dividends from foreign investments) generally is not subject to U.S. taxation. However under I.R.C. § 877A if a citizen gives up U.S. citizenship, the taxpayer may be treated as if all property is sold for fair market value the day before expatriation. Accordingly, an "exit tax" would be imposed on any built-in gain.

For example, suppose a nonresident U.S. citizen owns shares of stock in a U.S. company. The shares have a basis of $1 million and a fair market value of $10 million. On the sale of the stock, the taxpayer faces $9 million of income for U.S. tax purposes. In order to avoid any U.S. tax, suppose the taxpayer renounces U.S. citizenship and then sells the stock. In the absence of a provision like I.R.C. § 877A, the taxpayer could avoid U.S. tax. However, I.R.C. § 877A will apply to immediately tax the gain (although in some cases, a taxpayer can elect to defer the tax).

I.R.C. § 877A(a) generally imposes a "mark-to-market" regime on covered expatriates, providing that all property of a covered expatriate is treated as sold on the day before the expatriation date for its fair market value. The provision requires that any gain arising from the deemed sale is taken into account (subject to an exclusion amount which for 2014 was $680,000) for the taxable year of the deemed sale notwithstanding any other provisions of the Code. Any loss from the deemed sale generally is taken into account for the taxable year of the deemed sale to the extent otherwise provided in the Code. A taxpayer may elect to defer payment of tax attributable to property deemed sold. I.R.C. § 877A(b).

Generally, a covered expatriate is an expatriate (citizen or long-term resident) who: (1) has an average annual net income tax liability for the five preceding taxable years that exceeds a specified amount that is adjusted for inflation ($157,000 for 2014) (the "tax liability test"); (2) has a net worth of $2 million or more (the "net worth test"); or (3) fails to certify, under penalties of perjury, compliance with all U.S. Federal tax obligations for the five taxable years preceding the taxable year. I.R.C. § 877A(g).

I.R.C. § 877A(b) provides that a covered expatriate may make an irrevocable election ("deferral election") with respect to any property deemed sold by reason of section 877A(a) to defer the payment of the additional tax attributable to any such property ("deferral assets"). The deferral election is made on an asset-by-asset basis. In order to make the election with respect to any asset, the covered expatriate must provide adequate security and must irrevocably waive any right under any U.S. treaty that would preclude assessment or collection of any tax imposed by reason of I.R.C.

§ 877A. Any deferred tax plus interest is due upon the earlier disposition of the asset (actually, when the tax return is due) or death of the expatriate (no tax planning opportunity here).

§ 2.06 INTRODUCTION TO U.S. INCOME TAX TREATIES

The basic ground rules governing the taxation of both nonresidents and residents often serve as a backdrop to a series of bilateral income tax treaties. *See infra* Chapter 5. These treaties typically allocate the taxing authority over specified types of income to the treaty partners. Once a treaty has allocated taxing authority to a treaty partner, the domestic tax laws of that partner govern the ultimate tax treatment. For example, the treaty between the United States and the Netherlands provides that business profits of a Dutch resident are exempt from U.S. taxation unless the profits are attributable to a permanent establishment (*e.g.*, a fixed place of business) in the United States. If the business profits are attributable to a U.S. permanent establishment, they are subject to taxation under either I.R.C. § 871(b) (individuals) or I.R.C. § 882 (corporations); if not, the profits are not taxable in the United States even if under purely domestic law principles the income would be considered income effectively connected with the conduct of a U.S. trade or business (*e.g.*, continuous sales of inventory to U.S. purchasers through a U.S. independent agent). Treaties do not enlarge the taxing authority of the United States.

Treaties also typically reduce the rate of tax on certain "investment" income. While the U.S. domestic tax rate on this "investment" income is typically 30 percent (*see supra* § 2.03), treaties may reduce the applicable rate to 15, 5 or in some cases 0 percent. *See infra* Chapter 5.

A treaty may also determine residence where an individual under domestic law principles is a nontreaty resident of both the United States and its treaty partner. Many treaties contain residency tie-breaker provisions that may make an individual a nonresident of the United States even though that individual meets the substantial presence test of I.R.C. § 7701(b). *See infra* § 5.05(C).

CHAPTER 3
SOURCE RULES

§ 3.01   THE INCOME SOURCE RULES

The source rules are important both to: (1) U.S. citizens, residents, and domestic corporations; and (2) nonresident alien individuals and foreign corporations. For the former, the foreign tax credit for income taxes paid to foreign countries is available to offset U.S. income taxes on foreign source income. For example, if Japan taxes income of a U.S. corporation that under U.S. tax rules is U.S. source income, the income taxes paid to Japan may not be creditable as an offset against taxes payable to the United States on the income. I.R.C. § 904. *See infra* § 8.06.

For nonresident aliens and foreign corporations, the source rules are important for two reasons. In the case of income from a U.S. trade or business, it is generally the case that income must be from U.S. sources to be effectively connected income and therefore subject to taxation under I.R.C. §§ 871(b) (individuals) and 882 (corporations). *But see* I.R.C. § 864(c)(4). In the case of nonbusiness income (*i.e.*, FDAP income), the 30 percent withholding tax is applicable only to U.S. source income. For example, if a nonresident alien investor receives a dividend that is deemed not to be U.S. source income, there is no U.S. taxation. I.R.C. §§ 871(a) and 881. What follows is a summary of the source rules for particular types of income. *See* I.R.C. §§ 861–863, 865 and 884(f).

(A) INTEREST

(1) Domestic Payor

In general, interest is sourced by reference to the residence of the payor. Accordingly, interest paid by a domestic corporation, noncorporate resident of the United States, the federal government, or an agency or instrumentality of the federal government is U.S. source interest. A domestic partnership is considered a U.S. resident for purposes of the interest source rule only if the partnership is engaged in a trade or business in the United States at any time during the taxable year. Reg. § 1.861–2(a)(1). In determining the source of an interest payment, the place of payment, the place where the debt is located, the recipient's location, the currency used to make the payment all are irrelevant factors.

One exception to the residence-of-the-payor rule treats the payment of interest by a foreign branch of a U.S. bank on deposits as foreign source interest even though the juridical payor is a U.S. bank. I.R.C. § 861(a)(1)(A).

(2) Foreign Payor

In general, interest paid by a foreign corporation is foreign source income under I.R.C. § 862(a)(1). Accordingly a foreign lender is not subject to a 30 percent tax on the receipt of interest paid by a foreign corporation. However, where a foreign corporation is engaged in a trade or business in the United States through its U.S. branch, interest payments paid (or deemed to be paid) by the U.S. branch are treated as if paid by a domestic corporation. I.R.C. § 884(f). Accordingly, such interest is taxable under either I.R.C. §§ 871(a) or 881. *See* the discussion of the branch profits tax *supra* at § 4.05. Interest paid by a foreign partnership with a U.S. trade or business is treated in a similar manner to interest paid by a foreign corporation—the interest paid will be considered U.S. source income only if it is paid by a U.S. trade or business of the partnership (or allocable to income that is effectively connected or is treated as effectively connected with the conduct of a U.S. trade or business). I.R.C. § 861(a)(1)(B). However, to be eligible for this treatment, the foreign partnership must be predominantly engaged in the active conduct of a trade or business outside the United States. If the partnership is not predominantly engaged in the active conduct of a foreign trade or business, then *all* interest paid by the partnership will be treated as U.S. source income. Reg. § 1.861–2(a)(2).

Substitute interest payments (*e.g.*, payments made by a foreign borrower of securities to the foreign lender) are treated as U.S. source income if the interest accruing on the transferred security would have been U.S. source income. Reg. § 1.861–2(a)(7); *see supra* § 3.01(A).

(B) DIVIDENDS

(1) Domestic Payor

Generally, a dividend paid by a domestic corporation is U.S. source income. I.R.C. § 861(a)(2)(A). It normally follows that such U.S. source income received by a nonresident alien or foreign corporation is subject to the 30 percent tax under I.R.C. §§ 871(a) or 881 (unless an applicable treaty reduces the tax rate). A dividend paid by a U.S. payor is taxable in the United States because the United States provides the economic environment in which the dividend-paying corporation conducts business. *But see* I.R.C. §§ 871(i) and 881(d) discussed *infra* at § 3.01(B)(2).

(2) Foreign Payor

Generally, a dividend paid by a foreign corporation to foreign shareholders is not U.S. source income and is not subject to a 30 percent tax in the United States. I.R.C. § 861(a)(2)(B). However, if the foreign corporation is engaged in a U.S. trade or business, a portion of any dividend payment may be treated as U.S. source income. If 25 percent or more of a foreign corporation's gross income for the three preceding years is U.S. business income, the portion of the dividend that is attributable to the corporation's U.S. business income is considered U.S. source income. Notwithstanding this rule, there will be no withholding tax on such a dividend because the foreign corporation will be subject to the branch profits tax instead. I.R.C. §§ 884(e)(3) and 871(i)(2)(D). *See infra* § 4.05.

A substitute dividend payment (*e.g.*, a payment made by a borrower of stock to the lender of stock which is equivalent to a dividend payment) is sourced in the same manner as the dividend payment itself. Reg. § 1.861–3(a)(6). *See supra* § 3.01(B).

(C) PERSONAL SERVICES

The source rule for services is straightforward: compensation for services performed in the United States is U.S. source income subject to a de minimis exception. Typically, a nonresident alien performing services in the United States is deemed to be engaged in a trade or business in the United States, and the compensation is treated as effectively connected income which is taxable under I.R.C. § 871(b). However to the extent that compensation is paid for services performed outside the United States, generally the compensation is not subject to U.S. taxation. *See* Reg. § 1.861–4(b). If a corporation receives income in the nature of personal services performed by an employee or other agent, the corporation's compensation is sourced in the place where the employee or agent performs the services. *See, e.g., Bank of America v. United States*, 680 F.2d 142 (Ct.Cl. 1982). *See also Commissioner v. Hawaiian Philippine Co.*, 100 F.2d 988 (9th Cir. 1939) (corporations can generate "personal" services).

The *de minimis* exception to the place-of-performance rule provides that compensation for services performed by a nonresident alien individual temporarily present in the United States is foreign source income if the individual is not present in the United States for more than 90 days during the taxable year and the compensation does not exceed $3,000, a figure rendered virtually meaningless by the ravages of inflation since 1954, the year of enactment. Furthermore the payments must be from a foreign employer not engaged in a trade or business in the United States or the foreign office of a U.S. employer. I.R.C. § 864(b)(1).

The payments covered by this place-of-performance rule include not only direct compensation but also fringe benefits (*e.g.*, pension payments), sales commissions, amounts received under a covenant not to compete, and even advertising income. *See Commissioner v. Piedras Negras Broadcasting Co.*, 127 F.2d 260 (5th Cir. 1942) (advertising revenues of Mexican radio station were foreign source income even though U.S. customers bought radio time to advertise to U.S. customers).

Not surprisingly, it is not always clear where services are performed. For example, suppose a Canadian hockey player is paid $1,000,000 a year by a U.S. hockey team. That portion of the salary attributable to games played in Canada is not taxed in the United States because it is foreign source income not effectively connected with the conduct of a U.S. trade or business. Should any portion of the

$1,000,000 be allocable to pre-season activities? To post-season playoffs? To the off-season since the taxpayer was expected to report to his team in good shape? Since the taxpayer spent the off-season and much of the pre-season and play-offs in Canada, allocation of salary to those periods would lower the taxpayer's U.S. tax liability. *See Stemkowski v. Commissioner*, 690 F.2d 40 (2d Cir. 1982) (services include pre- and post-season but not off-season).

Questions also arise as to whether a particular payment is for services rendered or for something else. In *Karrer v. United States*, 152 F.Supp. 66 (Ct.Cl. 1957), a Swiss national, a scientist, maintained that he was compensated for services performed in Switzerland by a Swiss corporation for work culminating in several patents. The taxpayer maintained that the payments received were foreign source income not subject to U.S. taxation even though the payments were based on U.S. sales of the synthetic vitamins developed from his work. The IRS argued unsuccessfully that the appropriate source rule was the one dealing with royalties— I.R.C. § 861(a)(4)—and that the payments received for the use of a patent in the United States were U.S. source income. In *Cook v. United States*, 599 F.2d 400 (Ct.Cl.1979), a sculptor's income on the sale of a sculpture was sourced in the country where the sculptor worked rather than in the country where the sculpture was sold.

In some cases, it may not be clear whether a payment is for services or the sale of property. For example, suppose that X Corp., a country X corporation, operates a server in country S from which customers for a fee can download financial reports. If USCo, a U.S. company downloads the report, is the fee a payment for services or a payment for property? Generally, in situations where the supplier (*i.e.*, X Corp.) never owned the property but created it solely for the customer (*i.e.*, USCo), the payment is considered a payment for services performed rather than for the property. *See Boulez v. Commissioner*, 83 T.C. 584 (U.S. Tax Ct.1984) (fee for services rather than a royalty for transfer of property because taxpayer created the property for the end-user).

Suppose a U.S. financial services company earns fees for services performed to process transactions made by customers using third-party ATM machines located outside the United States. The processing is done through the use of its computers, software and other equipment located in the United States. In CCA201205007, the IRS determined that based on where the processing took place, the services income should be U.S. income. Does the same reasoning apply to other types of services provided by computers directly to customers (*e.g.*, multi-party gaming, database searches)? Does that mean that a U.S. taxpayer can change U.S. source income to foreign source income by placing servers outside the United States while the software that makes the services possible is developed inside the United States? These are unresolved issues.

The Code provides specific source rules for specific types of services income. For example, one half of the income from furnishing transportation (*e.g.*, income of a shipping company or airline) is U.S. source income if the trip begins or ends in the United States. I.R.C. § 863(c)(2)(A). If the trip begins and ends in the United States, all income is from U.S. sources even if some part of the trip is over international waters or a foreign country. A round trip is treated as two trips, an outbound and inbound trip. This special source rule for transportation income does not apply to salaries and wages of transportation employees.

International communications income of a U.S. taxpayer is treated as 50 percent from U.S. sources and 50 percent from foreign sources. I.R.C. § 863(e)(1)(A). International communications income of a foreign taxpayer is usually foreign source income unless the income is attributable to a U.S. office or other fixed place of business or to a controlled foreign corporation in which case 50 percent of the income is U.S. sourced income. Reg. § 1.863–9(b). Income from communications between two points in the United States is U.S. source income, even if routed through a satellite.

(D) RENTALS AND ROYALTIES

Rentals from the lease of tangible property are sourced where the property is located. I.R.C. §§ 861(a)(4) and 862(a)(4). For example, if a foreign corporation leases computer hardware to another foreign corporation which uses the hardware in the United States, rental payments are U.S. source income notwithstanding, the residence of the lessor or lessee, or where payments take place.

Royalties from the license of intangible property including patents, copyrights, knowhow or other intellectual property are sourced according to where the intangibles are used. I.R.C. §§ 861(a)(4) and 862(a)(4). Essentially, the focus should be on where the intangible is legally protected. If the intangible is legally protected in more than one jurisdiction (*e.g.*, a worldwide copyright license), the focus should be on what legal protection the licensee is truly paying for. For example, if a U.S. taxpayer develops computer software abroad and licenses it to a foreign licensee under a contract signed abroad who pays royalties abroad, the royalties are U.S. source income if the licensee uses the software in its U.S. trade or business. In this situation, it is the permission to use the copyright in the U.S. without infringing, that justifies the royalty payments. If a patent, copyright, or other intangible is sold outright rather than licensed, but the sales proceeds are contingent on the productivity, use, or disposition of the intangible by the purchaser (*e.g.*, purchase price equal to 2% of gross sales), the source of the sales proceeds is determined as if such payments are royalties. I.R.C. § 865(d).

Suppose that a licensor from Bermuda licenses its worldwide rights in computer software to a Dutch licensee which sublicenses the intangible throughout the world including the U.S. rights to a U.S. sub-licensee. In the absence of a treaty between the United States and the Netherlands, the royalty paid by the U.S. sub-licensee to the Dutch sub-licensor for the right to exploit the U.S. rights in the software would be U.S. source FDAP income subject to U.S. withholding tax. I.R.C. §§ 881 and 1442. However, the applicable treaty does not permit U.S. withholding on such a payment. What about the royalty payment from the Dutch licensee (sub-licensor) to the Bermudan licensor? Should the portion of that payment attributable to royalties received from the U.S. sub-licensee be treated as U.S. source income even though paid by a non-U.S. payor to a non-U.S. payee? The possibility that the United States would collect multiple withholding taxes on royalties that are paid pursuant to sublicensing of an intangible (*e.g.*, X receives royalties from Y which receives royalties from Z which receives royalties from a U.S. sub-licensee) is referred to as the "cascading royalty" problem.

In *SDI Netherlands B.V. v. Commissioner*, 107 T.C. 161 (U.S. Tax Ct.1996), the court rejected the cascading royalty approach, ruling that the payment from the Dutch licensee (sub-licensor) to the Bermudan licensor was not U.S. source income even to the extent the payment is attributable to royalties received by the sub-licensor from a U.S. sub-licensee exploiting the U.S. intangible rights. The court did not suggest how I.R.C. § 861(a)(4) applies to determine the source of the payment from the Dutch licensee in this situation. Note that in *SDI Netherlands*, 107 T.C. 161 (U.S. Tax Ct.1996), the IRS did not argue that the Dutch licensee (sub-licensor) was merely a conduit so that the royalty was really being paid from the U.S. sub-licensee to the Bermudan licensor. If that were true, then both under the current treaty and under U.S. domestic law (*see e.g.*, I.R.C. § 7701(*l*) and Reg. § 1.881–3), the payment from the U.S. licensee would have been U.S. source income subject to a 30 percent tax under I.R.C. § 881.

Often it is not easy to determine the character of a particular payment that is received. Only after the character is determined can the appropriate source rule be applied. For example, suppose that a computer software company "licenses" computer software to customers in exchange for a royalty. A customer can acquire the software on a shrink-wrapped CD at local stores or by downloading. Conceivably, the payment might constitute a royalty, rental income from the lease of the CD or application itself, sales proceeds from the sale of the copyright or sales proceeds from the sale of a CD or application itself. Regulations attempt to distinguish a copyright right from a copyrighted article with respect to computer software. A copyright right includes the right to make copies of a computer program for distribution to the public, the right to prepare derivative computer programs, the right to make a public performance or the right to publicly display the program. Reg. § 1.861–18(c)(2).

Once it is determined whether a copyright right or a copyrighted article has been transferred, then the issue is whether the entire copyright right or copyrighted article has been transferred or rather there has been a lease or license. In the example above, typically there is no transfer of a copyright right by the software provider, notwithstanding the license. Instead, a person who acquires the software is acquiring a copyrighted article. Because the acquirer obtains full rights in the CD or software application, a sale has taken place and any proceeds are sales proceeds. On the other hand if an acquirer were permitted to make copies of the software and distribute them to the public, the transfer would be the transfer of a copyright right and any proceeds received by the software provider would either constitute a royalty or sales proceeds from the sale of an intangible depending on whether the acquirer has licensed the royalty (*e.g.*, the right to distribute for a limited period of time) or obtained full rights in the copyright.

For a discussion of whether a payment constitutes services or royalties, *see Sergio Garcia v. Commissioner*, 140 T.C. 141 (2013).

(E) REAL PROPERTY

Gain or loss from the disposition of U.S. real property or stock of a U.S. real property holding corporation (as defined in I.R.C. § 897(c)) is U.S. source income. Gain from the sale of real property located outside the United States is foreign source income.

(F) PERSONAL PROPERTY

For purposes of determining source, the term "personal property" essentially includes all property (both tangible and intangible) that is not real property.

(1) Purchased Inventory

Gain from the sale of purchased inventory is sourced where the sale takes place—generally the place where title passes. I.R.C. §§ 865(b) and 861(a)(6). For example, gain from the sale of inventory purchased in France and sold in the United States is U.S. source income while gain from the sale of inventory purchased in the United States and sold in France is foreign source income.

The title passage rule for purchased inventory allows taxpayers great latitude. U.S. residents that sell inventory for use abroad can arrange for title to pass abroad creating foreign source income that enhances the ability to credit foreign income taxes. *See* also *Liggett Group Inc. v. Commissioner*, T.C. Memo. 1990–18 (U.S. Tax Ct.1990) (U.S. seller, purchasing goods from a foreign supplier, generated foreign source income on sales to U.S. purchaser where both the legal title and economic ownership (*e.g.*, benefits and burden of ownership) passed abroad).

But there are limits to acceptable title-passage manipulation. If a transaction is structured with the primary purpose of tax avoidance, the title-passage rule may not apply. Instead the risk of loss, location of negotiations, execution of the agreement, location of the property itself; and the place of payment may be relevant in determining source. Reg. § 1.861–7(c). If a nonresident maintains an office or other fixed

place of business in the United States, income from
the sale of inventory (and other personal property)
attributable to such place of business is sourced in
the United States regardless of where title passes.
I.R.C. § 865(e)(2)(A). However, if the inventory is
sold for use outside the United States and a foreign
fixed place of business materially participates in the
sale, any gain on the sale is treated as foreign
source income. I.R.C. § 865(e)(2)(B).

(2) Produced Personal Property

The title-passage rule applies to personal
property (including inventory) that is purchased and
resold. The rule does not apply to personal property
(including inventory) that is produced by the
taxpayer. For example, suppose a foreign
corporation has a Spanish factory that
manufactures thermostats which are shipped to a
U.S. warehouse where sales representatives sell the
thermostats to U.S. purchasers. Income from the
sale of such property is allocated for source purposes
between the country of production and the country
of sale. I.R.C. §§ 865(b) and 863(b)(2). Both the
country of production and the country of sales
contribute to the value of the produced inventory.
Once the income has been sourced under I.R.C.
§ 863(b), taxation in the United States depends on
whether the income is effectively connected income
under either I.R.C. §§ 864(c)(3) or (4). In the
example above, the foreign source portion of the
gain attributable to the production is not subject to
U.S. taxation. The U.S. source sales portion of the
gain should be taxable as income effectively

connected with the conduct of a U.S. trade or business under I.R.C. §§ 864(c)(3) and 882.

The regulations specify a 3-step process for sourcing income from manufactured inventory. First, gross income is allocated to the sales activity and the production activity under one of the specified methods. Second, the gross income allocated to the sales activity and the production activity is then sourced. The sales activity gross income is sourced based on the title passage rule. I.R.C. § 861(a)(6). The production activity gross income is sourced according to the relative domestic and foreign production assets. Third, expenses are allocated in accordance with regulations discussed *infra* in § 3.02. Reg. § 1.863–3.

In allocating income between the production and sales activity, the regulations use the "50/50" method as the default. Under that method, 50 percent of the gross income is considered attributable to the sales activity and the other 50 percent is considered attributable to the production activity. Under the 50/50 method, once the allocation has been made, the income allocated to production is sourced based on where the production assets are located. Production assets are tangible and intangible assets that are directly used to produce inventory. In the example above, if all the manufacturing assets are in Spain, 50 percent of the gross income will be foreign source income not subject to U.S. tax. If title to the thermostats is transferred in the United States, the other 50 percent would be U.S. source income which would be effectively connected to the conduct of a U.S. trade or business and therefore subject to U.S. taxation. If the taxpayer had half of its manufacturing assets in Spain and half of it manufacturing assets in the U.S. and title to the thermostats was passed in the U.S., then 75 percent of its income would be U.S. source (*i.e.*, half of the 50 percent profit attributable to manufacturing and all of the 50 percent profit attributable to sales activity).

In lieu of the 50/50 method, a taxpayer can elect to use the independent factory price (IFP) method if an IFP can be fairly established. In the example above, suppose that the foreign corporation regularly sold the inventory to independent distributors that resold the thermostats in the United States. In the example above assuming all manufacturing in Spain, suppose that the cost of goods sold for each thermostat was $10 and the gross proceeds from sales to U.S. purchasers was $100. Under the 50/50 method, $45 of profit would be treated as foreign source and $45 would be treated as U.S. source on each sale, assuming all production takes place in Spain. However, if the foreign corporation could establish that independent distributors bought the same inventory for $60 per thermostat, then $50 of the gain would be allocated to the production activity (and treated as foreign source because the production assets are located in Spain) and $40 of the gross income from each thermostat would be treated as sales income and sourced in the United States if title passes there.

A taxpayer may elect to source gain from manufactured inventory based upon its books of account rather than the 50/50 or IFP methods if it receives in advance permission of the IRS. The taxpayer must establish that the books and records are unaffected by tax considerations and that receipts and expenditures clearly reflect income. Reg. § 1.863–3(b)(3).

The source rule for manufactured inventory also plays a significant role for U.S. taxpayers operating abroad. For example, if USCO, a U.S. corporation manufactures inventory in the United States and passes title to the inventory abroad, 50 percent of the income generated will be foreign source income. Often, the foreign country in which the sales are made may not impose a tax on the sales income if title passage is the only connection to the source country. As a result, USCO would generate untaxed, foreign source income which may be useful in absorbing any excess foreign tax credits generated from other business operations. *See infra* § 13.03.

(3) Intangible Property

Gain from the sale of any patent, copyright, secret process or formula, goodwill, trademark, trade brand, or similar intangible is sourced in one of two ways depending on the nature of the sale. If the sales proceeds are contingent on the productivity, use, or disposition of the intangible, any gain is sourced as if the payments received were royalties (*i.e.*, source is determined by where the property is used). I.R.C. § 865(d). For example, if a nonresident alien sells a patent to a U.S. purchaser to be used in producing home security alarm systems in the United States in exchange for 5 percent of the gross sales proceeds of the systems, the gain from the patent sale is U.S. source income because the patent is used in the United States. I.R.C. § 861(a)(4).

If the sales proceeds are not contingent on the use of the intangible, any gain is sourced by reference to the residence of the seller. I.R.C. §§ 865(a) and (g). In the example above, if the nonresident alien sold the patent for a flat $800,000, any gain from the sale would be foreign source income. If the sales contract has both a non-contingent and contingent aspect (*e.g.*, sale for $800,000 plus 2 percent of gross sales proceeds), the amounts received will receive bifurcated treatment in accordance with the rules above.

There is a special source rule for goodwill. Noncontingent payments received for the transfer of goodwill are sourced in the country where the goodwill was generated. I.R.C. § 865(d)(3).

(4) Depreciable Personal Property

Gain from the sale of business equipment, automobiles, machinery and other depreciable personal property or from any amortizable intangible property (*e.g.*, patent, copyright, trademark, goodwill) may consist of two components for tax purposes: depreciation (or amortization) adjustments and appreciation (including inflationary gain). I.R.C. § 865(c). For example, suppose business machinery was purchased for

$10,000 and that $3,000 of depreciation deductions were taken for U.S. tax purposes (reducing the machine's basis to $7,000) before the machinery was sold for $12,000. Of the $5,000 gain, $3,000 represents depreciation adjustments to the asset's basis for previous depreciation deductions and $2,000 represents capital appreciation (or inflation). To the extent that the previous depreciation deductions reduced U.S. source income, the depreciation adjustments are treated as U.S. source income regardless of the residence of the owner or the place where title passes. To the extent that previous depreciation deductions were taken against foreign source income, the depreciation adjustments are treated as foreign source income. Any other gain (*e.g.*, capital appreciation) is sourced like gains from inventory by determining where title passes. I.R.C. § 865(c)(2).

(5) Other Personal Property

The general rule of I.R.C. § 865(a) which applies to nondepreciable personal property is essentially a residual rule although it does apply to sales of stock (but *see* I.R.C. § 1248 discussed *infra* at § 10.06), securities, partnership interests and to the sale of intangibles where the sales proceeds are not contingent on the use of the intangible. Generally, income from the sale of nondepreciable personal property (*e.g.*, stock) by a U.S. resident is U.S. source income, while any gain from a sale by a nonresident produces foreign source income. For sales by a partnership, the rule is applied at the partner level. I.R.C. § 865(i)(5). If a U.S. resident maintains an office or other fixed place of business outside the United States, income from the sale of property attributable to that office is treated as foreign source income if the foreign country imposes at least a 10 percent tax on income from such a sale. I.R.C. § 865(e).

There is another exception to the residence-of-the-seller rule pertaining to stock dispositions. If a U.S. resident sells stock of a foreign affiliate (as defined in I.R.C. § 1504(a)) in a foreign country where the affiliate derived more than 50 percent of its gross income from an active trade or business during the preceding three years, any gain is foreign source income. I.R.C. § 865(f). Even if a U.S. taxpayer sells stock of a foreign corporation which is not a foreign affiliate, any gain is foreign source income if a treaty between the purchaser's country and the United States so provides and the U.S. taxpayer chooses the benefits of the treaty. I.R.C. § 865(h). For a U.S. taxpayer, treating such gains as foreign source income may mean that any foreign taxes imposed on that gain are creditable against U.S. tax liability. In contrast, foreign taxes imposed on U.S. source income are not creditable against U.S. taxes on that income.

(6) Sales Through Offices or Fixed Places of Businesses in the United States

Notwithstanding the other source rules pertaining to the sale of personal property, if a nonresident maintains an office or other fixed place of business in the United States to which the gain from a sale is attributable, the gain is treated as U.S. source income. I.R.C. § 865(e)(2)(A). There is an exception for inventory property sold for use outside the United States through a foreign fixed place of business that materially participated in the sale. I.R.C. § 865(e)(2)(B).

Notwithstanding certain specified source rules, if a U.S. resident maintains an office or other fixed place of business in a foreign country, income from the sale of personal property attributable to such office is treated as foreign source income if there is at least a 10 percent income tax actually paid in a foreign country. I.R.C. § 865(e)(1).

(G) OTHER GROSS INCOME

Scholarships, fellowship grants, prizes and awards are considered to be FDAP income subject to the 30 percent withholding tax if they are from U.S. sources and if the payment is included in gross income, *e.g.*, a prize, or a scholarship that does not satisfy the requirements of I.R.C. § 117. Reg. §§ 1.871–7(a)(2) and 1.1441–2. The source of a payment made to a nonresident as a scholarship etc. is the country of residence of the person making the payment. Reg. § 1.863–1(d)(2). For example, if a student from Hong Kong receives a scholarship from her government to study at a U.S. university, the payment would be foreign source income and would not be taxable by the United States. Conversely, a payment by a U.S. foundation for study at a U.S.

university would be U.S. source income. If a nonresident conducts activities outside the United States, the scholarship has a foreign source regardless of the residence of the payor. For example, if a U.S. university grants a scholarship to a Hong Kong student for field work done abroad, the income will be foreign source income.

Suppose a foreign parent corporation guarantees a loan made by a bank to the foreign parent's U.S. subsidiary in order to reduce the interest rate on the loan. If the U.S. subsidiary pays a guarantee fee to its foreign parent to compensate for the guarantee, I.R.C. § 861(a)(9) provides that the payment generates U.S. income.

A "notional principal contract" is defined as a financial instrument that provides for the payment of amounts by one party to another at specified intervals calculated by reference to a specified rate on a notional principal amount in exchange for specified consideration. For example, suppose a nonresident enters into an exchange with a U.S. party to pay the U.S. party 10 percent annually on a $1 million notional principal amount in exchange for the U.S. party's payment on a $1 million notional principal amount of interest equal to the London Interbank Offered Rate (LIBOR) plus three percentage points. Note that the $1 million is notional because it is used merely as a reference; no $1 million payment is made by either party.

The nonresident might engage in this transaction because of an outstanding obligation to pay interest measured by LIBOR plus 3 percentage points owed

to someone else which the nonresident wishes to
transform from a risky payment (if LIBOR should
rise unexpectedly) into a fixed 10 percent interest
obligation. The U.S. party may be willing to
undertake some risk, betting that the 10 percent
payment received will exceed the LIBOR plus 3
percentage points paid. However, suppose that in
year 1, LIBOR is 9 percent. Therefore the net flow of
income is $20,000 of income from the U.S. payor to
the nonresident. Is that payment subject to taxation
as FDAP income? Generally, income under a
notional principal contract is sourced in the country
of the recipient's residence. The income would be
treated as foreign source income not subject to
FDAP taxation under I.R.C. § 871(a) (or I.R.C.
§ 881). Reg. § 1.863–7(a).

However, I.R.C. § 871(m) treats certain notional
principal contract payments as "dividend
equivalents" which are treated as U.S. source
income. For example, suppose the nonresident
agrees to swap interest payments on a $10 million
notional principal contract with a U.S. counterparty
who agrees to swap a payment based on the
dividends paid on $10 million of stock in a U.S.
company. Any net amount paid to the nonresident
will not be foreign source income under Reg.
§ 1.863–7(a), but instead will be U.S. income.
Similar treatment results for other substitute
dividend transactions.

What is the source rule for items where there are
no specific source rules? Where an item of income is
not characterized by statute or regulation, courts

have sourced the item by comparison and analogy with the most closely related items of income specified within the statutes. *Bank of America v. United States*, 680 F.2d 142, 147 (Ct. Cl. 1982).

(H) RESIDENCE FOR SOURCE RULE PURPOSES

There is a special definition of "residence" for purposes of determining the source of income that is different from the definition of "residence" under I.R.C. § 7701(b) for overall taxing purposes. For source purposes, a U.S. citizen or resident alien under I.R.C. § 7701(b) who does not have a "tax home" (*see* Reg. § 1.911–2(b) and I.R.C. § 162(a)(2)) in the United States is a nonresident. I.R.C. § 865(g). Conversely, a nonresident alien who has a tax home in the United States is a U.S. resident for purposes of the source rule under I.R.C. § 865. Generally, a taxpayer's "tax home" is located at the taxpayer's regular or principal place of business.

§ 3.02   DEDUCTION ALLOCATION RULES

(A) IN GENERAL

The 30 percent tax on FDAP income of a nonresident is imposed on gross income; no deductions are allowed. However, the tax on a nonresident's income that is effectively connected with the conduct of a trade or business is imposed on taxable income. I.R.C. §§ 861(b), 871(b), 882, and 873. The allocation and apportionment of expenses serves an important function for foreign taxpayers.

To the extent that expenses are allocated and apportioned against income effectively connected to the conduct of a U.S. trade or business, a foreign taxpayer's income subject to U.S. tax liability is decreased. Keep in mind that what the United States does under its domestic law has no necessary effect on how expenses will be treated by the nonresident's home country.

Allocation and apportionment of deductions also plays an important role for U.S. residents and citizens doing business or investing abroad. These taxpayers are taxable on worldwide income so that all deductible expenses potentially reduce U.S. tax liability. Furthermore, these taxpayers can offset their U.S. tax liability with foreign income taxes paid on their foreign source taxable income (*i.e.*, taking deductions into account) if those foreign taxes do not exceed the U.S. tax potentially imposed on that income. To the extent expenses are allocated and apportioned against foreign source income, a U.S. taxpayer may have a smaller foreign tax credit. For this reason, U.S. taxpayers generally prefer expenses to be allocated and apportioned against U.S. source income.

To illustrate, suppose that U.S. Co. earns trade or business income of $100 in Italy and $100 in the United States. U.S. Co. also incurs a $100 deductible expense. As a result, net taxable income for U.S. purposes is $100. Assume that both Italy and the United States impose a 35 percent tax on taxable income. If the $100 expense is allocated and apportioned against the $100 earned in the United

States, U.S. Co. is able to credit the $35 Italian tax against the $35 U.S. tax on the Italian income that would otherwise be imposed (*i.e.*, U.S. Co. is taxed on worldwide income). In total, U.S. Co. would pay $35 in tax to the Italian government and $0 to the U.S. government. However, if the expense under U.S. tax rules is allocated and apportioned against the Italian income, then U.S. Co. is taxed $35 by the United States on the $100 of U.S. source income; there is no additional U.S. tax on the $0 net Italian income. Moreover, U.S. Co. is not able to credit the $35 tax paid to Italy against its U.S. tax liability because under U.S. source rules, U.S. Co. has no net foreign source income (even though Italy finds $100 of foreign source income). In total, U.S. Co. would pay a $35 tax to the United States and $35 to Italy. While the unused Italian foreign tax credit may be usable in another year, or alternatively a taxpayer could choose to deduct foreign taxes thus reducing U.S. taxable income to $65 and U.S. tax liability to $22.75, it is nevertheless advantageous when expenses are allocated and apportioned against U.S. source income.

The Code does not, for the most part, specify with precision how expenses should be allocated between U.S. and foreign sources. But in general a taxpayer is required to: (1) allocate deductions to a class of gross income; and then, if a statutory provision requires, (2) apportion deductions within the class of gross income between the statutory grouping (*e.g.*, effectively connected income for a nonresident taxpayer and foreign source income for a U.S. taxpayer) and the residual grouping (*i.e.*, everything else). Reg. § 1.861–8(a)(2). Often expenses bear a definite relationship to a class of gross income in which case no further allocation is necessary although it may be necessary to apportion the income between U.S. and foreign sources (or for a nonresident, between effectively connected income and all other income). For example, depreciation deductions and other direct business expenses deductible under I.R.C. § 162 can often be allocated to specific income.

To illustrate the operation of these rules: suppose that Forco, a foreign corporation, purchases and sells computer hardware in the United States through a U.S. branch and in foreign markets through foreign branches. Forco also sells computer books exclusively in foreign countries. For the taxable year, Forco has gross income of $2,000,000 of which $800,000 is from the sale of computer equipment and is effectively connected to the conduct of a trade or business in the United States, $700,000 is from sales of computer equipment outside the United States, and $500,000 is from sales of computer books outside the United States. Forco's marketing department incurs deductible expenses of $400,000 with respect to all of Forco's products and $100,000 for advertising relating only to Forco's books.

Under these facts, the general marketing expense of $400,000 is allocated to the class of gross income from sales of all of Forco's products, and the $100,000 advertising expense is allocated to gross income from the sale of books. For purposes of determining the amount of effectively connected income under I.R.C. § 882(c) with respect to the sale of computer equipment, it is necessary to apportion the $400,000 marketing expense between the gross income in the statutory grouping of effectively connected income and the residual grouping of non-effectively connected income. In this instance the amount apportioned to U.S. effectively connected sales is based on gross income from sales as follows:

$$\$400,000 \ \times \ \frac{\$800,000}{\$2,000,000} = \ \$160,000$$

The remaining $240,000 of general marketing expense is apportioned to the residual grouping of sales of computer equipment and books outside the United States. Because the $100,000 advertising expense is definitely related to a class of income (*i.e.*, book sales) that is in the residual grouping, there is no apportionment. Consequently, the net effectively connected income equals $800,000 minus $160,000, or $640,000.

In the example, just considered, if the taxpayer were a U.S. corporation the same process would be necessary but for a different purpose. For U.S. taxpayers the allocation and apportionment process is necessary to determine the foreign tax credit. *See infra* Chapter 8. For U.S. taxpayers, it is the foreign source income that is the statutory grouping and the U.S. source income is the residual grouping.

(B) INTEREST

(1) U.S. Corporations

The allocation and apportionment of interest expense often plays a significant in determining a taxpayer's tax posture. Some interest is directly allocated to a specific class of income if the loan proceeds are applied to purchase and improve real property or depreciable personal property and the creditor can look only to the identified property for security. Reg. § 1.861–10T(b). But if money is borrowed for general business purposes, the interest accrued or paid (depending on method of accounting) is first allocated against all of the taxpayer's gross income and then is apportioned under I.R.C. § 864(e) between U.S. and foreign sources generally according to the basis of all of the taxpayer's assets (in some cases a fair market value method can be elected). Moreover, for purposes of this apportionment, the assets of all affiliated corporations (generally members of a U.S. consolidated group but sometimes other corporations are included as well) are taken into account. I.R.C. § 1504. This allocation based on assets is premised on the notion that money is fungible making it difficult to trace accurately interest expense to a particular item of income.

Suppose that a U.S. parent corporation with $30 of interest expense on a $400 loan owns two assets: stock of a wholly-owned U.S. subsidiary with a basis of $600 and stock of a foreign subsidiary (that has no earnings and profits) with a basis of $200. The

U.S. subsidiary owns assets used to produce U.S. source income with a basis of $700 and assets used to produce foreign source income with a basis of $100. Because a foreign subsidiary is generally not part of an affiliated group, there is no "look-through" to the assets of the foreign corporation for purposes of allocating interest (although the basis of the stock in the foreign corporation is adjusted for a foreign corporation's earnings and profits under I.R.C. § 864(e)(4)). However, the parent is deemed to own the U.S. subsidiary's U.S. assets with a basis of $700 and the foreign assets with a basis of $100. In total, the U.S. parent is deemed to own foreign assets with a basis of $300 ($200 basis in the foreign stock and $100 basis in the U.S. subsidiary's foreign assets) and U.S. assets with a basis of $700 (the U.S. subsidiary's basis in its assets used to produce U.S. source income). Accordingly, 30 percent of the $30 interest expense of the U.S. parent corporation, or $9, is apportioned against foreign source income and the other $21 of interest expense is allocated against U.S. source income. The same result would occur if the U.S. subsidiary had borrowed the money and paid the interest. Notice that how the borrowed funds are actually used is irrelevant in determining the allocation and apportionment of interest expense. Notice also that the amount of gross U.S. source or foreign source income taxpayer generates is irrelevant. The formula is mechanical.

One important modification in calculating the tax book value basis of stock of a foreign corporation is the "basis bump" for earnings and profits (E&P) of 10 percent owned foreign corporations. In a typical case for a wholly-owned foreign subsidiary, the stock basis would be adjusted upwards for E&P of the foreign subsidiary or downwards if there was an E&P deficit. Reg. § 1.861–12(c)(2).

Suppose instead that the foreign subsidiary, rather than the U.S. parent, has a need for the borrowed funds. Suppose further that the U.S. parent has $60 of U.S. source income and $60 of foreign source income before taking into consideration any interest paid on the $400 loan. The foreign subsidiary could borrow the $400 directly in which case the $30 interest expense may have no impact on the U.S. parent's U.S. liability. Alternatively, the U.S. parent could borrow $400 and lend it to the foreign subsidiary which would pay $30 of interest to the parent which would pay $30 of interest to the bank. Notice that the U.S. parent has no additional net income for U.S. tax purposes—it has $30 of additional foreign source interest income but a $30 deduction for interest paid to the bank. However, if the parent borrows the money and lends it to the foreign subsidiary, the parent may create more foreign source income and less U.S. source income which may allow a bigger foreign tax credit thereby lowering the parent's worldwide income taxes.

For example, if the $30 interest expense is allocated according to asset value as indicated above, the U.S. parent and the U.S. subsidiary have $700 of assets used to produce U.S. source income and now $700 of assets used to produce foreign source income (the $300 discussed above plus a $400 tax basis in the note from the foreign subsidiary). Accordingly, $15 of the interest expense is apportioned against foreign source income (which also includes the interest paid from the foreign subsidiary to the U.S. parent) and $15 against U.S. source income. Although the net amount of taxable income (*i.e.*, $120) does not change, the U.S. parent has $15 of additional foreign source income and $15 less U.S. source income. The U.S. parent would have $75 of foreign source income (*i.e.*, $90 (which includes the $30 interest income) minus the $15 interest expense) and $45 of U.S. source income ($60 minus the $15 interest expense).

To prevent this type of manipulation, the IRS has adopted a netting rule which, when it applies, counters tax avoidance by allocating a U.S. taxpayer's interest deduction to any interest received from a foreign subsidiary. Reg. § 1.861–10(e). If the rule applied in the example, the U.S. parent would allocate the $30 of interest paid to the bank against the $30 of interest received from its foreign subsidiary, thereby defeating any advantage of borrowing and relending as opposed to the foreign subsidiary directly borrowing from the bank.

The mechanics of the netting rule are quite detailed but essentially the rule is implicated for a taxable year if two conditions are met: first, if the amount of related group indebtedness (*i.e.*, borrowing from a related U.S. corporation) increases compared to the amount of indebtedness for a 5-year testing period (Regs. § 1.861–10(e)(2)); second, if the amount of excess U.S. shareholder indebtedness (*i.e.*, borrowing from unrelated lenders by U.S. members of the corporate group increases compared to the amount of indebtedness for a 5-year testing period (Regs. § 1.861–10(e)(3)). So for example, for a given year the interest netting rule may apply if there is both an increase in borrowing by a U.S. parent corporation from unrelated lenders and an increase in indebtedness owed by a foreign subsidiary to the U.S. parent.

As noted above, generally a foreign corporation is not part of the U.S. borrowers affiliated group and so there is no look-through to its assets but rather the stock of foreign corporation owned by the U.S. corporation is taken into account. However, if a foreign corporation generates effectively connected income (essentially, U.S. source business income) that is more than 50 percent of the gross income for the taxable year, then the assets held by the foreign corporation are taken into account for interest expense allocation and apportionment, assuming at least 80 percent of the vote or value of the foreign corporation's stock is owned directly or indirectly by members of the affiliated group. I.R.C. § 864(e)(5).

A U.S. taxpayer with interest expense can use asset basis for purposes of allocating and apportioning interest expense, as illustrated above. This is known as the tax book value method. There is also an alternative tax book value method. Because U.S. depreciable assets are generally depreciated using accelerated depreciation methods while foreign assets held by a U.S. taxpayer are depreciated using a straight-line method, a U.S.

taxpayer's calculation under the tax book method may result in apportioning more interest expense against foreign source income for purposes of calculating the foreign tax credit. The alternative tax book value method allows a taxpayer to elect to calculate the tax book value of all depreciable tangible property under the straight-line method in apportioning certain expenses, including interest for foreign tax credit limitation purposes. This may result in less interest expense apportioned against foreign source income.

Alternatively, a U.S. taxpayer can elect to use the fair market value (FMV) method of allocating and apportioning interest expense. Reg. § 1.861–9T(h). While the rules for applying the fair market value method are complex, the FMV method may be attractive for a U.S. taxpayer where there is more appreciation in U.S. assets than in foreign assets. For example, suppose a U.S. corporation with appreciated U.S. assets purchases stock of a foreign corporation. Because the fair market value of the foreign assets (*i.e.*, stock of the newly purchased target) is equal to the basis of the stock while the basis of the U.S. assets is less than the fair market value of the assets, the FMV method of allocating interest may result in more interest expense allocated and apportioned against U.S. source income than would be the case under the tax book value method. By allocating more interest expense against U.S. source income, a U.S. taxpayer may be able to reduce the U.S. tax bill if sufficient foreign taxes have been paid to offset any U.S. tax on the foreign source income.

For example, suppose that U.S. Co. holds U.S. assets with a basis of $10 and a FMV of $90 and stock of a newly purchased foreign corporation with a basis and a fair market value of 90 (and no earnings and profits). Suppose further that U.S. Co. has interest expense of $20, foreign source income of $60 and U.S. source income of $60. Assume that foreign taxes paid with respect to the foreign source income are sufficient to offset any potential U.S. tax on that income.

Cutting through some of the detail, under the tax book value method $18 (*i.e.*, $90 basis/$100 total basis) of interest expense would be allocated and apportioned against foreign source income and only $2 would be allocated and apportioned against U.S. source income. As a result, there would be $58 of net U.S. source income which would result in a U.S. tax of $20.30 (.35 tax rate × $58). (The potential U.S. tax on the foreign source income may be offset by a credit for the foreign taxes paid.)

However, if the FMV method were used instead, then (ignoring the FMV method details) only $10 of interest expense would be allocated against foreign source income (*i.e.*, $90 FMV/$180 total FMV) and $10 would be allocated and apportioned against U.S. source income, resulting in a $17.50 U.S. tax on the $50 of net U.S. source income. The potential U.S. tax on the $50 of foreign source income would be offset by available foreign tax credits. Use of the FMV method in this case may result in lower U.S. tax because more expense is allocated against U.S. source income. Note that whether the taxpayer uses the tax book value method or the FMV method will have no effect on how the foreign country determines the foreign tax due under its own tax laws.

(2) Foreign Corporations Engaged in a U.S. Trade or Business

The interest allocation and apportionment rules described above apply to U.S. corporations. Foreign corporations engaged in a U.S. trade or business, particularly foreign banks, benefit from allocation rules under Reg. § 1.882–5 which generally have the effect of apportioning a larger interest deduction against U.S. source income than the asset allocation method of Reg. § 1.861–8 et seq. Foreign corporations (particularly banks) had complained that the cost of borrowing money (*i.e.*, interest) to lend in the United States is higher than the cost of borrowing money at home (*e.g.*, often through non-interest bearing deposits) and that allocation of interest based on the asset value of a loan portfolio underestimates the cost of maintaining the U.S. portion of that portfolio.

In the 3-step process under Reg. § 1.882–5, a foreign corporation first determines the value of U.S. assets (typically adjusted basis) that generate U.S. effectively connected income. Next the foreign corporation determines its U.S. connected liabilities by multiplying those U.S. assets by a specified fixed ratio of 50 percent (95 percent for a bank) or by the actual ratio of worldwide liabilities to worldwide assets. In the third step, the foreign corporation determines the interest allocable to the U.S. connected liabilities under the adjusted U.S.-booked liabilities method (ABLM) or the separate currency pools method (SCPM), which is more sensitive to currency fluctuation.

To illustrate at a high level, suppose that Forco, a foreign corporation, has a U.S. branch. For the taxable year, Forco has $500 of assets used to generate U.S. effectively connected income and $3,000 of worldwide assets. Forco's worldwide liabilities are $2,400 of which $300 appear on the books of the U.S. branch. The branch shows a $30 interest payment. The interest rate on Forco's U.S. dollar liabilities booked outside the United States (*e.g.*, dollar denominated loans made by Forco's home office) as well as its foreign currency denominated loans is 8 percent. Forco's worldwide interest payment is $198 ($30 in the United States plus 8 percent × $2,100, or $168 on loans outside the United States). Assume that Forco will use ABLM in the third step.

The U.S. connected liabilities of Forco under the actual ratio method is $2,400/$3,000 × $500, or $400. The interest apportioned against the U.S. connected liabilities under the ABLM method is equal to the $30 of interest shown on the books of the branch plus the U.S. connected liabilities in excess of those shown on the U.S. books (*i.e.*, $100) multiplied by the interest rate on U.S. dollar liabilities booked outside the United States (*i.e.*, 8 percent). In sum, Forco can apportion $38.00 of interest expense against U.S. source effectively connected income. If interest expense for Forco were allocated under the asset method applicable to U.S. taxpayers, only $33 of interest ($500/$3,000 × $198) would have been allocated and apportioned to its income effectively connected with the conduct of a U.S. trade or business.

(3) Deductibility of Interest Expense

The discussion above is focused on how to allocate and apportion interest expense, but U.S. corporations owned by foreign corporations also must contend with whether interest paid (however allocated and apportioned) is deductible. In general, I.R.C. § 163 provides for the deduction of interest expense. However, as discussed *infra* in § 4.04(A)(5), interest paid from a U.S. subsidiary to its foreign parent (or other related foreign owners) may be disallowed as a deduction under I.R.C. § 163(j) to the extent that the interest is not subject to a full U.S. tax in the hands of the recipient and where the U.S. subsidiary is deemed to be thinly capitalized. Even if interest is paid to an unrelated party, to the extent that the loan is guaranteed by a foreign related party, the interest deduction may be disallowed.

Even in situations where I.R.C. § 163(j) does not pose a problem, an interest expense deduction may be disallowed to a U.S. accrual basis taxpayer where the interest is payable to a related party. Under I.R.C. § 267(a)(3) a U.S. taxpayer is essentially put on the cash method of accounting for purposes of deducting interest paid to a related foreign party unless the foreign related party's accrued income is taxable in the United States (*e.g.*, gross subpart F income). Similar rules apply to other deductible payments made to related foreign parties (*e.g.*, royalties). Any deductible expense that has accrued will be deductible when payment is made or is considered to be made.

(C) RESEARCH AND EXPERIMENTAL EXPENDITURES

The allocation of research and experimental expenditures (often referred to as R&E, R&D or research and development expenditures) is an issue of great importance to U.S. corporations and great difficulty for the IRS. To the extent that research and experimental expenditures are allocated and apportioned against foreign source income, foreign source taxable income is reduced and so might the foreign tax credit be reduced for income taxes paid abroad. U.S. taxpayers normally want to allocate and apportion as much of these expenses as possible to U.S. source income to maximize the foreign tax credit. *See infra* Chapter 7.06. It is often not possible to allocate and apportion research and experimental expenditures with precision. By allocating a specified percentage of the research and experimental expenditures on the basis of where the research activities take place, Congress recognized that research and experimental expenditures do not always result in the direct production of income.

Under I.R.C. § 864(g), taxpayers are required to allocate research and experimentation expenses undertaken solely to meet legal requirements imposed by a government to the jurisdiction of that government (assuming the expenditures are not expected to generate income outside the jurisdiction). For example, where a taxpayer performs tests on a product in response to a requirement of the U.S. Food and Drug Administration, the costs of testing shall be allocated solely to gross income from U.S. sources. After accounting for such legal requirements, a taxpayer is required to allocate the remaining expenses either using the sales or the gross income method. Under the sales method, 50 percent of the deduction for research and experimentation shall be apportioned exclusively to the geographic location where the activities accounting for more than half the deduction were performed. The remainder is apportioned on the basis of where the sales resulting from the research take place. Reg. § 1.861–17.

For example, suppose that a U.S. manufacturer which derives 60 percent of its gross sales revenue from abroad incurs $100 million of research and experimental expenditures in the United States related to production of the assets that are sold. Fifty percent of $100 million, or $50 million is apportioned to U.S. sources. Of the remaining $50 million, 60 percent, or $30 million, is apportioned to foreign sources, and the remaining $20 million is apportioned to U.S. sources. Notice that 70 percent of the $100 million of the research and experimental expenditures are apportioned to U.S. income even though U.S. sales revenue only accounts for 40 percent of total sales revenue. This produces a favorable outcome for a U.S. taxpayer trying to maximize foreign source income (by apportioning deductions to U.S. source income) to increase the potential foreign tax credit.

A taxpayer can choose an alternative method of apportionment based on gross income. Reg. § 1.861–17(b)(1)(ii). Under this method 25 percent of any U.S. deduction for research and experimentation is apportioned exclusively to the geographic location where the activities accounting for more than half the deduction were performed. The remainder is apportioned on the basis of gross income so long as the result of the apportionment is at least 50 percent of the result under the sales method.

In the example above, suppose that the U.S. manufacturer had 30 percent of its gross income from sources outside the United States. Under the gross income method, 25 percent of the $100 million expenditure would be apportioned to U.S. sources. Of the remaining $75 million, 30 percent, or $22.5 million, would be apportioned to foreign source income. This method would produce even more foreign source income than under the sales method, thereby maximizing the potential for a foreign tax credit. If the U.S. manufacturer generated only 10 percent of its gross income from sources outside the United States, $15 million of expenditures, or 50 percent of the result under the sales method, would be apportioned to foreign source income (even though 10 percent × $75 million = $7.5 million).

(D) LOSSES

Suppose that USCO, which has foreign operations, suffers a loss in the conduct of its business. The source of that loss is important in determining USCO's foreign tax credit. For example, suppose that USCO has $100 of U.S. source income and $100 of foreign source income on which a $35 foreign tax is imposed. If USCO also has a $60 loss which is treated as U.S. source loss, then USCO will face a U.S. tax on the $40 of net U.S. source income. The potential $35 U.S. tax on the $100 of foreign source income may be offset by the $35 foreign tax credit. On the other hand, if the $60 loss is allocated against foreign source income, then USCO faces a U.S. tax on $100, rather than $40, of U.S. source income (Again, the potential U.S. tax on the foreign source income will be offset by the foreign taxes paid.) If income from the activity which produced a loss would have been foreign source income, then the loss generally will be allocated and apportioned against foreign source income. I.R.C. § 865(j); Reg. § 1.865–1. While this rule applies to the sale of personal property (with some exceptions including inventory) at a loss, the allocation and apportionment of losses from the sale of inventory will be sourced in the same manner, albeit under different authority. Reg. § 1.861–8.

Suppose that USCO disposes of stock in a foreign corporation at a loss. If the stock paid dividends, they would have been treated as foreign source income. I.R.C. § 861(a)(2). On the other hand, if the stock had been sold at a gain, the gain might have been U.S. source income. I.R.C. § 865(a). If the stock sold were stock of an affiliate that conducted a trade or business in a foreign country, any gain might have been treated as foreign source income. So given these possible treatments for income or gain associated with the stock, how should a loss be allocated and apportioned?

In general, loss from the sale of stock is sourced in the same manner as gain (*i.e.*, residence of the seller) ignoring whether the stock sold is stock of an affiliate (I.R.C. § 865(f)) or would have been treated as a foreign source dividend if sold at a gain (I.R.C. § 1248). Reg. § 1.865–2. However, if the stock sale is attributable to an office or other fixed place of business in a foreign country, the loss is allocated against foreign source income if a gain on the sale of stock would have been taxable by the foreign country at a 10 percent or greater rate. Reg. § 1.865–2(a)(2). Also, a loss on the sale of stock in a foreign corporation is allocated against foreign source income to the extent that dividends paid during the previous 24 months were treated as foreign source income. Reg. § 1.865–2(b)(1).

PART 2

U.S. ACTIVITIES OF FOREIGN TAXPAYERS

CHAPTER 4
TAXING RULES

§ 4.01   OVERVIEW

Income earned by nonresidents generally falls under one of two taxing regimes. For a nonresident (individual or corporation) "engaged in a trade or business" in the United States, the net income that is "effectively connected" with the conduct of that trade or business is taxed in the same manner as net income earned by a U.S. resident (individual or corporation). I.R.C. § 871(b) (individuals) and I.R.C. § 882 (corporations). Fixed or Determinable Annual or Periodical gains, profits, and income (*i.e.*, basically investment income often referred to as FDAP income) from U.S. sources earned by a nonresident is typically taxed on a gross basis at a flat 30 percent rate (or lower treaty rate). I.R.C. §§ 871(a) (individuals) and 881 (corporations).

What follows is a consideration of these two taxing regimes as well as other taxing provisions affecting nonresidents. Then the administrative provisions that enforce this taxing framework are addressed. *See supra* Chapter 3 for a discussion of the source rules which play an important role in the taxing regimes discussed in this chapter.

§ 4.02 "ENGAGED IN A TRADE OR BUSINESS" IN THE UNITED STATES

If a nonresident conducts a U.S. trade or business, the income effectively connected with the conduct of the trade or business is taxed in the same manner as business income of a U.S. resident. I.R.C. §§ 871(b) (individuals) and 882 (corporations). If there is no U.S. trade or business, the United States basically taxes only certain U.S. source income— generally investment income—at a 30 percent (or lower treaty) rate applied to gross income. I.R.C. §§ 871(a) (individuals) and 881 (corporations). Partners in a partnership are considered to be engaged in a trade or business in the United States if the partnership is engaged in a trade or business in the United States. I.R.C. § 875(1). A partnership is considered to be engaged in a trade or business in the United States if a partner is so engaged and is acting as an agent of the partnership. *See, e.g., Donroy, Ltd. v. United States*, 301 F.2d 200 (9th Cir. 1962).

The international tax provisions of the Code provide little guidance as to what constitutes a U.S. trade or business. *See* I.R.C. § 864(b). Certainly, passive investment activity does not rise to the level of a trade or business. For example, a nonresident individual or foreign corporation merely collecting interest or dividends from a U.S. payer is not engaged in a trade or business in the United States. The gross interest or dividend income (with no deductions permitted) normally would be subject to tax at a 30 percent (or lower treaty) rate. I.R.C.

§§ 871(a) or 881. Similarly, a foreign investor collecting rental income on U.S. property from a tenant under a net lease (*i.e.*, where the tenant is responsible for maintenance, taxes, and insurance) is not considered engaged in a trade or business and would normally be subject to the 30 percent tax. *But see* I.R.C. §§ 871(d), 882(d).

A nonresident is considered to be engaged in a USTB if its activities in the United are "considerable . . . as well as continuous and regular." *Pinchot v. Commissioner*, 113 F.2d 718, 719 (2d Cir. 1940). The standard for determining the existence of a USTB thus is both qualitative and quantitative. *See Scottish American Investment Co., Ltd. v. Commissioner*, 12 T.C. 49, 59 (1949) ("[I]t is a matter of degree, based upon both a quantitative and a qualitative analysis of the services performed, as to where the line of demarcation should be drawn.")

Activities conducted by a nonresident alien or a foreign corporation in the United States through an agent pose the most difficult questions concerning what constitutes a U.S. trade or business. For example, in *Lewenhaupt v. Commissioner*, 20 T.C. 151 (Tax Ct. 1953), the taxpayer, a resident of Sweden, was the owner of U.S. real property which was managed by a U.S. agent. The agent was given power of attorney and used the power to buy and sell real property, execute leases, collect rents, arrange for repairs, pay taxes and mortgage interest, and arrange for insurance. The court found that these activities were "considerable, continuous, and regular" and constituted the conduct of a U.S. trade or business by the principal, even where the agent was an independent agent.

There are special agency rules for nonresidents trading in stocks, securities or commodities. If a foreign taxpayer actively trades stocks, securities or commodities, the activity can rise to the level of a trade or business when made through a resident independent broker if the transactions are directed through an office of the taxpayer located in the United States. I.R.C. § 864(b)(2)(C). However, in the absence of a U.S. office, nonresidents, including dealers, may trade in stocks, securities or commodities through a resident broker or other independent agent without establishing a U.S. trade or business. I.R.C. § 864(b)(2)(A)(i) and (B)(i). A nonresident who is not a dealer may trade for the investor's own account through an employee or other dependent agent without having a U.S. trade or business even if the nonresident operates through a U.S. office. I.R.C. § 864(b)(2)(A)(ii) and (B)(ii). *See InverWorld, Inc. v. Commissioner*, T.C. Memo. 1996–301 (U.S. Tax Ct.1996) for a thorough analysis of the "engaged in a trade or business" requirement.

The threshold for business activities in the United States to constitute a U.S. trade or business is low. Certainly the sale of inventory on a regular basis resulting from activities in the United States constitutes a U.S. trade or business. *See, e.g., Handfield v. Commissioner*, 23 T.C. 633 (Tax Ct. 1955). But the IRS has taken the position that a foreign taxpayer present in the United States to demonstrate its product and solicit orders was engaged in a trade or business in the United States even in the absence of a U.S. office. Rev. Rul. 56–165, 1956–1 C.B. 849.

In some instances, it is clear that the taxpayer is engaged in a trade or business, but it is not clear whether the trade or business is in the United States. In *United States v. Balanovski,* 236 F.2d 298 (2d Cir. 1956), a taxpayer came to the United States to purchase trucks and other equipment. The trucks and equipment purchased were then sold to the Argentine government. Upon receiving bids from American suppliers, the taxpayer would submit the bids at a markup to the Argentine government. If the government approved the price, taxpayer would purchase the equipment with funds that were wired to the United States by the Argentine government. Taxpayer operated out of a hotel room with the help of a secretary. The level of taxpayer's activities including the solicitation of orders, the inspection of merchandise, the purchase and sale of the merchandise convinced the court that the taxpayer was engaged in a trade or business and that the trade or business was conducted in the United States rather than in Argentina. Accordingly, the taxpayer was taxed on income arising from the sales to the Argentine government.

In contrast, in *Commissioner v. Spermacet Whaling & Shipping Co.,* 281 F.2d 646 (1960), *aff'g* Tax Court, 30 T.C. 618 (1958), the court concluded that there was no *U.S.* trade or business where the taxpayer, a foreign corporation, was collecting sperm oil from whales caught on high seas and selling it in the U.S. through a U.S. middleman. All activities for the collection and production of such oil were performed entirely outside of U.S. including reconditioning and equipping a ship for an expedition, employing 300 people out of Norway, fishing for whales and executing all contracts. The only activities that took place in the U.S. were maintenance of a bank account, purchases of fuel oil, meeting of the board of directors of a foreign corporation and passage of title to the oil.

The performance of personal services in the United States by a nonresident is a U.S. trade or business. I.R.C. § 864(b). For example, a single performance by a visiting entertainer or athlete in the United States constitutes a U.S. trade or business. *See e.g.*, Rev. Rul. 70–543, 1970–2 C.B. 172. Rendering a *de minimis* level of services does not constitute a trade or business if: (1) the services are performed while the taxpayer is temporarily present in the United States; (2) the taxpayer is present in the United States for no more than 90 days during the taxable year; (3) the compensation for the services in the United States does not exceed $3,000; and (4) the employer is not engaged in a trade or business in the United States or a foreign office of a U.S. person. Treaties often broaden this *de minimis* rule. *See infra* Chapter 5.

In recent years, a number of private equity funds (generally partnerships) often with foreign investors have purchased all manner of debt instruments in the United States (*e.g.*, mortgages, distressed business loans, etc.). The goal of the investors is buy loans at a discount and then sell or settle them at or near the face value. This type of activity raises many issue that have not been fully resolved. Arguably, the mere purchase and sale of debt instruments should fall into the I.R.C. § 864(b)(2) securities trading exception. However, if the fund originates loans directly or indirectly through a pre-wired arrangement to buy loans originated by a related or unrelated lender, that activity if considerable, continuous and regular is likely a trade or business whether done directly or through a dependent or independent agent. *See* GLAM 2009–010. Even if a fund doesn't originate loans, there is a risk that a workout of existing loans may rise to the level of a trade or business (each loan that undergoes a significant modification under Reg. § 1.1001–3 is considered to be settled and reissued).

§ 4.03 "EFFECTIVELY CONNECTED" INCOME

(A) U.S. SOURCE INCOME

If a nonresident alien or foreign corporation is engaged in a trade or business in the United States, the taxpayer is taxable at rates generally applicable to U.S. residents (or citizens) on income that is "effectively connected" with the conduct of the U.S. trade or business. The term "effectively connected" is defined in I.R.C. § 864(c). If a taxpayer is engaged in a trade or business in the United States, generally, all sales, services, or manufacturing income from U.S. sources is effectively connected income. I.R.C. § 864(c)(3) and (2). For example, suppose that a foreign corporation is engaged in a trade or business in the United States of selling electronic equipment to U.S. customers through its U.S. branch. Any income generated by the U.S. branch is clearly effectively connected income. In addition, any income generated from the sale of equipment (or any other inventory in the United States) by the home office without any involvement of the U.S. branch may be effectively connected income if title to the inventory passes in the United States. Reg. § 1.864–4(b). Income from the performance of services in the United States is effectively connected income. *See* I.R.C. § 864(c)(2) and Reg. § 1.864–4(c)(3).

Income that would normally be U.S. source investment income (that is, FDAP income) is effectively connected income if either: (1) the income is derived from assets used in the conduct of the U.S. trade or business ("asset use"); or (2) the activities of the trade or business are a material factor in the realization of the income ("business activities"). I.R.C. § 864(c)(2). For example, the "asset-use" test is satisfied if a taxpayer receives interest from an account receivable arising in the trade or business. The "business-activities" test determines if dividends derived by dealers in securities or royalties derived from a patent licensing business or service fees derived from a services business are considered effectively connected income. Reg. § 1.864–4(c)(3). For a thorough analysis of the "effectively connected" requirement, *see InverWorld, Inc. v. Commissioner*, T.C. Memo. 1996–301 (U.S. Tax Ct.1996).

(B) FOREIGN SOURCE INCOME

Generally, income from foreign sources is not treated as effectively connected income and is therefore not taxable in the United States. I.R.C. § 864(c)(4)(A). However, there are exceptions for certain income from foreign sources that is "attributable to" a U.S. "office or fixed place of business." The foreign source income that is swept into the U.S. taxing net is generally the type of income the source of which could be easily manipulated to avoid U.S. taxation.

Rents or royalties from intangible property, located or used outside the United States which are derived in the active conduct of a U.S. trade or business can be effectively connected income. I.R.C. § 864(c)(4)(B)(i). For example, if a foreign corporation engaged in a U.S. trade or business of licensing patents licenses Mexican patents or trademarks through its U.S. office, income generated by the licensing of those intangibles to unrelated parties may be effectively connected income if the income is attributable to the U.S. office. Note that if the royalties are from related parties, the income is not treated as effectively connected income. I.R.C. § 864(c)(4)(D).

Dividends or interest from stock or securities derived from a U.S. trade or business by banks or other financial institutions or by a corporation whose principal business is trading stock or securities for its own account are effectively connected income even if the income is from foreign sources. I.R.C. § 864(c)(4)(B)(ii). For example, a Japanese bank with a U.S. branch which earns interest from loans to Canadian borrowers has effectively connected income if the income is attributable to the U.S. branch (*i.e.*, the loans are made by the U.S. branch). Note that if the interest is from related parties, the income is not treated as effectively connected income. I.R.C. § 864(c)(4)(D).

Suppose that a nonresident is engaged in a trade or business in the United States through a U.S. branch but arranges to sell inventory with title passing abroad even though the inventory is intended for use in the United States. Under I.R.C. § 864(c)(4)(B)(iii), any foreign source gain from the inventory sale is treated as effectively connected income which is taxable in the United States. However, if a foreign office of the taxpayer materially participates in the sale and the inventory is not used in the United States, gain is not considered effectively connected income. While this provision applies to foreign source income, in most situations of the type described, the income produced will be treated as U.S. source income under I.R.C. § 865(e)(2) and, therefore, treated as effectively connected income under I.R.C. § 864(c)(3). That is, the more recent source rule in I.R.C. § 865(e)(2) has made I.R.C. § 864(c)(4)(B)(iii) largely irrelevant.

The foreign source income described above is treated as U.S. source effectively connected income under I.R.C. § 865(e)(2) if it is attributable to an "office or other fixed place of business" in the United States. Generally, a foreign taxpayer is deemed to have an "office or other fixed place of business" in the United States if it has a store or plant or an office where the taxpayer engages in a trade or business. Reg. § 1.864–7. An office or fixed place of business of an agent does not satisfy this requirement unless the agent: (1) possesses and regularly exercises the authority to negotiate and conclude contracts for the principal or maintains a stock of merchandise from which he regularly fills orders on behalf of the principal; and (2) is not an independent agent. I.R.C. § 864(c)(5)(A).

For purposes of I.R.C. § 864(c)(4)(B), income is "attributable to" a U.S. office if: (1) the office is a material factor in the production of income; and (2) the income is realized in the ordinary course of the trade or business of the office. I.R.C. § 864(c)(5)(B). For example, an office would be considered to be a material factor in the production of income if it participated in soliciting an order, negotiating a contract, or performing other significant services for the consummation of the sale. Reg. § 1.864–6(b)(2).

Each category of income that is treated as effectively connected with a U.S. trade or business is expanded to include economic equivalents of such income (*i.e.*, economic equivalents of certain foreign-source: (1) rents and royalties; (2) dividends and interest; and (3) income on sales or exchanges of goods in the ordinary course of business). Thus, such economic equivalents are treated as U.S.-

effectively connected income in the same circumstances that foreign-source rents, royalties, dividends, interest, or certain inventory sales are treated as U.S.-effectively connected income. I.R.C. § 864(c)(4)(B). For example, foreign-source interest and dividend equivalents (*e.g.*, a swap) are treated as U.S.-effectively connected income if the income is attributable to a U.S. office of the foreign person, and such income is derived by such foreign person in the active conduct of a banking, financing, or similar business within the United States, or the foreign person is a corporation whose principal business is trading in stocks or securities for its own account.

(C) INCOME EFFECTIVELY CONNECTED TO A PRE-EXISTING TRADE OR BUSINESS

The preceding discussion focuses on whether U.S. and foreign source income from a *current* trade or business is effectively connected income. But suppose a foreign taxpayer in its last year of conducting a trade or business in the United States sells its inventory or performs services with payments to accrue and be due over the next ten years. As the payments accrue or are received, the foreign taxpayer is no longer engaged in a trade or business in the United States. Nevertheless, under I.R.C. § 864(c)(6), the payments are characterized as they would have been taken into account in the year in which the sale took place or the services were performed. If the income would have been effectively connected income in the year of sale (or performance) had the entire purchase price been received, the income will be effectively connected income even if received after the year of sale.

A related provision addresses the situation where a foreign taxpayer ceases to conduct a trade or business in the United States and then disposes of property used in that trade or business, such as plant or equipment. If the property had been sold while the foreign taxpayer was engaged in a trade or business in the United States, the income would have been effectively connected income. But once the foreign taxpayer has ceased to conduct the trade or business, in the absence of a corrective provision, the income from the sale would not be effectively connected income, nor would it be subject to a gross base tax under I.R.C. § 871(a) (individuals) or I.R.C. § 881 (corporations). However, under I.R.C. § 864(c)(7), property that is business property retains its character for ten years after business use ceases; any gain from its sale will be effectively connected income.

(D) EFFECTIVELY CONNECTED INCOME ELECTION

There are some situations where a foreign taxpayer may prefer to have income treated as if it were effectively connected to the conduct of a U.S. trade or business even though it is not. Nonresident alien individuals and foreign corporations that own U.S. real property as an investment can elect to treat the rental income as effectively connected income. I.R.C. §§ 871(d) and 882(d). This "net basis" election allows a holder of U.S. real property held as an investment the benefit of business deductions for depreciation and interest expense rather than being taxed at a flat 30 percent rate on gross rental income. Often a higher nominal tax rate applied to net income is more favorable to a taxpayer than a lower rate applied to gross income. Whether or not a nonresident makes a net basis election, any gain or loss on the sale of U.S. real property is taxed as if the taxpayer were engaged in a U.S. trade or business and as if any gain or loss on the sale were effectively connected with such trade or business even if the nonresident was a passive investor. I.R.C. § 897.

§ 4.04 NONBUSINESS INCOME FROM U.S. SOURCES

Under I.R.C. §§ 871(a) and 881(a) nonresident aliens and foreign corporations are subject to a 30 percent tax (or lower treaty rate) on several types of nonbusiness income. The tax is imposed at a flat 30 percent rate without any deductions or other allowances for costs incurred in producing the income and is typically collected through withholding. The tax applies to interest, dividends, rents, royalties, and other "**F**ixed or **D**eterminable **A**nnual or **P**eriodical" income (FDAP income) if the income is: (1) includible in gross income; (2) from U.S. sources; and (3) not effectively connected with the conduct of a U.S. trade or business. Accordingly, tax-exempt interest from state and municipal obligations generally is not taxable when received by nonresidents. Similarly, FDAP income from sources outside the United States is not taxable when received by a nonresident. FDAP income from sources within the United States that is effectively connected with the conduct of a U.S. trade or business is taxable on a net basis in the manner described *supra* in § 4.03. *See* the final clause of I.R.C. §§ 871(a), 881. Actual payment is not necessarily a prerequisite to taxation of FDAP income. *See Central Gas de Chihuahua, S.A. v. Commissioner*, 102 T.C. No. 19, 102 T.C. 515 (U.S. Tax Ct.1994)(U.S. source rental income reallocated from a related corporation was subject to tax under I.R.C. § 881 even though no actual payment was received).

The 30 percent tax on gross FDAP income should be contrasted with the tax on net business income that applies to income effectively connected to the conduct of a U.S. trade or business. The decision to tax FDAP income on a gross basis, generally through a flat 30 percent withholding tax, is more a concession to economic reality than it is a policy decision. While a nonresident engaged in a trade or business in the United States often has assets (*e.g.*, factory, office, machinery) that may be seized if the nonresident fails to pay the required tax, the nonresident with FDAP income may escape U.S. tax jurisdiction if no withholding tax is collected before payment is received.

A brief consideration of various categories of FDAP income follows.

(A) INTEREST

The term "interest" includes both original issue discount as well as unstated interest (*i.e.*, the portion of a deferred payment under a contract of sale that is treated as interest). Notwithstanding these inclusions, interest received by nonresident investors from unrelated borrowers often is not subject to the 30 percent tax because of the "portfolio interest" exception discussed *infra*.

(1) Original Issue Discount

An original issue discount obligation is one where the face value exceeds the issue price. For example, suppose that a foreign corporation makes a $6 million loan to a U.S. corporation and receives in exchange a debt instrument which provides for no stated interest but rather the payment of $9 million in 5 years from the date the loan was made. The $3 million difference between the issue price and the redemption price is treated as interest which must be accrued for tax purposes by both the lender and the borrower regardless of their methods of accounting. I.R.C. § 1273. This rule does not apply to short-term OID instruments. I.R.C. § 871(g)(1)(B). The original issue discount is treated as if interest payments were actually paid by the borrower to the lender which in turn are loaned back to the borrower. However, the original issue discount accrued by a nonresident lender is not subject to the 30 percent tax on investment income until the debt instrument is sold, exchanged or retired. I.R.C. §§ 871(a)(1)(C) and 881(a)(3).

(2) Portfolio Interest

U.S. source interest received by a nonresident is not subject to a 30 percent tax if the interest paid is "portfolio interest." I.R.C. §§ 871(h) and 881(c). The purpose of this exemption is to allow U.S. borrowers to compete for loans with borrowers from other countries which often do not tax interest payments made to foreign lenders. For example, suppose a U.K. lender is considering a $100 million loan to U.S. Co., a U.S. corporation or Forco, a comparable Swiss corporation. If the interest payable by U.S. Co. would be subject to a 30 percent U.S. withholding tax under I.R.C. §§ 881 and 1442 (assuming the U.K. lender would not qualify for benefits under the U.S.-U.K. treaty) but interest payable by Forco would not be subject to a withholding tax in Switzerland, the loan to Forco may become relatively more attractive assuming comparable interest rates and levels of risk.

In enacting the portfolio interest exemption, Congress sought to restrict its benefits to the intended beneficiaries (i.e., U.S. borrowers and unrelated foreign lenders) rather than unintended beneficiaries such as foreign lenders related to the U.S. borrower or any U.S. lenders (or subsequent U.S. purchasers of the debt instruments). To protect against the use of the portfolio exemption by related foreign lenders, the exemption does not apply to interest payments made to a foreign lender who owns (directly or indirectly) 10 percent or more of the voting power of the stock of the borrower. I.R.C. § 871(h)(3). For purposes of the 10 percent test, evaluation of a partnership which owns 10 percent or more of a U.S. payor of interest takes place at the partner level. Accordingly, if 100 unrelated partners each owns 1 percent of a partnership which owns 100 percent of a U.S. interest payor, the portfolio interest exemption should be available with respect to interest paid on a loan from the partnership to the U.S. borrower. Reg. § 1.871–14(g).

To protect against the use of the portfolio exemption by any U.S. lenders, to qualify for the portfolio interest exemption interest must be paid on registered obligations (*i.e.*, where the issuer records the owner of the instrument and surrender of the old instrument or a book entry is required for any transfer) and if the issuer generally obtains a statement that the beneficial owner is not a U.S. person. I.R.C. § 871(h)(2)(B). Interest on bearer obligations (*i.e.*, where no book entry is made) do not qualify for the portfolio interest exemption.

Because portfolio interest can escape U.S. withholding, but dividends paid by U.S. corporations are subject to a 30 percent gross base withholding tax, foreign investors might seek to disguise a dividend payment as an interest payment. Conceptually, a dividend is more dependent on the ups-and-downs of the dividend-paying corporation than interest paid by the same corporation. That is, loans are generally less risky than equity investments in part because lenders have a higher priority as a creditor than the shareholders. To prevent the unintended use of the portfolio interest exemption for more speculative income flows—"contingent interest"—I.R.C. § 871(h)(4) denies the portfolio interest exemption for any interest determined by reference to the receipts, sales, income, or asset appreciation of the debtor (or a related person). Moreover, if the interest rate is tied to the dividend rate of the payor, the portfolio interest exemption is not available. For example, if a nonresident corporation makes a $1,000,000 loan to an unrelated U.S. borrower with interest in the amount of 5 percent a year, plus 1 percent of the borrower's gross sales, the noncontingent $50,000 interest payment may qualify for the portfolio interest exemption. The interest tied to the borrower's sales, while still treated as interest (assuming the "loan" is treated as debt for U.S. tax purposes), would be subject to the 30 percent rate specified in I.R.C. § 881 (unless a lower treaty rate applies).

(3) Conduit Financing

Suppose that a foreign corporation is contemplating a loan to its U.S. subsidiary. Interest paid by the subsidiary will not qualify for the portfolio interest exemption because the parties are related. I.R.C. § 871(c)(3). Suppose instead that the foreign parent makes a loan to an unrelated foreign borrower (intermediate entity) who on-lends the funds to the U.S. subsidiary. Taken at face value, the interest payment from the U.S. subsidiary to the foreign unrelated party could qualify for the portfolio interest exemption. The interest paid from the unrelated intermediate entity to the foreign parent would normally not be subject to a U.S.

withholding tax. To counteract this type of arrangement, Congress authorized Treasury to promulgate multiparty financing (*i.e.,* conduit financing) regulations under I.R.C. § 7701(*l*).

The purpose of these Regulations (found in Reg. § 1.881–3) is to prevent foreign taxpayers from using intermediate entities to obtain the unintended benefit of reduced withholding (*e.g.,* through the portfolio exemption or through treaty reduction of withholding tax). The IRS has the authority to disregard, for purposes of section 881, the participation of one or more intermediate entities in a "financing arrangement" where such entities are acting as "conduit entities." Reg. § 1.881–3. A "financing arrangement" is a series of two or more financing transactions (*e.g.,* lending money, leasing or licensing property), whereby one party (financing entity) loans money or other property through one or more parties (intermediate entities) to another party (financed entity).

An intermediate entity will be considered a "conduit entity" if certain conditions exist. First, the participation of the intermediate entity in the financing arrangement must reduce the tax imposed by Code section 881. Second, the participation of the intermediate entity is pursuant to a tax avoidance plan. Finally, the intermediate entity is either: (1) related to the financing entity or the financed entity; or (2) unrelated, but "would not have participated in the financing arrangement on substantially the same terms *but* for the fact that the financing entity engaged in the financing transaction with the intermediate entity."

If a financing arrangement is found to be a conduit financing arrangement, payments from the financed entity to the intermediate entity will be recharacterized as if the payments were made directly to the financing entity. To return to the example above, interest payments from the U.S. subsidiary would be treated as if they were made to the foreign parent corporation so that the portfolio interest exemption would not be available if the intermediate entity would not normally have participated in such a transaction on substantially the same terms.

The conduit financing regulations also come into play where a non-treaty lender facing a 30 percent U.S. withholding tax on interest paid by a U.S. borrower arranges a back-to-back loan arrangement through a treaty resident that qualifies for a favorable withholding rate on interest under the applicable treaty with the United States. It is likely in this situation, that the conduit financing regulations will treat this arrangement as a direct loan from the non-treaty lender that is subject to 30 percent withholding tax.

(4) Bank Deposits

Interest earned by a nonresident investor on U.S. bank deposits is not subject to the 30 percent tax on FDAP income even though the income is U.S. source income. I.R.C. §§ 871(i) and 881(d). Deposit interest that is effectively connected with the conduct of a

U.S. trade or business is taxable as business income. *See supra* § 4.03(A).

(5) Interest Substitutes

Suppose that Forco, a foreign corporation makes a loan to Subco, a U.S. subsidiary. Interest payments are subject to a 30 percent withholding tax under I.R.C. § 881. Now suppose that Forco lends the Subco note to PF, a U.S. tax-exempt pension fund for a two-year period. Pursuant to the loan agreement, PF agrees to make a substitute payment to Forco in the amount of any interest payment PF receives from Subco. Is the substitute payment subject to I.R.C. § 881 even though it is not an interest payment? The Regulations clarify that the substitute payment will have the same character as the underlying interest payment and will be subject to I.R.C. § 882 whether the borrower is a U.S. or foreign borrower. Reg. § 1.881–7(b). The same treatment applies if Forco sells the debt instrument under a contract that entitles it to repurchase or repossess the debt instrument after two years (*i.e.*, a "repo"). If Forco could have qualified for the portfolio interest exemption (*i.e.*, 0 percent withholding) had the interest payment been paid directly to it, then the substitute payment can qualify for the portfolio interest exemption as well.

(6) Interest Stripping (I.R.C. § 163(j))

Suppose that Forco, a foreign corporation, owns 100% of USCO, a U.S. corporation. USCO is capitalized with both debt and equity. Notice that when USCO pays interest to Forco, USCO is likely to generate an interest deduction that reduces the U.S. tax base. However, the interest payment would be FDAP income to Forco and would be subject to a 30% U.S. withholding tax. I.R.C. §§ 881 and 1442. But now suppose that Forco resides in a treaty jurisdiction and that under the applicable treaty, the United States is not allowed to tax interest paid to Forco. In this situation, the deduction reduces the U.S. tax base (*i.e.*, USCO's taxable income) without an offsetting inclusion in the U.S. tax base.

Concerned about this interest stripping potential, Congress enacted a provision that serves as a quasi-thin capitalization ("thin cap") rule. In general terms, if a U.S. corporation pays interest to a related person and if no U.S. tax is imposed with respect to the interest paid, under some circumstances, the U.S. interest deduction is disallowed. The disallowed interest expense may be carried forward and may be permitted in subsequent years. This rule applies with respect to interest paid to a related lender who is not subject to full U.S. taxation on the interest received (*e.g.*, because of the application of a treaty). In order for this interest stripping rule to apply, the ratio of debt to equity (essentially liabilities divided by the difference between tax basis of assets minus liabilities) must exceed 1.5 to 1. Even if interest is not directly paid to a "tax-exempt" related party, § 163(j) might apply where there is a disqualified guarantee by a related foreign lender of a loan from an unrelated lender to USCO.

In its glorious detail, § 163(j) limits the deductibility of interest paid to, or on debt guaranteed by, a foreign related person (or a U.S. tax-exempt related person), if: (i) the debtor's debt-to-equity ratio exceeds 1.5-to-1, and (ii) the debtor's net interest expense exceeds 50 percent of its "adjusted taxable income" ("ATI"). ATI is essentially taxable income computed without any deductions for net interest expense or certain non-cash items such as net operating loss carryforwards or carrybacks, depreciation, amortization, and depletion. Putting jargon aside, interest expense will raise a § 163(j) issue where the interest paid represents more than half of the cash available to the corporation after taking into account all other cash expenditures. If both conditions (i) and (ii) are met, the disallowance applies only to "disqualified interest."

Interest is "disqualified interest" if it is: (i) paid to a related party and there is no U.S. tax imposed on the interest, or (ii) paid to an unrelated party on debt guaranteed by a foreign related person (or a related tax-exempt U.S. person) and there is no gross basis U.S. withholding tax imposed on the interest. Interest fits within the first category only if paid to a U.S. person that is tax-exempt or paid to a foreign person where the U.S. gross basis 30 percent interest withholding tax has been reduced under a tax treaty. For purposes of both categories, if the 30 percent interest withholding tax rate is reduced under a tax treaty, the amount of the interest that is disqualified interest is prorated based upon the amount by which the withholding tax rate is reduced by the treaty. Note that under I.R.C. § 163(j)(6)(D), the guarantee rule applies even if the lender is subject to full U.S. net basis taxation on the interest income.

Disallowed disqualified interest may be carried forward indefinitely and deducted in any future year to the extent that net interest expense in that year is less than 50 percent of ATI. If 50 percent of ATI exceeds net interest expense in any year (after taking into account any disallowed interest carried forward), the "excess limitation" may be carried forward for three taxable years.

The disallowance under § 163(j) not only applies to U.S. subsidiaries of foreign parents, but can also apply to limit the deduction of interest otherwise permitted to the U.S. branch of a foreign corporation under Reg. § 1.882–5 where that interest is deemed to be paid to a tax-exempt, related recipient (*see e.g.,* 884(f)(2)).

For the past several years, Congress has considered tightening the rules under § 163(j). Among the contemplated changes were: 1) elimination of the 1.5-to-1 safe harbor; 2) lowering the ATI threshold from 50% to 35%, or even 25%; 3) setting a 10-year carryforward on excess interest; 4) ending the carryforward for excess limitation.

(B) DIVIDENDS

Dividends from U.S. sources (*e.g.*, from a U.S. payor) are generally subject to the 30 percent withholding tax.

Dividends paid by a foreign corporation with substantial U.S. earnings can result in U.S. source income under I.R.C. § 861(a)(2)(B). However, the 30 percent withholding tax does not apply because of the operation of the branch profits tax. *See infra* § 4.05. Congress has explicitly clarified that FDAP taxation does not apply to dividends paid by a foreign corporation. I.R.C. § 871(i)(2)(D).

Just as there can be substitute interest payments where a foreign taxpayer lends a debt instrument, there can be substitute dividend payments where a foreign owner of stock lends the stock to a person and receives a substitute payment equivalent to a dividend distribution on the loaned stock. *See supra* § 4.04(A)(4). Substitute dividend payments are treated as FDAP income in the same manner as an actual dividend. *See* I.R.C. § 871(m) as well as Reg. §§ 1.871–7(b)(2) and 1.881–2(b)(2). If the actual dividend paid to a foreign stock borrower is subject to U.S. FDAP taxation, the tax on the foreign-to-foreign substitute dividend is equal the tax that would have been imposed if the dividend was paid directly to the lender minus any U.S. tax paid by the borrower. For example, if the borrower was subject to a 5 percent U.S. withholding tax because of the application of a treaty between the borrower's country and the United States, the substitute payment would be subject to a 25 percent U.S. withholding tax (*i.e.*, 30 percent minus 5 percent) if the lender was a resident of a country that did not have a treaty with the United States. *See* Notice 2010–46; 2010–1 C.B. 757

(C) RENTS AND ROYALTIES

Rental income received by a nonresident is subject to the 30 percent withholding tax if the activities of the nonresident (or agent) in managing the property do not amount to the conduct of a trade or business in the United States. If the activities do amount to a U.S. trade or business, the income from such activities is taxable as business income. *See supra* § 4.02. For an election to treat FDAP rental income as effectively connected income, *see supra* § 4.03(D).

Although not specifically listed in I.R.C. §§ 871(a) or 881, royalty payments are subject to the 30 percent withholding tax if the royalty income is not effectively connected with the conduct of a U.S. trade or business. Reg. §§ 1.861–5 and 1.871–7(b). Royalties are taxable whether received in installments or in a lump sum. *See Commissioner v. Wodehouse*, 337 U.S. 369 (1949). Moreover, gain from a sale of royalty-producing property is treated as a royalty if payments are contingent on the property's productivity, use, or disposition. I.R.C. § 871(a)(1)(D).

(D) INCOME FROM SERVICES

Although salaries and wages are listed as FDAP income (largely for historical reasons), they are almost never subject to the 30 percent tax. Instead, a taxpayer rendering services in the United States is considered to be in a trade or business so that services income is taxable as effectively connected income. *See supra* § 4.02.

Pensions and other distributions from retirement plans are potentially subject to the 30 percent withholding tax. I.R.C. § 871(a)(1)(B). However, a nonresident does not have gross income for annuity payments received under a qualified retirement plan. I.R.C. § 871(f). The exclusion applies if all of the personal services giving rise to the annuity were either: (1) performed outside the United States while the taxpayer was a nonresident; or (2) within the United States while the taxpayer was temporarily present (*i.e.*, 90 days or less) earning a *de minimis* amount of income (*i.e.*, $3,000 or less). Furthermore, if fewer than 90 percent of the participants in the retirement plan are citizens or residents of the United States when the nonresident's annuity begins, there is no exclusion unless the nonresident's country of residence either: (1) grants a substantially equivalent exclusion to U.S. residents and citizens; or is a beneficiary developing country under the Trade Act of 1974.

These domestic rules governing pensions are often altered by applicable treaty provisions. *See infra* Chapter 5. For example, Article 18 of the 2006 U.S. Model treaty bars the United States from taxing most pensions received from U.S. sources by residents of the other contracting state.

(E) SOCIAL SECURITY BENEFITS

Eighty-five percent of any monthly old age, survivors, and disability benefits (OASDI) or railroad retirement benefits received by a nonresident is subject to a 30 percent tax under I.R.C. § 871(a)(3).

(F) OTHER FDAP INCOME

Other FDAP income subject to the 30 percent withholding tax includes alimony, commissions, prizes, and gambling winnings. Guarantee fees paid by a U.S. borrower to a related foreign company which guarantees a bank loan can constitute FDAP income. I.R.C. § 861(a)(9).

(G) CAPITAL GAINS

Capital gains received by a nonresident from the sale of property are almost never subject to the 30 percent withholding tax—with one significant exception for U.S. real property interests. For example, if a nonresident sells stock in a U.S. corporation at a gain, typically the United States cannot tax the gain. However, gains from the sale of property that are effectively connected (or are deemed to be effectively connected) with the conduct of a U.S. trade or business are taxable as business income. *See infra* § 4.06(B) for a discussion of gains from the disposition of U.S. real property interests. Section 871(a)(2) does tax all U.S. capital gains for nonresidents that are present in the United States for 183 days or more during a taxable year. However, the provision predates changes in the residency rules. It is now the case that an individual who is present in the United States for 183 days or more during the taxable year often will be considered a U.S. resident taxable on worldwide income (including capital gains) and so I.R.C. § 871(a)(2) will not apply. *See* I.R.C. § 7701(b). It is possible that a person might not satisfy the 183-day test under § 7701(b) (certain days where the taxpayer is present in the United States may not count (*e.g.,* taxpayer is a foreign government diplomat)) but might satisfy the 183-day test under § 871(a)(2) which does not refer to the method of counting days under § 7701(b). *See supra* § 2.04.

§ 4.05   THE BRANCH PROFITS TAX

(A) THE BRANCH PROFITS TAX ON BRANCH EARNINGS

Prior to the enactment of the branch profits tax in 1986, a foreign corporation owned by foreign investors and doing business in the United States was taxed at the corporate level under the regular corporate graduated rates on its income effectively connected with a U.S. trade or business. I.R.C. §§ 882 and 11. If the foreign investors operated in the United States through a domestic corporation, the outcome was the same. However, differences in treatment arose when the corporation distributed the corporate earnings to the foreign owners.

For a domestic corporation, the dividend was subject to a 30 percent tax rate (or reduced treaty rate) under I.R.C. § 881 with the tax collected through withholding. I.R.C. § 1442. For a foreign corporation, prior to the Tax Reform Act of 1986, it was much less likely that a dividend paid to foreign investors would be subject to any U.S. tax either because of a favorable income tax treaty or because the dividend would be foreign source income not subject to the 30 percent tax under I.R.C. §§ 871(a) or 881 due to the distributing corporation's mix of foreign and U.S. income. *See* I.R.C. § 861(a)(2).

The purpose of the branch profits tax is to subject the income earned by foreign corporations operating in the United States to two levels of taxation like income earned and distributed by U.S. corporations operating in the United States. In the latter case, the income is taxed at a maximum marginal rate of 35 percent when earned by a U.S. corporation and is subject to a maximum 30 percent tax when the corporation makes a dividend payment. I.R.C. § 881(a). In the case of a foreign corporation, under the branch profits regime, income is taxed at a maximum marginal rate of 35 percent when it is earned, and an additional 30 percent branch profits tax is imposed when the income is repatriated from the U.S. branch to the foreign home office by the foreign corporation (or deemed to be repatriated because it is not reinvested in "U.S. assets"). In effect, the branch profits tax provision treats the U.S. branch as if it were a U.S. subsidiary of the foreign corporation.

Note that the branch profits tax results in two taxes on the foreign corporation with the U.S. branch—one tax when the income is earned and one tax when the earnings are repatriated or deemed repatriated. In the case of a U.S. corporation, there is only one tax imposed on the corporation that earns the income. The second tax in this case is imposed on the shareholder when the earnings are distributed as a dividend. The branch profits tax is a proxy for this second level of tax that would be imposed on a dividend from a U.S. corporation to a foreign shareholder.

The 30 percent branch profits tax is levied on the "dividend equivalent amount" in lieu of a secondary withholding tax on dividends paid by the foreign corporation to its shareholders. I.R.C. § 884(e)(3). The "dividend equivalent amount" equals the foreign corporation's earnings and profits that are effectively connected with the conduct of a trade or business in the United States subject to certain specified adjustments. I.R.C. § 884(b). To the extent that the effectively connected earnings and profits are invested in qualifying U.S. assets, the dividend equivalent amount (DEA) is decreased. This DEA base to which the branch profits tax applies is decreased because the branch is deemed not to have repatriated the earnings to the corporation's home country. Conversely, to the extent that a foreign corporation's investment in qualifying U.S. assets decreases (because of an actual repatriation of assets or because U.S. property of the branch which previously was invested in qualifying U.S. assets is converted into other nonqualifying assets), the dividend equivalent amount increases. The increase in the dividend equivalent amount reflects the fact that effectively connect earnings of a previous year are being repatriated or are treated as having been repatriated. Generally, qualifying U.S. assets consist of money and property used by the foreign corporation to conduct a trade or business in the United States. I.R.C. § 884(c)(2).

To illustrate how the branch profits tax might operate, suppose that Forco is incorporated in a foreign country which does not have a treaty with the United States. In Year 1, Forco earns $4 million of net income from business operations conducted by its U.S. branch. At a flat 35 percent tax rate, Forco will pay $1.4 million in U.S. income tax on its effectively connected income. I.R.C. § 882. If the remaining $2.6 million is repatriated to Forco's home office (or is invested in nonqualifying U.S. assets), the branch profits tax provision imposes an additional 30 percent tax, or $780,000. However, if Forco reinvests the $2.6 million in its U.S. business, there is no immediate branch profits tax liability.

Suppose that Forco does reinvest the proceeds in its U.S. trade or business in Year 1 so that the branch profits tax does not apply. In Year 2, Forco earns no net income but transfers $300,000 from the U.S. business to the home office. The $300,000 repatriation is subject to the 30 percent branch profits tax because Forco's dividend equivalent amount is increased by the disinvestment in qualifying U.S. assets.

(B) THE BRANCH PROFITS TAX ON INTEREST

Along with the branch profits tax on repatriated earnings, the Code imposes a 30 percent tax on interest paid (or deemed paid) by a branch of a foreign corporation engaged in a U.S. trade or business. In the absence of I.R.C. § 884(f) which imposes this branch level tax on interest, it would be possible for a foreign corporation to decrease or even avoid the branch profits tax by making interest payments to its foreign investors. To the extent that the deductible interest payments are allocable to the branch's earnings, the interest payments would decrease taxable income, effectively connected earnings and profits and, ultimately, the dividend equivalent amount on which the branch profits tax is based. In the example above, if Forco distributed all of its $4 million of net income to its foreign investors in the form of deductible interest, Forco would have no taxable income, no effectively connected earnings and profits, and no dividend equivalent amount for branch profits tax purposes.

Forco would also not have any effectively connected income for regular tax liability purposes but that would be true whether Forco was a foreign or domestic corporation. However, if Forco were a domestic corporation, the U.S. source interest payments would be subject to the 30 percent tax under I.R.C. §§ 871(a) or 881. In the absence of I.R.C. § 884(f), interest payments by a foreign corporation would often be foreign source income not subject to a 30 percent tax. I.R.C. § 884(f) seeks to remove this difference.

Code section I.R.C. § 884(f) contains two rules for taxing interest paid by the U.S. branch of a foreign corporation. I.R.C. § 884(f)(1)(A) provides that, for a foreign corporation engaged in a U.S. trade or business, interest paid by the U.S. trade or business (*i.e.*, where the loan is on the books of the branch) is treated as if paid by a domestic corporation. Consequently, under I.R.C. § 861(a)(1) the interest is U.S. source income generally subject to a flat 30 percent tax under I.R.C. §§ 871(a) or 881. However, if the interest payment qualifies as portfolio interest, there is no U.S. taxation. *See supra* § 4.04(A)(2).

I.R.C. § 884(f)(1)(B) provides that, to the extent that the amount of interest allowable as a deduction under Reg. § 1.882–5 in computing taxable income of the U.S. branch exceeds the interest actually paid by the branch, the excess shall be treated as interest paid by a fictional U.S. subsidiary (the branch) to the parent, thereby subjecting the notional interest payment to a 30 percent tax under I.R.C. § 881. The portfolio interest exemption will not apply to this excess interest because it is deemed to be paid to a related entity (*i.e.*, the home office). I.R.C. § 871(h)(3).

(C) THE BRANCH PROFITS TAX AND SECONDARY WITHHOLDING ON DIVIDENDS

A foreign corporation with a U.S. branch is subject to the regular U.S. corporate income tax under I.R.C. § 882 on income which is effectively connected with a U.S. trade or business. Such income is also subject to the branch profits tax to the extent the income is not reinvested in qualifying U.S. assets, as defined in I.R.C. § 884(c)(2). There is no further tax when the foreign corporation makes a dividend distribution to its foreign investors. I.R.C. §§ 884(e)(3)(A) and 871(i)(2)(D).

(D) THE BRANCH PROFITS TAX AND INCOME TAX TREATIES

The statutory rate for both the branch profits tax and the branch profits tax on interest is 30 percent. However, as explained in Chapter 5, the dividend article (or branch profits tax article) of an applicable treaty may reduce the rate of tax on repatriated branch profits to 5 percent or even eliminate the branch profits tax. Similarly the rate of withholding tax on interest paid by a branch or treated as paid by a branch often is reduced under the applicable treaty interest article often to 10 percent or 0 percent.

§ 4.06   FOREIGN INVESTMENT IN U.S. REAL PROPERTY

(A) OPERATIONAL INCOME

Suppose a foreign investor owns U.S. real property that produces rental income. If the foreign investor is considered to be engaged in a U.S. trade or business, the net rental income (gross rental income minus deductions for depreciation, maintenance, mortgage interest etc.) is effectively connected income taxable in the same manner as other business income of a U.S. taxpayer. I.R.C. §§ 871(b) or 882. If a foreign investor is not engaged in a trade or business in the United States, the gross rental income is taxed at a 30 percent rate under I.R.C. §§ 871(a) or 881. Normally, a foreign investor prefers the benefit of offsetting deductions, including depreciation and interest expense, compared with a tax on gross income. Under I.R.C. §§ 871(d) or 881(d), a foreign investor not engaged in a trade or business in the United States can elect to treat the rental income as effectively connected income which can be offset by any appropriate deductions before applying the tax rates under I.R.C. §§ 1 or 11. This "net basis" election is irrevocable once made.

To illustrate, suppose that Forco, a foreign corporation, owns an apartment building in the United States that produces $2 million of rental income. To avoid the 30 percent withholding tax on the rental income, Forco might prefer to make the net basis election and face a 35 percent tax on net income. If Forco has $1.5 million of expenses (*e.g.*, depreciation, interest expense, maintenance) in connection with the apartment building, a higher nominal rate applied to $500,000 of net income produces a lower U.S. tax bill ($500,000 × 35% = $175,000) than a lower nominal rate applied to $2 million of gross income ($2 million × 30% = $600,000).

Suppose that a nonresident alien or foreign corporation with U.S. real property derives no gross income but incurs expenses in connection with the property. Can the taxpayer make a net basis election in order to use the deductions to offset other income the taxpayer may have from activities that are effectively connected with the conduct of a U.S. trade or business? In Revenue Ruling 91–7, 1991–1 C.B. 110, the IRS ruled that a nonresident may not make a net basis election with respect to U.S. real property for a taxable year in which the taxpayer does not derive any income from such property. However, it should not be difficult for a nonresident with U.S. real property to generate some gross income from the property in order to make the net basis election. In Revenue Ruling 92–74, 1992–2 C.B. 156, the IRS ruled that the excess of deductions attributable to U.S. real property over income from the property may be used to offset income from the conduct of a U.S. trade or business, and, if necessary, may be carried back or forward to other years as a net operating loss. The ruling applies to a foreign corporation only but logically should be extended to nonresident aliens as well.

(B) DISPOSITIONAL INCOME

Gain from the sale of U.S. real property by a nonresident engaged in a trade or business of buying and selling real property is treated as effectively connected income taxable in the United States even in the absence of a special provision. However, a foreign investor not engaged in a trade or business normally—absent a special provision— would not have U.S. taxable gain (or loss) on the sale of a capital asset (*e.g.,* real property) because a capital gain of a nonresident is not normally subject to the 30 percent withholding tax. I.R.C. §§ 871(a) and 881.

Concerned with increasing foreign ownership of U.S. real property, in 1980 Congress enacted I.R.C. § 897 (the Foreign Investment in Real Property Tax Act, or FIRPTA) which treats gain from the sale of a

"United States real property interest" as if the taxpayer is engaged in a trade or business in the United States, and as if the gain is effectively connected income. I.R.C. § 897(a). A United States real property interest can include not only a fee interest in U.S. real property but leaseholds, options, and natural resources. If a nonresident holds U.S. real property through a partnership or trust, the sale by the entity of U.S. real property or the sale by the nonresident of the interest in the entity may produce effectively connected income. I.R.C. §§ 875 and 897(g). The Code "looks through" the entity and attributes the sale by the entity to the participants or treats the sale of the entity interest partially as a sale of the U.S. real property held by the entity.

The look-through paradigm does not apply to a corporate entity which is treated instead as a separate taxpaying entity. A sale by a foreign corporation of U.S. real property is not attributed to the shareholder. Instead, the foreign corporation is taxed on any gain as if the gain were effectively connected income. I.R.C. § 897. Because the foreign corporation is taxed on gain from the sale of U.S. real property under I.R.C. § 897, a foreign shareholder who sells appreciated stock in the foreign corporation is not taxable on the sale. If a U.S. corporation sells U.S. real property, the corporation is, of course, taxable under I.R.C. § 11. If a foreign shareholder sells appreciated stock of a U.S. corporation most of the assets of which are U.S. real property, the shareholder may be s taxed on any gain (which is treated as effectively connected income).

An equity interest in a U.S. corporation is a "U.S. real property interest" (USRPI) and therefore subject to I.R.C. § 897 if the corporation is a "U.S. real property holding corporation" (USRPHC). I.R.C. § 897(c)(2). (There is an exception for stock of a U.S. corporation which is regularly traded on an established securities market where a foreign taxpayer owns 5 percent or less.) A U.S. corporation is a USRPHC if on any "determination date" (*see* below) during the previous five years the fair market value of the corporation's USRPIs equaled at least 50 percent of the sum of the fair market value of the corporation's total worldwide real property interests plus business assets. For example, if, on a determination date during the applicable period, a domestic corporation owns U.S. real property with a fair market value of $100,000, foreign real property with a fair market value of $75,000 and business assets with a fair market value of $50,000, it is not a USRPHC and the stock is not a USRPI ($100,000/$225,000). If the corporation disposes of $25,000 of business assets (*e.g.,* distribution to its shareholders), it would become a USRPHC ($100,000/$200,000), and any subsequent sale of the corporation's stock at a gain would be taxable in the United States.

A domestic corporation is a USRPHC during the five-year test period if it is a USRPHC on any "determination date." Generally, those dates are: (a) the last day of a corporation's tax year and (b) the date of each transaction that might cause a corporation to become a USRPHC. Such transactions include either the acquisition of a USRPI or the disposition of foreign real property or assets used in a trade or business. Reg. § 1.897–2(c). In the example above, the disposition of the $25,000 of business assets would trigger a determination date thereby rendering the corporation a USRPHC.

A look-through rule applies to determine whether a U.S. corporation is a U.S. real property holding corporation. If the U.S. corporation owns an interest in a transparent entity (*e.g.*, a partnership) or at least 50 percent (by value) of the stock of a U.S. or foreign corporation, a pro rata portion of the entity's assets is considered to be owned by the parent corporation. I.R.C. § 897(c)(5). If X Corp., a U.S. corporation, owns less than 50 percent (by value) of the stock of a second corporation, there is no "look-through." An "all-or-nothing" rule applies instead. If the second corporation is a USRPHC (or would be if it were a U.S. corporation), then the entire stock interest is treated as a USRPI in calculating whether X Corp. is a USRPHC. Note that while a foreign corporation can be a USRPHC for purposes of testing whether a U.S. corporation as a shareholder is a USRPHC (*see* I.R.C. § 897(c)(4)), stock of a foreign corporation is not a USRPI (*i.e.,* sale of stock of a foreign corporation by a foreign taxpayer is never taxable under sec. 897(a)).

If a class of stock is regularly traded on an established securities market, the stock will be a USRPI on in the case of a more than 5 percent holder (*i.e.,* a holder that owned more than a 5 percent interest during a 5-year look-back period). I.R.C. § 897(c)(3). If a seller is not a more than 5-percent shareholder, gain on the sale of the stock should not be subject to U.S. tax.

For example, suppose a foreign individual holds a 1 percent interest in the publicly-traded stock of a United States real estate investment trust (*i.e.,* a REIT). A REIT is a U.S. corporation having at least 100 shareholders that is treated as a pass-through entity (*i.e.,* not entity-level tax) essentially if almost all of its income is real estate related income and distributes 90 percent or more of its taxable income each year. Gain on the sale of the REIT stock is not taxable in the United States because the stock is publicly traded and the seller is not a more than 5 percent shareholder. Moreover, even if the stock of the REIT were not publicly traded, if foreign investors own less than 50 percent of the value of the REIT stock during the previous 5-year period (*i.e.,* the REIT is "domestically controlled"), gain on the sale of shares by any foreign investor— regardless of ownership level—is not taxable under I.R.C. § 897. I.R.C. § 897(h)(2).

If a U.S. corporation is a USRPHC, a disposition by a nonresident of any interest (other than an interest solely as a creditor) at a gain is subject to U.S. taxation. I.R.C. § 897(a). Hybrid securities as well as stock interests are covered. Dispositions other than sales can trigger U.S. taxation. Suppose that a nonresident holding U.S. real property exchanges the property for stock of a foreign corporation in a nonrecognition exchange qualifying under I.R.C. § 351. If there is no recognition on the exchange, the foreign taxpayer would then be free to sell the stock in a foreign corporation free of U.S. taxation. However, I.R.C. § 897(e) overrides all statutory nonrecognition provisions unless the property received in the transaction would be taxable in the United States if sold (*e.g.,* if the foreign owner gives up a FIRPTA interest and receives a FIRPTA interest in return—a "FIRPTA for FIRPTA" exchange). In the example, the foreign taxpayer may not be able to rely on I.R.C. § 351 because gain from the sale of stock in a foreign corporation by a nonresident is not taxable in the United States. However, even foreign-to-foreign exchanges can sometimes qualify for nonrecognition. *See* Reg. § 1.897–6T(b) and Notice 2006–46, 2006–1 C.B. 1044.

A number of the FIRPTA provisions address a variety of corporate and partnership transactions. *See* I.R.C. §§ 897(d) and (e). The detailed interplay of FIRPTA with corporate and partnership provisions is beyond the scope of this book. However, the thrust of these provisions is to ensure that if a transferor of a USRPI in what would otherwise be a tax-free transaction does not get back a USRPI (*i.e.,* a USRPI interest for a USRPI interest), then the transfer is taxable or the gain can be preserved.

§ 4.07   TRANSPORTATION INCOME

If a foreign corporation is engaged in a U.S. trade or business that generates transportation income and the income is effectively connected with the trade or business, it is subject to the regular U.S. corporate income tax. I.R.C. § 882. Transportation income is treated as being effectively connected if the foreign corporation has a fixed place of business within the United States that is involved in the earning of the income, and if substantially all (at least 90 percent) of the U.S. gross transportation income of the foreign corporation for the tax year is attributable to regularly scheduled transportation (or, for income from the leasing of a vessel or aircraft, is attributable to a fixed place of business in the United States).

However, if a foreign corporation has U.S.-source transportation income that is not effectively connected with a U.S. trade or business, then that income is subject to a 4 percent gross withholding tax under I.R.C. section 887(a). The 4 percent tax applies only to the extent that the foreign corporation's transportation income is derived from U.S. sources as determined in accordance with I.R.C. § 863(c)(2). Under those sourcing rules, transportation income is foreign sourced if it is derived from transportation between two non-U.S. locations, and as such, that income would not be subject to U.S. taxation. If the income is derived from transportation that either begins or ends in the United States, the transportation income is considered to be 50 percent U.S.-sourced and 50 percent foreign-sourced, with the U.S.-sourced portion being subject to the 4 percent withholding tax under I.R.C. § 887.

There are two exceptions under which income from the international operation of ships and aircraft can be exempted from gross and net-based U.S. taxes. First, most U.S. tax treaties contain a shipping and air transport article that generally provides that income derived by a corporation from the operation of ships or aircraft in international traffic is taxable only in the country in which the corporation is a resident. *See* Art. 8 of the U.S. Model discussed *infra* in § 5.05(D)(1). Thus, foreign corporations that are resident in a U.S. treaty partner country whose treaty provides for that exemption can avoid the U.S. taxes on transportation income imposed by I.R.C. § 887.

Second, a statutory exemption exists in I.R.C. § 883 that provides that gross transportation income derived by a foreign corporation from the international operation of ships or aircraft is exempt from U.S. taxation if the corporation's country of residence provides for a reciprocal exemption. A corresponding exemption from the 4 percent withholding tax under section 887 also exists under section 883. Thus, if the country where the foreign company is incorporated does not impose an income tax, or if it grants an equivalent exemption from its income tax for transportation income earned by U.S. corporations (either via domestic law or by an exchange of diplomatic notes), the foreign corporation will not be subject to U.S. taxation (either gross-or net-based) on its U.S.-source transportation income.

§ 4.08 TAXATION OF FOREIGN GOVERNMENTS

Historically, the United States has exempted from U.S. federal income tax certain types of U.S. source investment income derived by foreign governments. I.R.C. § 892. However, income which foreign governments derived from "commercial activities" has generally been taxable as if the income were earned by a foreign private corporation.

A foreign government (or subdivision) or its agent seeking exemption from U.S. taxation must satisfy two basic requirements: a status requirement and an income requirement. The foreign government must qualify as a "foreign government" for purposes of the provision, and the income it receives must be the type eligible for exemption under I.R.C. § 892. The term "foreign government" includes "a controlled entity" of a "foreign sovereign." A "controlled entity" is an entity (*e.g.*, a corporation) that essentially is wholly-owned by a single foreign sovereign, the earnings of which do not inure to the benefit of any individual, and whose assets would vest in the foreign sovereign upon dissolution. Reg. § 1.892–2T(a)(3). A pension trust for the benefit of foreign government employees can qualify as a "controlled entity." Reg. § 1.892–2T(c).

A foreign government (or controlled entity) is exempt from U.S. taxation on income from stocks, bonds or other securities and interest on bank deposits. I.R.C. § 892(a)(1). The exemption does not cover rental income from U.S. real property or any gain from the disposition of such property. However, gain from the sale of stock of a corporation owning U.S. real property can be exempt from U.S. taxation unless the foreign government holds a controlling interest in the corporation. Like rental income, income derived by a foreign government (or controlled entity) from the conduct of commercial activity is subject to U.S. taxation. I.R.C. § 892(a)(2).

Moreover, income received from or by a "controlled commercial entity" is subject to U.S. taxation. I.R.C. § 892(a)(2). A "controlled commercial entity" is an entity engaged in commercial activities anywhere in the world if the government holds (by value or voting interest) 50 percent or more of the total of such interests or a lesser amount if it holds effective control. For example, if the government of India owns a corporation that is engaged in commercial activities anywhere in the world, any income received by that corporation may be subject to U.S. taxation under normal U.S. taxing rules. Thus, if the corporation receives dividends or interest from a U.S. payer, the corporation may be taxable under I.R.C. § 881. A corporation is deemed to be engaged in commercial activities if it is a U.S. real property holding corporation or in the case of a foreign corporation would be a U.S. real property holding corporation if it were a U.S. corporation.

Proposed regulations under I.R.C. § 892 provide that an entity not otherwise engaged in commercial activities will not be deemed to be engaged in commercial activities solely because it holds an interest as a limited partner in a limited partnership, as defined in the Prop. Reg. § 1.892–5(d)(5)(iii)(B). In general, the partnership interest should not give any rights to participate in the management and conduct of the partnership's business at any time during the tax year. Even in proposed form, these regulations can be relied on. Although the commercial activity of a limited partnership will not cause a controlled entity of a foreign sovereign limited partner meeting the requirements of the exception for limited partnerships to be engaged in commercial activities, the controlled entity partner's distributive share of partnership income attributable to such commercial activity will be considered to be derived from the conduct of commercial activity, and therefore will not be exempt from taxation under section 892.

If a foreign government has income that is not exempt from U.S. taxation under I.R.C. § 892, the foreign government is treated as a foreign corporation for purposes of applying the U.S. domestic tax rules. Furthermore, the foreign government is treated as a corporate resident of its country, allowing the foreign government to qualify for tax benefits provided by an applicable income tax treaty with the United States. I.R.C. § 892(a)(3).

CHAPTER 5

THE ROLE OF INCOME TAX TREATIES

§ 5.01 THE BILATERAL INCOME TAX TREATY NETWORK

Many of the Code ground rules in the previous Chapters (and in the following Chapters dealing with U.S. taxpayers) are altered by more than 50 bilateral income tax treaties between the United States and its trading partners (referred to in tax treaties as "contracting states" rather than "countries"). The principal purpose of this income tax treaty network is to facilitate international trade and investment by lowering tax barriers to the international flow of goods and services. Lower overall taxation encourages trade and investment. Every contracting state involved in international commerce acts in two capacities for tax purposes. In some situations a contracting state claims the right to tax as the residence state of a taxpayer. In other situations a contracting state asserts tax jurisdiction based on the source of income earned by a nonresident.

While most contracting states have enacted domestic laws governing international transactions and providing unilateral relief from juridical double taxation, these unilateral efforts do not always eliminate jurisdictional overlaps. For example, if Canada under its domestic rules considers a taxpayer to be a resident of Canada while the United States under its rules considers the taxpayer to be a resident of the United States, there is likely to be double taxation of the income earned by that taxpayer. One purpose of an income tax treaty is to resolve such residence-residence conflicts.

Similarly, if a resident of the United States earns income in Germany, a tax treaty typically alleviates potential double taxation either by granting exclusive tax jurisdiction to the residence state (*e.g.*, under many U.S. treaties, only the residence state can tax interest income paid by a payor in the other contracting state) or providing for shared tax jurisdiction with the residence state entitled to residual taxation after taking source state taxation into account (*e.g.*, business profits attributable to a permanent establishment in the other contracting state).

Treaties also provide a degree of certainty and predictability so that taxpayers can arrange their affairs. The clarification of tax jurisdiction and the mutual agreement procedures for resolving treaty problems contained in a tax treaty help smooth out some of the rough edges for a taxpayer dealing with different states with different laws. Also the provisions in a treaty for the exchange of information between states help contracting states enforce their domestic tax provisions.

While the discussion of treaties has been placed in Part II dealing with U.S. activities of foreign taxpayers, treaties also address the tax treatment of U.S. taxpayers by the other contracting state and how that tax treatment is recognized for U.S. tax purposes.

§ 5.02   THE TREATY MAKING PROCESS IN THE UNITED STATES

The Executive Branch of the United States, as part of its authority to conduct the foreign relations of the United States has the exclusive authority to negotiate income tax treaties. The Department of Treasury, through the Assistant Secretary for Tax Policy and the International Tax Counsel do the actual negotiation. Once a treaty is signed by the President or the President's delegate, the treaty is transmitted to the Senate for its advice and consent. Typically the Senate Foreign Relations Committee conducts hearings before approving or rejecting a treaty. If a treaty is approved by the Committee, the full Senate votes on the treaty. Occasionally, the Senate will approve a treaty subject to a reservation in respect of a particular provision. In such a case, from the U.S. perspective the treaty may enter into force except in respect of such a provision. Once the Senate approves a treaty, it enters into force upon the exchange of instruments of ratification by the Executive Branch. From time to time, treaties are amended through bilateral Protocols which must also undergo the ratification process as described above.

§ 5.03   THE RELATIONSHIP OF INCOME TAX TREATIES AND THE CODE

Income tax treaties exist to limit a contracting state's tax jurisdiction in order to avoid international double taxation. To that end, a treaty provision should not be construed to restrict in any manner any exclusion, exemption, deduction or credit, or any allowance accorded by the domestic laws of the treaty partners. Stated differently, income tax treaties can reduce a taxpayer's U.S. tax liability but cannot generally increase it.

U.S. income tax treaties have the same force as domestic law (*i.e.*, both are the "supreme Law of the Land"). U.S. Const. art. VI, cl. 2. If a treaty conflicts with federal law (*e.g.*, a tax provision), generally, for domestic law purposes, the later-in-time rule prevails. *Whitney v. Robertson*, 124 U.S. 190 (1888). Whenever possible, courts try to construe treaty provisions and domestic tax laws harmoniously. If a taxpayer claims that a statutory provision is affected by a tax treaty, the taxpayer must disclose reliance on a treaty to modify application of a Code provision. I.R.C. § 6114.

The domestic later-in-time rule sometimes leads to a violation of international law. When Congress enacts a statutory provision that directly overrides a pre-existing treaty provision, the later enacted statute prevails for domestic law purposes. However, the United States is not relieved of its treaty obligations and failure to comply with a treaty results in a violation of international law. *See* Vienna Convention on the Law of Treaties, Art. 27

(not signed by the U.S.); Restatement of Foreign Relations Law of the United States, § 135(1)(b). There are no practical remedies for a such a violation of international law, except that the contracting state against which the breach was committed can terminate or partially terminate the treaty.

Notwithstanding the international law implications, I.R.C. § 7852(d) clearly states that neither a treaty provision nor a tax provision has preferential status (so that the domestic later-in-time rule applies). The uneasy relationship between U.S. treaties and domestic law is expressed in I.R.C. § 894(a) which provides that Code provisions should be applied "with due regard to any treaty obligation of the United States."

§ 5.04 DEVELOPMENT OF MODEL INCOME TAX TREATIES

The United States has had a dual purpose in treaty design: to harmonize its domestic tax rules with the rules of other states and at the same time to preserve domestic tax jurisdiction over citizens and residents. Historically, the United States has followed a series of model income tax treaties in negotiating its income tax treaties with other nations. Most recently, the starting point for U.S. treaty negotiations has been a U.S. model income tax treaty primarily developed in 1977 and revised in 1981, 1996, and 2006 ("U.S. Model"). In 2015, the United States announced that a new model was in the works. Some of the expected provisions are discussed below.

Many of the European and other trading partners of the United States use a model treaty developed by the Organization for Economic Cooperation and Development ("OECD Model"). The United States is also a member of the OECD. The member states of the OECD also have agreed to Commentaries on the OECD Model treaty. The OECD Model and Commentaries provide useful explanations of treaty provisions and are often cited by U.S. courts. *See e.g., National Westminster Bank, PLC v. United States,* 512 F.3d 1347 (Fed. Cir. 2008); *Taisei Fire & Marine Insurance Co., Ltd., et al. v. Commissioner,* 104 T.C. 535 (U.S. Tax Ct.1995).

While the two models are far more alike than different, there are some fundamental differences. Unlike the OECD Model, the U.S. Model "saves" the right (in the "saving clause") of a contracting state to tax its citizens even if they reside in the other contracting state. Under the U.S. Model, the residence of a corporation is the state of incorporation if there are competing claims of residence; under the OECD Model, residence is based on the place of effective management of the corporation. Where there is potential double taxation, the U.S. Model relies on the credit method (*i.e.,* a contracting state credits the taxes paid to the other contracting state on income earned in the other contracting state) for relief while the OECD Model recognizes the exemption method (*i.e.,* a contracting state exempts income earned in the other contracting state) as well as the credit method.

Still another difference between the two models lies in the treatment of interest income. The U.S. Model assigns exclusive tax jurisdiction to the state where the recipient resides while the OECD Model permits the source state (*i.e.*, where the payor resides) a limited right to tax interest paid to a resident of the other state. There are other important structural differences between the two Models as well. For example, the U.S. Model does not generally extend to state and local income tax laws while the OECD Model does. Finally, the U.S. Model focuses more attention on treaty shopping than the OECD Model by specifically limiting the availability of treaty benefits where a taxpayer seeks to use a treaty for tax avoidance reasons. *See* U.S. Model, 2006, Art. 22.

In addition to the U.S. and OECD Models, there is a 1980 UN Model (amended in 2001 and updated in 2010) intended as a guide for treaties between developed and developing states. While the U.S. and OECD Models tend to favor capital exporters (*i.e.*, the residence state), the UN Model favors capital importing states (*i.e.*, the source state) by assigning greater taxing authority to the source state with respect to both investment and business income. In negotiating with the United States, a developing state may rely on the UN Model as its starting point, but the UN Model has not reached the same level of acceptance as the OECD Model.

While the U.S. Model serves as a starting point for U.S. treaty negotiation, U.S. bilateral income tax treaties show a remarkable degree of individuality. Nevertheless, the 2006 U.S. Model income tax treaty is the focus of the discussion that follows.

§ 5.05   INCOME TAX TREATY PROVISIONS

Although there is some variation in income tax treaty provisions between the United States and its treaty partners, there are a number of typical provisions that are found in virtually all the U.S. income tax treaties.

(A) INTERPRETATION OF U.S. INCOME TAX TREATIES

All modern U.S. treaties contain a provision that establishes a hierarchy of interpretation rules that apply to treaty terms. *See* U.S. Model, 2006, Art. 3(2). First, many treaty terms are specifically defined in the treaty (*e.g.,* the definition of "interest"). If a term is not specifically defined, the context of the treaty, including all relevant background material involving the treaty, may require a particular definition. If the context of a treaty does not require a particular definition, the contracting state applying the treaty applies its own domestic tax law. Even if the other contracting state might reach a different conclusion with respect to a definition, it is obligated to honor the conclusion reached by the contracting state applying the treaty if under Art. 3(2) that state acted in accordance with the treaty.

It is generally accepted that any reference to domestic law of a contracting state refers to that law as it may change from time to time that is, a dynamic rather than a static interpretation. Dynamic interpretation does not mean that a state is free unilaterally to amend its domestic law for the exclusive purpose of altering the application of a treaty provision.

(B) SCOPE OF THE TREATY

Articles 1, 2, and 29 of the U.S. Model address the coverage of the treaty in respect of persons, taxes, territory and time. Generally, the treaty applies to residents of a contracting state. However, it is U.S. policy that a tax treaty can limit the ability of the United States to tax the residents of other states but should "save" for the United States the right to tax U.S. citizens and residents on their worldwide income. U.S. Model, Art., 2006, 1(4). For example under this "saving clause," a resident of the United Kingdom who is not a U.S. citizen can rely on Article 11 of the U.S.-United Kingdom treaty to avoid U.S. taxation of interest paid by a U.S. borrower. However if that U.K. resident were a U.S. citizen, the United States reserves the right under Article 1(4) to tax fully the interest income, as if the treaty were not in effect. Even if the interest is paid by a U.K. borrower to a resident of the United Kingdom, the United States will tax the interest if the U.K. resident is also a U.S. citizen, although the responsibility for avoiding double taxation in this situation lies with the United States. *See* U.S. Model, 2006, Art. 23(4).

Turning to the scope of coverage in respect of taxes, territory, and time, not surprisingly U.S. income tax treaties address federal income taxes. State and local income taxes are not covered much to the disappointment of U.S. treaty partners who would like protection from what they regard as unfair state taxation by some U.S. states which, using a formulary approach, sometimes tax income not related to activities in the state. *See infra* § 9.01. Treaties have no fixed duration and can be terminated by a contracting state with six months' notice. U.S. Model, 2006, Art. 29.

Under Article 1(2), a treaty should not be applied in a way which would deprive the taxpayer a benefit which would be available if the treaty had not come into effect. That is, a treaty cannot increase a taxpayer's U.S. tax liability compared to the tax consequences in the absence of a treaty. For example, if a resident of the other contracting state has business income and business losses from two different activities conducted in the United States, the taxpayer can elect to be taxed under the U.S. domestic tax rules if those rules produce a more favorable outcome (*e.g.*, the ability to offset the business income with the business losses) for the taxpayer than taxation under the applicable treaty. However, the taxpayer must behave consistently with respect to any single category of income (*e.g.*, the taxpayer cannot choose treaty benefits with respect to the business income and statutory treatment of the business losses). Rev. Rul. 84–17, 1984–1 C.B. 10. If different categories of income are unrelated (*e.g.,* business income and dividends), a taxpayer can claim statutory treatment with respect to one category and treaty benefits with respect to the other category.

(C) DEFINITIONS

Articles 3–5 of the U.S. Model contain definitions of key terms used throughout the treaty. The definition of the term "resident" is central to the application of a treaty because treaties often assign taxing authority to the state of residence. Each contracting state defines residence for individuals and companies under its domestic law. A partnership typically is not a resident of a contracting state unless it is taxed as an entity. However partners of a contracting state may be residents entitled to the application of a treaty to partnership income.

Because a contracting state applies its own domestic definition of the term "resident," an individual taxpayer may be a resident of both states. For example, T might be a U.S. resident by virtue of I.R.C. § 7701(b) and a French resident under French domestic law. Under the residency tie-breaker provision in Article 3(3) of the U.S.-France treaty (or Article 4(3)(a) of the U.S. Model treaty), T is a resident of the State in which T has a permanent home. If T has a home available in both states, T is a resident where his personal and economic relations (center of vital interests) are closer. If the center of vital interests cannot be determined, a "habitual abode" test is applied. In the absence of a habitual abode, citizenship will be the determining factor. If T is a citizen of both states or neither state, the contracting states promise to try to settle the question by mutual consent.

Suppose X Corp. is incorporated in the United States but its place of effective management is in a foreign state so that it is considered a resident by both states under their domestic laws. *See e.g.,* Article 4(1) of the U.S.-United Kingdom income tax treaty. The residency tie-breaker provision (Article 4(4)) in the U.S. Model treaty classifies X Corp. as a resident of the state of incorporation. Some treaties do not contain a definitive corporate tax tie-breaker but instead allow each state to tax as if the treaty were not in effect. *See e.g.,* Article 4(5) of the U.S.-United Kingdom income tax treaty.

One of the more challenging treaty issues is to determine the treaty residence of hybrid entities (*i.e.*, a flow-through or transparent entity for U.S. tax purposes but a corporation for foreign tax purposes) and reverse hybrid entities (*i.e.*, a corporation for U.S. tax purposes but a flow-through for foreign tax purposes). Hybrids and reverse hybrids are common under the check-the-box rules in Reg. §§ 301.7701–2 and –3. Essentially, the rule under U.S. domestic law and U.S. treaties is that the residence state determines residence and the source state follows the residence state determination. *See* I.R.C. § 894(c), Reg. § 1.894–1(d) and Art. 1(6) of the U.S. Model.

For example, suppose that Canadian investors own 100 percent of the interest in a Cayman Islands entity that is reverse hybrid. The Cayman Island entity receives interest from a United States payor. In deciding whether the treaty with Canada applies (there is no U.S. treaty with the Cayman Islands), the United States will look to how Canada treats the U.S. income earned by the Cayman entity. If the United States followed its own view, it would not apply the treaty because the income is earned by a Cayman Islands corporation, but if Canada taxes the income earned by the Cayman entity directly to the Canadian investors, the United States will apply the treaty with Canada. Reg. § 1.894–1(d)(1).

Now suppose that the Cayman Islands entity was a hybrid entity (*i.e.*, a flow-through entity for U.S. tax purposes but a corporation for Canadian tax purposes). If the United States followed its own view, it would apply the treaty with Canada because the United States sees the Cayman Islands entity as a flow-through. But Canada does not tax the investors on the income from the United States because Canada thinks the income was earned by a Cayman Islands corporation. Therefore, the United States would not apply the treaty with Canada in this situation. The same situation would apply if the hybrid were a U.S. Limited Liability Company (LLC) (rather than a Cayman Islands entity) which was treated as a corporation for Canadian purposes, but was transparent for U.S. tax purposes. The U.S. generally would not apply the Canadian treaty with respect to income earned in the United States where that income is not taxable in the hands of a Canadian resident.

Sometimes more than one treaty may apply at the same time. Suppose that Canadian investors own 100 percent of the interest in a U.K. entity that is treated as a flow-through entity by Canada and as a corporation by the U.K. Income earned in the U.S. will be subject to taxation in the hands of a resident in both the U.K. and in Canada. In this situation, the United States is obligated to apply both the treaty with the U.K. and the treaty with Canada. For example, if the UK treaty provided a maximum U.S. withholding rate of 0 percent and the Canadian treaty provided a maximum withholding rate of 10 percent, the United States should honor both treaties by withholding at 0 percent.

Suppose Corporation A, a resident of both Country X and Country Y under the laws of each country, is treated as a resident of Country Y and not of Country X for purposes of the X-Y treaty and, as a result, is not liable to tax in Country X by reason of its residence. Is it entitled to claim the benefits of the U.S.-X Convention as a resident of Country X or of the U.S.-Y Convention as a resident of Country Y?

Revenue Ruling 2004–76, 2004–2 C.B. 111, determines that if Corporation A is treated as a resident of Country Y and not of Country X for purposes of the X-Y treaty and, as a result, is not liable to tax in Country X by reason of its residence, it is not entitled to claim benefits under the U.S.-X treaty, because it is not a resident of Country X under the relevant article of the U.S.-X treaty. However, Corporation A is entitled to claim benefits under the U.S.-Y treaty as a resident of Country Y, if it satisfies the requirements of the applicable limitation on benefits article, if any, and other applicable requirements in order to receive benefits under the U.S.-Y treaty.

The approach described above where the U.S. looks to the treatment of the taxpayer in the residence country clearly applies to FDAP income. But I.R.C. § 894(c) does not apply to business profits or to the branch profits tax. However, in more recent treaties and protocols including those with Belgium, Canada, Japan and the United Kingdom, the treaties clarify that all income whether FDAP or otherwise will be entitled to treaty benefits if taxed in the hands of a qualifying treaty resident.

(D) CLASSIFICATION AND ASSIGNMENT RULES

Articles 6–21 of the U.S. Model are the classification and assignment rules that classify types of income and assign taxing authority over that income to one or both contracting states.

(1) Business Income

Generally, a resident of a contracting state is not taxed on business income derived in the other contracting state unless the business income is "attributable to" a "permanent establishment" (PE) located in the other contracting state. If there is no permanent establishment, income that would otherwise be taxable in the state in which such income is earned in the absence of a treaty is not taxable in that state. For example, a foreign corporation engaged in a trade or business in the United States but not through a permanent establishment (*e.g.*, regularly selling inventory in the United States from a foreign business office using local independent sales agents) generally would not be taxable in the United States under an applicable treaty.

The definition of the term "permanent establishment" varies from treaty to treaty but in general a permanent establishment takes the form of either a physical PE or an agency PE. A third PE category—a construction site PE—may exist where a building site or construction or installation project or drilling rig used for the exploration of natural resources lasts more than twelve months.

The physical permanent establishment refers to a fixed place of business (*e.g.*, a factory or office) through which the business of an enterprise is carried on. A presence in the United States which might rise to the level of a "trade or business" under U.S. domestic tax law may not constitute a permanent establishment under treaty principles. *See e.g.*, *De Amodio v. Commissioner*, 34 T.C. 894 (Tax Ct. 1960) (taxpayer's business activities in the U.S. conducted by independent agents). Note that whether a resident of a contracting state has a permanent establishment in the other contracting state is not a function of ownership. The issue is whether the taxpayer has the premises "at its constant disposal." OECD Commentary, Art. 5, ¶ 4.

Accordingly, a leased premises can be a permanent establishment.

Suppose that a foreign corporation conducts its business activities in the United States, not through its own employees, but rather through an agent that is paid a fee. To determine whether the foreign corporation has a U.S. permanent establishment is a two-step process. First, it might be the case that the agent's physical premises is "at the constant disposal" of the foreign principal (*e.g.*, employees of the foreign corporation use the premises as they please). If so, then the foreign corporation would have a physical PE in the United States. But suppose that the foreign corporation did not have the premises of the agent at its constant disposal. In some cases, the activities of the agent, as opposed to the physical location, may create a PE.

A dependent agent of the taxpayer with authority to conclude contracts in the name of the principal and which habitually exercises that authority may constitute a permanent establishment of the principal. However, an independent agent acting in the ordinary course of the agent's business does not constitute a permanent establishment of the principal. An agency permanent establishment is based on the activities of the agent, not the agent's physical location. For example, a traveling employee with no fixed base might constitute a permanent establishment for the employer if the employee habitually concludes contracts binding the employer.

In *Taisei Fire & Marine Insurance Co., Ltd., et al. v. Commissioner*, 104 T.C. 535 (U.S. Tax Ct.1995), four Japanese property and casualty insurance companies (insurance companies) executed management agreements with Fortress Re Inc., a North Carolina corporation. The management agreements authorized Fortress to act as the agent for each company to underwrite insurance on behalf of each company. Either party could terminate the agreement by giving six months' notice. Fortress retained "total control over the handling and disposition of claims on behalf of [the Japanese insurance companies]," and remained free to enter into other management agreements with other companies.

Although representatives of the insurance companies met on occasion in Japan for business reasons, they did not discuss their individual relationships with Fortress. Each year, a Fortress representative visited the offices of each of the insurance companies in Tokyo; other communications occurred via letter or telex, but not telephone. A representative of each of the four companies visited Fortress's offices one or two times each year.

The IRS asserted that these Japanese companies were not exempt from U.S. income tax, because their profits were attributable to a U.S. permanent establishment Fortress, which exercised on a regular basis its authority to bind its principals. The Tax Court held that Fortress was not a "permanent establishment" of the insurance companies. The court concluded that, during the years at issue, Fortress was legally and economically independent of the four companies and therefore even if Fortress concluded contracts, doing so as an independent agent did not create a permanent establishment.

Examining the question of legal independence, the court noted that, under the management agreements, Fortress had complete discretion to conduct reinsurance business on behalf of the petitioners. The court also pointed out that the petitioners held no interest in Fortress and rejected the IRS's contention that the petitioners "exercised 'comprehensive control' over Fortress by acting as a 'pool.'"

Turning to economic independence, the court noted that parties to the management agreements could terminate their contractual relationship on six months' notice. The court rejected the IRS's assertion that Fortress bore no entrepreneurial risk because its operating expenses were covered by management fees and because it was guaranteed business on behalf of the petitioners' creditworthiness. Analogizing the instant facts to the case of a large mutual fund that charges an annual fee to cover operating expenses, the court wrote: "Clearly, the mutual fund company would not be considered dependent on its thousands of investors."

If a parent corporation in state A has a subsidiary in state B, the subsidiary does not automatically constitute a permanent establishment of the parent merely because of the parent's ownership, enabling state B to tax some of the parent's profit. However, if the subsidiary acts as an agent of the parent with authority to conclude contracts in the name of the parent which is habitually exercised, then the subsidiary may constitute a permanent establishment of the parent (or if employees of the parent have the premises of the subsidiary at their constant disposal, there may be a physical PE). In a partnership context, the permanent establishment of a partnership or of any partner is attributed to all of the partners.

Article 5(4) of the U.S. Model specifically provides that a permanent establishment does not include: (1) the use of facilities or the maintenance of a stock of goods or merchandise in a contracting state for storage, display, delivery; (2) the maintenance of a stock of goods or merchandise solely for processing by another enterprise; (3) the maintenance of a fixed place of business for the purpose of purchasing goods or merchandise or collecting information; or (4) the maintenance of a fixed place of business solely for engaging in any other activity of a preparatory or auxiliary character. But once a taxpayer crosses the line from preparatory or auxiliary activities into a full-fledged set of business activities, a PE would exist and all business profits (including those attributable to the preparatory or auxiliary activities) attributable to the permanent establishment may be taxed in the source state (*i.e.*, the state where the permanent establishment is located).

Suppose that ResCo, an R state corporation, maintains a server in state S which is engaged in electronic commerce (*e.g.*, provides financial information on a web site for a fee). Can the server constitute a permanent establishment in state S, thereby permitting source state taxation of business profits attributable to the permanent establishment? Under most treaty language, neither the server (*i.e.*, the computer itself) nor the web site can constitute a permanent establishment. However, the Commentaries to the OECD Model Convention suggest that the premises where the server is located can constitute a permanent establishment if ResCo has that premises at its disposal. OECD Commentary, Art. 5, ¶ 42.1–42.10. There may be a permanent establishment whether ResCo owns the premises or leases it in a manner where ResCo controls the premises. Mere use of space on a third party's server (*e.g.,* a hosted web site) should not constitute a permanent establishment.

Generally the term "business profits" means income derived from the active conduct of a trade or business, including the performance of personal services and the rental of tangible personal property. The term "attributable to" generally refers to net income that is produced by the permanent establishment as if it were an independent entity operating at arm's-length. For a discussion of arm's length principles, *see infra* Chapter 9. Accordingly, the deductions reasonably connected with the production of income by the permanent establishment, including an appropriate amount of overhead, reduce the amount of income that is taxable by the state in which the permanent establishment is situated.

In *National Westminster Bank, PLC v. United States*, 512 F.3d 1347 (Fed. Cir. 2008) ("NatWest") the U.S. Court of Federal Claims held that the interest expense Regulations under Reg. § 1.882–5 (*see supra* § 3.02(B)) are inconsistent with the "separate enterprise" requirements of Art. 7 of the U.S.-U.K. income tax treaty because the Regulations rely on a formula and is not based on a deemed arm's length relationship between the U.S. branch and the U.K. home office.

If income generated by a permanent establishment is received by a resident after the permanent establishment ceases to exist, the income will be considered attributable to the permanent establishment. U.S. Model, 2006, Art. 7(7). This provision is the treaty counterpart to I.R.C. § 864(c)(6).

Certain types of business income are sometimes dealt with separately in the U.S. Model. For example, Article 8 of the U.S. Model provides that income (from direct operation or from rental activities) from shipping and air transport in international traffic is generally taxable in the state of residence of the entrepreneur rather than in the state in which the income is produced, even if the income is attributable to a permanent establishment in that state. This rule reflects a concern that difficulties in allocation may otherwise result in multiple taxation of shipping profits.

Article 6 of the U.S. Model provides that income from real property may be taxed in the state where the property is located. The income may also be taxed in the owner's state of residence if relief from double taxation is allowed for any situs state taxation. The real property article applies both to business and investment income from real property.

Articles 6, 7 and 8 of the U.S. Model deal with allocation of business profits within an enterprise. Article 9 of the U.S. Model allows business profits (and other income) to be allocated between associated enterprises to reflect an arm's-length relationship. Article 9 makes possible the application of I.R.C. § 482 and related provisions. *See infra* Chapter 9.

(2) Personal Services Income

Under the U.S. Model and newer treaties, where a taxpayer resident in contracting state R performs independent personal services (*e.g.*, consulting not as an employee) in contracting state S, the income generated by the services performed is taxable in contracting state S where the services are performed only to the extent that the income is attributable to a permanent establishment in contracting state S. *See* Art. 7. In older treaties, a separate article dealing with independent personal services essentially reached the same result.

Under Article 14 of the U.S. Model, if an individual resident of a contracting state performs dependent personal services (*i.e.*, services as an employee) in the other contracting state, the state in which such services are performed has taxing authority over any remuneration paid if any one of the following three conditions is satisfied: (1) the recipient is present in the state where services are performed for more than 183 days during the taxable year; (2) the remuneration is paid by, or on behalf of, a resident of that state; or (3) the remuneration is borne by (*i.e.*, is deducted by) a permanent establishment or fixed base that the employer maintains in that state. U.S. Model, 2006, Art. 14.

Pensions derived by an employee are taxable exclusively in the employee's state of residence. U.S. Model, 2006, Art. 17(1). *See also* Art. 18. The IRS takes the position that to qualify as a pension, payments must meet the following cumulative requirements: (i) the recipient has been employed for at least 5 years or he/she was 62 or older at the time the payment was made; (ii) the payment is made (a) on account of the employee's death or disability, (b) as part of a series of substantially equal payments over the employee's life expectancy (or over the life expectancy of the employee and his beneficiary), or (c) paid on account of the employee's retirement after 55; and (iii) all payments are made after the employee has separated from service or on or after the date at which the employee reached the age of 70.5. Deferred bonuses paid by the employer to the individual after retirement do not constitute 'pensions or other similar remuneration' under Article 17 but are covered by Article 14. Rev. Rul. 71–478, 1971–2 C.B. 490.

While Article 14 of the U.S. Model is the major provisions addressing income from the performance of personal services, particular types of income from services are addressed elsewhere in the U.S. Model. For example, income earned by artistes and sportsmen because of their high earning capacity is generally taxable in the state of performance even if the income earned is not attributable to a fixed base (*e.g.*, income from a 2 week musical tour). U.S. Model, 2006, Art. 16. Directors' fees and other compensation derived by a resident of a contracting state for services rendered in the other contracting state in the capacity as a member of the board of directors of a company in that other state may be taxed in the company's state even if the director does not have a fixed base in that state. U.S. Model, 2006, Art. 15. There are special rules for government employees (Article 19) and students and trainees (Article 20) as well.

(3) Investment Income

The U.S. Model contains specific provisions addressing the taxation of dividends, interest, royalties, rental income from real property, and capital gains. In the absence of a treaty, dividends from U.S. sources paid to a nonresident of the United States are normally subject to a 30 percent withholding tax on the gross amount paid. I.R.C. §§ 871(a) or 881. U.S. income tax treaties generally modify these rates through a reciprocal reduction of rates that the payor's state (*i.e.*, the source state) can impose on dividends distributed to a resident of the other contracting state. Under Article 10 of the

U.S. Model, the maximum source state treaty tax rate on dividends is 15 percent. Many treaties reduce the maximum rate to 5 percent for dividends paid to a corporation owning as little as 10 percent of the voting stock of the dividend-paying corporation. *See* U.S. Model, 2006, Art 10. By limiting the source state rate of taxation, treaties reduce the incidence of double taxation. However, to the extent that a dividend recipient is taxed both by the source state and the residence state, the residence state must relieve any double taxation. U.S. Model, 2006, Art. 23. More recent treaties and Protocols (*e.g.,* with the United Kingdom, Belgium, Denmark, Germany, the Netherlands, Mexico, Japan, Australia) eliminate the withholding on direct dividends from a subsidiary to a parent corporation in some cases so that dividends from a subsidiary can be paid to the parent corporation free of any source state withholding tax. This appears to be the trend in current U.S. treaty negotiations.

The U.S. branch profits tax was enacted as a substitute tax for any tax that might be payable on dividends paid by a foreign corporation out of U.S. earnings and profits. The 2006 U.S. Model clarifies that the United States may impose its branch profits tax on income repatriated from a U.S. branch to a foreign corporation's home office. The tax on that repatriation is the same as that which would be imposed on a U.S. corporation making a dividend payment to its foreign parent corporation; the applicable tax rate generally is 5 percent, but in some treaties with no withholding tax on dividends paid to certain qualified persons (*e.g.,* publicly-traded parent corporation), the branch profits tax may also not be imposed. U.S. Model, 2006, Art. 10(8).

The U.S. Model treats interest in a manner similar to dividends, limiting source state taxation, but there are important differences. Article 11 does not permit any taxation of interest by the source state (*i.e.*, the state where the payor resides) although there are U.S. treaties based on the OECD Model that do permit the source state to tax interest at a rate not exceeding 10 percent (*e.g.*, the treaty with Spain).

Like interest, royalties (*e.g.*, amounts paid for the use of copyrights, artistic or scientific works, patents, secret formulae, trademarks, know-how) derived and beneficially owned by a resident of a contracting state are taxable only in that state under Article 12 of the U.S. Model. However, many developing states, following the UN Model, do permit limited source state taxation typically at rates not exceeding 15–20 percent of the royalty. The United States has entered into treaties with many developing states (*e.g.*, India), permitting source state taxation of royalties.

Under those treaties that permit source state taxation, it can be very important to determine whether a particular payment is a royalty or constitutes business profits. For example, suppose that ResCo, a state R resident, is engaged in electronic commerce through a server located in state R. An unrelated customer, SourceCo, located in state S, acquires some type of digital output (*e.g.*, a report, software) for a fee. If state S regards the fee as a royalty, state S may withhold on the royalty. If state R regards the fee as business profits, then in its view state S has no right to tax because there is no permanent establishment in state S. Generally, in order to constitute a royalty in this context, a payment must be for the right to acquire an interest in the copyright that can then be exploited rather than the output of ResCo exploiting the copyright. *See* OECD Commentary, Art. 12, ¶¶ 12–19.

If interest, dividend, or royalty income derived by a recipient is attributable to a permanent establishment the recipient maintains in the other contracting state, then the income is treated as business profits fully taxable in the state where the permanent establishment is situated under the business profits article rather than being subject to a withholding tax. *See* U.S. Model, 2006, Arts. 10(6) (dividends), 11(4) (interest), and 12(3) (royalties).

While source state taxation of income from dividends, interest, and royalties is limited by the U.S. Model, income derived by a resident of a contracting state from real property situated in the other contracting state may be fully taxed under Article 6 in the state where the property is situated. If that state under its domestic provisions would tax income from real property on a gross income basis, Article 6(5) allows the recipient an election to tax such income on a net basis.

Taxing jurisdiction over gains from the disposition of investment property depends on the nature of the property. Gain from the disposition of real property or an interest in an entity whose property consists primarily of real property is subject to tax in the contracting state in which the property is situated under its domestic law. *See* U.S. Model, 2006, Art. 13. Gain from the alienation of personal property (*e.g.*, machinery and equipment) attributable to a permanent establishment is taxable in the contracting state where the permanent establishment is situated. Gain from the disposition of stock or securities is normally taxable exclusively in the state of the seller's residence.

(4) Other Income

Any income that is not specifically covered in the U.S. Model is subject to taxing authority exclusively in the residence state of the recipient. U.S. Model, Art. 21. For example, a contracting state is not free under its domestic law to tax guarantee fees paid by a U.S. subsidiary to its foreign parent corporation for a parent guarantee that helps the U.S. subsidiary secure a beneficial bank loan. It should be noted, however, that some U.S. treaties (*e.g.*, the treaty with Canada) do permit source state taxation of Other Income. Under those treaties, the United States would be able to collect a 30 percent withholding tax under its view that such guarantee fees are Other Income and not business profits. *See* I.R.C. §§ 861(a)(9) and 881.

(E) AVOIDANCE OF DOUBLE TAXATION

A major purpose of the U.S. bilateral income tax treaty network is to eliminate international double taxation. U.S. income tax treaties contain reciprocal commitments by each state when acting as a residence state to provide either a foreign tax credit for taxes paid in the source state or to exempt income earned in the other contracting state. For example, the United States grants a credit for any foreign income taxes paid on foreign source income while often the other contracting state exempts from its taxation U.S. source business income (and grants a credit for source state taxation of investment income). U.S. Model, 2006, Art. 23.

(F) LIMITATION ON BENEFITS

Not surprisingly, foreign taxpayers investing or doing business in the United States often will try to structure their affairs to take advantage of a favorable income tax treaty. This is sometimes referred to as "treaty shopping." While U.S. taxpayers can also engage in treaty shopping in an effort to lower foreign taxes on income earned abroad, the United States more than any other country has been preoccupied with the perceived treaty shopping problem. Treaty shopping generally takes one of two forms: a taxpayer of a state that has no treaty with the United States seeks the coverage of a favorable treaty, or a taxpayer of a U.S. treaty partner prefers the treaty of another state. Often, a foreign taxpayer investing in the United States may seek out a treaty that provides for a low rate of taxation by the United States on investment income generated in the United States.

Absent some restrictions on treaty shopping, a treaty with one state could become a treaty with the world. With increasing determination, the United States has sought to curtail treaty shopping on many fronts. In *Aiken Indus., Inc. v. Commissioner*, 56 T.C. 925 (U.S. Tax Ct.1971), a Bahamian company that loaned money to a U.S. subsidiary assigned the obligation to a Honduran subsidiary under the same terms (*i.e.*, payment schedule and interest rate) as the obligation from the U.S. subsidiary. The Honduran subsidiary realized no profit from the transaction since the interest it received from the U.S. corporation was immediately payable to the Bahamian corporation. The U.S. subsidiary claimed that no U.S. withholding tax was required under I.R.C. §§ 881 and 1442 in respect of the interest payments made to the Honduran company under the applicable treaty. There was no treaty between the United States and the Bahamas.

The tax court ruled that the Honduran corporation never "received" the interest payments as required under the U.S.-Honduras tax treaty because the receipt of the interest and the obligation to transmit the interest to the Bahamian corporation were inseparable. The tax court found that the treaty provision required more than temporary physical possession; the Honduran corporation was required to have complete dominion and control in order for the treaty to apply. Characterizing the Honduran corporation as a mere "conduit," the Tax Court noted that the transaction had no economic or business purpose but existed only to avoid U.S. taxation through the treaty benefits. *See* also Rev. Ruls. 84–152, 1984–2 C.B. 381 and 84–153, 1984–2 C.B. 183.

In its treaty negotiations, the United States now insists on the insertion of a limitations on benefits (LOB) provision. U.S. Model, 2006, Art. 22. A treaty LOB provision determines whether a treaty resident under Article 4 is a "qualified person" permitted to receive treaty benefits. The LOB provision functions as a supplement to a treaty residence article. The focus of the treaty LOB provisions is on corporate taxpayers. Individual taxpayers who are residents of a contracting state will be qualified persons. But for corporations, the LOB provisions are more involved.

While there is much variation in the nature of these provisions, a typical treaty might provide that certain treaty benefits are not available to a foreign corporation unless one of several tests is met. For example, if the stock of a corporation is publicly traded on a recognized stock exchange of either contracting state or a foreign corporation is owned by such a publicly-traded entity in the same country of residence, it may typically qualify for treaty benefits. U.S. Model, 2006, Art. 22(2)(c).

A corporation that cannot qualify under the publicly-traded test, may qualify under an ownership/base erosion test. *See* Article 22(2)(e). If no more than 50 percent of a corporation's stock is held by third-country taxpayers, the ownership test may be satisfied. For example, if Saudi Arabian investors form a Dutch company solely to invest in U.S. stock and securities, the company does not qualify for reduced U.S. tax rates under the Dutch treaty on interest and dividends paid by a U.S. payor.

Suppose the Saudi Arabian investors arrange for Dutch individuals to hold 51 percent of the Dutch company's stock while the Saudi investors hold the other 49 percent and capitalize the company with as much debt as possible. While this arrangement satisfies the stock ownership requirement, it may not satisfy the base erosion test which denies treaty benefits if a company's income is syphoned off in substantial part to meet deductible liabilities owed to nonresidents, thereby eroding the tax base of the residence state.

Even if a company does not satisfy both the stock ownership and base erosion tests, treaty benefits may be available under a "derivative benefits" provision in some treaties (*e.g.,* those with EU members). For example, suppose that a German corporation (publicly-traded on a German stock exchange) owns all of the stock of a Dutch corporation which receives a royalty payment from a U.S. licensee. The Dutch corporation could not satisfy either the publicly-traded (*i.e.,* not owned by a publicly-traded Dutch corporation) or ownership/base erosion tests, but there really is no treaty shopping in this situation because had the German corporation received the royalty, it would have received the same treaty benefits under the

U.S.-Germany treaty. Under the derivative benefits test, the treaty between the U.S. and the Netherlands will apply (the treaty "derives" its application from the fact that the benefits would have been available under the US-Germany treaty) if the ultimate owners of the Dutch entity are qualified treaty residents of certain countries (*e.g.,* the EU, European Economic Area or NAFTA) and if the tax consequences under the treaty with the Netherlands are no more favorable than would have been the case under the treaty with Germany.

Even if none of these tests is satisfied, a corporation may enjoy treaty benefits under an active trade or business test, although the corporation is not a qualified resident. For example, suppose that Taiwanese shareholders own all of the stock of a Japanese corporation which earns income in the United States. If the Japanese corporation conducts a trade or business in Japan and the income received from the United States is derived in connection with (or is incidental to) the Japanese business, the income may qualify for treaty benefits. If income is received from a related U.S. payor, the business activities in Japan must be substantial when compared with the business activities in the United States. Note that derivative benefits provision cannot generally piggy-back on the active trade or business test (*e.g.,* the treaty with Luxembourg is the exception). In the example above, if the German corporation could only meet the active trade or business test and was not publicly traded or German-owned, the Dutch corporation could not satisfy the derivative benefits requirements because it was not owned by an EU "qualified resident". U.S. Model, 2006, Art. 22(3).

Some U.S. treaties contain a headquarters test that will allow a holding company to qualify for treaty benefits if it functions as the headquarters for a corporate group operating in at least 5 countries and meets other requirements. Finally, the Competent Authority of the contracting state in which income is earned can grant treaty benefits if a taxpayer doesn't otherwise qualify. But in real life, this is not a practical way of planning into a structure.

(G) NONDISCRIMINATION

Because the fundamental purpose of an income tax treaty is to minimize the impact taxes have on the free flow of international trade, treaties typically contain mutual assurances that each treaty partner will not use excessive taxation as a protectionist device. In general, nationals and residents of each treaty state should play on a level playing field with nationals and residents of the other treaty state in the same circumstances. This nondiscrimination commitment takes the form of a promise by each partner in exercising its source-based and residence-based jurisdiction not to tax nationals and residents of the other contracting state more heavily than its own similarly situated nationals and residents. *See* U.S. Model, 2006, Art. 24.

A nondiscrimination article typically provides that a citizen of one contracting state that is resident in the other contracting state may not be treated less favorably than a citizen of the other contracting state in the same circumstances. Similarly a corporate resident of one contracting state doing business through a permanent establishment in the other contracting state cannot be treated less favorably than a corporation resident in the other contracting state. For example, if the United States imposed a higher tax on the business profits of a U.S. permanent establishment than on similar profits earned by a U.S. corporation, the provision would violate the nondiscrimination article.

Nondiscrimination articles also typically prevent a contracting state from denying a deduction for interest, royalties, or other disbursements paid to a resident of the other contracting state if those same payments would be deductible if paid to a resident of the state of the payor. For example, the United States denies an interest deduction under some circumstances for interest paid by a U.S. payor to a nonresident where under an applicable treaty there is a reduction in the normal 30 percent U.S. tax rate. I.R.C. § 163(j). However, there is no denial of a deduction for an identical interest payment paid to an identical recipient that is a U.S. resident. The application of I.R.C. § 163(j) in a treaty context appears to violate the nondiscrimination article, but is nevertheless U.S. domestic law. Similarly, some might argue that the branch profits tax being a second tax on a foreign corporation in addition to the regular tax violates nondiscrimination articles. Most recent U.S. treaties eliminate the problem by specifically providing that the imposition of the branch profits tax does not violate the treaty.

The presence of a nondiscrimination article in a treaty does not mean that all nonresidents must be taxed in the same manner as residents. The concept of discrimination implies a comparison of similarly situated persons. For example, nonresidents and foreign corporations may be subject to a 30 percent gross basis tax on FDAP income paid by a U.S. payor while U.S. individuals and corporations are taxed on similar income on a net basis under I.R.C. §§ 1 or 11. However, the 30 percent withholding tax is not considered discriminatory because nonresidents are not "similarly situated" to U.S. residents U.S. residents are taxed on worldwide income while nonresidents are generally taxed only on income that is connected to the United States through the source rules. The same reasoning allows different rules for exemptions, filing status, etc. to apply to nonresidents. To determine whether a contracting state is discriminating in violation of a treaty, no comparison can be made between a nonresident noncitizen of the United States and a nonresident citizen of the United States because they are not in the same circumstances the U.S. citizen is taxable on worldwide income while the non-U.S. citizen is not subject to worldwide taxation in the United States.

Unlike most other provisions in the treaty, the nondiscrimination article applies to taxes of every kind, including those imposed by states and other local authorities. That is, a state is not permitted to discriminate against nonresidents in a manner that violates Article 24. U.S. Model, 2006, Art. 24(7).

(H) MUTUAL AGREEMENT PROCEDURE

U.S. income tax treaties typically contain a mutual agreement procedure provision for resolving treaty disputes. *See* U.S. Model, 2006, Art. 25. Under such a provision, if a taxpayer claims that the action of the tax authorities of a contracting state has resulted, or will result, in taxation that violates the treaty, the competent authorities of both contracting states seek to reach an agreement to avoid double taxation. Under a mutual agreement article, the competent authorities of the contracting states can enter into a mutual agreement (which may modify domestic law) in order: (i) to resolve specific cases in which a taxpayer alleges violation of a treaty; (ii) to agree upon interpretation and application of a treaty provision; and (iii) to eliminate double taxation in cases not expressly provided for in the treaty. In the United States, the competent authority is the Secretary of the Treasury or his delegate which is the Assistant Commissioner (International).

Typical issues that may be resolved by mutual agreement include: the attribution of income to a permanent establishment; the allocation of income between related persons; the characterization of particular items of income; the application of source rules with respect to particular items of income; the meaning of a term; increases in amounts specified in the treaty to reflect monetary or economic developments; and the application of domestic law relating to penalties, fines and interest. Much of the work of the competent authorities is to allocate business profits and deductions between a permanent establishment in one state and a home office in the other state or to allocate income and deduction between related taxpayers in different states. For example, if a U.S. corporation sells goods to a wholly-owned Swiss subsidiary which resells to wholesalers throughout Europe, the competent authorities may be called upon to allocate gain between the U.S. and Swiss corporations for tax purposes.

The guidelines for requesting U.S. competent authority assistance are set forth in Rev. Proc. 2006–54, 2006–2 C.B. 1035.

(I)   EXCHANGE OF INFORMATION AND ADMINISTRATIVE ASSISTANCE

U.S. bilateral income tax treaties also contain provisions obligating a treaty partner to provide information to the other treaty partner for the purpose of enabling that other treaty partner to enforce its tax law. *See* U.S. Model, 2006, Art. 26. The partner that is asked for the information is authorized to use its administrative information gathering powers, including compulsory legal process, to obtain any necessary information. There are several types of exchanges that take place including: routine or automatic exchanges of information concerning names of payees and amounts of interest, dividends and royalties paid to residents of a treaty partner; exchanges made upon request by a treaty partner; simultaneous examinations of related taxpayers; spontaneous exchanges of information; and exchanges of industry-wide information. If the IRS issues a summons to a third-party record keeper seeking records of business transactions with the taxpayer pursuant to a treaty partner's request for information, the taxpayer must be provided with notice allowing an opportunity to quash the third-party summons. I.R.C. § 7609. There is no requirement that the IRS provide a taxpayer notice if it provides information in its own possession to a treaty partner, although the Treasury may allow an opportunity for administrative review of the decision to exchange information.

The United States also has entered into tax information exchange agreements (TIEAs) with countries that are not treaty partners to facilitate international cooperation in the enforcement of tax laws. In addition, the United States, has ratified the multilateral OECD Convention on Mutual Assistance in Tax Matters which also provides for information exchanges.

A treaty partner may decline to provide information if: it would require administrative measures which violate the law or administrative practice of either treaty partner; the information is not obtainable in the normal tax administration of either treaty partner; or the information requested would disclose any trade or business secret.

While the United States is willing to exchange information pursuant to its treaties, normally one country will not assist in collection of another country's taxes. *Holman v. Johnson*, 1775 WL 22 (Eng. 1775) (Lord Mansfield). It is difficult to defend this common law principle in the tax area when a foreign government can already seek to enforce a foreign judgment based on a breach of contract in a U.S. court. Why shouldn't a U.S. court enforce a foreign tax judgment (and vice versa) as long as the taxpayer has notice, the right to be heard, and the right to raise any constitutional due process defenses.

§ 5.06 THE FUTURE OF THE U.S. MODEL INCOME TAX TREATY

In May of 2015, the U.S. Treasury announced they were working on a revised version of the U.S. Model treaty. The expected changes are sweeping in nature and are consistent with changes that occurring throughout the world—most notably the OECD's Base Erosion and Profits Shifting initiative—BEPS which is discussed in more detail *infra* at § 13.06. The focus of BEPS and the proposed changes to the U.S. Model are to prevent double non-taxation—income that is not taxed or insignificantly taxed by any nation. For example suppose a U.K. parent corporation has two subsidiaries—a Luxembourg subsidiary and a U.S. subsidiary. If the Luxembourg subsidiary loans money to the U.S. subsidiary and drops the loan receivable into a U.S. branch of the Luxembourg subsidiary, deductible interest payments from the

U.S. subsidiary reduce the U.S. tax base. Generally, the interest accrued would not be taxable as income effectively connected with a U.S. trade or business (because the branch merely collects income). Luxembourg may nevertheless exempt the income because it thinks that taxing authority belongs to the United States. The result is no taxation of the interest income, and under the current U.S.-Luxembourg treaty, there is no U.S. withholding tax. The proposed revisions to the U.S. Model—if incorporated into the U.S.-Luxembourg treaty— would allow the United States to collect a 30 percent withholding tax where the income received by the U.S. branch is lightly taxed in the United States and Luxembourg.

Other anticipated changes include a denial of favorable treaty withholding rates for recently expatriated entities—those that have given up U.S. residence—and for certain taxpayers that enjoy special tax regimes that provide for reduced residence state taxation. Two other changes of note are a toughening up of limitation on benefits provisions in several respects (*e.g.*, in the derivative benefits provision, all entities in a chain of ownership must qualify for derivative benefits—not just the ultimate owner) and a provision that allows a contracting state to "turn off" the availability of some treaty benefits if the other contracting state enacts legislation after the treaty is signed that significantly reduces taxation.

Even when the new U.S. Model is officially released, it has no legal significance—it does not impact any existing treaties. It is simply a statement of the U.S. starting position for negotiating future treaties. The new U.S. Model is also noteworthy because usually U.S. Models incorporate provisions that are already found in some negotiated treaties. However, the sweeping changes proposed for the new Model include provisions not found in any existing U.S. treaties.

CHAPTER 6

FILING, WITHHOLDING, AND REPORTING REQUIREMENTS

§ 6.01   FILING REQUIREMENTS

If a nonresident is engaged in a trade or business in the United States, the taxpayer must file a tax return for that year even if the taxpayer has no effectively connected income for the year or is exempt from taxation by statute or treaty. I.R.C. § 6012. Historically, the IRS in regulations has taken the position that if no return is filed or if the return filed is not "true and accurate," a nonresident may not claim any deductions from gross income. I.R.C. §§ 874(a), 82(c)(2) and Reg. § 1.882–4. In *Swallows Holding, Ltd. v. Commissioner,* 515 F.3d 162 (3rd Cir. 2008), the court upheld the regulations.

If a nonresident is not engaged in a trade or business in the United States, the taxpayer often may not be required to file a return if the tax liability is fully satisfied by withholding at the source. Reg. §§ 1.6012–1(b)(2)(i) and 1.6012–2(g)(2)(i).

In many cases, a nonresident taking a position that a treaty of the United States overrules (or otherwise modifies) a U.S. domestic tax law must file a return and disclose this position on a statement (Form 8833) attached to the taxpayer's return. I.R.C. § 6114. For example, a nonresident who contends that the U.S. effectively connect income that it generates in not attributable to a U.S. permanent establishment or a foreign corporation that claims a treaty exemption from the U.S. branch profits tax is required to disclose that position under I.R.C. § 6114. Moreover, a foreign person entitled to a treaty reduction of the 30 percent statutory withholding rate on interest, dividends, etc. (*i.e.*, FDAP income) must provide the withholding agent with the necessary documentation (*e.g.*, a W–8BEN—BEN is short for "beneficial owner"; entities file a W–8BEN–E) prior to the time of payment in order to receive the treaty benefits. Reg. § 1.1441–6(b)(1). Even then, in some cases where the payments are from related parties and exceed more than $500,000, a taxpayer may still be required to file a Form 1120–F (along with a Form 8833). A foreign corporation failing to disclose a treaty-based reporting position can be subject to a penalty of $10,000 ($1,000 for other nonresidents). I.R.C. § 6712.

While an extensive discussion of all the filing requirements and Forms in both an inbound and outbound context is beyond the scope of this book, what follows is a brief summary of some of the more important filing requirements for both inbound and outbound taxpayers.

For a U.S. corporation, Schedule N, which is attached to the U.S. corporation's income tax return, is used to identify whether a U.S. corporation has any foreign operations. Certain U.S. citizens, residents, and corporations who own or acquire the stock of a foreign corporation (including stock treated as owned under constructive ownership rules) may be required to file Form 5471. Additionally, certain officers and directors of the foreign corporation may be required to file Form 5471. The category of the filer determines what information must be disclosed on the form. The information generally consists of an income statement, balance sheet, earnings and profits calculations, details of intercompany transactions, and disclosures concerning acquisitions, dispositions and mergers involving the foreign corporation.

Other important forms for a U.S. corporate taxpayer include the Form 1118 which is used to compute a corporation's foreign tax credit for income taxes paid or accrued to a foreign country or a U.S. possession and is filed as part of the taxpayer's corporate income tax return. Any corporation that claims a foreign tax credit must attach this form to its income tax return. This form is also used to calculate and track a corporation's "overall foreign losses," which can adversely impact a corporation's ability to use foreign tax credits.

Generally, Form 926 must be filed by a U.S. citizen or resident, domestic corporation, or an estate or trust (other than a foreign estate or trust) that transfers tangible or intangible property (even if unappreciated) to a foreign corporation. Form 926 is not used to report transfers relating to foreign estates and trusts and foreign partnerships (Forms

3520 and 8865, respectively, address these transfers).

A U.S. taxpayer which owns a foreign corporation (treated as a disregarded entity under the U.S. check-the-box regulations) is required to file a Form 8858 that provides information that may help the IRS enforce the branch currency provisions of I.R.C. § 987 when income is remitted from the branch back to the U.S.

For an inbound taxpayer, generally, a foreign corporation must file Form 1120–F if, during the taxable year, the corporation:

- Overpaid income tax that it wants refunded;

- Engaged in a trade or business in the United States, whether or not it had income from that trade or business;

- Had income, gains, losses treated as if they were effectively connected with a U.S. trade or business; or

- With some exceptions, had income from any U.S. source (even if its income is tax exempt under an income tax treaty or code section).

The return is due by the 15th day of the 6th month after the corporation's taxable year if the corporation does not have an office in the United States. Otherwise, the return is due by the 15th day of the 3rd month after the end of the corporation's taxable year. A six-month extension of time for filing the return, but not for paying tax, may be requested on Form 7004, *Application for Automatic Extension of Time to File Corporate Income Tax Return.*

Form 5472 reports intercompany transactions involving U.S. corporations (or foreign corporations that are engaged in a U.S. trade or business) and certain foreign and domestic related parties.

In addition to a nonresident filing a U.S. corporate tax return where appropriate, every partnership (domestic or foreign) that engages in a U.S. trade or business or has U.S. source income is required to file a Form 1065. It is due on the 15th day of the 4th month after the end of the partnership taxable year (*i.e.*, April 15th for a calendar year-end partnership). Foreign partnerships that are controlled by U.S. persons must file a Form 8865 even if not engaged in a U.S. business.

§ 6.02   SAILING PERMITS

Aside from any filing requirements, neither a resident alien nor a nonresident alien may depart from the United States without procuring a certificate of compliance with the federal income tax laws. I.R.C. § 6851(d)(1). This provision does not apply to temporary visitors or in the case where a resident alien is planning to return to the United States.

§ 6.03   THE NEED FOR WITHHOLDING

If a foreign taxpayer is not engaged in a trade or business in the United States but receives investment income from U.S. sources, any fixed or determinable annual or periodical income is subject to a 30 percent tax rate (or lower treaty rate). I.R.C. §§ 871(a) or 881. However, because the foreign taxpayer may not have business assets in the United States, it might be impossible to enforce the 30 percent tax against a foreign taxpayer that does not voluntarily pay. Accordingly, the Code contains a variety of withholding provisions which apply to the investment income of foreign taxpayers. A withholding agent who fails to withhold will be personally liable for the requisite tax, penalties, and interest. I.R.C. § 1461.

In general, withholding is required if the following six criteria are met: (a) the recipient is a foreign person; (b) the amount paid is U.S. source income; (c) the amount paid is fixed or determinable annual or periodical income (*i.e.*, generally passive investment income from interest, dividends, royalties, and some rents); (d) the amount paid is not income effectively connected to a U.S. trade or business; (e) the payor or some agent of the payor is a withholding agent; and (f) no exception applies.

§ 6.04   WITHHOLDING ON DIVIDENDS, INTEREST, AND OTHER PERIODIC PAYMENTS

When a U.S. or foreign payor makes a U.S. source dividend or interest payment (or other U.S. source payment to a foreign investor that is taxable under either I.R.C. §§ 871(a)(1) or 881), the payor may be obligated under I.R.C. §§ 1441 or 1442 to withhold 30 percent of the amount paid from U.S. sources that is not effectively connected with the foreign investor's conduct of a U.S. trade or business. No additional tax liability is imposed by I.R.C. § 1441; instead, the provision establishes a method of collecting taxes that are imposed and due under I.R.C. §§ 871 and 881 by transferring the initial tax payment responsibility to the payor.

The general withholding obligation arises when there are specified types of payments to a foreign person. Reg. § 1.1441–1(b). Payments to U.S. persons are not subject to the 30 percent withholding requirement of I.R.C. § 1441, but a backup withholding requirement of 31 percent may be imposed by I.R.C. § 3406 if a U.S. recipient fails to provide the required proof of U.S. residence or citizenship to the withholding agent (*e.g.,* a Form W–9). Conversely, payments to foreign persons are subject to 30 percent withholding under I.R.C. § 1441 but are not additionally subject to the backup withholding rules.

Determining the status of a payee as U.S. or foreign is not always easy. The Regulations contain a complicated series of presumptions which a withholding agent may use to ascertain the payee's residency in the absence of documentation as to the payee's status. Reg. § 1.1441–1(b)(3). A withholding agent, relying on these presumptions will not be liable for any tax or penalties that may result because the payee's actual residency was not as presumed. The presumptions are to be used only for determining a payee's status in reaching a decision to withhold; the presumptions are not to be used for granting a reduced rate of withholding under any income tax treaty. Moreover, withholding agents should be aware that the Regulations under I.R.C. § 1441 also contain rules for determining the status of entities that are disregarded under the check-the-box Regulations. *See infra* Chapter 13. Payments to a U.S. disregarded entity which is wholly owned by a foreign person are treated as made to a foreign person. Reg. § 1.1441–1(b)(2)(iii).

Normally, the amount withheld on a distribution to a foreign payee is 30 percent of the gross amount of the payment. I.R.C. §§ 871 and 881. A withholding agent may grant a reduced rate of withholding to a beneficial owner that is a foreign person entitled to a reduced rate of withholding in accordance with a tax treaty if appropriate documentation is provided. Reg. § 1.1441–1(b). Moreover, a withholding agent may be absolved of the withholding obligation when making a payment to a foreign person who assumes responsibility for withholding on that payment. Foreign persons eligible to assume this withholding responsibility fall into four categories: qualified intermediaries, U.S. branches of foreign entities, withholding foreign partnerships, or authorized foreign agents. *See infra* § 6.04(E).

(A) INCOME SUBJECT TO WITHHOLDING

The broad withholding requirement of I.R.C. § 1441 does not apply to all items of income. Items that are effectively connected with the conduct of a trade or business within the United States are exempt from withholding if appropriate documentation is presented to the withholding agent (*e.g.*, W–8ECI). Compensation paid to employees is subject to wage withholding rather than withholding under I.R.C. §§ 1441 or 1442. *See* Form 8233. An amount paid as a scholarship or fellowship for study, training or research in the United States (*i.e.*, amounts that do not represent compensation for services) to a nonresident alien individual temporarily present in the U.S. may constitute income to the nonresident if the scholarship is not excluded under I.R.C. § 117. That payment will be subject to a 14 percent withholding requirement, consistent with I.R.C. § 871(c).

In general, income from sources within the United States that is fixed or determinable, annual or periodical income (FDAP income) is subject to withholding. I.R.C. § 1441(b). There are exceptions from the withholding requirement for certain classes of income such as portfolio interest, bank deposit interest, and short-term original issue discount. Reg. § 1.1441–2(a). To be considered a short-term obligation, and thereby exempt from withholding, an obligation must be payable within 183 days of the original issue. I.R.C. § 871(g).

On all other original issue discount (OID) obligations, withholding is required where the payor is able to calculate the amount of OID paid to a foreign beneficial owner. Reg. § 1.1441–2(b)(3). A withholding agent must withhold on OID to the extent that it has actual knowledge of the portion of the payment constituting taxable OID to the beneficial owner or if that knowledge is reasonably available to the withholding agent. The withholding agent will be considered to have actual knowledge of the portion of the payment which constitutes taxable OID if it knows the beneficial owner's holding period, purchase price and the terms of the obligation.

When a foreign beneficial owner of an instrument carrying OID has the instrument redeemed by the corporation, the withholding agent must compute and withhold the requisite tax on the amount of OID that accrued while the foreign person held the obligation up to the time when the instrument is redeemed. Generally, no withholding is required if an OID instrument is sold unless the sale is part of a plan to avoid tax and the withholding agent has reason to know of the plan. Reg. § 1.1441–2(a). However, even in the absence of withholding tax the seller may have to file and pay tax on the accrued interest. Reg. § 1.1441–2(b)(3).

Often it will be necessary for a withholding agent to determine whether a payee is the beneficial owner of a payment or the agent of the beneficial owner. The term "beneficial owner" is defined as "the person who is the owner of the income for tax purposes and who beneficially owns that income." Reg. § 1.1441–1(c)(6). A person "owns" income to the extent that it is required under general U.S. tax principles to include the payment in gross income per I.R.C. § 61. A person who receives income in the capacity of a nominee, agent, or custodian for another person is not the beneficial owner of the income.

In general, the beneficial owners of a payment to a flow-through entity (*e.g.*, a partnership) are the persons who under U.S. tax principles are the owners of the income in their separate and individual capacities. For example, suppose that a payment is made to a partnership. Under generally applicable U.S. tax principles, the beneficial owners of partnership income are the partners in the partnership. Therefore, when a payment is made to that partnership, the beneficial owners of that payment are the partners in their separate and individual capacities. In determining the beneficial owners of payments to a partnership, the withholding agent may be required to look through multiple tiers of pass-through entities in order to find a beneficial owner that is not a conduit. Reg. § 1.1441–1(c)(6)(ii).

Typically, the amount subject to withholding is the gross (*i.e.*, full) amount of the payment. Reg. § 1.1441–3(a). However, a corporation may reduce the amount of a distribution which is treated as a dividend subject to withholding based on a reasonable estimate of available earnings and profits (either current or accumulated). No withholding is required on a distribution that is not paid out of available earnings and profits. Reg.

§ 1.1441–3(c)(2). If the corporation making the distribution later determines that it under withheld on the distribution, it will be liable for the amount under withheld and any related interest. The corporation will not incur a penalty so long as the estimate of available earnings and profits was reasonable. If the FDAP payment subject to withholding is a payment-in-kind (*e.g.*, property used to satisfy an interest obligation), the withholding agent is not obligated to convert the property to cash if the withholding agent is able to obtain payment from another source (*i.e.*, withhold an extra amount on the cash portion of an interest payment to the same recipient). The obligation to withhold is not discharged even when there is no alternative source from which to withhold, and as a result, a withholding agent is authorized to liquidate any property of the beneficial owner into cash if necessary to satisfy the withholding requirements. Reg. § 1.1441–3(e).

Withholding is required at the time when there is a payment of FDAP income to a foreign payee. Income subject to withholding is considered paid when it is includible in income under U.S. tax principles governing the cash basis method of accounting. Reg. § 1.1441–2(e). A payment may be deemed made even where there is no actual transfer of cash or other property. Accordingly, FDAP income reallocated from a related U.S. person to a foreign recipient under I.R.C. § 482 would be considered a payment for withholding purposes. Reg. § 1.1441–2(e)(2) and *Central de Gas de Chihuahua, S.A. v. Commissioner*, 102 T.C. No. 19, 102 T.C. 515 (U.S.

Tax Ct. 1994). Moreover, where a foreign person realizes income from the cancellation of a debt, withholding is required if the withholding agent has control over money or property owned by the recipient. Reg. §§ 1.1441–2(d) and 2(e)(1).

(B)   REDUCED RATES OF WITHHOLDING

Nonresidents receiving FDAP income may claim a reduced rate of withholding under a favorable treaty provision. Reg. § 1.1441–6. Withholding will be reduced to the level specified in a particular treaty if the beneficial owner of the payment is a resident of that treaty country and all of the other requirements to obtain benefits of the treaty are satisfied. Reg. § 1.1441–6(b). To prove that a treaty applies, the foreign beneficial owner of the income must provide the withholding agent with a beneficial owner withholding certificate (W–8BEN for individuals or W–8BEN–E for entities). This certificate should establish that the person who is considered to be the beneficial owner of the income under U.S. tax principles is a resident of the signatory treaty country or is somehow otherwise entitled to reduced withholding under that treaty. Reg. § 1.1441–6(b)(1). A beneficial owner withholding certificate is valid only if it is provided on a Form W–8BEN (or W–8BEN–E) or in some cases a substitute form. Reg. § 1.1441–1(e)(2). Generally, a withholding agent may rely upon the beneficial owner's Form W–8BEN(–E) and withhold at a reduced rate if the certificate is received before any payment is made. Reg. § 1.1441–1(e)(1).

(C) WHO IS A WITHHOLDING AGENT?

A withholding agent is any person that has the control, receipt, custody, disposal, or payment of an item of a foreign person subject to withholding, including a lessee, mortgagee, employer or the payor of dividends. Reg. § 1.1441–7(a). In general, the withholding agent is the last person in the United States who handles an item of income before it is paid over to a foreign person. Under I.R.C. § 1441(a), it is possible to have more than one withholding agent for a single income item. Even where several persons qualify as withholding agents with respect to a single payment, only one tax is required to be withheld and generally only one return must be filed.

The withholding agent is required to deposit any withheld tax in a Federal Reserve or other authorized bank. I.R.C. § 6302. The withholding agent must file an annual return on Form 1042 and a Form 1042S with respect to each foreign recipient. A copy of the Form 1042S goes to the foreign recipient. The withholding agent is personally liable to the IRS for any amount required to be withheld and is indemnified against any claims of the taxpayer. I.R.C. § 1461. Moreover, a withholding agent is obligated to withhold only to the extent that the agent has control over, or custody of, money or property of the payee from which to withhold the required amount. When a withholding agent does not have control over or custody of any money or property owned by the recipient or beneficial owner during the course of the year in which a payment occurs, the withholding agent will be absolved of the withholding obligation unless the payment is a distribution on stock or the lack of control or custody of money or property is a result of a pre-arranged plan to avoid withholding. Reg. § 1.1441–2(d).

If a withholding agent fails to withhold or under withholds, there is no defense that either another withholding agent failed to withhold or that legal counsel advised that withholding was unnecessary. However, a withholding agent may rely on documentation provided by the payee indicating that no withholding is required (*e.g.*, the income is effectively connected or the payee is a U.S. citizen or resident) if appropriate procedures are followed. Where the failure to file or withhold is a willful attempt to evade tax, the withholding agent will be liable for penalties imposed under I.R.C. § 6672, in addition to the withholding agent's liability for the underlying tax.

(D) PAYMENTS INVOLVING PARTNERSHIPS, TRUSTS AND ESTATES

If a FDAP payment is made to a pass-through entity, such as a partnership, the withholding obligation depends on whether the partnership is domestic or foreign. Reg. § 1.1441–5(a)(1). Generally, a withholding agent will be able to rely on documentation from the payee in determining the residence of the payee. A partnership is deemed to be foreign if it is created or organized outside the United States. I.R.C. § 7701(a)(5). A partnership will be presumed foreign under the following circumstances: actual knowledge of the employer identification number (EIN) indicates foreign status; correspondence with the payee is mailed to a foreign address; or the payment is made outside of the United States. Reg. § 1.1441–5(d)(2).

Payments to domestic partnerships are not subject to withholding under I.R.C. § 1441, even if some of the partners are foreign persons. Reg. § 1.1441–5(b)(1). Instead, a domestic partnership is the withholding agent for items of income included in the distributive share of a partner who is a foreign person. Assuming that the domestic partnership withholds on a foreign partner's distributive share of FDAP income received, there will be no withholding obligation when the income is actually distributed to the foreign partner. However, a U.S. partnership must withhold on any distributions of an amount subject to withholding (*i.e.*, an interest payment to a lender) or on making a guaranteed payment to a foreign partner. Reg. § 1.1441–5(b)(2). Similar rules apply to payments to U.S. trusts and estates on behalf of foreign beneficiaries.

A more substantial withholding obligation exists when payments are made to foreign partnerships. Generally, a payment to a foreign partnership is treated as if the payment were made directly to its partners. Reg. § 1.1441–5(c)(1). The partners individually—rather than the partnership—will be considered the payees for purposes of determining whether a payment was made to a U.S. or foreign person. If a partner is itself a partnership or another pass-through entity, the partners of the highest tier foreign partnership will be considered the payees. Reg. § 1.1441–5(c)(1)(i). Essentially, the lower tier partnerships will be looked through for tax purposes, until a partner is reached that is not a pass-through entity. As a result of the look-through, a foreign partner may claim treaty benefits to which the partner is entitled in its own right. To the extent that the payor is unable to determine the amount allocable to each foreign partner or in the event that some partners are not accounted for, the payor may be required to withhold at the highest applicable rate. Reg. § 1.1441–5(d)(3).

Suppose U.S. Co. makes a dividend payment of $120 to XYZ, a foreign partnership in Country X. XYZ is comprised of three equal partners, X, Y, and Z. In determining the correct rate of withholding, the withholding agent will look through XYZ and consider the residence of the individual partners, if appropriate documentation is provided. If X is a resident of country X which does not have a tax treaty with the United States, the withholding agent must withhold from the dividend payment 30 percent of the share of the dividend attributable to X. Because X,Y, and Z are equal partners, we can assume that X will be allocated $40 of the dividend. Therefore, on the payment to XYZ, the withholding agent must collect $12 of tax (30% of $40) and remit the $12 to the IRS on behalf of X. If Y is a U.S. resident, no withholding is required by I.R.C. § 1441 on Y's share of the dividend payment. Suppose that Z is a resident of the Netherlands which has a tax treaty with the U.S. Under that treaty, the rate of withholding on dividends is reduced to 15 percent. So the withholding agent must withhold $6 from the dividend payment to XYZ as tax on the $40 share of the payment allocable to Z. In sum, on the $120 dividend from U.S. Co., the withholding agent collects a total of $18 to remit to the IRS, and the payee XYZ actually receives a payment of only $102.

Nonetheless, a withholding agent may treat a payment as made to a foreign partnership—and not to its partners—if certain documentation is provided to the withholding agent which would indicate the payee is a withholding foreign partnership. Reg. § 1.1441–5(c)(1)(ii). In the case of a withholding foreign partnership, the withholding agent will not withhold on the payment to the entity, but rather the partnership itself will become liable for collecting the tax on the distributive shares of its foreign partners. Withholding foreign partnerships are discussed *infra* in § 6.04(E).

Consider also the scenario when a foreign partnership is engaged in a trade or business in the United States. Its effectively connected income is subject to U.S. taxation, but there is no withholding under I.R.C. § 1441 on this income. If the partnership then distributes its effectively connected income to its foreign partners, unless there is a withholding obligation, U.S. source income may escape U.S. taxation entirely (although the partners are obligated under I.R.C. § 875 to pay the tax due as a result of the partners' conduct of a U.S. trade or business).

I.R.C. § 1446 requires foreign and domestic partnerships to withhold with respect to a foreign partner's distributive share of income effectively connected with the conduct of a U.S. trade or business. This withholding obligation is, in effect, a prepayment of taxes due with respect to the foreign partners' shares of effectively connected income under I.R.C. § 875(1). If the amount withheld exceeds the substantive tax liability, the excess is refunded. The withholding rate is the highest applicable graduated rate for each partner (*e.g.*, 35% for a corporate partner). Withholding under I.R.C. § 1446 is required regardless of whether there is an actual distribution.

In tiered partnership situations, the withholding obligation can be pushed down to the bottom tier with proper documentation from the upper tier partnership. For example, suppose that USP1 and USP2, U.S. partnerships with foreign partners, own 100 percent of USP3, a U.S. partnership that generates U.S. effectively connected income. USP1 and USP2 would have I.R.C. § 1446 withholding obligations, but can shift the obligations to USP3 with proper documentation.

(E) PAYMENTS TO FOREIGN INTERMEDIARIES

In the case of investment income, payments often will be made to a foreign intermediary (*i.e.*, a person other than the beneficial owner). Examples of such intermediaries are a nominee recipient, a bank, a brokerage house or a foreign partnership. The

Regulations promulgated under I.R.C. § 1441 identify five different types of intermediaries. They are: (1) nonqualified intermediaries, (2) qualified intermediaries, (3) withholding foreign partnerships, (4) authorized foreign agents, and (5) U.S. branches of foreign financial institutions. Each of these intermediaries serves a slightly different function, and the filing and withholding obligations associated with each are also slightly different. Typically, a foreign intermediary will provide a W–8IMY (IMY for Intermediary) to a withholding agent, in some cases along with the appropriate W–8BEN(–E) for any beneficial owner. Withholding agents must identify situations where an intermediary is involved and take into account the effect of the intermediary on the withholding obligation. Where a qualified intermediary (QI) or withholding foreign partnership (WFP) exists, the withholding agent may be relieved of the withholding obligation if certain documentation is provided to the IRS by the intermediary. If the withholding agent is relieved of the withholding obligation, the QI or the WFP becomes responsible for withholding.

A nonqualified foreign intermediary (NQI) is a foreign person (*e.g.*, a foreign bank) receiving payments for which it is not the beneficial owner and who has not entered into a withholding agreement with the IRS. A withholding agent must obtain certain documentation from a nonqualified intermediary indicating the portion of the payment allocable to each person for whom the intermediary is collecting the payment. This information is necessary so that the withholding agent is able to withhold the appropriate amount. Reg. § 1.1441–1(e)(3)(iii). When a nonqualified intermediary fails to provide the necessary documentation, the withholding agent simply withholds at the statutory rate. Therefore, where a nonqualified intermediary is involved in a transaction, the withholding agent is not released from the responsibility of obtaining the required documentation.

In contrast, a foreign intermediary will be considered to be "qualified" if it has entered into an agreement with the IRS accepting certain information gathering responsibilities with respect to withholding. Reg. § 1.1441–1(e)(5). A qualified intermediary may be a foreign financial institution or clearing organization; a foreign branch or office of a U.S. financial institution or clearing organization; a foreign corporation claiming treaty benefits for its shareholders; or any other person with whom the IRS may choose to enter into a withholding agreement. Reg. § 1.1441–1(e)(5)(ii). Under a withholding agreement, a qualified intermediary generally will be subject to the same reporting and withholding provisions applicable to withholding agents. The terms of such an agreement may vary depending on the situation and on the circumstances of each qualified intermediary. A qualified intermediary may assume primary withholding responsibility, thereby agreeing to withhold and pay over the required amounts as if the intermediary were a withholding agent. The qualified intermediary must provide specified documentation to the withholding agent indicating that the intermediary has assumed the withholding obligation.

Obviously some intermediaries will not want to assume the legal liabilities inherent in the withholding obligation or to deal with the hassle and additional paperwork created by the new withholding responsibility. A qualified intermediary (QI) without primary withholding responsibility (non-PWR), unlike a QI with primary withholding responsibility (PWR), must collect beneficial owner documentation. But unlike a nonqualified intermediary, a non-PWR QI does not need to turn over the information to a withholding agent. Instead, the non-PWR QI provides the withholding agent with withholding rate pool information (*e.g.,* a U.S. beneficial owner pool, a 30% pool for nonresident beneficial owners not entitled to a treaty-reduced withholding rate, a 15% pool for beneficial owners entitled to a treaty-reduced withholding rate). This pool information allows the withholding agent to withhold in the aggregate the correct amount of tax.

An intermediary may, however, choose to enter into a withholding agreement with the IRS in order to use its status as a qualified intermediary with primary withholding responsibility (*i.e.,* as a withholding agent) to attract customers. For instance, a foreign investor who might be hesitant to invest in U.S. stocks or debt instruments due to various reporting requirements may be persuaded to invest through a qualified intermediary which has a less extensive reporting requirement than a comparable   nonqualified   intermediary. Furthermore, the burden created by entering into a withholding agreement with the IRS may be minimal for a large foreign bank or brokerage house which maintains adequate customer records.

Shifting primary withholding responsibility will generally be favorable to withholding agents. For example, suppose the qualified intermediary is a foreign financial institution investing in stock and securities of U.S. corporations on behalf of a group of customers. If the qualified intermediary assumes the primary withholding obligation, then the withholding agent will not face the burden of collecting and reporting on payments to multiple foreign beneficial owners. Instead, the qualified intermediary will be liable for reporting and paying over the requisite tax.

Suppose that U.S. Co. is a publicly traded, domestic corporation. FrenchBank is a French financial institution that offers brokerage services to its customers. FrenchBank reaches an agreement with the IRS to act as a qualified intermediary with primary withholding responsibility for payments made to its customers on stocks and other instruments held through FrenchBank accounts. In accordance with this agreement, FrenchBank notifies U.S. Co. of its status as a qualified intermediary. A, B, and C are customers of FrenchBank and through their FrenchBank accounts they each purchase 100 shares of U.S. Co. stock. U.S. Co. declares a dividend of $1/share and pays FrenchBank $300 to credit to the accounts of

A, B, and C. U.S. Co. does not withhold on the payment to FrenchBank; rather FrenchBank is obligated to withhold as a result of its agreement with the IRS. If A is a U.S. resident, FrenchBank is not required to withhold and can credit A's account the full $100 dividend. If B is a resident of France which has a tax treaty with the United States reducing withholding on dividend payments to 15 percent, FrenchBank must collect $15 of tax on the dividend payment to B and can credit B's account $85. If C is a resident of Argentina which does not have a tax treaty with the United States, FrenchBank must collect $30 of tax on the U.S. Co. dividend for C and can credit C's account $70. Therefore, FrenchBank withholds a total of $45 and remits it to the IRS. FrenchBank disburses the remainder to its clients: $100 to A, $85 to B, and $70 to C.

Moreover, foreign partnerships may enter into agreements with the IRS to assume primary withholding and reporting responsibility. Reg. § 1.1441–5(c)(2). A foreign partnership that has entered into such a withholding agreement is known as a withholding foreign partnership and serves the same purposes and functions as a qualified intermediary. Payments to a withholding foreign partnership are treated as if they are made to the partnership as an entity, rather than flowing through to the partners who are the beneficial owners of the payments. Provided certain documentation, the withholding agent merely reports that it made payments to the partnership; there is no withholding at the time of the payment to the withholding foreign partnership. In this manner, a foreign partnership is accorded the same treatment as a domestic partnership. To achieve this result, a withholding foreign partnership will be required to withhold at the same time and use the same procedures as U.S. partnerships with foreign partners. Reg. § 1.1441–5(c)(2)(iii). When a foreign partner is required by U.S. tax principles to recognize its distributive share of the partnership's taxable income, the withholding foreign partnership will be required to withhold the requisite tax and remit it to the IRS at that time.

Consider again, the XYZ partnership example discussed *supra* in § 6.04(D). XYZ, a foreign partnership in Country X, decides to enter into a withholding agreement with the IRS. XYZ informs U.S. Co. of XYZ's status as a withholding foreign partnership and provides U.S. Co. with the necessary documentation. Subsequently, U.S. Co. makes another $120 dividend payment to XYZ. Because of XYZ's new status as a withholding foreign partnership, the withholding obligation shifts to XYZ, and U.S. Co. is absolved of its § 1441 responsibility. U.S. Co. pays the full $120 dividend to XYZ and does not remit any tax to the IRS. Instead, XYZ is liable for the requisite withholding tax at the time prescribed by U.S. tax principles applicable to a domestic partnership (*e.g.*, withholding on a foreign partner's distributive share of FDAP income).

A U.S. branch of a foreign bank or insurance company may receive payments on behalf of a foreign person which does not have income effectively connected with the conduct of a U.S. trade or business. Reg. § 1.1441–1(e)(3)(v). Normally, a withholding agent would be required to withhold on a payment to a foreign payee (*e.g.*, the foreign bank) because the U.S. branch is not considered to be a legal entity. Instead, the U.S. branch may enter into an agreement with a withholding agent to be treated as U.S. person with respect to any payments received. Once the withholding agent receives the appropriate documentation, the withholding obligation will be removed from it. Rather, the U.S. branch will be treated as the withholding agent in a manner similar to that of a qualified intermediary.

A withholding agent may shift some of its responsibilities to an authorized foreign agent by mutual agreement. Reg. § 1.1441–7(c). This type of arrangement is advantageous to a withholding agent, because it allows the withholding agent to shift some or all of the burden of collecting documentation and reporting to the IRS. The acts of an authorized foreign agent will be considered the acts of the withholding agent for the purposes of satisfying the withholding obligation. The withholding agent is fully liable for the acts of the authorized foreign agent and continues to be liable if the authorized foreign agent fails to carry out its obligation.

As noted, a beneficial owner of income otherwise subject to FDAP withholding, typically files a W–8BEN(–E). An intermediary who collects a payment

for the beneficial owners (*e.g.*, a foreign bank or
foreign partnership) files a W–8IMY and in cases
where it is not a qualified intermediary it should
attach each appropriate W–8BEN(–E) so the
withholding agent knows how much to withhold. In
some cases, a FDAP payment (*e.g.*, payment for
services performed in the United States) is made to
a nonresident that is engaged in a U.S. trade or
business to which the income is effectively
connected. In these cases, the nonresident should
provide a W–8ECI which informs the potential
withholding agent not to withhold because the
nonresident is required to file a U.S. tax return (*e.g.*,
a Form 1120–F for a corporation or a Form 1040–
NR for an individual). Finally, foreign governments
(or their controlled entities) are exempt from
withholding under section 892 on certain types of
FDAP income. In these situations, a W–8EXP (EXP
for Exempt) should be provided to the withholding
agent.

§ 6.05   FIRPTA WITHHOLDING

When a foreign taxpayer is engaged in a trade or
business in the United States, normally there is no
required withholding on the trade or business
income. However, when a foreign taxpayer disposes
of U.S. real property, withholding is required on the
deemed effectively connected income. I.R.C. § 897.

In general, the purchaser of any U.S. real
property must withhold 10 percent of the amount
realized on a disposition. I.R.C. § 1445(a).
Withholding under I.R.C. § 1445(a) is an estimation

of the tax due as opposed to withholding under I.R.C. §§ 1441 and 1442 which generally collects without estimation the 30 percent tax imposed by I.R.C. §§ 871(a) or 881. Withholding is required of a purchaser of a partnership interest if 50 percent or more of the value of the partnership's gross assets consist of U.S. real property interests and 90 percent or more of the value of the gross assets consist of U.S. real property interests plus cash (or cash equivalents). Reg. § 1.1445–11T(d).

There are a number of important exceptions to the general rule. If the seller provides an affidavit that it is a United States person, no withholding is required. I.R.C. § 1445(b)(2). This is true even if a U.S. partnership with foreign partners sells a United States Real Property Interest to a purchaser. That is because the U.S. partnership itself is responsible for handling the withholding for its partners. If the asset sold is stock of a domestic corporation and the corporation provides an affidavit that it is not a U.S. real property holding corporation (and has not been one during the 5-year testing period), the purchaser is relieved of a withholding obligation. I.R.C. § 1445(b)(3). No withholding is required if the IRS provides a statement that the seller is exempt from tax or has made other satisfactory arrangements. Finally, no withholding is required if the purchaser acquires the property as a personal residence and the purchase price does not exceed $300,000—an increasingly difficult test to meet in today's housing market.

I.R.C. § 897 treats gain and loss from the disposition of a U.S. real property interest (a "USRPI") recognized by a foreign person "as if the taxpayer were engaged in a trade or business within the United States during the taxable year and as if such gain or loss were effectively connected with such trade or business" for purposes of imposing net income-based taxation under sections 871 and 882. When a foreign person disposes of a USRPI, I.R.C. § 1445 requires the transferee to withhold 10 percent of the total amount paid. A special rule, provided in I.R.C. § 1445(e)(1), applies when a domestic partnership with foreign partners disposes of a USRPI. Under that section, the partnership is required to withhold tax equal to 35 percent of the gain realized and allocable to the foreign partners. Similarly, there is a 35 percent withholding obligation on certain distributions of U.S. real property interests by a domestic or foreign corporation. I.R.C. §§ 1441(e)(2) and (3). Because the gain is effectively connected income in the hands of the U.S. partnership, then there is an overlap of two withholding regimes because the partnership will also be required to withhold on under I.R.C. § 1446. However, there is no double-withholding. In the case of an overlap, only section 1446 shall apply, thereby trumping I.R.C. § 1445. Reg. § 1.1446–3(c)(2)(i). In the case of a foreign partnership that has tax withheld by the transferee under section 1445(a), the Regulations permit the partnership a credit against its section 1446 liability. Reg. § 1.1446–3(c)(2)(ii).

§ 6.06   INFORMATION REPORTING

In addition to the return and withholding requirements, taxpayers may also be subject to information reporting requirements that are imposed to provide the IRS with information needed to verify a taxpayer's tax liability. For example, suppose that a U.S. subsidiary of a foreign corporation purchases inventory from its foreign parent and resells the inventory in the United States. If the purchase price paid by the U.S. subsidiary to the foreign parent is more than an arm's-length price, then the gain taxable in the United States from the subsidiary's sales to customers will be understated (and the foreign parent's income which is not typically taxable in the United States will be overstated). To determine whether, the subsidiary has paid an arm's-length price, it may be helpful to know the foreign parent's costs of production or the price which the foreign corporation sells to unrelated purchasers, if any.

Congress has enacted I.R.C. §§ 6038A and 6038C which require certain U.S. taxpayers or foreign taxpayers doing business in the United States to provide a variety of information to enable the IRS to police arm's-length pricing between related taxpayers. The details of these disclosure provisions and the intercompany pricing problem in general are discussed *infra* at § 9.11.

§ 6.07   FATCA REPORTING AND WITHHOLDING

(A)   BACKGROUND

It has been estimated that the United States loses hundreds of billions in tax revenues each year as a result of offshore tax abuse primarily from the use of concealed and undeclared accounts held by U.S. taxpayers or their controlled foreign entities. In 2009 Congress enacted the "Foreign Account Tax Compliance Act of 2009" ("FATCA"). *See* I.R.C. §§ 1471–1474 and accompanying Regulations. The FATCA withholding rules are coordinated with existing withholding rules to prevent duplicate withholding.

These rules are designed to combat offshore tax evasion by requiring non-U.S. financial institutions (foreign financial institutions or FFIs) and other offshore vehicles to report certain information pertaining to U.S. taxpayers holding financial assets abroad. The intent behind the law is to require FFIs to identify and report U.S. persons holding assets abroad and for certain non-financial foreign entities (NFFEs) to identify substantial U.S. owners. In order to comply with these rules, FFIs are required to enter into an FFI Agreement with the U.S. Treasury or comply with intergovernmental agreements (IGAs) entered into by their local government. U.S. withholding agents (USWAs) must document all of their relationships with foreign entities in order to assist with the enforcement of the rules. Failure to enter into an agreement or provide required documentation will result in the imposition of a 30% withholding tax on certain payments made to such customers and counterparties. The intent of FATCA is not impose a withholding tax but rather to use the threat of the tax as a stick to compel disclosure.

For example, a payment of interest from a U.S. payor to an FFI will be subject to 30 percent FATCA withholding tax if the FFI is not a "participating FFI" (*i.e.*, one that has entered into an FFI Agreement with the IRS) or has not agreed to comply with any applicable intergovernmental agreement (IGA) with its local government. The tax imposed under I.R.C. § 1471 applies notwithstanding what would be required under I.R.C. § 1441. Even a participating FFI will be required to withhold on a payment to a non-participating FFI based on the applicable pass-thru percentage discussed below.

(B) WITHHOLDABLE PAYMENTS

FATCA regulations define withholdable payments as "[a]ny payment of U.S. source FDAP1 income; and [f]or any sales or other dispositions occurring after December 31, 2016, any gross proceeds from the sale or other disposition of any property of a type that can produce interest or dividends that are U.S. source FDAP income." Reg. § 1.1473–1(a)(1)(i). In addition, FATCA does not align directly with many of the withholding exceptions regarding U.S. source FDAP payments expressly granted in other Code sections. For example, a payment of U.S.

source portfolio interest or bank deposit interest, both exempt from withholding under I.R.C. § 1441, are treated as withholdable payments for FATCA purposes. While FATCA implements a 30 percent withholding tax on some payments if certain requirements are not met, certain payments are exempt from withholding. Grandfathered obligations, certain short term obligations, effectively connected income (ECI), excluded non-financial payments (*i.e.,* payments made in the ordinary course of business such as wages, rental income, software license payments), gross proceeds from the sale of excluded property, fractional shares and offshore payments of U.S. FDAP income prior to 2017 are all types of exempt payments.

(C) FOREIGN FINANCIAL INSTITUTION (FFI)

An FFI is generally any non-U.S. entity that functions as a financial institution (*e.g.*, a bank) custodial institution that hold financial assets for third parties, investment entity (*e.g.*, investment or portfolio management company) or insurance company. In addition certain holding companies or treasury centers may be treated as FFIs. A treasury center is defined as an entity primarily involved in financing transactions (*e.g.*, making loans, taking deposits, entering into hedges) for members of its affiliated group. Not all corporate holding companies or treasury centers are subject to FATCA. The holding companies and treasury centers that are primarily affected or those which are part of an affiliated group that has a foreign financial institution (*e.g.*, a bank) as a member or a holding company or treasury center in a private equity type structure.

Even though an entity falls under the definition of an FFI, it may still be excluded where the regulations deem the chances of U.S. persons hiding assets to be low. For example, if the entity is an excepted nonfinancial group entity or a non-profit organization, it is excluded. Many nonfinancial groups that are engaged in active business but have a treasury center entity that enters into hedging activities or other financing activities for the group would be excluded from the definition of an FFI. Similarly, holding companies in nonfinancial group can be excluded as they are generally used for organizational, regulatory or tax purposes.

If an entity falls under the definition of an FFI and is not excluded from the definition, it can nevertheless fall under a deemed-compliant FFI category. Generally deemed-compliant FFIs have less impact in terms of what they are required to do to comply with FATCA, but the impact varies depending on the category of deemed-compliant status. There are three categories of FFIs with varying responsibilities including registered deemed-compliant FFIs, certified deemed-compliant FFIs and owner-documented FFIs. While registered deemed-compliant FFIs will have to manage most of the administrative burdens common to participating FFIs, certified deemed-compliant FFIs will have far fewer administrative requirements because they do not need to register with the IRS. Certified deemed-compliant FFIs include, but are not limited to, nonregistering foreign local banks (*i.e.,* those not likely to have U.S. customers), and low value account FFIs (*e.g.*, no accounts exciting $50,000 and no more than $50 million in assets). The final deemed-compliant status category, an owner-documented FFI, is meant for smaller passive investment vehicles. Treating them as an owner-documented FFI whereby U.S. owner information is provided to the withholding agent and subsequently reported to the IRS serves the same purpose behind FATCA.

(D) NON-FINANCIAL FOREIGN ENTITY (NFFE)

If an entity does not fall under the definition of an FFI or is otherwise excluded from the definition, the entity would be considered a NFFE. Generally if the NFFE is not an excepted NFFE (including an active NFFE described below), the NFFE (*i.e.*, passive NFFE) will have to provide its withholding agent with information on any substantial U.S. owners, or if none exist, a certification to that effect.

Excepted entities include publicly traded corporations and affiliates and active NFFEs. These types of entities generally will likely not be vehicles for U.S. persons to hide their assets because of the nature of their activities. Most U.S. persons tend to use passive vehicles to shield their income rather than conducting an actual business activity, which is why entities that do not qualify for an excepted NFFE status are required to provide substantial U.S. owner certifications.

Active NFFEs are entities that conduct an actual business activity other than holding assets that produce investment income such as interest, dividends, rents, etc. Any entity may be classified as an Active NFFE if: less than 50 percent of its gross income for the preceding calendar year is passive income; and less than 50 percent of the weighted average percentage of assets (tested quarterly) held are assets that produce or are held for the production of passive income.

Any NFFE that is not otherwise excepted will be a passive NFFE and must provide withholding agents with a certification regarding its substantial U.S. owners (if any). Substantial U.S. owners include any specified U.S. person directly or indirectly owning more than 10 percent of the passive NFFE. In IGA countries the term "controlling person" is used instead of substantial U.S. owner, and refers to persons who are considered as having control over an entity. The definition of "control" is interpreted in accordance with the Financial Action Tax Force Recommendations and may vary depending on the IGA country. For example, it is possible that under a particular IGA country, a controlling person may be defined as having ownership of 25% or more or an entity.

(E) FATCA OBLIGATIONS

When a U.S. withholding agent makes a withholdable payment, FATCA's enforcement mechanism is a 30 percent withholding tax on payments made to persons that do not qualify for a FATCA withholding exemption. USWAs must annually report aggregate FATCA withholding on Form 1042 and file Forms 1042–S with respect to each payee for any withholdable payments. The FATCA status of a payee is determined most clearly by a valid Form W–8 or W–9 that can be associated with the payee at the time of payment. For purposes of identifying a payee where the payment is made to a flow-through entity or intermediary, if the flow-through entity or intermediary is not the payee (as defined above) the USWA may associate a payment with a withholding certificate using an intermediary withholding certificate (*e.g.*, a Form W–8IMY) from the flow-through entity that includes documentation of the actual payee or payees of the payment.

Participating FFIs must follow certain procedures to identify and document the FATCA status of each of its account holders to determine whether the account is a U.S. account, non-U.S. account or an account held by a recalcitrant account holder (essentially a holder not providing documentation) or nonparticipating FFI. Participating FFIs can generally document account holders with a Form W–8 or Form W–9.

Under the FFI agreement, a participating FFI agrees to withhold 30 percent on any withholdable payment made to a recalcitrant account holder or nonparticipating FFI. The withholding must take place at the time of payment. A participating FFI acting as a nonqualified intermediary (NQI), non-withholding foreign partnership or non-withholding foreign trust may delegate its withholding responsibility to its withholding agent by providing the information necessary for that withholding agent to withhold and report on any payments *e.g.*, providing a Form W–8IMY, withholding statement, etc. Participating FFIs are however required to withhold to the extent the withholding agent fails to withhold the correct amount.

Under the FFI agreement, a participating FFI agrees to report on specified U.S. individuals, specified U.S. owners of accounts held by owner-documented FFIs, and substantial U.S. owners of accounts held by passive NFFEs. The information is reported on Form 8966. Generally, the information reported consists of identifying information as well as the value of the account and payments with respect to the account.

§ 6.08   PENALTY PROVISIONS

Congress has enacted a welter of penalty and interest provisions to ensure that taxpayers comply with the Code's requirements. For example, there are penalties for failure to file a tax return or to pay tax (§ 6651), for failure to file information returns (§ 6662), failure to pay estimated income tax (§ 6655) and for failure to deposit withheld taxes (§ 6656).

Two of the more important penalty provisions are I.R.C. § 6662 which provides accuracy-related penalties and I.R.C. § 6694 which penalizes a tax preparer when a position on a return lacks a realistic possibility of being sustained on its merits and that position is not disclosed.

Section 6662 penalizes a taxpayer for any underpayment of tax required to be shown on a return which is attributable to specified factors including negligence (or worse), any substantial understatement of income tax or any substantial valuation misstatement. Generally, the penalty is equal to 20 percent of any underpayment but can be 40 percent for substantial valuation misstatements or 75 percent in the event of fraud.

Negligence is defined to include any failure to make a reasonable attempt to comply with the tax laws. If a position lacks a "reasonable basis," negligence penalties may result. Reg. § 1.6662–3(b). Disregarding existing rules or regulations (*e.g.,* Regulations, revenue rulings) also can trigger the penalty, although if a taxpayer discloses the existence of the adverse rule and has a "reasonable basis" for the position taken, the penalty can be avoided. Many practitioners think they can take have a reasonable basis for a position if they have a 20 percent likelihood of success in the event of litigation.

Of particular importance is the substantial understatement factor. A substantial understatement occurs if the amount stated on the return exceeds 10 percent of the correct tax liability or $5,000 ($10,000 for a corporation). § 6662(d)(1)(A). No penalty is imposed on an understatement if "substantial authority" exists (some practitioners use a 40 percent likelihood of success benchmark) for the taxpayer's position, or if there is disclosure of the taxpayer's position and there is a "reasonable basis." While substantial authority might include cases, rulings, legislative history, private letter rulings, etc., conclusions reached in articles treatises, legal periodicals, or opinion letters do not constitute substantial authority. Reg. § 1.6662–4(d)(3).

For a discussion of the tax shelter listing and reporting requirements, *see infra* § 13.05.

PART 3

FOREIGN ACTIVITIES OF U.S. TAXPAYERS

CHAPTER 7

INTRODUCTION TO U.S. BUSINESS ACTIVITY IN FOREIGN COUNTRIES

§ 7.01   INTRODUCTION

In this part of the book, the U.S. treatment of U.S. taxpayers doing business or investing abroad is considered. U.S. citizens and residents are taxable on their worldwide income. This feature of the income tax system raises at least three major issues involving U.S. taxpayers. First, to the extent that the United States taxes a U.S. taxpayer's worldwide income and the same income is also taxed by the foreign country in which it is earned (*i.e.,* the source country), how is international double taxation avoided? As is discussed in Chapter 8 *infra,* the primary method of avoiding double taxation in the United States is through the use of a foreign tax credit which essentially allows a U.S. taxpayer to decrease U.S. tax liability on foreign source income dollar-for-dollar by the amount of any foreign income taxes paid on the foreign source income. Alternatively, for certain earned income there is an exclusion from gross income and therefore no U.S. taxation as indicated in § 7.02. Many other countries relieve double taxation by exempting business income earned in other jurisdictions while using a credit mechanism for investment income earned and taxed in other jurisdictions.

The second major issue involving the U.S. tax treatment of U.S. taxpayers earning income abroad concerns the attempt by some taxpayers to place foreign income beyond U.S. tax jurisdiction. This might be desirable from a taxpayer's standpoint if the foreign source income would be subject to little or no tax in the foreign jurisdiction. Because U.S. taxpayers are taxed on worldwide income, merely shifting U.S. source income (*e.g.*, sales income, investment income) abroad so that it becomes foreign source income would not place the income beyond U.S. tax jurisdiction. However, if income can be shifted to a foreign corporation related to the U.S. taxpayer, it might be possible to avoid or defer U.S. taxation.

Sometimes a U.S. taxpayer can shift income outside U.S. tax jurisdiction by structuring transactions with related foreign parties in a non-arm's-length manner. Chapter 9 *infra* considers the transfer pricing rules which primarily are designed to prevent the artificial shifting of income from a U.S. corporation to a related foreign corporation. In other cases, a U.S. taxpayer is able to structure its affairs so that a foreign corporation rather than the U.S. taxpayer earns income. If such income earned by a foreign corporation is not related to U.S. activities, normally it would not be taxable in the United States. However, Chapter 10 describes situations where a foreign corporation controlled by U.S. taxpayers earns income outside the United States that nevertheless is subject to U.S. taxation.

A third major tax issue involving U.S. taxpayers earning income abroad is the treatment of transactions denominated in a foreign currency. Chapter 11 *infra* describes how foreign currency gains and losses are computed and treated for U.S. tax purposes.

§ 7.02   CITIZENS AND RESIDENTS OF THE UNITED STATES LIVING ABROAD

(A) INTRODUCTION

Normally, U.S. citizens and residents are taxable on their worldwide income. However, U.S. citizens and residents who work abroad have historically been able to exclude for tax purposes foreign source earned income and certain excessive housing cost amounts. The congressional purpose behind this exclusion is to make U.S. businesses more competitive abroad by making the use of U.S. employees abroad less expensive (*i.e.,* lower employer reimbursements for extra tax expenses incurred because of overseas transfers).

The exclusion under I.R.C. § 911 for certain income earned abroad is basically a substitute for the foreign tax credit on that income. In the absence of I.R.C. § 911, a U.S. taxpayer with earned income abroad would pay U.S. taxes on that income but could reduce the U.S. taxes by the amount of foreign taxes paid on such income. But notice that I.R.C. § 911 permits an exclusion from gross income even if the income earned abroad is not taxed (or is taxed at a lower rate than it would be taxed in the United States) by the foreign country.

(B) FOREIGN INCOME EXCLUSION

Under I.R.C. § 911 for 2015, a qualified individual can exclude as much as $100,800 of foreign earned income from taxable gross income. This amount is indexed for inflation. A "qualified individual" is one who is a bona fide resident of a foreign country for at least a taxable year or is present in a foreign country for at least 330 days during any consecutive twelve months. I.R.C. § 911(d)(1). In addition, the exclusion under I.R.C. § 911 is only available if the taxpayer's tax home (*i.e.*, regular place of business) is in the foreign country. For purposes of I.R.C. § 911, "residence" is defined under U.S. tax principles by looking at factors including: the taxpayer's intention; establishment of a home in the foreign country for an indefinite period of time; and, participation in the activities of the community. *See* Reg. § 1.911–2(c); *Sochurek v. Commissioner*, 300 F.2d 34 (7th Cir. 1962). In a liberal interpretation of I.R.C. § 911, an airline pilot for a Japanese airline was deemed to be a "resident" of Japan for purposes of I.R.C. § 911 even though the pilot's wife remained in the couple's historic home in Alaska, the pilot did not speak Japanese, and was not integrated into the Japanese community. *Jones v. Commissioner*, 927 F.2d 849 (5th Cir. 1991). The court found a strong congressional intent to encourage foreign trade by placing U.S. employees seeking foreign employment in an equal position with noncitizens working abroad whose income is exempt in their home countries.

An individual does not have to be taxed as a resident by the foreign country in order to qualify under I.R.C. § 911. Also, a national of a foreign country resident in the United States under I.R.C. § 7701(b) is entitled to the exclusion under I.R.C. § 911(d) for foreign income under most treaty nondiscrimination articles. Rev. Rul. 91–58, 1991–2 C.B. 340.

The exclusion is limited to compensation (pensions and annuities are not covered) not exceeding $100,800 for personal services actually rendered while overseas; it does not cover personal services rendered in anticipation of, or after the conclusion of, an overseas assignment or over international waters. I.R.C. §§ 911(b)(1)(A) and (d)(2) and *Rogers v. Commissioner*, 783 F.3d 320 (D.C. Cir. 2015). Suppose that a U.S. taxpayer residing in Mexico is engaged in the publishing business in Mexico. Can the taxpayer exclude $110,800 of income from taxation? Under I.R.C. § 911(d)(2)(B), where both personal services and capital (*e.g.*, printing presses) are material income-producing factors, not more than 30 percent of the net profits are treated as earned income subject to exclusion. Capital is a material income-producing factor if the operation of the business requires substantial inventories or substantial investments in plant, machinery, or other equipment, but not if the capital is incidental to the production of income (*e.g.,* computers for general office use). *Rousku v.*

Commissioner, 56 T.C. 548 (Tax Ct. 1971). If services performed abroad culminate in a product that is either sold or licensed, it is often difficult to determine whether the proceeds are foreign earned income. The IRS has acknowledged that royalties paid to a writer of literary works is earned income for purposes of I.R.C. § 911. Rev. Rul. 80–254, 1980–2 C.B. 222.

(C) HOUSING COST AMOUNT

In addition to the exclusion for foreign earned income, a qualified U.S. taxpayer can "exclude" from gross income a housing cost amount. The base housing amount used in calculating the foreign housing cost exclusion in a taxable year is 16 percent of the amount (computed on a daily basis) of the foreign earned income exclusion limitation (*i.e.,* $110,800 for 2015), multiplied by the number of days of foreign residence or presence in that year— $17,728 per year for 2015.

Reasonable foreign housing expenses in excess of the base housing amount remain excluded from gross income (or, if paid by the taxpayer, are deductible), but the amount of the exclusion is limited to 30 percent of the maximum amount of a taxpayer's foreign earned income exclusion. The IRS is given authority to issue regulations or other guidance providing for the adjustment of this 30-percent housing cost limitation based on geographic differences in housing costs relative to housing costs in the United States. Under the 30 percent rule, the maximum amount of the foreign housing cost exclusion in 2015 is (assuming foreign residence or presence on all days in the year) $15,512 (($110,800 × 30 percent)—($110,800 × 16 percent)). Certain expenses are ineligible for the exclusion including the costs of purchasing a house or apartment, capital improvements, furniture, mortgage interest, property taxes, wages of housekeepers, gardeners or other laborers, and any costs that are lavish and extravagant. I.R.C. § 911(c)(3). While I.R.C. § 911 uses the term "exclusion," a taxpayer incurring qualifying housing expenses excludes from gross income the amount used by the taxpayer to pay the housing costs.

Where a U.S. taxpayer's employer provides a housing allowance, the housing cost amount can be excluded from gross income. A payment by an employer that is not denominated as a housing cost allowance can still be excluded from gross income under I.R.C. § 911(c). Where the employer does not provide a housing allowance, a qualified U.S. taxpayer can exclude (*i.e.,* deduct) the housing cost amount from gross income, but the exclusion is limited to the taxpayer's foreign earned income not already excluded. I.R.C. § 911(c)(4). Any excess housing cost may be carried forward one year only and deducted then subject to the same limitation.

§ 7.03   EXPORT INCENTIVES

(A)   BACKGROUND

In 1962, the U.S. Congress enacted the foreign base company rules, in an effort to curtail the movement of U.S. export profits into foreign subsidiaries in tax haven jurisdictions. From a tax perspective, exporting immediately became more costly. In 1971, Congress enacted the domestic international sales corporation (DISC) legislation, the practical effect of which was to exempt a portion of U.S. exporters' profits by funneling export sales through a domestic subsidiary of the U.S. exporter.

The DISC framework angered U.S. trading partners and, following a decision by a panel established under the General Agreement on Tariffs and Trade that the DISC legislation constituted an illegal subsidy, was largely withdrawn in favor of the foreign sales corporation (FSC) legislation. The U.S. Congress hoped that the FSC legislation would comply with international trade law because of the statutorily required foreign character of the FSC.

From 1984 until late 2000, the United States offered its exporters a federal income tax subsidy for operating through foreign sales corporations. In 1999, a panel formed by the World Trade Organization held the FSC regime to be an unlawful subsidy. In 2000, the Appeals Body of the WTO confirmed the illegality of FSCs and required the United States to eliminate the subsidy.

Congress quickly fashioned a new law, embodied in the FSC Repeal and Extraterritorial Income Exclusion Act 2000. It significantly changed how export sales were taxed by the creation of so-called "extraterritorial income." The practical outcome was a continuation of the FSC's benefits, now available under a new concept, intended to meet the WTO objections to the FSC regime.

This second replacement for the DISC—known as the extraterritorial income exclusion (ETI)—also underwent World Trade Organization review and was also deemed to constitute an illegal subsidy.

(B) REPLACEMENT FOR THE ETI REGIME

Congress has replaced the ETI regime with another production incentive. However, this new incentive is not targeted to export sales. Instead, the incentive is available for domestic production irrespective of the final destination of the produced merchandise. I.R.C. § 199(a)(1) allows a deduction equal to 9 percent (6% rate for oil related income) of the lesser of: (a) the qualified production activities income (QPAI) of the taxpayer for the taxable year; or (b) taxable income or in the case of an individual, adjusted gross income (AGI). The deduction for a taxable year is limited to 50 percent of the W–2 wages paid by the taxpayer. I.R.C. § 199(b)(1).

QPAI is the excess of domestic production gross receipts (DPGR) over the sum of: (a) the cost of goods sold (CGS) allocable to such receipts; (b) other deductions, expenses, or losses directly allocable to such receipts; and (c) a ratable portion of deductions, expenses, and losses not directly allocable to such receipts or another class of income. I.R.C. § 199(c)(1). Extensive and intricate Regulations have been promulgated to deal with the proper allocation of items of income, deduction, expense and losses for purposes of computing QPAI.

DPGR refers to the taxpayer's gross receipts (not including receipts from related parties) that are derived from: (i) any lease, rental, license, sale, exchange, or other disposition of (I) qualifying production property (QPP) that was manufactured, produced, grown, or extracted (MPGE) by the taxpayer in whole or in significant part within the United States; (II) any qualified film produced by the taxpayer; or (III) electricity, natural gas, or potable water (collectively, utilities) produced by the taxpayer in the United States; (ii) construction performed in the United States; or (iii) engineering or architectural services performed in the United States for construction projects in the United States. I.R.C. § 199(c)(4)(A). QPP is limited to: (A) tangible personal property; (B) any computer software; and (C) certain sound recordings. I.R.C. § 199(c)(5).

CHAPTER 8

THE FOREIGN TAX CREDIT

§ 8.01   OVERVIEW

(A) RELIEVING DOUBLE TAXATION

Suppose that a U.S. taxpayer (individual or corporation) earns $100,000 of income in Germany. Assuming a flat 35 percent rate of taxation in the United States, the U.S. taxpayer, taxable on worldwide income, potentially faces $35,000 in U.S. taxes. If Germany also taxes the income at a 35 percent rate, the taxpayer may pay an additional $35,000 in taxes. In effect, the U.S. taxpayer might pay taxes at a 70 percent rate before even considering any German or U.S. local taxes. If the taxpayer earns $100,000 in the United States, there is only a $35,000 tax liability (aside from state and local income taxes).

While it is apparent that there is international double taxation, it is not apparent what should be done to ameliorate the situation. There are many possibilities. First, perhaps nothing should be done—neither Germany nor the United States should make any adjustments. But this solution treats the U.S. taxpayer earning foreign source income inequitably when compared to a U.S. taxpayer earning U.S. source income. In addition to the issue of equity or fairness, the failure to relieve such double taxation may cause some taxpayers to structure their affairs to avoid producing income in Germany even though, in the absence of tax considerations, the German investment is more productive than a competing U.S. investment.

A second possibility is that Germany should do something—either exclude the income from its tax jurisdiction or give a credit for U.S. taxes paid thereby reducing German taxation to $0. This solution runs counter to a basic international tax norm—the country of source (*i.e.,* the place where income is earned) has taxing priority over the country of residence (*i.e.,* the place where the taxpayer resides). This international taxation norm recognizes that the source country's economic environment is likely to have played a larger role in the production of income than the economic environment of the residence state. If the income is earned in Germany, Germany has first crack at taxation, and if any adjustment is to be made, the United States as a residence country must make it.

A third possibility is for the United States as the country of residence to relieve the double taxation. The United States could meet this requirement in one of several ways. For example, the United States could allow the taxpayer a deduction for the income taxes paid to Germany just as a deduction would be allowed for any other reasonable cost of earning income in Germany. Indeed, German taxes could be treated like state income taxes in the United States which are deductible. If a deduction were permitted, the U.S. taxpayer would still pay $35,000 in taxes to Germany, but for U.S. tax purposes the taxable income would be $100,000 minus $35,000, or $65,000 on which U.S. federal taxes would be $22,750. In total, national income taxes (*i.e.,* those of Germany and the United States) would be $57,750 which is less than a $70,000 tax liability if no deduction is permitted. Still, this would leave the taxpayer earning income in Germany paying an extra layer of taxes that a taxpayer earning income in the United States would not have to pay, undoubtedly deterring some taxpayers from making otherwise profitable investments in Germany.

Alternatively, the United States simply could exempt the German income from U.S. taxation. Under this approach, which is the prevailing approach among many countries, Germany would collect $35,000 in taxes and the United States $0 on the German income. The taxpayer would be equitably treated when compared with a U.S. taxpayer earning $100,000 in the United States, and a taxpayer debating an investment in the United States or the same one in Germany would not be influenced by the national income tax consequences. This is the approach taken by I.R.C. § 911 discussed in § 7.02 *supra* which permits a qualified individual to exclude a specified amount of foreign earned income. But suppose that Germany does not tax the income or taxes it at a rate less than 35 percent. In such a case, the U.S. taxpayer earning income in Germany is better off than a U.S. taxpayer earning the same income at home. In such a case, a pre-tax decision to invest in the United States rather than Germany might be reversed in light of the lower German taxes.

Concerned with this problem, the United States has adopted a tax credit rather than an exemption method for relieving double taxation. Under the tax credit method, the United States essentially taxes the $100,000 earned in Germany but allows a credit against the $35,000 U.S. tax liability for the income taxes paid to Germany on that income. If Germany taxes the income at a flat 35 percent rate, the taxpayer owes no U.S. taxes because the taxpayer credits the $35,000 in taxes paid to Germany against the $35,000 U.S. tax liability.

Note that to the extent foreign taxes are creditable against U.S. tax liability, a U.S. taxpayer may on one level be largely indifferent about the German taxes. The imposition of German taxes does not cost the taxpayer any additional money because the taxpayer would have paid the United States $35,000 in taxes if there were no German taxes. (All things being equal, U.S. taxpayers might prefer the tax money to go to the United States as between the United States and a foreign country.)

The tax credit method at this point may seem no different than if the U.S. taxpayer were allowed to exempt the German income, but there is an important difference. Suppose that the rate Germany imposes on the German income is only 10 percent so that the U.S. taxpayer pays $10,000 in taxes to Germany. Under an exclusion method, the United States would not tax the German income. But the tax credit method allows the United States to impose a $35,000 tax on the $100,000 of German income and then to allow a $10,000 foreign tax credit for the taxes paid to Germany. So the United States still collects $25,000 of tax revenue from the German income, and the overall tax burden on the U.S. taxpayer earning income abroad is not more favorable (as it would be under the exclusion method) than a U.S. taxpayer earning income in the United States.

Now suppose that the German tax rate is 50 percent and further assume that the U.S. taxpayer in addition to the $100,000 of German income has $100,000 of income earned in the United States. The German tax on the $100,000 of German income is $50,000. Assuming a 35 percent tax rate, the U.S. tax on the $200,000 of worldwide income is $70,000. If the United States grants a full foreign tax credit for the $50,000 German tax liability, the total U.S. tax actually paid by the taxpayer will be $20,000. It is true that the taxpayer's total income tax liability (*i.e.*, in Germany and the United States) is $70,000 ($50,000 paid to Germany and $20,000 paid to the United States) on $200,000 of total income just as it would be for a U.S. taxpayer earning $200,000 in the United States. However, if the $50,000 in German taxes is fully creditable, the U.S. taxpayer ends up paying $20,000 of U.S. taxes (instead of $35,000) on $100,000 of U.S. source income. In effect, taxes paid to Germany would reduce U.S. taxes on U.S. source income from 35 percent to 20 percent.

The U.S. tax system does not allow a foreign country's income taxes to reduce U.S. income taxes on U.S. source income. As explained in more detail *infra* in § 8.06, limitations are placed on the creditability of foreign income taxes. The U.S. taxpayer is allowed to credit only $35,000 of German taxes (*i.e.,* the German taxes can offset the U.S. taxes on the $100,000 of German income). The taxpayer's total tax bill is $50,000 of German taxes and $35,000 of U.S. taxes (on the $100,000 of U.S. source income). To the extent that a U.S. taxpayer cannot credit foreign income taxes against U.S. income taxes on the same income, there is double taxation. But the United States is unwilling to relieve double taxation that in its view is caused by unwarranted taxation by another country (or by the taxpayer's decision to generate income in high-tax jurisdiction). Any foreign tax credits that are limited in this manner may be available as credits in other years under a tax credit carryforward/carryback mechanism.

In this situation where the taxpayer has excess foreign tax credits, international tax planning would focus on ways to turn the U.S. income into foreign source income. Suppose that the U.S. taxpayer were able to turn all of the U.S. source income into foreign source income in a manner that would not trigger any additional foreign tax. Now the taxpayer would have $200,000 of foreign source income. The potential U.S. tax is $70,000, but the taxpayer may qualify for a tax credit for the $50,000 tax paid in Germany. Notice that in this situation the German tax would not be offsetting U.S. tax on U.S. source income. With the tax credit, the U.S. tax bill would be $20,000. The result is an overall tax bill of $70,000 rather than the $85,000 tax bill that existed before turning the U.S. source income into foreign source income. Changing the source of income from U.S. source to foreign source income in this case results in a tax savings.

How might a taxpayer and a tax advisor turn U.S. source income into foreign source income in a manner that does not trigger any additional foreign taxes? There are many ways this could occur. For example, suppose that the taxpayer was generating U.S. source income by selling purchased inventory to foreign customers with title passing in the United States. If the taxpayer transfers title abroad, the sales income will be foreign source income. I.R.C. § 861(a)(6). If the taxpayer manufactured the inventory and passed title outside the U.S. rather than inside the U.S., 50 percent of the income would be foreign source. I.R.C. § 863(b). Changing where title passes normally will not affect how a foreign country taxes the sale. Another way to affect source of income would be to decrease expenses currently allocated and apportioned against foreign source income and have them allocated and apportioned against U.S. source income instead. In the example above, if $100,000 of expenses that were currently allocated and apportioned against the German source income were instead allocated and apportioned against the U.S. income, foreign source income would increase by $100,000 and U.S. source income would decrease by $100,000. Again, the U.S. rules would not impact how a foreign country taxes under its own set of rules.

While there are possible tax planning opportunities to maximize the use of excess foreign tax credits, source cannot be changed by merely waving a wand. Changing the source of income often will involve changes in the way business is conducted. Furthermore, tax planning is best done when business decisions are implemented in a tax-efficient manner rather than making business decisions merely to facilitate tax planning. Also as discussed below, there are some limits on the ability of a taxpayer to lump together all foreign source income in determining the appropriate foreign tax credit.

(B) THE STATUTORY FRAMEWORK

I.R.C. § 901(a) authorizes the foreign tax credit subject to the limitations of I.R.C. § 904. The foreign tax credit is elective, and if the taxpayer elects to take the credit, no deduction for foreign taxes paid is available. I.R.C. § 275(a)(4)(A). In most circumstances, a taxpayer will elect to take a credit which offsets U.S. taxes dollar-for-dollar rather than a deduction which may only offset U.S. taxes by 35 cents for every dollar deducted if the tax rate is 35 percent. Of course if foreign taxes are not creditable, then the deduction under I.R.C. § 164(a)(3) becomes attractive. Also, a deduction may be preferable if a U.S. taxpayer has excess credits. For example, if T has $100 of U.S. source income, $100 of business income from country A (subject to a $30 country A income tax), and a $100 business loss from country B, no foreign tax credit can be taken because T has $0 foreign source income overall. However, if T deducts the $30 income tax paid to country A, then T's taxable income is reduced from $100 to $70. It should be noted that even in this situation, a credit may be preferable because of the ability to carry unused credits to other taxable years. I.R.C. § 904(c).

The credit is available for United States citizens and residents including U.S. corporations. I.R.C. § 901(b). Under some circumstances the credit is also available for nonresident aliens and foreign corporations engaged in a trade or business in the United States. I.R.C. § 906. The credit is available for foreign income taxes and for any other tax paid in lieu of an income tax. I.R.C. §§ 901(b) and 903.

Generally the taxpayer accounts for the foreign tax credit in a manner consistent with the taxpayer's method of accounting. However, I.R.C. § 905 permits a taxpayer to claim a foreign tax credit in the year the foreign taxes accrue even if the taxpayer is a cash basis taxpayer. On the receipt (or deemed receipt) of certain dividends, some shareholders are permitted an indirect tax credit for any foreign taxes the paying corporation paid on its foreign source income used to make the dividend distributions. I.R.C. §§ 902 (actual dividend) and 960 (deemed inclusion). Finally, the foreign tax credit provisions contain special rules for the treatment of taxes paid on certain types of income, notably oil and gas income. I.R.C. § 907.

In some cases, taxpayers have been able to arrange their affairs so that foreign tax credits were available even though the underlying income that gave rise to those credits was not immediately subject to U.S. tax. This availability of credits without the underlying income enabled U.S. taxpayers to use the credits to offset potential U.S. tax on other low-taxed foreign source income. For example, suppose a U.S. taxpayer earns $100 of foreign source business income that is taxed at a 35 percent rate by a foreign country (high-taxed income) and $100 of foreign source business income that is not taxed at all by a foreign country (low-taxed income). The result would be $200 of income that is potentially subject to a $70 U.S. federal income tax, but there would be a $35 dollar foreign tax credit—reducing the U.S. tax to $35. The overall tax for the taxpayer would be $70—a 35 percent effective tax rate. Now suppose that the taxpayer is able to avoid including the high-taxed income for U.S. tax purposes but can somehow still claim the $35 foreign tax credit. Now the taxpayer would pay $0 U.S. tax ($35 potential U.S. tax on low-taxed income offset with $35 foreign tax credit) and have an overall tax burden of $35 on the $200 of income—a 17.5 percent effective tax rate.

How taxpayers have accomplished this result is discussed in § 8.03(F) along with how I.R.C. § 909 operates to curtail the ability to take foreign tax credits until the underlying income is taxable in the U.S.

§ 8.02   ELIGIBILITY

Under I.R.C. § 901(b), U.S. citizens and domestic corporations may credit income taxes paid to foreign countries, except that no credit is available for income taxes paid to any foreign country which the United States does not recognize, or maintain diplomatic relations with, or which provides support for acts of international terrorism. I.R.C. § 901(j). Resident aliens also are eligible for the foreign tax credit. However, I.R.C. § 901(c) authorizes the President to disallow the foreign tax credit to resident aliens who are citizens of a foreign country that does not allow U.S. citizens resident there a similar credit for taxes paid to the United States or other countries.

A foreign corporation or nonresident alien engaged in a trade or business in the United States is taxed on effectively connected income. I.R.C. §§ 871(b) or 882. It is possible that foreign source income may be effectively connected income. I.R.C. § 864(c)(4). For example, suppose that a Peruvian corporation engaged in a software licensing business in the United States licenses the use of computer software to a licensee in France. The Peruvian corporation may have foreign source royalty income that is subject to U.S. taxation as effectively connected income. I.R.C. § 864(c)(4)(B)(i). If France also taxes such income, the Peruvian corporation may be able to credit the French income taxes against U.S. taxes on the U.S. royalty income. I.R.C. § 906.

Any eligible taxpayer that is a member of a partnership or trust may claim as a credit a proportionate share of the qualifying foreign taxes paid by the entity. I.R.C. § 901(b)(5).

§ 8.03 CREDITABLE TAXES

In order for a taxpayer to receive a U.S. foreign tax credit for an amount paid to a foreign government, there are several requirements that must be met. Not all payments to a foreign government are creditable taxes. First, the foreign levy must be a tax, not a voluntary payment and not a payment for a specific right or service (*e.g.,* a royalty payment). Second, it may be necessary to determine whether the payment is a separate tax or part of a unified tax in order to evaluate creditability. Third, it is necessary to determine if the tax is an income tax when viewed through the lens of U.S. tax principles. Fourth, if the tax is not an income tax, it may still be creditable as an "in-lieu-of" tax under I.R.C. § 903. If a foreign levy is a creditable income tax, then it is necessary to determine who can claim the credit and what is the amount of the creditable tax that is paid.

(A) IS THE FOREIGN LEVY A TAX?

Essentially, a tax is a forced payment collected by a governmental authority in exchange for a variety of governmental services (*e.g.,* roads, schools, national defense). If the payment is voluntary, it is not creditable. Reg. § 1.901–2(e)(5). A taxpayer must exhaust all effective and practical means of lowering foreign tax payments but need not tilt at windmills. For example, if the IRS makes a transfer pricing adjustment under I.R.C. § 482 that allocates income from a foreign subsidiary to a U.S. parent, the foreign subsidiary must try to reduce the foreign tax paid. Reg. § 1.901–2(e)(5)(ii) Exs. 2 and 3. *See Procter & Gamble Co. v. U.S.*, 2010–2 U.S. Tax Cas. (CCH) P50,593 (SD Ohio 2010), where the taxpayer failed to pursue whether under the U.S.-Japan treaty, Japan would be willing to reduce taxes it imposed on what Korea taxed as Korean source income. However, a taxpayer need not litigate a foreign tax liability if the taxpayer has obtained in good faith from a foreign tax advisor an opinion that litigation would be unsuccessful. Reg. § 1.901–2(e)(5)(i). Recently, Treasury has expanded the concept of "voluntary" to encompass some carefully crafted transactions designed to provide foreign tax credits to U.S. investors while also allowing a foreign counterparty to claim a duplicative foreign tax benefit. Treasury has determined that in the absence of the structured transaction, no foreign tax credit would be available and therefore the payment is not compulsory. Reg. § 1.901–2(e)(5)(iv).

Even if a foreign levy is not voluntary, it will not be creditable unless it is a payment to a foreign government as a taxing authority. Reg. § 1.901–2(a)(2)(i). A thorny issue concerning creditability is whether a purported tax payment is in fact a payment for a "specific economic benefit" in which case it is not creditable. A tax payment theoretically is a payment in return for a variety of nonspecific government services (*e.g.*, national defense, use of the highways, national health care). The creditability Regulations attempt to distinguish between this variety of broad government services and a payment for a specific economic benefit (*e.g.*, the right to extract oil from the ground). Reg.

§ 1.901–2(a)(2). The term "specific economic benefit" means an economic benefit that is not made substantially available on substantially the same terms to substantially all persons who are subject to the generally imposed income tax. Reg. § 1.901–2(a)(2)(ii).

In *Exxon Corp. v. Commissioner*, 113 T.C. 338 (Tax Ct. 1999), the Tax Court held that the U.K. Petroleum Revenue Tax (PRT) was a creditable foreign income tax—a conclusion that was affirmed in a related case by the Supreme Court in a *PPL Corp. v. Commissioner*, 133 S. Ct. 1897 (2013). The Tax Court determined that the PRT taken in its entirety did not constitute a royalty payment because the taxpayer did not receive any special benefit for paying the tax. Even though there was some evidence that the tax was imposed because the U.K. had earlier sold the right to explore in the North Sea for what in hindsight was a bargain price, the Court did not regard the PRT as a delayed royalty payment.

In some cases, a U.S. taxpayer pays a foreign tax that includes a payment for a specific economic benefit as well as payment for general governmental services. For purposes of determining the amount creditable, the payment is bifurcated into two components: a noncreditable payment for a specific economic benefit and a creditable payment for the excess paid if the payment otherwise satisfies the creditability requirements. Reg. § 1.901–2(a)(2)(i). The taxpayer is referred to as a "dual capacity taxpayer." Reg. § 1.901–2A. A dual capacity taxpayer must establish the creditable portion of the payment under either the "facts and circumstances" method or the safe harbor method. The facts and circumstances method is exactly what it sounds like: if the taxpayer can establish that an otherwise creditable levy is not paid in exchange for a specific economic benefit, the payment is creditable. Reg. § 1.901–2A(c)(2).

The safe harbor method employs the following formula to determine the creditable portion of a levy paid by a dual capacity taxpayer:

$$(A - B - C) \times \frac{D}{1 - D}$$

where:

A = gross receipts

B = expenses computed under the general foreign income tax rules

C = the total "tax" paid by the dual capacity taxpayer

D = the general tax rate.

To understand the formula, consider the following example. Country X imposes a levy on every corporation doing business in Country X on 40 percent of its Country X net business income. Net income is computed under U.S. tax principles except that a corporation engaged in mineral exploitation in Country X is not permitted to recover its exploration expenditures. Mineral deposits in

Country X are owned by the government which exacts a royalty in exchange for the mining privilege. Assuming that the nonrecovery of exploration expenses does not render the entire income tax noncreditable, a taxpayer engaged in mining is a dual capacity taxpayer paying a general income tax and a levy for the right to extract minerals. For the taxable year in question, U.S. Co., a U.S. corporation engaged in a trade or business in Country X, has gross receipts of $120,000, deductible general business expenses of $20,000 and a tax liability of $40,000. In addition, U.S. Co. incurs exploration expenses that would be deductible under normal U.S. income tax principles of $30,000.

Under the safe harbor method, U.S. Co.'s creditable income tax would be $20,000 (($120,000 − $50,000 − $40,000) × .40 divided by (1 − .40)) and the other $20,000 would be treated as a payment for a specific economic benefit. Stated differently, if Country X had allowed normal deductions, U.S. Co. would have only paid $20,000 of income tax at a 40 percent rate on net income of $120,000 minus $20,000 of general business expenses minus $30,000 of exploration expenses minus $20,000 paid for a specific economic benefit.

(B) IS THE TAX A SEPARATE TAX OR PART OF A BROADER TAX?

If the levy in question is determined to be a tax, it is necessary to ascertain whether the tax stands alone or is part of a broader tax. For example, suppose that a U.S. taxpayer is subject to a foreign tax on the gross revenues resulting from sales in that foreign country. Viewed as a tax in and of itself, the tax on gross sales revenue may not qualify as a creditable income tax if no allowance is made for the cost of goods sold. However, if the levy is deemed to be part of an overall tax system that viewed in its entirety is a creditable income tax for U.S. tax purposes, then the levy may be creditable. Conversely, suppose that a U.S. taxpayer pays a foreign tax, based on the net sales income generated in the foreign country. Viewed as a separate tax, the levy may be a creditable income tax. However, if the levy is deemed to be part of an overall tax that has other features that render the tax not creditable against U.S. tax liability, the levy on net sale income will not be a creditable tax.

The creditability of a tax is determined by looking at all taxpayers subject to the tax rather than on a taxpayer-by-taxpayer basis. Reg. § 1.901–2(a)(1). In determining whether a levy is a separate tax or part of a broader tax, the Regulations offer several general principles. Reg. § 1.901–2(d)(1). The determination of whether a levy is a separate levy or part of a broader levy is made by looking at U.S. rather than foreign tax principles. Foreign labeling is not relevant. A levy imposed by one taxing authority (*e.g.,* national government) is always separate from a levy imposed by another taxing authority (*e.g.,* local government). A levy is a separate levy if the tax base differs in kind for different classes of taxpayers. For example, a gross base withholding tax on nonresidents is a separate tax from a net income tax on residents. Similarly a gross base withholding tax imposed on nonresidents is a separate tax from a net business tax imposed on nonresidents. Reg. § 1.901–2(d)(3) Ex. 2.

(C)   IS THE TAX AN INCOME TAX?

Because the foreign tax credit is aimed at preventing international double taxation of income, the only payment allowed as a tax credit against U.S. income tax liability is a foreign *income* tax under I.R.C. § 901. Foreign taxes that are income taxes in the U.S. sense can qualify for a tax credit even if imposed by a political subdivision or local authority of a foreign country. By contrast, U.S. state and local taxes are not creditable, but can only be deducted.

Foreign taxes which are not income taxes in a U.S. sense may be deductible for U.S. tax purposes under I.R.C. § 164(a)(3). The issue of what constitutes a creditable foreign income tax is a difficult one. Countries implement all manner of user fees, royalty payments, and profit-splitting arrangements which are sometimes difficult to distinguish from an income tax. Even an exaction that looks like an income tax may not really be an income tax because the tax revenue is rebated to the taxpayer, or the taxpayer receives a direct or indirect subsidy from the government.

The Code provides little guidance as to what constitutes a creditable income tax. The Regulations issued by the IRS labor mightily to distinguish an income tax from other payments. Essentially, the

Regulations provide that a foreign tax is creditable only if its "predominant character . . . is that of an income tax in the U.S. sense." Stated differently, in order to be creditable, a foreign tax must be "likely to reach net gain." Reg. §§ 1.901–2(a)(1)(ii) and (3)(i).

A foreign tax is considered "likely to reach net gain" if it satisfies three requirements: realization, gross receipts, and net income. The "realization" requirement is met, if on the basis of its predominant character, a foreign tax is imposed only upon, or subsequent to, the occurrence of an event that would result in realization under the Code. Reg. § 1.901–2(b)(2). For example, a foreign tax that is generally imposed on mere asset appreciation prior to a sale or other disposition probably would not be creditable. It is possible for a foreign tax imposed prior to a realization event to be creditable if the foreign country does not tax the same income again upon realization, and either the imposition of the tax is based on the difference in property values during the taxable year or the pre-realization event is the physical transfer of inventory. In addition, pre-realization taxation may be creditable if the income taxed is recapture income from deductions (or credits) previously taken by the taxpayer. For example, suppose that a taxpayer purchases an asset for $10,000 and is permitted a depreciation deduction of $3,000 thereby reducing the basis to $7,000 while the fair market value of the property remains at $10,000. A foreign tax on $3,000 of recapture income imposed prior to a sale or disposition does not disqualify a foreign tax from being creditable.

The "gross receipts" requirement is satisfied if the foreign tax uses a tax base of gross receipts from the disposition of property, or if there is no disposition, or the disposition is between related parties, the tax base is computed under a method that is likely not to exceed the fair market value of the property involved. Reg. § 1.901–2(b)(3). For example, a foreign tax based on the assumption that gross receipts from extraction income equal 105 percent of the fair market value of petroleum extracted would not be creditable if the tax is designed to produce an amount that is greater than actual gross receipts. However, if a tax not based on gross receipts is intended to reach the same tax base, it may be creditable. For example, suppose that country A imposes a "headquarters tax" on the country A branch of a U.S. corporation equal to 110 percent of expenses where the branch manages the business activities of the U.S. corporation and its related corporations. If the tax is imposed because of the difficulties of measuring the actual gross receipts of the branch from its management activities, and the headquarters tax base is not likely to be greater than actual gross receipts, the tax may be creditable.

The "net income" requirement is satisfied if a foreign tax is computed by reducing gross receipts by the costs of producing the income (including capital expenditures) determined under "reasonable principles." Reg. § 1.901–2(b)(4). A foreign tax law is deemed to permit the recovery of significant costs even if there are timing differences when compared with U.S. law unless the timing differences effectively deny the deduction. For example, expenses that are deducted under U.S. tax principles may be capitalized under foreign tax principles and recovered on a recurring basis over time or upon the occurrence of a future event (*e.g.*, a sale). Such treatment would not endanger the creditability of a foreign income tax unless the delayed recovery was tantamount to a denial (*e.g.*, capitalization of a U.S.-deductible expense over 100 years). Even if a foreign tax law does not permit the recovery of a significant cost, the tax may be creditable if there is an allowance that effectively compensates for the denial.

While the net income requirement is aimed at producing a tax base similar to that under U.S. tax principles, in some rare circumstances a foreign tax whose base is gross receipts may still be creditable if the tax is almost certain to reach some net gain because the expenses of producing income will almost never be so high as to offset gross receipts. Reg. § 1.901–2(b)(4). For example, suppose a foreign tax is imposed at a 30 percent rate on gross wages earned by an employee with no employee deductions permitted. Because the expenses of employees attributable to wage income are almost always insignificant compared to the gross wages realized, employees subject to the tax are almost certain to have net gain. Accordingly, the tax would satisfy the net income requirement. Reg. § 1.901–2(b)(4) Ex. 3. Gross base withholding taxes similar in nature to the U.S. withholding tax with respect to dividends, interest, rents, royalties and other fixed and determinable annual periodical income can be creditable income taxes. *Bank of America National Trust & Savings Ass'n v. United States*, 459 F.2d 513 (Cl. Ct. 1972).

In some cases, a tax that does not appear to reach net income on its face nevertheless may be a creditable income tax. In *PPL Corp. v. Comm'r,* 133 S. Ct. 1897 (2013), the Supreme Court after reviewing and discussing the I.R.C. § 901 requirements held that a U.K. windfall tax on excess profits was a creditable foreign income tax. The Court determined that the tax taken in its entirety was an income tax even though it was nominally based on the difference between the company's valuation based on purchase price and subsequent performance and on its face did not appear to tax net profits or to meet other income tax criteria. The court found that the difference between the two different valuations was based on net income.

In determining whether a foreign tax satisfies the net income requirement, one of the factors taken into account is whether a loss in one activity (*e.g.*, a contract involving oil and gas exploration) in a trade or business is allowed to offset profits in another activity (*e.g.*, a separate contract) in the same trade or business. If an offset is allowed, it need not be in the same taxable period in order to insure creditability. Furthermore, the fact that no offset is allowed against a different activity in a trade or business does not defeat creditability if an offset is allowed against profitable activity of the same contract in another taxable period. It is not necessary that a foreign tax permit an offset against profits from a different trade or business or profits from investment activity or that losses be allowed to offset profits from related entities in order for a foreign tax to be creditable. Reg. § 1.901–2(b)(4)(ii).

A foreign tax which otherwise might satisfy the creditability requirements is nevertheless not creditable if the tax is designed to tax U.S. residents or citizens only to the extent each $1 of foreign tax reduces U.S. tax liability by $1 (*i.e.,* a "soak-up" tax). For example, a foreign tax that is only imposed if, or to the extent that, it is creditable against U.S. taxes would not be a creditable tax. Reg. § 1.901– 2(c). This type of selective tax whose application is dependent on U.S. creditability, like those foreign taxes permitting rebates or which directly subsidize the taxpayer, is not creditable because it is not an income tax in the U.S. sense.

(D) TAXES IN LIEU OF AN INCOME TAX

In some cases, a tax that does not qualify as a creditable foreign income tax may nevertheless be creditable as an "in-lieu-of" tax under I.R.C. § 903 if the tax is imposed in lieu of a tax on income that is generally imposed. In order for a tax to qualify as an in-lieu-of tax, the foreign country must have a general income tax law that would apply to the taxpayer but for the in-lieu-of tax, and the general income tax is not imposed on the taxpayer because of the in-lieu-of tax. Reg. § 1.903–1(a)(2) and (b). However to qualify for a foreign tax credit, the taxpayer cannot be subject to the general income tax and subject to the in-lieu-of tax.

It is not a requirement that the in-lieu-of tax be imposed because of administrative difficulty in applying the generally imposed income tax. Reg. § 1.903–1(a). Nor is the base of the in-lieu-of tax required to be net income in order for the imposition to be creditable. There is also no requirement that the burden of the in-lieu-of tax be the same as or less than the tax burden that would have resulted under the generally imposed income tax. Reg. § 1.903–1(b). However, a "soak-up" in-lieu-of tax, like a soak-up income tax, will not be creditable. Reg. § 1.903–1(b)(2).

As an example of an in-lieu-of tax, suppose that Country X has a tax that is generally imposed on realized net income of nonresident corporations attributable to a trade or business carried on in Country X. The tax applies to all nonresident corporations, except that corporations engaged in the insurance business are subject to a charge on gross receipts. The tax applicable to nonresident corporations engaged in insurance activities would satisfy the in-lieu-of requirement. Reg. § 1.903–1(b)(1).

A gross base income tax imposed on nonresidents as a substitute for a general comprehensive net base income tax applicable to residents qualifies as an in-lieu-of tax that is creditable. Reg. § 1.903–1(b)(3) Ex. 1. Accordingly, a withholding tax on dividends, interest, and royalties imposed by a foreign country similar to the tax imposed by I.R.C. §§ 871(a) and 881 would qualify as an in-lieu-of tax and is creditable in the United States.

(E) WHO CAN CLAIM THE FOREIGN TAX CREDIT?

Under I.R.C. § 901(b), U.S. citizens, residents and domestic corporations are entitled to a foreign tax credit. A U.S. partner in a partnership (or a beneficiary in an estate or trust) can claim a credit for a proportionate share of foreign tax paid by the entity. I.R.C. §§ 901(b)(5) (individual partners) and 702(a)(6) (corporations). Also, nonresidents that are subject to U.S. tax on income effectively connected with the conduct of a U.S. trade or business may be able to credit foreign taxes paid with respect to that income. I.R.C. § 906.

Sometimes it is not clear who the taxpayer is with respect to a foreign tax payment. Suppose that a U.S. resident R owns a foreign entity E located in country E that is treated for U.S. tax purposes as a corporation but is treated as a transparent, pass-through entity by country E. If country E imposes a tax on R resulting from the activities of E, who is deemed to pay the tax—E, the person that the United States considers as the income earner or R, the person country E considers to be the income earner? The Regulations consider the taxpayer of a foreign tax to be the person on whom foreign law imposes legal liability for tax. Reg. § 1.901–2(f)(1). This is known as the "technical taxpayer" rule. Yet, the longstanding case of *Biddle v. Commissioner*, 302 U.S. 573 (1938) is often cited for the proposition that U.S. rather than foreign standards apply in determining U.S. tax consequences.

A taxpayer who is legally liable for a foreign tax that is paid is deemed to pay the tax even if the payment is made by someone else. Reg. § 1.901–2(f)(2). Moreover, even if the foreign government itself assumes the responsibility for a U.S. taxpayer's foreign tax, a credit may be available if the government's assumption of the tax liability is compensation for services rendered or goods sold or leased to the government by the U.S. taxpayer. This Regulation permits a U.S. taxpayer to enter into a "net contract" with a foreign government that assures a taxpayer a fixed after-tax contract price for services rendered or goods sold or leased to the foreign government. *Amoco Corp. v. Commissioner*, 138 F.3d 1139 (7th Cir. 1998). Any tax liability that is assumed by another party (*e.g.*, a foreign government) is considered income for U.S. tax purposes. Reg. § 1.901–2(f)(2)(ii).

Suppose USCo owns all of the "stock" in Forco1 which is a disregarded entity for U.S. tax purposes but a corporation for Country X purposes. Forco1 owns all of stock of Forco2, a regarded Country X corporation. Forco1 and Forco2 form a Country X consolidated group. Under country X law, the parent of the consolidated group is responsible for any taxes on group income. Suppose that Forco 2 earns $100 and Country X imposes an income tax of $35 on Forco1. Does that mean that USCo can take a tax credit for the taxes imposed on disregarded Forco1 (and potentially utilize that credit to offset U.S. tax on some other foreign source income that USCo has generated)? Reg. § 1.901–2(f)(3) essentially aligns the tax with the underlying income within a consolidated group regardless of who the technical taxpayer is under local law. So in this example the taxes would be deemed to reside at Forco2 and would be available only when taxable distributions were made (or were deemed to be made) by Forco2.

The "who is the taxpayer" issue has offered some tax planning opportunities. Suppose a U.S. taxpayer has $100 of foreign source income (not subject to foreign tax) and owns stock of a foreign corporation that earns $100 of active business income on which a $35 foreign tax is paid. Under these facts, the U.S. taxpayer faces a $35 U.S. tax on the $100 of foreign source income. The active income earned by the foreign subsidiary typically is not taxable in the hands of the taxpayer. Now assume that the foreign corporation is a reverse hybrid—an entity that is treated as a corporation for U.S. purposes but a flow-through for foreign tax purposes. From a U.S. perspective, the income is still earned by the foreign subsidiary and is not subject to U.S. tax in the hands of the U.S. shareholder. But under the technical taxpayer rule, the foreign country imposes the tax on the U.S. taxpayer that earns the income through a flow-through. That is, the United States applies U.S. tax principles to determine who earns the income but looks to foreign tax rules to determine who paid the tax. As a result, the taxpayer has historically been able to use the $35 foreign tax to offset the potential U.S. tax on the $100 of foreign source income in the same tax basket. Separating the taxes paid from the earnings that gave rise to the tax, saves the U.S. taxpayer $35 of tax in this example.

Taxpayers do not have unlimited ability to separate earnings from taxes. For example, Regulations in the partnership area prevent a partnership from allocating tax expense (and the resulting credits) to one partner and the underlying income to a different partner. Reg. § 1.704–1(b)(4)(viii). Section 909, discussed immediately below, also is aimed at preventing taxpayers from separating foreign taxes from the underlying earnings that gave rise to the taxes in order to discourage taxpayers from accessing the foreign tax credits (to offset U.S. tax on other low-taxed foreign source income) while leaving the foreign earnings outside the U.S. tax net.

(F)　WHEN CAN THE FOREIGN TAX CREDIT BE CLAIMED?

In 2010, I.R.C. § 909 was enacted to address situations where foreign income taxes have been separated from the related income *(i.e.,* the foreign tax credits have been made available to a U.S. taxpayer, but the underlying income is not yet subject to U.S. taxation). If there is a foreign tax credit splitting event (FTCSE) with respect to a foreign income tax paid or accrued by a taxpayer, such tax is not be taken into account for federal tax purposes before the taxable year in which the related income is taken into account by the taxpayer—that is, the split tax is suspended. Accordingly, foreign tax credits (or deductions) are available only when the underlying income is taxable. The rule is aimed at limiting taxpayers' ability to use foreign tax credits on income that is not yet taxable in the U.S. to offset U.S. tax on other foreign source income that the U.S. taxpayer has generated.

For purposes of I.R.C. § 909, there is a FTCSE with respect to a foreign income tax if the related income is (or will be) taken into account by a "covered person" (essentially, a related party). I.R.C. §§ 909(d)(1) and (4) and Reg. § 1.909–1(a)(4). I.R.C. § 909 does not suspend foreign income taxes if the same person pays the tax but takes into account the related income in a different taxable period (or periods) due to, for example, timing differences between the U.S. and foreign tax accounting rules.

Reg. § 1.909–2 identifies four splitter arrangements that give rise to a FTCSE. The four splitter arrangements involve: (1) reverse hybrid structures; (2) loss-sharing; (3) hybrid instruments; and (4) partnership inter-branch payment.

To illustrate the impact of section 909, revisit the reverse hybrid structure discussed above in subsection (e) (*i.e.*, foreign reverse hybrid earns active income but foreign tax is imposed on U.S. parent). Under I.R.C. § 909, the foreign taxes imposed on the income are not taken into account for U.S. tax purposes (*i.e.*, they are suspended) until the underlying income of the reverse hybrid becomes taxable in the U.S (*e.g.,* a dividend is distributed).

As an illustration of the second identified tax splitting event (loss sharing), suppose that USCo owns 100 percent of the stock of FC1 which owns 100% of the stock of FC2 and FC3. FC2 owns all of the "stock" of DRE, a disregarded entity for U.S. tax purposes but a corporation for local country purposes. FC1, FC2, FC3 and DRE are all located in Country A. Country A (*e.g.,* the United Kingdom) does not allow consolidation for tax purposes but does allow a company with losses to share the loss with any group member it designates. Suppose that FC2 and FC3 each earn 100 of income and DRE has a loss of 100. From a U.S. perspective FC2 has 0 income (and should attract no Country A tax) and FC3 with 100 of income should attract Country A tax—foreign tax and foreign income aligned. But if DRE shares its loss with FC3, then the FC3 with 100 of earnings would have no Country A tax while FC2 with no earnings from a U.S. perspective would attract Country A tax—foreign taxes and foreign income are split. In this type of fact pattern, the foreign taxes that are in the tax pool at FC2 cannot be utilized by USCo (*e.g.,* if FC2 accumulated a small amount of earnings, a distribution of those earnings to FC1 and then to USCo would bring back the FC2 tax pool for use by USCo) before the income at FC3 is repatriated to USCo.

The third type of splitter arrangement involves hybrid instruments—instruments that are treated as equity for U.S. purposes (U.S. equity hybrid interest) but debt for foreign purposes—and vice versa (U.S. debt hybrid interest). For example suppose that USCo owns 100 percent of the stock of FC1 which owns 100 percent of the stock of FC2. FC1 and FC2 both Country A corporations. FC2 earns 20 but accrues an interest deduction under Country A law (but not under U.S. law because the instrument is considered as equity for U.S. tax purposes and dividends cannot be accrued) to FC1. FC1 pays Country A tax. However, from a U.S. perspective because the payment to FC1 should not have been deductible the underlying earnings that gave rise to the tax are at FC2—a splitter. Similar results can be achieved using a U.S. debt hybrid instrument. As with the other splitters, I.R.C. § 909 will not permit USCo to utilize the FC1 foreign taxes before the underlying income from FC2 is repatriated to the United States.

The fourth splitter arrangement involves inter-branch disregarded payments under a partnership. For example, suppose USCo owns 100 percent of the stock of FA corporation and FB corporation which form the AB partnership. Without going into detail, it is possible through partnership allocations to arrange for the foreign taxes to end up in the hands of one partner (*e.g.*, FA) while the underlying income ends up in the hands of the other partner (FB). While that can be accomplished, again the foreign taxes cannot be utilized by USCo until the underlying income is repatriated to the United States.

I.R.C. 909's impact on tax arbitrage transactions is discussed in more detail below in Chapter 13.

(G) WHAT IS THE AMOUNT OF THE CREDITABLE FOREIGN INCOME TAX?

Even if a foreign income tax satisfies the realization, gross proceeds, and net income requirements, an amount paid to a foreign government is not creditable to the extent that it is reasonably certain that the amount will be refunded, credited, rebated or forgiven. Reg. § 1.901–2(e)(2). For example, a U.S. taxpayer subject to a 30 percent withholding tax by country X on a dividend payment may not claim a credit for the withholding if pursuant to the U.S.-X income tax treaty the taxpayer can file a refund claim. Reg. § 1.901–2(e)(2)(ii) Ex. 1.

If a foreign government either directly or indirectly returns a portion of a tax payment as a subsidy, the tax payment to the extent of the subsidy is not creditable. I.R.C. § 901(i). For example, suppose Brazil imposes a 30 percent tax on interest paid from a Brazilian borrower to a foreign lender. A Brazilian borrower pays $100,000 in interest to a U.S. lender of which $30,000 is withheld for payment to the government. If the government either rebates the $30,000 to the lender or to the Brazilian borrower, the tax is not creditable. The U.S. lender who receives $70,000 of net income would be willing to include an extra $30,000 of income in order to receive a $30,000 tax credit. The "extra" $30,000 inclusion would result in an additional $10,500 of U.S. tax if the lender pays taxes at a 35 percent rate. However, a $30,000 tax credit, if available, would provide a dollar-for-dollar offset against U.S. tax liability that would not only offset any additional tax but may effectively decrease U.S. tax on the taxpayer's other foreign source income. Similarly, if a tax payment is directly linked to a government subsidy (*e.g.*, the government provides office space to the lender), the tax is not creditable.

Suppose foreign government F imposes both a noncreditable tax based on asset value (assets tax) and a creditable income tax. Suppose further that the assets tax is allowed as a credit against the income tax. If a U.S. taxpayer has a $4,000 assets tax liability and a $10,000 income tax liability, the taxpayer can take a credit for $6,000. Reg. § 1.901–2(e)(4) and Reg. § 1.903–1(b)(3) Ex. 5. If the rule in country F is that a taxpayer pays whichever is greater, the assets tax or the income tax, then the taxpayer could take a $10,000 foreign tax credit. If the rule in country F is that a taxpayer pay whichever is less, then the taxpayer could take no credit.

Under some circumstances, a tax that qualifies as a creditable foreign tax may not be fully creditable and may be permanently disallowed when there is a base difference with respect to the amount of taxable income in a foreign country resulting from inconsistent views of asset basis. To illustrate, suppose that USCO buys the "stock" of a German disregarded entity for $150 million. From a U.S.

perspective, USCO has bought the underlying assets for $150 million, but for German purposes, USCO has bought stock and the basis of the underlying assets carries over. This may lead to a situation where for U.S. purposes, the basis of the assets is $150 million but for German purposes the basis of the assets is, for example, $120 million. Assume that the property purchased is amortizable both in Germany and U.S. over 15 years (*e.g.*, goodwill or other intangibles). For U.S. tax purposes the annual amortization would be $10 million but for German purposes, the amortization would be $8 million. Holding all else constant, the German taxable income each year will be $2 million less under U.S. law than under German law. The "policy" behind I.R.C. § 901(m) is that if there is $2 million of German phantom income from a U.S. perspective, then the German tax on that "phantom income" (*e.g.*, $600,000 assuming a 30 percent German tax rate) should not be creditable in the U.S. From a U.S. perspective, there is no income to the extent offset by the excess amortization deduction allowed under U.S. law, and therefore no German tax credit for German taxes imposed on that "phantom income."

Under I.R.C. § 901(m), certain foreign income taxes paid or accrued on "covered asset acquisition" (CAA) transactions may be permanently disallowed. These transactions are the target of I.R.C. § 901(m) because they result in stepped-up bases in assets that are eligible for cost recovery for U.S. tax purposes, without a corresponding increase to tax basis for foreign tax purposes. For example, when a taxpayer makes a I.R.C. § 338(g) election as part of a qualified stock purchase of a foreign target, the target is treated as having sold its assets to a new foreign target for fair market value. The deemed asset acquisition treatment also results in the new foreign target taking a cost-basis in the assets deemed purchased from the target. However, because the election is only relevant for U.S. purposes, there is no corresponding increase to the target's asset-basis for foreign tax purposes. The difference may result in a permanent difference in the amounts available for cost-recovery deduction for U.S. and foreign tax purposes.

While perhaps the two most common events that would trigger I.R.C. § 901(m) might be the purchase of stock in a disregarded foreign entity and an I.R.C. § 338(g) election, any transaction that gives rise to an asset basis difference may be problematic. Where I.R.C. § 901(m) applies, the disqualified portion of any foreign taxes paid are deductible for U.S. tax purposes.

Notice 2014–44, 2014–2 C.B. 270 has announced Treasury's intention to issue Regulations that clarify that once a CAA has occurred, section 901(m) is "turned off" only when there has been a "disposition" (the Statutory Disposition Rule) of the relevant foreign assets (RFAs) such that gain or loss is recognized by the United States, the foreign country or both. For example, suppose that USP, a U.S. corporation, wholly owns a foreign corporation (FSub), which purchases 100 percent of a foreign corporation (FT). An election is made under an

I.R.C. § 338(g) with respect to FT, such that the acquisition is a CAA. The RFAs are those owned by FT. Shortly after the acquisition, FT files a check-the-box election to be disregarded as an entity separate from its owner, resulting in a tax-free liquidation under an I.R.C. § 332. No gain or loss is recognized with respect to the RFAs for U.S. or foreign income tax purposes. Nevertheless, some taxpayers had taken the position that the transaction constitutes a disposition of RFAs, and the Statutory Disposition Rule provides that no basis differences will be allocated to any year following the liquidation. That position is no longer tenable.

For further discussion of I.R.C. § 901(m), *see* Chapter 13.

§ 8.04   COMPUTING THE DIRECT CREDIT

The computation of the direct foreign tax credit under I.R.C. § 901 is not complicated. If a taxpayer pays a creditable foreign income tax of $15,000 and the taxpayer's U.S. income tax liability before the foreign tax credit is $60,000, the taxpayer only pays $45,000 to the U.S. government. The credit reduces U.S. tax liability dollar-for-dollar. However, it is important to note that the tax credit permitted under I.R.C. § 901 is subject to the limitations under I.R.C. § 904, discussed in § 8.06 and I.R.C. § 909, discussed in § 8.03. Without additional information concerning the nature and source of the income that generated the foreign tax, the amount of the foreign tax credit permitted for a particular taxable year cannot be determined.

§ 8.05 COMPUTING THE INDIRECT CREDIT

(A) OVERVIEW

If a U.S. corporation conducts business abroad through an unincorporated branch, the branch income is taxable in the United States and is likely to be taxed in the country in which it is earned. The U.S. corporation (subject to limitations under I.R.C. § 904) can credit the foreign income taxes against the U.S. tax liability. Suppose instead that the U.S. corporation operates abroad through a subsidiary. Normally, the income earned by the subsidiary is not taxable in the United States because the income is earned by a foreign corporation abroad. *But see* the discussion of subpart F *infra* in Chapter 10. Not surprisingly, the U.S. parent corporation cannot credit the foreign income taxes paid by the foreign subsidiary. However when the foreign subsidiary makes a dividend distribution to the U.S. parent corporation, the dividend is normally taxable in the United States. Upon the distribution, the U.S. parent corporation may be permitted an indirect tax credit for the foreign taxes on the income that was earned by the foreign subsidiary out of which the dividend distribution was made. Note that the U.S. parent corporation is not entitled to the dividends-received deduction that is ordinarily available to dividends received by a parent corporation from a domestic subsidiary under I.R.C. § 243, except to the extent that the foreign subsidiary earns U.S. source business income. I.R.C. §§ 245 and 243(e).

In sum, a U.S. corporation operating through a foreign branch is taxable in the United States on the branch income and can credit foreign income taxes on the branch income. Normally, a U.S. corporation operating abroad through a foreign subsidiary is not immediately taxable on the subsidiary's income, nor is there a foreign tax credit for the foreign taxes paid by the subsidiary. However, once the subsidiary distributes the foreign earnings in the form of a dividend, the U.S. parent is taxable on the income and at that point may receive a foreign tax credit for foreign taxes paid by the distributing corporation with respect to income used to make the dividend payment. In those cases where a foreign corporation is a controlled foreign corporation which has subpart F income taxable immediately to a U.S. parent, the U.S. parent can qualify for a foreign tax credit for the foreign income taxes associated with the foreign income that is included in the U.S. corporation's taxable income. *See infra* Chapter 10 for a discussion of subpart F.

(B) MINIMUM OWNERSHIP REQUIREMENTS

In order to qualify for the indirect tax credit, a domestic corporation must own at least 10 percent of a foreign corporation's voting stock. I.R.C. § 902(a). This requirement is easily met in the context of a parent-subsidiary arrangement and is intended to make the indirect tax credit unavailable where a domestic corporation owns stock of a foreign corporation as a portfolio investment. Note that there is no indirect tax credit for dividends received by an *individual* owning at least 10 percent of the voting stock of a foreign corporation doing business abroad even though that individual is taxed on the dividend originating from foreign earnings that are taxed by a foreign country. If that same individual carries on the business abroad directly rather than through a corporation, the foreign income is subject to U.S. tax but a foreign tax credit under I.R.C. § 901 is available. The same result would occur if the individual operated through a hybrid entity (*i.e.*, a flow-through for U.S. purposes but a corporation for foreign purposes).

If a domestic corporation owns stock in a foreign corporation through a partnership, an aggregate approach to the partnership interest can result in an indirect foreign tax credit. I.R.C. § 902(c)(7). For example, suppose that U.S. Co. is a 50 percent partner in a foreign partnership that owns 100 percent of the stock of Forco. For purposes of I.R.C. § 902, U.S. Co. is a 50 percent owner of Forco.

The ownership requirement becomes more complicated when there are multiple levels of foreign subsidiaries. The indirect tax credit can apply to sixth-tier subsidiaries. I.R.C. §§ 902(b)(1) and (2) where any foreign corporation below the third tier is a controlled foreign corporation. For lower-tier subsidiaries, the ownership percentages are multiplied together and the indirect credit applies if the resulting product is at least 5 percent. I.R.C. § 902(b)(2). For example, suppose U.S. Co.

owns 40 percent of the voting stock of Forco1 which in turn owns 10 percent of Forco2 which owns 70 percent of Forco3—all of the Forco companies being foreign corporations. Each corporation satisfies the 10 percent minimum ownership requirement of I.R.C. §§ 902(a), (b)(1), (b)(2). However, the 5 percent ownership requirement of I.R.C. § 902(b)(3) is not satisfied with respect to Forco2 and Forco3 because U.S. Co.'s 40 percent ownership of Forco1 when multiplied by Forco1's 10 percent ownership of Forco2—4 percent does not satisfy the 5 percent threshold. (The 5 percent test is also not satisfied for Forco3 because the product is only 2.8 percent—40 percent × 10 percent × 70 percent.) Consequently, only the foreign income taxes paid by Forco1 may qualify for the indirect tax credit.

If Forco1 owns 15 percent of the voting stock of Forco2, the foreign income taxes of Forco2 may qualify for the indirect tax credit because the product of the ownership percentages—6 percent (40 percent × 15 percent)—exceeds the 5 percent threshold. Taxes paid by Forco3 still would not qualify for the indirect tax credit because the product of ownership percentages is only 4.2 percent (40 percent × 15 percent × 70 percent). If Forco1 owns 20 percent of Forco2, then foreign income taxes paid by Forco3 may qualify for the indirect tax credit because the ownership percentage would be 5.6 percent (40 percent × 20 percent × 70 percent).

If the 5 percent test is satisfied with regard to lower-tier subsidiaries, then foreign taxes paid by the first-tier subsidiary may include the taxes it is deemed to have paid with respect to dividends distributed by the lower-tier corporations. In short, the U.S. parent corporation receives a larger foreign tax credit on dividends it receives from the first-tier subsidiary which has itself received dividends from lower-tier subsidiaries.

(C) AMOUNT OF TAX DEEMED PAID

Assuming that the foreign income taxes paid by a foreign subsidiary are creditable income taxes and that the minimum ownership requirements are satisfied, the portion of the foreign taxes deemed paid by a U.S. parent corporation is determined under I.R.C. § 902(a) according to the following formula:

$$\text{Post-1986 Foreign Income Taxes} \times \frac{\text{Dividends}}{\text{Post-1986 Undistributed Earnings}}$$

The purpose of the formula is to allocate a portion of the foreign income taxes paid by a foreign subsidiary to the dividend distribution. The formula for computing the indirect tax credit was altered by the Tax Reform Act of 1986, but because dividends are deemed to come from the most recent earnings first, the pre-1986 rules rarely come into play. The term "post-1986 foreign income taxes" refers to taxes paid after 1986, including the year in question to the extent that the taxes have not already been deemed paid by the corporate parent. I.R.C. § 902(c)(2). The term "post-1986 undistributed earnings" refers essentially to the corporation's earnings and profits determined under U.S. tax principles (*see* I.R.C. §§ 316, 964) that a corporation has accumulated (*i.e.,* distributions reduce post-1986 undistributed earnings) after 1986 and through the year of distribution. *See United States v. Goodyear Tire and Rubber Co.,* 493 U.S. 132 (1989).

Suppose that a newly-formed, wholly-owned foreign subsidiary of a U.S. corporation earned $1 million in its first year on which it paid $250,000 in foreign income taxes. The foreign corporation therefore has $750,000 of earnings and profits for its only year of existence (*i.e.,* for the post-1986 period)—$1 million of earnings minus the $250,000 tax payment. If the foreign subsidiary distributes a $75,000 dividend at the end of its first year, the domestic parent corporation is deemed to have paid $25,000 of the $250,000 in foreign income taxes actually paid by the foreign subsidiary determined as follows:

$$\$250,000 \ \times \ \frac{\$75,000}{\$750,000}$$

At first glance, it appears that the parent corporation will report dividend income of $75,000 and be able to credit $25,000 in foreign taxes against its U.S. tax liability. But if that were the case, the effective tax rate on the distributed income would be 33 1/3 percent ($25,000 tax on $75,000 of income) when the foreign tax rate was actually 25 percent ($250,000 tax on $1 million of income).

Instead, the indirect foreign tax credit actually treats the domestic parent corporation as if it directly paid the allocable portion of income taxes borne by the distribution. It is as if the foreign subsidiary distributed not only the $75,000 dividend but also $25,000 additional dollars which the U.S. parent then uses to discharge the foreign income tax liability of the subsidiary on the earnings used to generate the dividend. Stated differently, the U.S. parent corporation must "gross up" the deemed tax payment and treat the grossed-up amount as part of the dividend distribution. I.R.C. § 78. In sum, the domestic parent corporation reports $100,000 of dividend income and can take a $25,000 foreign tax credit so that the effective tax rate on the distributed income is 25 percent ($25,000 tax on $100,000 dividend)—the same rate applied to the foreign subsidiary.

Notice that the foreign subsidiary had $750,000 available for distribution after paying foreign income taxes. It actually distributed $75,000, or 10 percent of the $750,000 available earnings. That 10 percent distribution carried with it a deemed tax payment of $25,000 or 10 percent of the foreign taxes paid. The $225,000 in foreign taxes *not* deemed paid by the domestic parent corporation are those associated with the $675,000 that the foreign subsidiary did not distribute. For purposes of calculating the indirect tax credit in the next year, the foreign subsidiary is deemed to have post-1986 foreign income taxes of $225,000 and post-1986 undistributed earnings of $675,000 as of the beginning of the year.

To see how the indirect foreign tax credit works with multiple tiers, suppose in the previous example that the foreign subsidiary, Forco1, owned 100 percent of Forco2, a second tier subsidiary of the domestic parent corporation. For the year at issue, Forco2 had $600,000 of accumulated and current earnings and profits ("E&P") on which it paid $100,000 in foreign income taxes (reducing E&P to $500,000). Forco2 made a $250,000 dividend distribution (that does not result in subpart F income) during the year which Forco1 received in addition to its $1 million of earned income. Under I.R.C. § 902, Forco1 is deemed to have paid $50,000 of the foreign income taxes paid by Forco2 ($100,000 × $250,000/$500,000) in addition to the $250,000 of income taxes actually paid. Although Forco1 is not a U.S. taxpayer, the taxes it is deemed to pay are important to the U.S. parent. On the dividend distribution of $75,000 by Forco1 to the U.S. parent corporation, the amount of the deemed foreign income tax paid by the domestic parent is $22,500 determined as follows:

$$\$300,000 \ \times \ \frac{\$75,000}{\$1,000,000}$$

Notice that the net increase to the undistributed earnings of Forco1 is the $250,000 dividend received from Forco2. The $50,000 of Forco2 taxes deemed paid by Forco1 is not grossed up under I.R.C. § 78 but rather moves direct from the Forco 2 tax pool to the Forco 1 tax pool. Reg. § 1.902–1(c)(2)(ii) In sum, the parent corporation would report a dividend of

$97,500 ($75,000 dividend + $22,500 deemed taxes paid) and a foreign tax credit of $22,500.

To make things more complicated still, a dividend distribution from a foreign subsidiary to a U.S. parent corporation may involve both the indirect and direct tax credit. Suppose in the previous example the country in which Forco1 was located imposed a 10 percent withholding tax (*i.e.,* $7,500) on the actual $75,000 dividend distribution. Because that tax is directly withheld from the distribution (so that the domestic parent receives $67,500 in cash but reports a $75,000 dividend plus the amount of indirect taxes deemed paid), there is no need to gross up the withholding payment. Under I.R.C. § 901, the domestic parent corporation would report a dividend of $97,500 and be entitled to a direct tax credit of $7,500 and an indirect tax credit of $22,500, or a total tax credit of $30,000 which may be subject to limitation under I.R.C. § 904.

One final aspect of the indirect foreign tax credit under I.R.C. § 902 deserves comment. Suppose that a U.S. corporation receives a dividend from a foreign subsidiary that has income effectively connected with the conduct of a U.S. trade or business. Under I.R.C. § 245, the dividends attributable to the effectively connected income are eligible for a dividends-received deduction of up to 100 percent depending on the degree of ownership. *See* I.R.C. §§ 243(e) and 245(b). To the extent that I.R.C. § 245 applies, no foreign tax credit is available for taxes attributable to the dividend from U.S. effectively connected income. I.R.C. § 245(a)(8).

§ 8.06   LIMITATIONS ON THE FOREIGN TAX CREDIT

(A) OVERVIEW

Worried about tax-motivated, opportunistic behavior, Congress has imposed a minimum holding period for purposes of crediting foreign taxes associated with both direct and indirect foreign source dividends. In general, a taxpayer qualifies for a credit with respect to a dividend only if a 16-day holding period for the dividend-paying stock (46-day holding period for certain dividends on preferred stock) is satisfied. I.R.C. § 901(k). Otherwise, a taxpayer can deduct any withholding tax and need not gross up any underlying taxes under I.R.C. § 78 in the case of any indirect credit that is disallowed.

There is a similar 16-day minimum holding period in order to take a direct credit for other withholding taxes. For example, a U.S. taxpayer that acquires a royalty license (or a note) will be entitled to a foreign tax credit for any withholding tax imposed on the payments of a royalty (or interest) if the license (or note) was held for at least 16 days (during a 31-day period centered around the event giving rise to the payment). I.R.C. § 901(*l*).

Determining the foreign tax credit would be complicated enough even if there were no limitations. But with the limitations discussed below, the computation can boggle the mind. What follows is an overview of what Congress was attempting to accomplish in enacting such labyrinthine provisions.

Suppose T, a U.S. taxpayer (corporation or individual), earns net income of $100,000 from business activities in Mexico and $200,000 of income from U.S. sources. Assume that the U.S. tax rate is a flat 35 percent while the Mexican rate is 50 percent. The U.S. tax liability on the $300,000 of worldwide income is $105,000. Absent a limitation provision, T could credit the $50,000 of Mexican taxes against the U.S. tax liability, leaving a net U.S. tax liability of $55,000, or an effective tax rate of only 27.5 rather than 35 percent on the $200,000 of U.S. source income. In order to prevent foreign income taxes from reducing U.S. income taxes on U.S. source income, I.R.C. § 904 limits the foreign tax credit to foreign income taxes imposed on foreign source income to the extent those taxes do not exceed the U.S. income tax on that foreign source income.

Specifically, I.R.C. § 904 provides that the total amount of the foreign tax credit cannot exceed the same proportion of the tax against which the credit is taken which the taxpayer's foreign source taxable income bears to worldwide taxable income. Stated differently:

$$\frac{X}{\text{U.S. income tax}} = \frac{\text{Foreign source income}}{\text{Worldwide taxable income}}$$

where X = the amount of creditable foreign income taxes that can be credited for the taxable year. Solving the equation for X yields the following formulation:

$$X = \text{U.S. income tax} \times \frac{\text{Foreign source income}}{\text{Worldwide taxable income}}$$

Foreign source income is sometimes referred to as the numerator of the I.R.C. § 904(a) limitation formula, and worldwide taxable income is referred to as the denominator. Under a graduated rate system, this formula treats foreign source income as bearing the average rate of tax borne by all of the taxpayer's income.

Applying the formula to the problem above results in a U.S. income tax credit for the current year of $35,000 of the $50,000 Mexican income tax and a U.S tax collection of $70,000—essentially $200,000 of U.S. source income taxed at a 35 percent tax rate:

$$\frac{X}{\$90,000} = \frac{\$100,000}{\$300,000}$$

Under I.R.C. § 904(c), any excess creditable taxes that cannot be immediately credited because of the I.R.C. § 904(a) limitation can be carried back one year (necessitating an amended return) and carried forward ten years, subject always to the I.R.C. § 904(a) limitation. But note that the excess credits cannot be deducted. I.R.C. §§ 904(c), 275(a)(4)(A).

Now suppose that T arranges for $100,000 of the U.S. source income (*e.g.*, investment income that may be easily moveable) to be earned in the Cayman Islands, a foreign jurisdiction which imposes no income tax. Now T has $200,000 of foreign source income and $100,000 of U.S. source income. If the I.R.C. § 904(a) formula allows T to look at "overall" foreign income, the entire $50,000 in Mexican taxes is immediately creditable; indeed, T could credit up to $70,000 of Mexican income taxes if they were imposed:

$$\frac{X}{\$90,000} = \frac{\$200,000}{\$300,000}$$

In effect under this "overall" method, the taxpayer would be permitted to average the highly-taxed Mexican income with the nontaxed Cayman Islands income so that the United States would only collect $55,000 of U.S. tax instead of $70,000 in the example above where the was $200,000 of U.S. source income. For various periods in U.S. tax history, the taxpayer was permitted to use this "overall" method of determining the foreign tax credit limitation.

However to prevent the type of averaging just illustrated, Congress has also during the history of the U.S. tax system from time-to-time enacted a "per country" limitation. Under the "per country" limitation, foreign income taxes from each country are subjected to the I.R.C. § 904(a) limitation separately so that the numerator of the I.R.C. § 904(a) ratio (*i.e.,* foreign source income) is applied country-by-country. In the previous example then, only $35,000 of the Mexican income taxes would be immediately creditable. Up to $35,000 of Cayman Islands income taxes would also have been creditable but there are no taxes imposed and the taxpayer cannot credit the excess Mexican income taxes under the Cayman Islands limitation. Crediting $35,000 of Mexican tax against the potential $105,000 U.S. tax liability on $300,000 would leave a $70,000 residual U.S. tax.

The "per-country" limitation method appears to be a perfect solution to the perceived averaging problem. But consider this additional problem that the per-country limitation creates. Suppose that T has the $100,000 of Mexican income on which $50,000 of Mexican income taxes are paid, $100,000 of U.S. income and a $100,000 loss from the start of a new business in China. In total, T has $100,000 of net income on which there is a $35,000 U.S. income tax. If the "per-country" method is used, the taxpayer can credit $35,000 of Mexican taxes against the $35,000 U.S. tax liability:

$$\frac{X}{\$30,000} = \frac{\$100,000}{\$100,000}$$

If T is allowed to credit $35,000 of Mexican income taxes, the U.S. tax liability is eliminated even though T has earned $100,000 of U.S. source income. For this situation, the "per-country" method results in lower U.S. taxes than the "overall" method which would force T to combine the $100,000 of Mexican income with the $100,000 Chinese loss in the I.R.C. § 904(a) numerator, thereby producing no foreign tax credit:

$$\frac{X}{\$30,000} = \frac{\$0}{\$100,000}$$

It is this conundrum of the "overall" method being preferable in some situations and the "per country" limitation method being preferable in some situations in terms of protecting U.S. taxation of U.S. source income that has led to a shifting back-and-forth over the years in the way in which I.R.C. § 904(a) limitation is applied. The current system, as explained below, offers yet another regimen for protecting U.S. taxation of U.S. source income.

(B) SEPARATE "BASKETS"

The Tax Reform Act of 1986 reaffirmed the "overall" method of limiting the foreign tax credit, but the overall method is applied separately to different types of income. Each specially designated type of income is placed into a "basket" to which the I.R.C. § 904(a) limitation is applied. I.R.C. § 904(d). The complexity involved in applying I.R.C. § 904 to the separate baskets have turned many a sane tax professional (is "sane tax professional" an oxymoron?) into a "basket case." Nevertheless, the basic Congressional intent is not difficult to understand. Congress wanted to prevent U.S. taxpayers from arranging their affairs to maximize the foreign tax credit at the expense of U.S. taxes on U.S. source income.

The I.R.C. § 904(d) limitation for each basket can be stated as follows:

$$X = \text{U.S. income tax} \times \frac{\text{Foreign source income in the basket}}{\text{Worldwide taxable income}}$$

where X = the amount of creditable foreign income taxes that can be credited for the taxable year. Solving the equation for X yields the following formulation:

$$\frac{X}{\$30,000} = \frac{\$0}{\$100,000}$$

For years beginning after September 31, 2006, there are only two baskets—the passive basket and the general basket. Prior to that time, I.R.C. § 904(d) created as many as nine separate baskets. It was not an administrable provision, but it endured for 20 years.

To illustrate how the current basket mechanism works, consider again the examples discussed. The $100,000 of Mexican income is generated from business activities and is therefore placed in the general income basket. I.R.C. § 904(d)(1)(B). The $100,000 of investment income from the Cayman Islands would be placed in the passive income basket and treated separately. Applying the I.R.C. § 904(a) formula to the general income basket produces only $35,000 of creditable Mexican taxes:

$$\frac{X}{\$90,000} = \frac{\$100,000}{\$300,000}$$

This produces the same result as the "per country" limitation. (Note that separate baskets apply even if the passive interest income is earned in the same country as the business income.) But, recall that the "per country" limitation failed to protect U.S. source income in the situation where T earned $100,000 of Mexican income and suffered a $100,000 business loss in China. However, applying the baskets to this situation yields a "correct" result, a result that protects the $30,000 U.S. income tax on the $100,000 of U.S. income. Both the Mexican income and the Chinese loss are placed in the general basket (I.R.C. § 904(d)(1)(B)) so that no Mexican taxes are creditable for the taxable year because the numerator in the I.R.C. § 904(a) ratio is $0:

$$\frac{X}{\$30,000} = \frac{\$0}{\$100,000}$$

In sum, the use of the basket method is intended to provide some of the advantages of the "per country" limitation in preventing averaging of high- and low-taxed income and the advantages of the "overall" limitation in offsetting foreign losses against foreign income for purposes of determining the numerator in the I.R.C. § 904(a) formula.

Computing the foreign tax credit limitation is a daunting task requiring a lot of information. As an act of simplification, Congress has waived the limitation for certain de minimis foreign taxes paid by individuals. An individual with $300 ($600 for joint filers) or less of creditable foreign taxes is exempt from the foreign tax credit limitation, provided that the taxpayer has no foreign source income other than qualified passive income. I.R.C. § 904(k).

(1) Passive Income Basket

Passive income (*e.g.*, interest and dividends) can be quite portable. For example, a U.S. corporation may be able to arrange its affairs so that interest income that was formerly U.S. source income (*e.g.*, interest from U.S. corporate bonds) becomes foreign source income (*e.g.*, the taxpayer purchases foreign bonds) often subject to little or no foreign taxation. The relative ease of changing the source of investment income in the absence of some limitation would allow the taxpayer to average high-taxed business income with low-taxed investment income.

The most important categories of income that fall into the passive income basket include dividends, interest, rents, royalties, annuities, net capital gains, and commodities transactions. I.R.C. §§ 904(d)(2)(A)(i), 954(c)(1). There are some important exceptions to these inclusions. Rents and royalties derived in an active trade or business from a related or an unrelated person may not be considered passive. Reg. § 1.904–4(b)(2). There is another important exception for high-taxed passive income which is referred to in the legislative history as the "high-tax kick-out." I.R.C.

§ 904(d)(2)(A)(iii)(II). The motivation behind this exception is similar to the motivation for the passive income basket in the first place. Just as Congress does not want taxpayers to average foreign source high-taxed business income with foreign source low-taxed passive income for purposes of determining the foreign tax credit, it does not want taxpayers to average high-taxed passive income with low-taxed passive income. The term "high-taxed passive income" refers to income subject to an effective foreign tax rate exceeding the highest applicable U.S. rate (*i.e.,* corporate or individual, depending on the taxpayer) on the income. I.R.C. § 904(d)(2)(F). When high-taxed income is removed from the passive income basket, it is placed in the general income basket of I.R.C. § 904(d)(1)(B) along with the underlying taxes.

Suppose that U.S. Co. receives from an unrelated foreign taxpayer $1,000 of interest which bears a 10 percent foreign income tax and $1,000 of rental income from a passive real property investment in India that is subject to a 30 percent Indian withholding tax. At first glance, it appears that both of the income items fall into the passive income basket. However, suppose that the parent incurs $400 of expenses that are allocable to the rental income. Now the effective tax rate on the rental income is 50 percent ($300 tax/$600 net income) which exceeds the highest corporate tax rate of 35 percent. Therefore the rental income must be placed in the general basket with any active business income.

Financial services income (*e.g.,* interest earned by a bank) is not considered passive income. The term "financial services income" includes certain types of income received or accrued by a person predominantly engaged in the active conduct of a banking, insurance, financing, or similar business. Code Sec. 904(d)(2)(C) and Reg. § 1.904–4(e)(1). It also includes income derived from an insurance company's investment of its unearned premiums or reserves, as well as subpart F "insurance income" as defined under Code Sec. 953(a), passive income, and export financing interest (*i.e.,* interest on loans to customers buying certain exported inventory) that is subject to at least a five percent foreign withholding tax.

(2) Look-Through Rules

Income may appear to be passive income (*e.g.,* dividends, interest, royalties, rents from a related taxpayer), but under a look-through ruled may end up characterized as general basket income. Where a foreign subsidiary is a controlled foreign corporation, a U.S. taxpayer owning at least 10 percent of the voting stock must "look through" any distribution of dividends, interest, rents and royalties to the distributing corporation's underlying income. I.R.C. § 904(d)(3). The look-through rules apply as well to a deemed distribution by a controlled foreign corporation with subpart F income. *See infra* Chapter 10. A controlled foreign corporation is a corporation more than 50 percent of the stock of which measured by voting stock or value is owned by U.S. shareholders (*i.e.,* U.S.

persons owning at least 10 percent of the voting stock).

The purpose of the "look-through" rule is to equate the treatment of a controlled foreign corporation with a branch for foreign tax credit basketing purposes. Accordingly, for tax credit basketing purposes, a U.S. parent is treated as earning the income earned by a foreign subsidiary. If the U.S. parent is taxable on income (*e.g.*, foreign personal holding company income) as it is earned under subpart F, then the income taxed to the U.S. parent is placed in those baskets that are appropriate for the income earned by the foreign subsidiary. If the U.S. parent is not taxed on income earned by the foreign subsidiary until it is distributed in the form of a dividend, interest, royalties, or rent, the distribution is allocated to baskets in accordance with the income of the foreign subsidiary that is deemed to be used to make the distribution.

An important aspect of the "look-through" rule is the allocation of the distribution made by a controlled foreign corporation to the income earned by that corporation. A dividend subject to the look-through rule is allocated pro rata to the income earned by the distributing corporation. Reg. § 1.904–5(c)(4). Interest, royalties, and rent paid by a controlled foreign corporation to a U.S. taxpayer owning 10 percent or more of the corporation's voting stock are allocated to the recipient's baskets in the same way as deductible payments are allocated to income generally. *See supra* § 4.02. For example, typically royalty and rental payments are allocable to the income of the controlled foreign corporation that those deductions helped generate. However, there is a special rule for allocating interest payments. Interest payments received by a U.S. shareholder from a controlled foreign corporation are allocated first to passive income earned by the controlled foreign corporation. Then interest expense is apportioned among classes of gross income in proportion to asset value (or modified gross income). Reg. § 1.904–5(c)(2).

As an illustration of the look-through rules, suppose that a U.S. parent of a controlled foreign corporation (CFC) receives a dividend. The dividend does not automatically fall into the general or passive income basket for purposes of determining the foreign tax credit limitation on any associated foreign income taxes. Instead, the dividend is apportioned according to earnings of the controlled foreign corporation. Reg. § 1.904–5(c)(4). Suppose that 80 percent of the controlled foreign corporation's income is from manufacturing activities, 20 percent is a dividend from a portfolio investment. A proportionate amount of any dividend received by the U.S. parent is allocated to each basket corresponding to the underlying controlled foreign corporation's income (*e.g.*, 80 percent of the distribution to the general (*i.e.*, the (B)) basket, 20 percent of the distribution to the passive (A) basket).

Suppose that U.S. Co., which owns exactly 50 percent of the stock of Forco, receives a dividend from Forco. The other 50 percent of the stock of Forco is held by an unrelated foreign joint venture partner. The CFC look-through rule does not apply because U.S. shareholders (*i.e.,* U.S. Co.) do not own more than 50 percent of the stock of Forco. However, there is a special look-through rule for dividends from corporations where the U.S. shareholder owns at least 10 percent of the voting stock, but U.S. shareholders do not own more than 50 percent of the vote or value of the stock of the corporation (sometimes referred to as a "10/50" corporation— U.S. shareholders own more than 10 percent and not more than 50 percent). The special rule does not provide exactly the same look-through that is available with respect to payments from a CFC but doesn't automatically put distributions in the passive basket either. Dividends from such a 10/50 corporation receive look-through treatment while interest rents, and royalties would be treated as passive income for foreign tax credit basket purposes. I.R.C. § 904(d)(4).

(3) General Basket

The general basket in I.R.C. § 904(d)(1)(B) is defined to include any income that does not go in the passive basket. I.R.C. § 904(d)(2)(A)(ii). Typically, foreign source business profits would be general basket income. If a wholly-owned foreign subsidiary earns business profits and repatriates those earnings to the U.S. parent in the form of dividends, interest, rents or royalties, under the look-through rule, the income should be treated as general basket income.

Suppose that a foreign country imposes a tax on an item received by a U.S. taxpayer that is income for foreign tax purposes but not for U.S. purposes. For example, suppose a wholly-owned foreign subsidiary makes a distribution that would be treated as a return of capital for U.S. tax purposes (*e.g.,* there are no earnings and profits) but is a dividend subject to a foreign tax for foreign country purposes. What basket does the foreign tax go into where no income was generated? Under I.R.C. § 904(d)(2)(H), where there is a tax base difference the taxes are placed in the general basket.

(C) TREATMENT OF FOREIGN LOSSES

Because U.S. taxpayers are taxed on worldwide income, a foreign loss has the potential of decreasing U.S. taxes on U.S. income. That seems appropriate in light of the fact that foreign gains increase U.S. taxes. But, suppose a U.S. taxpayer has an overall foreign loss (OFL) in one year and foreign income in a subsequent year that is not offset by the earlier foreign loss (*e.g.*, the loss was in one country and the income was in a different country). An overall foreign loss arises when foreign deductions exceed foreign source income. The excess loss is then available to offset U.S. source income. Once an OFL (the excess of foreign source deductions over foreign source income) offsets U.S. income, it becomes an "OFL account." In the absence of a corrective provision, the impact over a two year period would be to lower U.S. taxation of U.S. source net income.

To illustrate, suppose that U.S. Co. earns $1,000 of U.S. source business income and suffers a $1,000 loss from business operations in Germany. The U.S. taxation for the year is $0 on the worldwide income of $0. In the next year, U.S. Co. earns $1,000 from U.S. business operations and $1,000 from business operations in Switzerland. Assuming a flat 35 percent rate, the U.S. tax on the $2,000 of worldwide income is $700. If the Swiss income tax is also a flat 35 percent rate, U.S. Co. is able to credit the $350 of Swiss tax on $1,000 of Swiss income against the U.S. tax liability, resulting in a $350 U.S. tax liability. Over the two year period, the United States collected only $350 on $2,000 of U.S. source income for an effective tax rate of 17 1/2 percent. That result arises because on net foreign income of $0 over a two-year period, the taxpayer paid $350 of foreign taxes which were creditable against U.S. taxes.

To prevent this result, I.R.C. § 904(f)(1) generally requires U.S. Co. to treat the foreign source income earned in the second year as domestic source income for purposes of the foreign tax credit. With this resourcing, none of the Swiss income tax is creditable in the second year under the I.R.C. § 904(a) limitation because the numerator (*i.e.,* foreign source income) of the I.R.C. § 904(a) fraction is $0. Notice that over a two year period, the correct result is reached from a U.S. standpoint: U.S. Co. earned $2,000 of U.S. source income and pays $700 in U.S. income taxes. Unfortunately, U.S. Co. earned $0 net foreign income but still paid a $350 Swiss income tax. Those Swiss taxes may be available in the prior year or in the next ten years under I.R.C. § 904(c).

The recapture rule for OFL accounts under I.R.C. § 904(f)(1) is actually more lenient than indicated above. In many cases, only 50 percent (or greater if the taxpayer so elects) of a taxpayer's foreign earnings (limited by the amount of the OFL) is resourced as U.S. source income for purposes of the foreign tax credit limitation. Taxes on the other 50 percent of the foreign earnings are still creditable. In the example, $175 of the Swiss income taxes would still be immediately creditable ($700 × ($500 foreign source income/$2,000) worldwide income) reducing U.S. tax liability in the second year to $525.

The principle of recapturing foreign losses by recharacterizing future foreign source income also applies where foreign losses in one basket offset income in another basket. (Remember that foreign losses offset U.S. source income only if there are foreign losses left after offsetting foreign source income.) The following rules apply under I.R.C. § 904(f)(5): (1) for any taxable year, a foreign loss in one basket (separate limitation loss) is allocated to income in the other basket before offsetting U.S. source income; (2) in a subsequent taxable year, foreign income attributable to the loss basket is first treated as U.S. source income to the extent U.S. source income was previously offset (OFL account recapture) and then is treated as foreign source income placed in the other basket the income of which was previously offset (separate limitation loss recapture).

To illustrate, suppose that U.S. Co. earns $200 of U.S. source business income, and $30 of foreign passive income. U.S. Co. also incurs a $40 foreign general category loss (*e.g.*, a loss from business operations in France) for the year. Under I.R.C. § 904(f), the $40 general basket loss is first applied against income in the passive basket. Consequently, no foreign tax credit is immediately available with respect to foreign income taxes imposed on income in the passive basket. The remaining $10 loss in the general basket offsets U.S. source income decreasing U.S. taxes on that income. At the end of the year, U.S. Co. has an OFL account of $10 with respect to the general basket and an SLL (separate limitation loss) in the general basket of $30.

In the following taxable year, U.S. Co. earns $50 of foreign passive income and $50 of foreign general category income. Because U.S. Co. generated a $10 general basket OFL in the previous year and a $30 SLL with respect to the general basket, $10 of the general basket income is treated as U.S. source income and $30 of the $50 general basket income is recharacterized as income from the basket whose income was offset in the previous year—$30 as passive income. Thus for foreign tax purposes, U.S. Co. has $80 of foreign passive income. This leaves $10 in the foreign general category basket.

The recapture rule for overall foreign losses only applies to income in a subsequent year in the basket which gave rise to the loss in the earlier year. *See*

1986–3 C.B. (vol. 4) II–591. In the example above, if U.S. Co. in the following year has no income in the general category basket, then no recapture is required under I.R.C. § 904(f).

I.R.C. § 904(f)(3) also provides for a recapture of foreign losses on a disposition of trade or business property used outside the United States. Gain that would normally be foreign source income or perhaps not even recognized for U.S. tax purposes (*see, e.g.*, I.R.C. § 351) is recaptured as U.S. source income to the extent of any unrecaptured OFLs. Suppose that U.S. Co. (which has an OFL account) wholly owns the stock of Forco1. If U.S. Co. contributes the stock of Forco1 to Forco 2 (also wholly-owned), the transaction would qualify under I.R.C. § 351 and there would be no OFL account recapture. Now suppose that the stock of Forco1 is contributed to Forco2, a newly-created joint venture where U.S. Co. receives 50 percent of the stock and the other joint venture contributor (who contributed other assets equal in value to the stock of Forco 1) also receives 50 percent of the stock of Forco2. In this situation, notwithstanding I.R.C. § 351, U.S. Co. will have to recognize gain to the extent of its OFL account (previous foreign losses that offset U.S. source income) because its ownership in Forco2 is less than its ownership in Forco1. Note there is a cliff effect here. Even if U.S. Co. received 99 percent of the stock of Forco2, there would be the same OFL account recapture.

OFL account recapture is a significant problem for many U.S. multinationals. Recharacterizing a foreign source dividend as a U.S. source dividend means that foreign tax credits cannot be used to offset the potential U.S. tax on such a dividend. Those credits might be the excess credits that a U.S. multinational has accumulated or the indirect foreign taxes (under I.R.C. § 902) that are associated with the dividend. The result is that many foreign multinationals in OFL account positions have chosen not to repatriate foreign earnings to the United States.

What causes this OFL account problem? Historically, it has been the way U.S. interest expense is allocated and apportioned. *See* the discussion at § 3.02(B)(1). Under the asset method, if U.S. interest expense is allocated and apportioned against foreign source income (because the U.S. consolidated group has foreign assets such as the stock of its foreign subsidiaries) and no foreign source income is generated (*e.g.*, the foreign subsidiaries do not pay dividends), then the combination of foreign source deductions and no foreign source income can create an OFL which then will offset U.S. source income resulting in an OFL account. This creates the OFL account recapture problem.

(D) TREATMENT OF U.S. LOSSES

If a U.S. taxpayer has income from foreign sources but a loss from U.S. sources, the U.S. loss is allocated among the taxpayer's foreign income baskets. I.R.C. § 904(f)(5)(D). If a U.S. taxpayer has both a loss from U.S. source income and a loss in a foreign income basket, the loss from the foreign basket is allocated against foreign source income in the other basket and then the U.S. loss is allocated to the income remaining in that basket.

If an overall domestic loss (ODL) in one year offset foreign income, there is a counterpart to the OFL rules in a subsequent year that changes U.S. source income to foreign source income. I.R.C. § 904(g). To illustrate, suppose in year 1 U.S. Co. has a $1,000 U.S. loss and $1,000 of foreign source income. In year 2, U.S. Co. has $1,000 of U.S. source income and $1,000 of foreign source income. Because the U.S. source loss in year 1 offset foreign source income, the U.S. source income in year 2 should be treated as foreign source income. That is, in year 1 U.S. Co. reports no net income, and in year 2 U.S. Co. should report $2,000 of foreign source income to reflect accurately the source of the net income earned during the 2-year period (*i.e.*, no net U.S. income and $2,000 of net foreign source income). However, under I.R.C. § 904(g)(1), 50 percent of the $1,000 U.S. source income in year 2 is treated as foreign source income. This is consistent with the 50 percent recapture rule for OFLs discussed above. An ODL is a positive attribute for a U.S. taxpayer. ODL recapture may permit a U.S. taxpayer to utilize foreign tax credits more efficiently (because there will be $1,500 of foreign source income in year 2 rather than $1,000 of foreign source income).

For ordering rules with respect to OFLs, SLLs, and ODLs, *see* Reg. § 1.904(g)–3T.

(E) FOREIGN TAX CREDIT SOURCE RULES

The limitation formula in I.R.C. § 904(a) as applied to the two baskets of I.R.C. § 904(d) is intended, in part, to allow a foreign tax credit only for foreign income taxes on foreign source income. While I.R.C. § 904(d) was enacted to prevent taxpayers from averaging low-taxed passive income with high-taxed business income, I.R.C. § 904(h) was enacted to prevent taxpayers from turning U.S. source income into foreign source income in order to increase the foreign tax credit.

Suppose that U.S. Co. has passive income which is taxed by a foreign country but which is considered U.S. source income by the United States (*e.g.*, Hong Kong imposes a withholding tax on a royalty paid by an unrelated Hong Kong licensee to U.S. Co.—not derived in an active trade or business—for the use of software that the licensee deploys in the United States). The foreign taxes on this passive income are not creditable against the U.S. taxes on the income because the numerator of the I.R.C. § 904(a) limitation formula is $0—no foreign source income. But suppose that U.S. Co. has additional funds it wants to invest in U.S. corporate bonds. In order to credit fully the foreign taxes on the U.S. source income, U.S. Co. lends the additional funds to a controlled foreign subsidiary which then invests the funds in U.S. corporate bonds. The interest payments received by U.S. Co. from the subsidiary would be foreign source income under I.R.C. § 861(a)(1) (in the absence of a special rule), assigned to the passive income basket under the look-through rules of I.R.C. § 904(d)(3). If that foreign source interest income is subject to little or no foreign taxes, U.S. Co. may be able to credit the foreign taxes on the U.S. income because now there is foreign source income for purposes of the I.R.C. § 904 limitation.

The special source rule of § 904(h) re-sources the interest payments as U.S. source income by looking through the controlled subsidiary to determine the actual source of the income (*i.e.*, interest paid by a U.S. payor). I.R.C. § 904(h) undermines the taxpayer's attempt to turn U.S. source income into foreign source income in order to increase the foreign tax credit. The effect of I.R.C. § 904(h) is to preserve U.S. taxation of U.S. source income.

§ 8.07   TAX REDETERMINATIONS

It is not uncommon that in a year after a U.S. taxpayer takes a foreign tax credit, the foreign taxing authority may redetermine the foreign taxes. For example, an audit may require additional taxes due or perhaps the taxpayer receives a tax refund. In some cases, the amount of foreign taxes paid for U.S. tax purposes changes because of currency fluctuations between the time of accrual and that of payment. I.R.C. § 905(c) addresses tax redeterminations. It will come as no surprise that the rules are quite intricate, but essentially the rules are as follows. Any redetermination that affects a direct tax (*e.g.*, a withholding tax or taxes imposed on a foreign branch of a U.S. corporation) requires a U.S. taxpayer to file an amended return to reflect the redetermination. Any redetermination that affects an indirect tax under I.R.C. § 902 (*e.g.*, a foreign subsidiary is assessed a higher income tax, the subsidiary receives a refund, currency fluctuations result in a difference between the dollar value of accrued and paid taxes), generally is taken into account prospectively by making the appropriate change to the tax and E&P pools. These changes will impact any subsequent inclusions and credit usage by a U.S. taxpayer. Temporary Regulations that were issued under I.R.C. § 905(c) have sunset, creating some uncertainty as to what rules apply However, because the Temporary Regulations were issued as Proposed and Temporary Regulations, the IRS has ruled that taxpayers can rely on the Proposed Regulations even though the Temporary Regulations are no longer in effect. *See* CCA201145015.

§ 8.08   EFFECT OF TREATIES ON THE FOREIGN TAX CREDIT

To have trudged through the rules governing the foreign tax credit only to learn that the rules do not apply to income from U.S. treaty partners would be cruel indeed. But not surprisingly, U.S. bilateral income tax treaties do address the crediting of foreign income taxes. For example, in the U.S. Model Income Tax Treaty, Article 23 provides relief from double taxation generally in accordance with U.S. domestic law rules governing relief from double taxation. However, treaty relief from double taxation under some treaties may be more favorable for a taxpayer than under U.S. domestic law rules providing relief from double taxation (*e.g.,* the source rules used in limiting the foreign tax credit may provide the taxpayer a larger foreign tax credit under the treaty than under U.S. domestic law). Where treaty resourcing rules permit a foreign tax credit that would not be available under U.S. domestic law, the item of income is put in a separate treaty basket to prohibit any cross-crediting of taxes. I.R.C. § 904(d)(6).

§ 8.09   CHANGES TO THE INTEREST EXPENSE ALLOCATION RULES

Under the current system of interest expense allocation which is based on the concept of fungibility, U.S. taxpayers often find themselves in a position where either they cannot fully credit foreign taxes paid or where an overall foreign loss is created. *See supra* § 8.06(C). This occurs because interest may be allocated against foreign source income in cases where it should not be. I.R.C. § 864(f) for tax years beginning in 2021 (starting date has been repeatedly postponed) is scheduled to change the method of interest expense allocation to take into account interest expense of controlled foreign corporations that are supporting foreign operations. If you and the author are still interested in international tax in the year 2021, we can revisit how the rules will work at that time.

From time to time, there have also been proposals to defer any interest expense allocated against foreign source income where the U.S. taxation of that income has been deferred (*i.e.,* a controlled foreign corporation has not made a distribution of earnings to the U.S. parent). There are those that would say that current interest expense allocation and apportionment rules unfairly apportion income against foreign source income, and now there are proposals to compound that inappropriate result by deferring the interest expense so apportioned. It remains to be seen if Congress will enact this legislation.

CHAPTER 9

INTERCOMPANY PRICING[1]

§ 9.01 OVERVIEW

Suppose Parentco, a U.S. corporation, has a wholly-owned foreign subsidiary, Hungarian Subco, organized and operated in Hungary. Parentco manufactures tractor parts in the U.S. and sells them to Hungarian Subco which in turn sells the parts to unrelated Hungarian customers. If the tax burden in Hungary is lower than those in the United States, or Hungary offers special tax incentives that are available for income earned in Hungary, or perhaps Hungarian Subco has large net operating losses, it may be advantageous for Parentco and its subsidiary to structure transactions so that much or all of the combined profit of Parentco and Hungarian Subco is recognized by Subco. For example, assume that for a particular transaction the cost of manufacturing is $60,000 and that the final sales price received by Hungarian Subco is $150,000 on sales to Hungarian customers, a $90,000 combined profit. In the absence of a remedial provision, if Parentco sells the tractor parts to Subco for $60,000, then Subco would

---

[1]   Much of this chapter was prepared by Ivan Gutierrez and George Soba, who have specialized in transfer pricing issues and financial economic analysis for many years. In addition, The Members of the Deloitte Tax LLP Transfer Pricing Consultant Think Tank have provided very helpful background material.

report $90,000 of income on the ultimate sale and Parentco would report $0. Normally, Subco may not be liable for U.S. taxes because it is a foreign corporation earning foreign source business income. If Hungarian tax rates are low, the overall tax liability of Parentco and its subsidiary may be minimized.

Conversely, if Hungarian Parentco is a foreign corporation which manufactures the tractor parts and sells them to Subco, a U.S. corporation, which resells the tractor parts throughout the United States, Subco might pay $150,000 to Parentco. Parentco would report a $90,000 gain which normally would escape U.S. taxation, and Subco would report $0. Because Parentco and Subco are related, the amount paid by Subco to Parentco is artificial because the amount paid remains within the controlled group. But in the absence of a remedial provision, the tax savings achieved by manipulating prices can be significant.

Incorrect transfer pricing can easily lead to international double taxation. Suppose that in Table 1 below, country A (*e.g.,* the United States) under its transfer pricing rules determines that in addition to the $200 reported as income, an additional $400 of income reported by a foreign subsidiary in country B is really taxable in the United States. Assume that country B does not agree and continues to tax the $800 of income reported on the return. The results are as follows:

Table 1 - Detrimental Impact of Double Taxation on Effective Tax Rate (ETR)	Parent (Country A)	Subsidiary (Country B)	Consolidated
Total profit reported on tax return	200	800	1,000
Tax rate	40%	40%	
Tax liability before Country A transfer pricing adjustment	80	320	400
Global ETR			40%
Double taxation effect on ETR			
Total profit after 400 Country A adjustment	600	800	1,000
Tax rate	40%	40%	
Tax liability after Country A transfer pricing adjustment	240	320	560
Global ETR			56%

The other side of the coin is that more accurate transfer pricing can be used to lower effective tax rates. In Table 2, incorrect transfer pricing might result in $600 of additional taxable income in country A where it really should be taxable income in country B. Doing the transfer pricing correctly can lead to a significant effective tax rate reduction—from 34 percent to 16 percent.

Table 2 - Potential Benefit of Transfer Pricing on Global Effective Tax Rate (ETR)	Parent (Country A)	Subsidiary (Country B)	Consolidated
Total profit reported on tax return	800	200	1,000
Tax rate	40%	10%	
Tax liability before change to transfer price	320	20	340
Global ETR			34%
ETR Effect of Transfer Pricing Change			
Total profit after using transfer pricing to shift 400 of income	200	800	1,000
Tax rate	40%	10%	
Tax liability after 400 transfer pricing change	80	80	160
Global ETR			16%

Transfer pricing addressed in I.R.C. § 482 represents the policies and procedures associated with the way in which a company prices goods, services, and intangibles transferred within an organization. From an international tax standpoint, transfer pricing concerns itself with transactions between affiliates domiciled in different taxing jurisdictions. Transfer pricing is significant for both taxpayers and tax administrations because it affects the allocation of profits from intra-group transactions, which impacts the income and expenses reported, and therefore taxable profits of related companies that operate in different taxing jurisdictions. One of the most challenging issues that arise from an international tax perspective is determining income and expenses that can reasonably be considered to arise within a territory.

Taxing authorities as well as multinational enterprises ("MNEs") continue to pay increasing attention to transfer pricing. It is not only large MNEs, but potentially every company engaging in cross-border transactions with related parties that must focus on transfer pricing. An issue under I.R.C. § 482 can arise when related parties are involved in any of the following situations:

- Sales and/or purchases of tangible property;
- Sales and/or use of intangible property;
- Provision and/or receipt of services or know-how;

- Joint development of intangibles with a related party, or
- Loans and guarantees.

Transfer pricing examinations by tax authorities can lead to tax adjustments and even penalties. Over 50 countries have enacted transfer pricing documentation rules.

§ 9.02   ARM'S LENGTH PRINCIPLE

The increase in the globalization of businesses has meant that tax authorities and MNEs are facing ever more complex tax issues that could potentially cause double or less than single taxation. The "arm's length principle" attempts to measure the value of a transaction "as if" the parties do not have the relationship between them that, in fact, exists (*i.e.,* as if the related parties were independent, unrelated parties). Thus, the profits subject to tax in a particular jurisdiction would not be impacted by the fact that a relationship does exist between the parties.

The arm's length standard has been adopted by the Organization for Cooperation and Economic Development ("OECD") and is the standard used globally to resolve transfer pricing disputes with the dual purpose of safeguarding each jurisdiction's tax base and avoiding the imposition of double tax on taxpayers.

The arm's length principle has received a tremendous amount of scrutiny from scholars and practitioners. The literature surrounding the arm's length principle yields two main conclusions. First, there is little reason to expect that observations of actual arm's length prices even exist for most goods traded by multinational corporations. Second, in cases where such direct arm's length price observations are unavailable, profit based applications of the arm's length principle yield, at best, a range of prices within which any price could be characterized as an arm's length price. This latter conclusion is referred to as the "continuum price problem," and is considered the source of many lengthy and expensive disputes between governmental authorities and taxpayers.

§ 9.03 CONTROLLED AND UNCONTROLLED TRANSACTIONS

Uncontrolled transactions are those business transactions that take place between two unrelated entities and involve the sale or purchase of tangible or intangible property or the provision of services. These transactions are also referred to as "unrelated" or "third-party" transactions.

Transactions that take place between related entities that sell or purchase tangible or intangible property or provide services are considered "controlled" transactions, and are the focus of transfer pricing analysis. These transactions are also referred to as "related party" transactions.

There is no objective definition of control under I.R.C. § 482 or the regulations thereunder. Control is a matter that is determined based on the totality of facts and circumstances and includes any kind of control, direct or indirect, whether legally enforceable or whether exercisable or exercised. Therefore, control is not limited to legal ownership, but depends on all the facts and circumstances.

§ 9.04 OVERVIEW OF TRANSFER PRICING METHODOLOGIES

The two approaches generally used to assess whether cross-border, related party transactions produce arm's length results are: 1) transaction-based methodologies; and 2) profit-based methodologies. Transaction-based methods require the identification of prices or margins from individual transactions or groups of transactions involving related entities, and comparing these results to the price or margin information involving independent third parties. The profit-based methods seek to benchmark the profits earned by controlled entities and unrelated parties performing similar functions and incurring similar risks.

The transaction-based methods include the Comparable Uncontrolled Price ("CUP") method, the Comparable Uncontrolled Transaction ("CUT") method (essentially, the CUP method applied to intangibles), the resale price method ("RPM"), and the cost plus method. The profit-based methods include the profit split and the Comparable Profits Method (CPM)/Transactional Net Margin Method ("TNMM[2]").

---

[2] The TNMM is CPM's counterpart under the OECD Transfer Pricing Guidelines.

The U.S. regulations specify the following methods to analyze tangible property transactions: CUP, Resale Price, Cost Plus, Profit Split (Comparable and Residual), and Comparable Profits Method. To analyze intangible property transactions, the U.S. regulations specify: CUT, Profit Split (Comparable and Residual), and CPM.

The OECD Guidelines specify the following methods: CUP, Resale Price, Cost Plus, Profit Split (Comparable and Residual), and TNMM.

§ 9.05 TRANSACTION-BASED METHODOLOGIES

(A) COMPARABLE UNCONTROLLED PRICE METHOD

The Comparable Uncontrolled Price ("CUP") method compares the amounts charged in controlled transactions with the amounts charged in comparable third party transactions. Comparable uncontrolled transactions may be between two unrelated parties or between one of the related parties and an unrelated party. The CUP method is generally the most reliable measure of an arm's length result if the transaction is identical, or if only minor readily quantifiable differences exist for which appropriate adjustments are made.

The CUP method requires a high degree of comparability of products and functions. Comparability can be enhanced by making adjustments to the prices being compared, said adjustments seek to control for the effect that the quantifiable differences referred above have on the prices. Adjustments likely to be required include adjustments for differences in:

- product quality;
- sales volume;
- contractual terms (such as payment terms, shipping liability, etc.);
- geographic market;
- embedded intangibles; and
- foreign currency risks.

For illustrative purposes, consider an example where a parent company ("Canco"), located in Canada manufactures "product X". Canco sells product X to both related ("USCO") and unrelated distributors in the United States and the circumstances surrounding the controlled and uncontrolled transactions are substantially the same. Under the CUP method, if Canco sells product X to the unrelated distributors for $10/unit, then Canco should sell product X to USCO at the same price, *i.e.,* $10/unit, to satisfy the arm's length principle. However, assume that Canco arranges for and pays to ship product X to USCO whereas the unrelated entities pick up product X directly from Canco's manufacturing facility. Because Canco performs more activities for USCO than it does for the unrelated parties, it should be compensated accordingly. Assuming the additional compensation Canco should receive for performing the additional activities equals $1/unit, then Canco should charge USCO $11/unit.

CUP Example

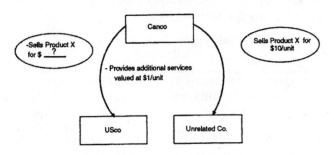

The price to USco should be $11/unit which equals the price to unrelated Co. plus the cost of providing additional services.

In practice, there may be more than one comparable transaction, which would result in a range of potentially arm's length results rather than an individual result.

(B) COMPARABLE UNCONTROLLED TRANSACTION METHOD

The Comparable Uncontrolled Transaction ("CUT") method compares the amount charged in a controlled transfer of intangible property to the amount charged in a comparable uncontrolled transaction. Essentially, it is the CUP method applied to intangibles. An intangible is defined as an asset that comprises of any of the following items and has a substantial value independent of the services of any individual:

- Patents, inventions, formulae, processes, designs, patterns, or know-how;
- Copyrights and literary, musical, or artistic compositions;
- Trademarks, trade names, or brand names;
- Franchises, licenses, or contracts;
- Methods, programs, systems, procedures, campaigns, surveys, studies, forecasts, estimates, customer lists, or technical data; and
- Other similar items.

For purposes of applying the CUT method, comparable intangible property must be used in connection with similar products or processes, within the same general industry or market, and have similar profit potential. Profit potential ideally is measured by the net present value of the benefits from the intangible based on prospective extraordinary revenues to be realized or costs to be saved. However, under Reg. § 1.482–4 more subjective factors may be considered to determine profit potential, such as:

- the terms of transfer, including the exploitation rights granted in the intangible, the exclusive or nonexclusive character of any rights granted, and any restrictions in use including limits on the geographic area in which the rights may be exploited;
- stage of development of the intangible;

- right to receive periodic updates, revisions, or modifications of the intangible;

- duration of license, contract or other agreement and any termination or renegotiation rights;

- uniqueness of the property and the period for which it remains unique;

- economic or product liability risks assumed by the transferee;

- exclusivity;

- existence and extent of collateral transactions or ongoing business relationships between the transferee and the transferor; and

- the functions performed by the transferor and transferee.

In this CUT example, assume that Foreign Parent ("FP"), located in the U.K., licenses the use of its trademark/trade name to USCO, a related party located in the U.S. In addition, FP also licenses the use of the same trademark/trade name to an Unrelated Co. located in the U.S. at the rate of 4.0 percent of sales. The circumstances affecting USCO and Unrelated Co. are similar, as are their license terms. Thus, the royalty rate between FP and USCO is comparable to the royalty paid by Unrelated Co. to FP and should be priced accordingly.

CUT Example

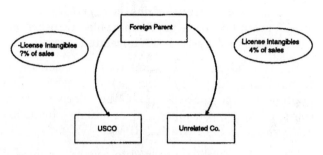

The royalty paid by US co should be equal the royalty paid by Unrelated Co.

(C) RESALE PRICE METHOD

The resale price method ("RPM") compares the gross margin earned in the controlled transaction to the gross margins earned in comparable uncontrolled transactions. The RPM is most often used for distributors that resell products without physically altering or adding substantial value. Under this method, the arm's length price at which a distributor would purchase finished products from a related party is determined by subtracting the appropriate gross profit from the applicable resale price of the property involved in the controlled transaction.

The RPM requires detailed comparisons of functions performed, risks borne, and contractual terms of controlled and uncontrolled transactions. A higher degree of comparability is more likely to exist between controlled and uncontrolled transactions involving the same reseller (*i.e.,* internal RPM), in which case the appropriate gross profit to be earned in the controlled transactions is derived from the gross profit earned in comparable transactions between the taxpayer and an unrelated party.

In the absence of comparable uncontrolled transactions involving the same reseller, an appropriate comparison may be derived from comparable uncontrolled transactions involving other resellers (*i.e.,* external RPM).

The RPM is unlikely to lead to accurate results if there are significant differences in the:

- level of market for which the products are being sold;
- functions performed;
- type of products; or
- embedded intangibles.

A reasonable number of adjustments may be made to compensate for the lack of comparability between controlled and uncontrolled transactions including:

- inventory turnover;
- contractual terms;
- transportation costs; and
- other measurable differences.

Returning to the previous example of Canco and USCO, assume that USCO buys teddy bears from Canco and it complements its product portfolio with toy racing cars purchased from unrelated manufacturers. Although each of the individual products is similar to one another (*i.e.,* both are children's toys), they are not exactly the same. Assume that no reasonable and objective adjustments could be made to the unit prices to eliminate the effect of such differences and establish a comparable price.

To apply the RPM, compare the gross margins earned by USCO on products purchased from Canco to the gross margins earned by USCO on products purchased from the unrelated manufacturers. Other factors to consider in such an analysis would be the similarity of the terms and conditions, the volumes purchased, and the market conditions faced by Canco and the unrelated manufacturers. USCO's gross margins on purchases of racing cars from unrelated manufacturers form an arm's length range of gross margins. For example, consider the following gross margins resulting from USCO's purchases of toy racing cars from five manufacturers under terms comparable with those in purchases from Canco:

Unrelated Manufacturer 1	29%
Unrelated Manufacturer 2	32%
Unrelated Manufacturer 3	33%
Unrelated Manufacturer 4	35%
Unrelated Manufacturer 5	36%

The interquartile range (*i.e.,* the middle 50 percent of returns observed among the comparable companies) of gross margins would be 32% to 35%, with a median of 33%. Thus, to satisfy the arm' length principle, USCO's purchases of teddy bears from its related parties should be set at a price that will allow USCO to earn a gross margin of between 32% and 35% on the sale to third party customers.

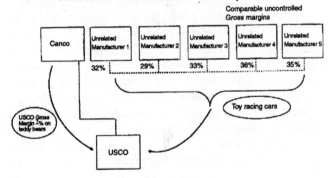

Resale Price Method Example

(D) COST PLUS METHOD

The cost plus method (*see* Reg. § 1.482–3) compares gross margins of controlled and uncontrolled transactions. Under this method, the arm's length sales price to a related party is determined by adding the appropriate gross profit to the controlled taxpayer's cost of producing the property involved in the controlled transaction. The cost plus method is most often used to assess the mark-up earned by manufacturers selling to related parties.

The cost plus method requires detailed comparisons of the goods produced, functions performed, risks borne, manufacturing complexity, cost structures and embedded intangibles between controlled and uncontrolled transactions. Higher comparability is most likely found among controlled and uncontrolled sales of property by the same seller (*i.e.,* internal cost plus method). In the absence of such transactions, an appropriate comparison may be derived from comparable uncontrolled transactions involving other producers (*i.e.,* external cost plus method).

The cost plus method is less likely to be reliable if material differences exist between the controlled and uncontrolled transactions with respect to:

- intangibles;
- cost structure;
- business experience;
- management efficiency;
- functions performed; and
- products.

A reasonable number of adjustments may be made to compensate for the lack of comparability between controlled and uncontrolled transactions including:

- inventory turnover;
- contractual terms; and
- transportation costs and
- other measurable differences.

The degree of consistency in accounting practices between the controlled transaction and the uncontrolled comparables that materially affect the gross profit mark-up will impact the reliability of the result. For example, if differences in inventory and other cost accounting practices would materially affect the gross profit mark-up, the ability to make objective adjustments for such differences would materially impact the reliability of the result. Further, the controlled transaction and the comparable uncontrolled transaction should be consistent in the reporting of costs between cost of goods sold and operating expenses.

Consider the following fact pattern, in which USCO manufactures similar but not identical products both for Canco and for unrelated parties. In both cases, USCO acts as a contract manufacturer which means, in general, that USCO does not undertake sales and marketing activities; it does not develop its own products, and typically uses patents and designs owned by the purchaser. Further, USCO does not assume significant inventory and production planning risks.

Application of the cost plus method requires a comparison of the gross profits generated relative to the manufacturing costs (gross costs) incurred based on sales to Canco and unrelated companies. For example, consider the gross mark-ups realized by USCO when selling products manufactured for five different unrelated parties:

Unrelated Co1	42%
Unrelated Co2	45%
Unrelated Co3	41%
Unrelated Co4	44%
Unrelated Co5	39%

The interquartile range of gross mark-ups would be 41% to 44%, with a median of 42%. This indicates that USCO needs to earn a gross mark-up between 41% and 44% for transactions with Canco to satisfy the arm's length principle. Any result outside this range would indicate the need for an adjustment to the current transfer pricing.

Cost Plus Method Example

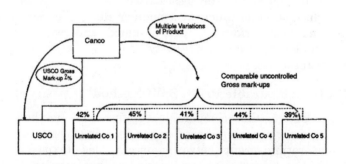

§ 9.06   PROFIT-BASED METHODOLOGIES

Given the high degree of comparability required to apply the transactional methods, these methods are not used as frequently as the profit based methods unless reliable internal data are available. Arm's length references may be derived from transactions between third parties for which public data is available. However, one must pay close attention to potential differences between the controlled and uncontrolled transactions which could impact the condition being examined (*i.e.,* the gross margin earned by the taxpayer), a common example of such differences are inconsistencies in the reporting of costs between cost of goods sold and operating expenses.

(A) PROFIT SPLIT METHODS

The profit split methods allocate the combined operating profits or losses from controlled transactions in proportion to the relative contributions made by each party in creating the combined profits or losses. Relative contributions must be determined in a manner that reflects the functions performed, risks assumed, and resources employed by each party to the controlled transaction.

(1) Comparable Profit Split Method

Under the comparable profit split method, transfer prices are based on the division of combined operating profit between uncontrolled taxpayers whose transactions and activities are similar to those of the controlled taxpayers in the relevant business activity. Under this method, the uncontrolled parties' shares of the combined operating profit or loss is used to allocate the combined operating profit or loss of the relevant business activity between the related parties.

This method is not often used because it is extremely difficult to find two companies in an uncontrolled circumstance with similar functions, risks, and transactions as well as detailed information on how they allocate the business' profits between them.

(2) Residual Profit Split Method

The residual profit split method involves two steps. First, operating income is allocated to each party in the controlled transactions to provide a market return for their routine contributions to the relevant business activity. Second, any residual profit or loss is divided among the controlled parties based on the relative value of their contributions of any valuable intangible property to the relevant business activity. This method is particularly suited to transactions involving highly profitable intangibles that are contributed by more than one party to the transaction.

Consider the following example where both the manufacturer and the distributor contribute to the development of intangible property. In this example, assume that the manufacturer's product is recognized by the industry as a better quality product than any competitors and therefore can command a higher price among consumers. In addition, the distributor has access to a comprehensive distribution network and through its expertise in the local market designs marketing campaigns that appeal to the particular characteristics of its target consumers and is able to more effectively convey to its customers the benefits of the product's superior quality. The distributor's increased market coverage generates sales high enough to allow the manufacturer to operate at very high levels of utilization that it would otherwise not have access to on its own, in addition, the localized marketing effort contributes to the higher price that the products command in that market. For purposes of this example, assume that the total operating profit available for these transactions is $100.

(a) Step 1—Allocate Routine Returns

The first step is to allocate routine returns for the manufacturing and distribution activities undertaken by each company respectively. Routine returns are the profitability levels that the manufacturing and distribution companies would earn absent the intangibles used in the manufacture and distribution of the product. For simplicity, assume that the routine profit associated with the distribution activities is $18 and that the routine profit associated with the manufacturing activities is $22. Assume that these profit levels (derived from "profit level indicators" discussed below) were computed comparing the operating margin (operating profit divided by sales) and mark-up on total costs earned by comparable distributors and manufacturers, respectively. This would leave $60 ($100–$18–$22) of profit remaining to be split between the distributor and manufacturer based on their relative contributions from valuable intangible property.

Profit level indicators are financial ratios that measure the relationships among profits, costs incurred and resources employed. For example, the rate of return on capital employed is the ratio of operating profit to operating assets.

(b)   Step 2—Allocate Non-Routine Returns

There are various ways to allocate the non-routine returns, but generally, the method used should quantitatively reflect the relative value of non-routine contributions made by each party involved in the transaction. For this example, the relative "value-adding" costs incurred by each party are taken into account. For the distributor, the example includes the costs of the senior sales, marketing, and customer service personnel, as well as costs incurred to launch various campaigns that have proven successful for the company. Assume these costs total $5. For the manufacturer, the example includes the costs of the quality control department, as well as the senior management of the engineering area. Assume these costs total $8.

Therefore, the total cost associated with generating the residual returns is $13. The relative split of residual profits is calculated as follows:

Manufacturer's Contribution	8/13 = 61.5%
Distributor's Contribution	5/13 = 38.5%
Total Residual	$60
Manufacturer's Share of Residual	61.5% * $60 = $36.9
Distributor's Share of Residual	38.5% * $60 = $23.1

(B) COMPARABLE PROFITS METHOD

The Comparable Profits Method ("CPM") evaluates whether the amount charged in a controlled transaction is at arm's length by comparing the profitability of one of the entities involved in the controlled transaction (the "tested party") to that of companies that are comparable in terms of functions performed, risks borne and assets employed. The tested party should not use intangible property or unique assets that distinguish it from unrelated comparable companies.

The degree of comparability between the tested party and the comparable company affects the reliability of the CPM analysis. Reliability may also be adversely affected by varying cost structures, differences in business experience, or differences in management efficiency. However, less functional comparability is required for reliable results than under the transactional methods (*e.g.,* the CUP method, the RPM, or the cost plus method). In addition, less product similarity is required for reliable results under the CPM than under the transactional methods.

The comparable profits method examines the operating profit margin relative to an appropriate base (*e.g.,* costs, sales, assets), in contrast with the RPM and Cost Plus both of which examine gross profits. In this regard, the CPM is less sensitive to differences in accounting classifications between costs and expense items between the tested party and the comparable companies.

The fact that the reliability of results under the CPM is, relatively, less dependent on product and functional comparability and less sensitive to inconsistencies in accounting practices means that this is the transfer pricing method most frequently used by tax payers as it commonly allows for a broader sample of arm's length references.

Adjustments that may be required include those for differences in:

- accounting classifications;
- credit terms;
- inventory;
- currency risk; and
- business circumstances.

To illustrate, assume that USCO's Foreign Parent ("FP") sources and manufactures semi-finished vehicle parts (the "Subassemblies") and sells the Subassemblies to USCO. USCO, in turn, USCO assembles and distributes the finished vehicles in the United States. FP does not allow unrelated parties to assemble its vehicles. USCO's does not own any valuable intangibles associated with the manufacturing process or product, and FP owns all valuable intangibles and conducts additional research to increase manufacturing efficiencies. USCO's responsibility is to assemble the vehicles and distribute them to customers located in the United States. Assume that USCO is the tested party in this transaction.

Given this fact pattern, the return on assets (or operating profits relative assets employed) is used to analyze the company's intercompany pricing. Assume the identification of five comparable companies with their return on assets as set forth below.

Unrelated Co1	4.7%
Unrelated Co2	6.1%
Unrelated Co3	7.2%
Unrelated Co4	5.8%
Unrelated Co5	2.5%

The interquartile range is 4.7% to 6.1% with a median of 5.8%. This indicates that USCO needs to earn a return on assets between 4.7% and 6.1% for its transactions with FP to satisfy the arm's length principle. Any result outside this range would indicate the need for an adjustment to the current price at which the company purchases the Subassemblies.

Comparable Profits Method Example

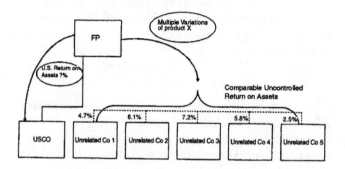

§ 9.07   OTHER KEY FEATURES UNDER
I.R.C. § 482 AND THE REGULATIONS

I.R.C. § 482 which has been in the U.S. Code in one form or another since 1917, is intended to insure that transactions between related taxpayers take place on an "arm's length" basis that is consistent with transactions between two independent parties.

The purpose of I.R.C. § 482 is to ensure that taxpayers clearly reflect income attributable to controlled transactions, and to prevent the avoidance of taxes with respect to such transactions. The United States Treasury Regulations for I.R.C. § 482 provide a detailed guide to the implementation of the arm's length principle.

(A) BEST METHOD RULE

The arm's length result of a controlled transaction must be determined under the method that provides the most reliable measure of the arm's length result. There is no strict priority of methods, and no method will invariably be considered to be more reliable than the others. Reg. § 1.482–1(c).

The following factors are taken into account when determining the best method: (i) the degree of comparability between the controlled and uncontrolled transactions; and (ii) the quality of the data and assumptions used in the analysis.

The degree of comparability is assessed by:

- functions;
- contractual terms;
- risks;
- economic conditions; and
- nature of goods and services supplied.

The quality of data and assumptions is assessed by:

- completeness and accuracy of data;
- reliability of assumptions; and
- sensitivity of results to deficiencies in data and assumptions.

(B) ARM'S LENGTH RANGE

As a result of the application of any of the specified transfer pricing methods the taxpayer may arrive at a single arm's length reference if it is determined that a single uncontrolled transaction presents a high enough degree of comparability or if a number of comparable uncontrolled transactions derive in the same arm's length reference. However, more often than not the application of the methods derives in a number of results all of which could reasonably be considered as arm's length. In such cases, Reg. § 1.482–1(e)(2)(iii)(C) requires reliability of the analysis to be increased by adjusting the range through the application of a statistical method (*e.g.,* the interquartile range discussed above). Put simply, the interquartile range represents the middle 50 percent of prices or returns observed in the uncontrolled transactions.

(C) COMPARABILITY ANALYSIS

The regulations generally require use of the interquartile range to increase the reliability of the comparison unless there are sufficient data to identify, and to make adjustments to eliminate the effects of, all material differences between the tested party and the comparable companies.

Because a transaction is evaluated by comparing the results of the controlled transaction to the results of the uncontrolled transaction, factors that could affect prices or profits must be included in the analysis and adjustments made where warranted. The regulations under Reg. § 1.482–1(d)(3) indicate five factors that would be considered:

- Functional analysis;
- Contractual terms;

- Risk;
- Economic conditions; and
- Property and services.

(1) Functional Analysis

The functional analysis requires an understanding of the functions performed and associated resources employed (*e.g.*, plant and equipment, use of "valuable intangibles"). The functional analysis identifies the significant activities of the related parties and may include:

- Research and development;
- Product design and engineering;
- Manufacturing, production, and process engineering;
- Purchasing and materials management;
- Marketing and distribution functions, including inventory management, warranty administration, and advertising activities;
- Transportation and warehousing; and
- Managerial, legal, accounting and finance, credit and collection, training, and personnel management services.

(2) Contractual Terms

Contractual terms that could result in adjustments to the transfer price include:

- The form of consideration charged or paid;
- Sales or purchase volume;

- The scope and terms of warranties provided;
- Rights to updates, revisions, or modifications;
- The duration of relevant license, contract, or other agreements, and termination or renegotiation rights;
- Collateral transactions or ongoing business relationships between the buyer and the seller, including arrangements for the provision of ancillary or subsidiary services; and
- Extension of credit and payment terms.

If the terms of the agreement are written and made in advance, then these terms will be respected as long as they are consistent with the economic substance of the underlying transactions. However, greatest weight will be given to the actual conduct of the parties. If there is no written agreement, the IRS may impute a contractual agreement between the controlled taxpayers.

(3) Risk

The third factor defines significant risk that could affect prices or profits. Relevant risks to consider include:

- Market risk, including fluctuations in cost, demand pricing and inventory levels;
- Risks associated with the success or failure of research and development activities;

- Financial risks, including fluctuations in foreign currency rates of exchange and interest rates;
- Credit and collection risks;
- Product liability risks; and
- General business risks related to the ownership of property, plant, and equipment.

(4) Economic Conditions

The fourth factor is economic conditions—which requires an evaluation of the significant economic conditions that could affect the prices that would be charged or paid, or the profit earned in each transaction.

(5) Property or Services

The fifth factor focuses on an evaluation of property or services transferred with the transaction. The comparison includes any embedded intangibles, physical likeness, or similarity of the terms.

(D) SELECTION OF THE TESTED PARTY

Under I.R.C. § 482 regulations, the tested party (*e.g.,* in a sales transaction the related seller or related purchaser) will be the participant in the controlled transactions whose operating profit attributable to the controlled transactions can be verified using the most reliable data and requiring the fewest and most reliable adjustments, and for which reliable data regarding uncontrolled comparable companies can be located. Generally, the tested party is the party with the least complex functions and does not own valuable intangibles.

(E) MULTIPLE YEAR DATA

Data from multiple years usually must be considered when applying CPM. Generally three years (the tested year and the two preceding years) of data are used for the tested party and the comparable companies unless the specific facts of the case warrant a longer or shorter period (*i.e.,* such as the effect of business cycles in the tested party's industry or effect of the life cycles of product or intangible). If the tested party's results fall within the interquartile range for the appropriate averaging period, it is deemed to have satisfied the requirements of CPM. If the tested party multiple year results fall outside the interquartile range for the appropriate averaging period, the tested party's and comparable companies single year results are used to determine any adjustment.

(F) PERIODIC ADJUSTMENTS

Payments to a related party for a license or transfer of an intangible must be "commensurate with the income" attributable to the intangible. I.R.C. § 482 (second sentence). The practical effect of the "commensurate with income" language is that royalty arrangements between related parties can be periodically adjusted by the IRS to reflect changing market conditions. A taxpayer should also manage its valuable intangible assets proactively and modify its intercompany royalty rate as these assets gain or lose value.

For example, royalty payments deemed received by a U.S. corporation from intangible property licensed to its foreign subsidiary might be adjusted periodically to reflect how the property actually performs in the hands of the licensee. If five or ten years after the original license the intangible becomes extremely valuable, that increase in value (*i.e.,* increased sublicensing royalties or increased sales of property incorporating the intangible) may be taxable to the licensor even if the royalty rates at the time of the original license were reasonable under the facts known at that time. This provision represents an extraordinary view of what an arm's length transaction is—substituting an ex post determination for an ex ante determination. The fact that a royalty agreement at the time it was concluded provided for arm's length payments does not guarantee that an adjustment will not be made in a subsequent year. Reg. § 1.482–4(f)(2).

There are some protections from the periodic adjustments rule. If the CUT method was used to determine an "arm's length" royalty in year 1 and the intangible transfer in the uncontrolled transaction was made under substantially the same circumstances as those in the controlled transaction, no adjustment may be made in a subsequent year. Reg. § 1.482–4(f)(2)(ii)(A). For example, if a U.S. pharmaceutical company licenses a patented drug to an unrelated manufacturer for use in country Y on an arm's length basis and grants a substantially identical license of the patent to P's subsidiary in country X, no adjustment will be made for a subsequent year under the "commensurate with income" standard. Reg. § 1.482–4(c)(4)(iii) Ex. 1.

If the CUT method is used with respect to an uncontrolled transfer of a different but comparable intangible, no later adjustment will be made if certain specified requirements are met, including a finding that the aggregate profits actually earned (or cost savings realized) by the controlled taxpayer from the exploitation of the intangible are not less than 80 percent nor more than 120 percent of the prospective profits (or cost savings) that were foreseeable when the comparability of the uncontrolled agreement was established. Where the arm's length royalty in year 1 is determined under a method other than CUT, there are more stringent requirements in order to prevent a subsequent adjustment under the "commensurate with income" standard.

§ 9.08   PENALTIES

The I.R.C. § 6662 regulations were drafted at least partially as a result of *United States v. Derr*, 968 F.2d 943 (9th Cir. 1992). The IRS requested certain financial data from Chevron. In response to this request, Chevron supplied over one million pages of documents to the IRS. As one might speculate, this response created a lengthy confrontational process, as well as large legal fees. Finalization of the I.R.C. § 6662 regulations effectively shifted the burden of providing transfer pricing documentation from the IRS to the taxpayer.

The purpose of the I.R.C. § 6662 penalty regulations as stated in the preamble is to encourage taxpayers to make a serious effort to comply with the "arm's length" standard. The preamble follows by stating its intent for taxpayers to report arm's length results on their tax returns. A taxpayer's last two obligations under I.R.C. § 6662 are to document its transfer pricing analysis in a formal report and be prepared to provide this documentation to the IRS upon request.

Taxpayers may avoid penalties by meeting the contemporaneous documentation requirements under Reg. § 1.6662–6(d). These regulations require contemporaneous documentation (documentation in existence at the time the taxpayer file its tax return) that shows that the taxpayer reasonably concluded that the transfer pricing methodology chosen and its application provide the most reliable measure of an arm's-length result under the best method rule. Taxpayers must be able to explain how they selected their pricing method and the reasons for their rejection of other possible methods.

If a taxpayer does not have contemporaneous documentation and the IRS concludes that a transfer pricing adjustment is appropriate, the taxpayer may be subject to the following penalties:

	Transactional	**Net Adjustment**
Substantial Valuation Misstatement (20% Penalty of the Underpayment of Tax)	Price or value is 200% or more (50% or less) than the correct amount	Net adjustment exceeds the lessor of $5 million or 10% of gross receipts
Gross Valuation Misstatement (40% Penalty of the Underpayment of Tax)	Price or value is 400% or more (25% or less) than the correct amount	Net adjustment exceeds the lessor of $20 million or 20% of gross receipts

The transactional penalty tests a specific transaction and there is no netting of transactions, while the net adjustment penalty is based on the net Section 482 adjustments, which are the sum of all increases in taxable income less any decreases in taxable income.

§ 9.09 APPLICATION OF I.R.C. § 482 PRINCIPLES

(A) CUSTOMS CONSIDERATIONS

Aside from the application of I.R.C. § 482, there is a special rule to prevent a U.S. purchaser from inflating the price paid to a related foreign corporation in order to minimize the gain on eventual resale. I.R.C. § 1059A now prevents a U.S. purchaser of inventory from a related party from taking as its basis for determining gain on resale an amount greater than the price used in determining the amount of customs duties. While this provision may bring a certain consistency, it may not end attempts to shift income abroad. Some taxpayers may prefer to pay higher customs duties in order to inflate basis for income tax purposes.

(B)   OTHER I.R.C. § 482 ADJUSTMENTS

Where the IRS makes an adjustment under I.R.C. § 482 to the income of one related party, a correlative adjustment must also be made to the income of the other related party. Reg. § 1.482–1(g)(2). For example, if U.S. Co. sells property to Subco, a foreign corporation, and the IRS adjusts the purchase price upwards under I.R.C. § 482, an adjustment downwards should be made for the income recognized by the related purchaser on the ultimate sale of the property to unrelated purchasers. Or if U.S. Co. makes an interest-free loan to Subco, the interest imputed to U.S. Co. should be treated as interest paid by Subco for purposes of determining whether Subco has an interest deduction under I.R.C. § 163.

In a domestic context, such correlative adjustments usually mean an increase in the tax liability of one party and a decrease in the tax liability of the other party. In an international context, the United States may not have tax jurisdiction over a related party resident in a foreign country. However, to the extent that the income of a foreign corporation is relevant for U.S. tax purposes (*e.g.*, for purposes of determining the indirect foreign tax credit), the earnings and profits account of the related foreign corporation reflects the correlative adjustments.

Suppose that U.S. Co. only charges Subco, a foreign corporation, $10,000 for property Subco purchases from U.S. Co. instead of $15,000, the arm's length price. If the IRS allocates $5,000 of additional income to U.S. Co., U.S. Co. will not have in fact received the extra $5,000 from Subco. The IRS has administratively ruled that a taxpayer to whom income is allocated may receive a dividend from the related party in the year of the I.R.C. § 482 allocation which is excludable from U.S. income if the transaction which gave rise to the I.R.C. § 482 adjustment did not have as one its principal purposes the avoidance of U.S. federal income tax. Rev. Proc. 99–32, 1999–2 C.B. 296. Alternatively, the taxpayer can set up an account receivable on its books which can then be paid by the related party with no further tax consequence.

As children we are often taught that "two wrongs don't make a right." That is not always the case in tax law. A taxpayer can avoid a proposed adjustment under I.R.C. § 482 in some cases by showing that it engaged in other transactions not at arm's length to their detriment. For example, if Parentco overcharges Subco for services by $25,000, but also permits Subco free use of property with a fair rental value of $25,000, no I.R.C. § 482 adjustment is warranted. Reg. § 1.482–1(g)(4) Ex. 1.

(C) I.R.C. § 482 AND FOREIGN TAX CREDIT

When an I.R.C. § 482 adjustment is made increasing the amount of income taxable to a U.S. corporation and decreasing the amount of a related foreign corporation's income, the adjustment may have an effect on the foreign tax credit. For example, if U.S. Co. received a dividend from Subco that carries with it an indirect tax credit under I.R.C. § 902, a reallocation of income from Subco to U.S. Co. may decrease the amount of foreign taxes paid by Subco which can be credited by U.S. Co. However, unless the foreign country recognizes the reallocation and refunds any taxes collected, the reallocation may increase U.S. taxes without any correlative decrease in foreign taxes.

U.S. Co. may still be able to claim the full indirect tax credit under I.R.C. § 902 even on the reallocated income if U.S. Co. can establish that Subco has exhausted its administrative remedies in seeking a refund of the foreign taxes on the reallocated income. Otherwise, the foreign taxes paid on the reallocated income are treated as a contribution to the foreign government not qualifying for the foreign tax credit.

(D) I.R.C. § 482 AND U.S. TREATIES

Suppose that UKCo is a U.K. holding company that owns 100 percent of the stock of IrishCo, an Irish manufacturing company. IrishCo manufactures computer storage devices which it manufactures for $100. IrishCo sells the devices to USCo, a wholly-owned U.S. corporation, which resells to unrelated distributors for $200. Which country gets to tax the $100 profit? Ireland might claim that the arm's length price for the sale to USCo is $200 so that all of the profit is taxable in Ireland. The United States might claim that the arm's length price should be $100, so that the $100 profit is taxable in the United States. Finally, the United Kingdom might argue that both Ireland and the United States are wrong. The arm's length price ought to be $150. Moreover in the view of the United Kingdom, IrishCo ought to be deemed to have paid a $50 royalty to UKCo for various manufacturing intangibles (*e.g.,* patents, knowhow), and the USCo ought to be deemed to pay a $50 royalty to UKCo for various marketing intangibles (*e.g.,* trademarks, customer lists). Under this U.K. view, the United Kingdom should be able to tax the $100 profit. Hopefully, the three countries involved will be able to resolve their differences, often through the mutual agreement procedures in the applicable treaties, so that the related taxpayers do not have to confront $300 of taxable income when only $100 of net income was earned. Unfortunately, sometimes agreement cannot be reached and a taxpayer faces multiple taxation of the same income. This example highlights the importance of performing transfer pricing analysis and even entering into legal agreements that further support a company's intended intercompany policy.

Under Article 9 (Associated Enterprises) of the U.S. Model Income Tax Treaty (*see   supra* § 5.05(D)(1)), each contracting state is authorized to determine the income of persons subject to its taxing jurisdiction on an arm's length basis in any situation where related parties make intercorporate arrangements which would not be made between independent enterprises. Generally, the standards under I.R.C. § 482 do not violate the associated enterprises article of most treaties, although most treaties do not explicitly recognize a profit split as a legitimate method of allocating profits. Under most treaties, if the United States makes a reallocation, the other country agrees to make corresponding adjustments if it agrees with the allocation. If the other country does not agree with the reallocation of income, the two countries agree to reach a compromise under the mutual agreement procedures contained in the treaty. If the countries fail to reach a compromise, a taxpayer may confront international double taxation as a result of the failure to agree.

§ 9.10   ADVANCE PRICING AGREEMENTS

In an effort to ensure compliance with I.R.C. § 482, and at the same time provide taxpayers with some certainty in planning their business transactions, the IRS has set forth procedures for obtaining an "advance pricing agreement" (APA). Rev. Proc. 2006–9, 2006–1 C.B. 278, as modified by Rev. Proc. 2008–31, 2008–1 C.B. 1133. Several countries have adopted procedures for taxpayers to enter into bilateral or multilateral APAs. An APA is a binding agreement between the IRS and a taxpayer and applies an agreed-upon transfer pricing methodology to specified transactions between the taxpayer and a related party. Because the term of an APA is generally three to five years, an APA provides a taxpayer with some level of certainty before a transaction is consummated, rather than having to justify pricing after a transaction is consummated. From a business perspective, an APA makes it easier to evaluate whether to undertake a transaction.

§ 9.11   COST-SHARING

(A) COST SHARING AGREEMENTS

A cost-sharing agreement governs how two or more parties agree to share the risks and costs of development of an intangible in proportion to their shares of reasonably anticipated benefits from exploitation of their interests in the intangible. Reg. § 1.482–7(b)(1). A cost-sharing agreement is qualified if: it includes two or more participants which expect to use the intangible in the active conduct of a trade or business; the agreement contains certain specified information, including each participant's interest in the intangible, each participant's share of the development costs for the intangible, and the method by which costs will be determined; and the agreement provides for adjustments to each participant's interest in the intangible to account for changes in the economic relationship between the participants. If there is a qualified cost-sharing agreement then, all of the participants are considered owners of the intangible so that no royalty payment for the use of the cost shared intangibles will be imputed under I.R.C. § 482.

At the center of the cost sharing regulations is the goal that each participant's share of costs is reasonably related to the anticipated benefits. This can be challenging because the determination often involves projected costs and benefits. During the life of the agreement, the participants make payments to each other to adjust the costs of the project to prearranged proportions. The base amount includes all costs, including wages and salaries of the research staff and a reasonable allowance for overhead, related to performing general and basic research and development activities.

The treatment of stock-based compensation in the calculation of the cost base to determine cost-sharing payments has been a significant issue facing taxpayers and the IRS. *See* Reg. § 1.482–7(d)(3). Essentially, it is the IRS view that companies are required to include the value of stock options in calculating the fully-loaded cost of employees involved in qualified cost-sharing arrangements By including stock-based compensation in the calculation of cost-sharing payments, the result will likely be more income to a U.S. owner of intangibles (resulting from smaller deductions for the net R & D expenses of that U.S. owner) and a higher tax liability. However, in *Altera Corp. v. Commissioner*, 145 T.C. No. 3 (2015), the court found invalid that part of the transfer pricing cost sharing regulations that require taxpayers to include stock based compensation in the pool of costs that need to be shared in a qualified cost sharing arrangement.

The benefits are based on the additional income to be generated or costs to be saved by the use of the covered intangible. These benefits may be projected using input units used, produced or sold by each participant, operating profits of each participant or any other method that provides reliable projections of the benefits derived from the use of the intangible.

For example, suppose that Parentco, a U.S. corporation, and Subco, its wholly-owned foreign subsidiary, enter into a cost sharing arrangement to develop new and improved household cleaning products. Both participants have sold such products for many years and have stable market shares. The products under development are unlikely to produce extraordinary profits. If the parties divide costs on the basis of current sales of existing household cleaning products, it will be considered a reasonable projection of estimated benefits. Reg. § 1.482–7(e)(2)(iii)(B) Ex. 2. If actual benefits turn out to be different than the projections, the IRS may make an adjustment of costs, consistent with the "commensurate with income" requirement of I.R.C. § 482. However, under the Cost Sharing Regulations no adjustment will be made if the ratio of present value of the Foreign Subsidiary's actual operating income from all of its activities associated with the development and exploitation of the cost shared intangibles to the present value of its cost sharing and preliminary or contemporaneous transaction or PCT payments is greater than 0.667 or less than 1.5 for taxpayers that have substantially complied with the documentation requirements (a "Qualified Cost

Sharing Arrangement"); the threshold is narrower, standing between 0.8 and 1.25, for taxpayers that have not substantially complied with documentation requirements. As one might speculate, cost sharing arrangements require constant management.

If one of the participants to a cost sharing arrangement has existing valuable intangibles, then other participants must make a buy-in payment at the arm's length price as compensation for use of the intangible. Reg. § 1.482–7(c). Similarly, if a participant leaves a cost sharing arrangement, then the other participant(s) must make buy-out payments in proportion to the value of the exiting party's interest in the jointly developed intangible.

(B) THE INVESTOR MODEL AND THE INCOME METHOD

Under the current regulations, taxpayers are required to base their valuations of buy-in payments (referred to as preliminary or contemporaneous transactions or PCTs) on a hypothetically constructed "reference transaction" in which the contributor grants perpetual and exclusive territorial rights in the covered intangibles under a cost sharing agreement (CSA) to the CSA participants. Several new valuation methods are specified, and the IRS is given broader powers to impose periodic adjustments when results are considered to diverge from predicted outcomes.

The regulations adopt the theoretical "investor model." The rules generally require taxpayers to adopt inflexible prescribed contractual and economic arrangements to which taxpayers can make only limited *ex post* adjustments. The changes stem from the IRS belief that taxpayers' application of the current methods for determining buy-in payments resulted in underpayments by foreign subsidiaries to U.S. parents, and that taxpayers failed to appropriately value all the resources and capabilities that, in many cases, the foreign affiliate received. The IRS was also concerned that unrelated parties did not enter into cost sharing agreements of the form and substance of those generally being adopted by related parties.

Under the income method, PCTs will be an amount such that a controlled participant's present value of pursuing the alternative of entering into a CSA equals the present value of its best realistic alternative. In arrangements where the existing intangibles prior to the CSA are owned in the U.S., the foreign participants' best realistic alternative to entering into the CSA would be to license intangibles from an uncontrolled licensor while the best realistic alternative of the U.S. participant would be to develop the intangible and license it to an uncontrolled licensee. Reg. § 1.482–7(g)(4). The PCT payment would be the difference between the licensing alternatives above and the proposed Cost Sharing alternative. Generally, the application of the investor model results in limiting the returns of participants that do not contribute pre-existing intangibles (often the non-U.S. participants) to an investor's return for its share of the development costs.

§ 9.12 CONTROLLED SERVICES TRANSACTIONS

When one corporation performs services for, or on behalf of, a related corporation, the corporation purchasing the services is deemed to pay an arm's length price to the corporation performing the services. The IRS has wrestled with whether the arm's length price should not only cover actual costs of performing the services but should also include a profit mark-up.

For example, if in-house accountants at Parentco perform services for Subco, The arm's length payment to Parentco should include deemed payments for both the direct and indirect costs of providing the services. The direct costs might include employee salaries and benefits; indirect expenses might include a portion of depreciation, rent, property taxes and other overhead expenses of Parentco attributable to its accounting services. But should there also be a deemed payment from Subco to Parentco for some level of profit in performing the services?

Historically, intercompany payments for services generally did not require a profit mark-up. However, current regulations require a profit mark-up for certain services performed for related parties. Still there are some services where the arm's length price is considered to be the cost to the related party performing the service with no additional mark-up (the services cost method or SCM). Reg. § 1.482–9(b).

(A) SERVICES COST METHOD

The services cost method evaluates the arm's-length nature of the services transaction by reference to the total cost of providing the service with no additional charge or mark-up. In addition to the services cost method, the temporary regulations contain rules for shared service arrangements, which for the first time permit cost sharing for services. The services cost method and the new rules for shared services arrangements are intended to preserve the salutary aspects of the cost safe harbor of the current regulations by allowing certain routine back-office and other low-value services to continue to be charged out at cost.

For a service to qualify for the services cost method, the service cannot:

- contribute to the key competitive advantages, core capabilities, or fundamental risks of success or failure of the renderer, the recipient, or both; or

- be a specifically excluded service (listed below).

If the service is not excluded, then the regulations provide two categories of services that will be eligible for the services cost method. The first category, "specified covered services," includes services specified by the IRS in a proposed revenue procedure. The second category of services eligible for the services cost method are "low margin covered services," which are services that have a median comparable mark-up on "total services costs" of less than or equal to 7.0 percent. The figure below illustrates the process to qualify to use the services cost method.

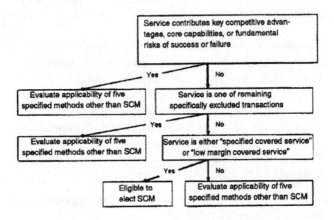

Services do not qualify for the services cost method unless a taxpayer can reasonably conclude in its business judgment that the services do not contribute significantly to key competitive advantages, core capabilities, or fundamental chances of success or failure in one or more trades or businesses of the renderer, the recipient, or both. Regs. § 1.482–9(b)(2). While the IRS indicated in the preamble that it anticipates accepting taxpayer's judgment in this matter in most cases, the preamble also makes it clear that the IRS is not bound by the taxpayer's determination. This test is intended to replace the integral test contained in the current rules and to force taxpayers to conduct a more robust transfer pricing analysis of these important activities.

The regulations' exclusion of services that provide a key competitive advantage or fundamental chances of success or failure of the business is likely to exclude many, if not most, services provided by senior managers in a company. Arguably, the services provided by senior-level operations managers in most companies will be considered fundamental to the success of those operations. This is also likely to be the case for managers in virtually every important department in a typical company, especially large multinationals with complex organizations. Presumably, individuals who render services that may be considered to provide a key competitive advantage or that are fundamental to the success of the business also perform more routine services, such as providing counseling to employees, attending company functions, and training. The temporary regulations appear to permit taxpayers to segregate these routine activities. However, in many cases it may not be practical to separate an individual's routine activities from other activities.

Although the IRS indicated in the preamble to the regulations that it will respect taxpayers' judgment in most cases, documenting the rationale for the characterization of services may be both time-consuming and a challenge in a number of situations.

In addition to services excluded under the subjective test, the following services are specifically excluded from the application of the services cost method:

- manufacturing;
- production;
- extraction, exploration, or processing of natural resources;
- construction;
- reselling, distribution, acting as a sales or purchasing agent, or acting under a commission or other similar arrangement;
- research, development, or experimentation;
- engineering or scientific operations;
- financial transactions, including guarantees; and
- insurance or reinsurance.

(B) SHARED SERVICES ARRANGEMENTS

The introduction of shared services arrangements is the second major change contained in the regulations that is intended to address taxpayers' comments on the proposed simplified cost-based method. The major advantages of shared services arrangements are that:

- if a taxpayer reasonably allocates cost among affiliates, the IRS will not adjust the allocation, even though another method may be more reasonable;
- taxpayers are permitted to aggregate or group service costs even though not all services in the group will similarly benefit all participants; and

- the arrangements are likely to be consistent with similar arrangements adopted by other OECD countries.

To qualify as a shared services arrangement, the agreement must:

- include two or more participants;
- include as participants all controlled taxpayers that reasonably anticipate a benefit from one or more covered services specified in the shared services arrangement; and
- be structured so that each covered service (or each reasonable aggregation of services) confers a benefit on at least one participant in the shared services arrangement. Reg. § 1.482–9(b)(5)(ii)(A).

Under a shared services arrangement, the arm's-length charge to each participant is the portion of the total costs of the services otherwise determined under the services cost method that is properly allocated to that participant. A participant's allocation must reflect the participant's respective share of reasonably anticipated benefits from the services. Reasonably anticipated benefits will depend on the service being provided and usually are computed using allocation keys such as sales or head count. Importantly, the regulations provide that if the taxpayer has reasonably allocated the benefits to reflect the reasonably anticipated benefits, the IRS will not adjust the basis for allocation.

In addition, the regulations provide a special aggregation rule that applies only to shared services arrangements. The special rule permits taxpayers to aggregate or group services for purposes of allocation even though not all participants will benefit equally from each service based on the allocation key. For example, this rule will permit taxpayers to use an allocation key such as sales or head count without having to show that the allocation key was appropriate for each service and for each participant. Thus, as long as the overall allocation is reasonable, the fact that one participant receives more relative benefits from one or more services than other participants will not cause the IRS to challenge the taxpayer's allocation.

As a procedural matter, the taxpayer also must prepare and maintain sufficient documentation to establish that the regulatory requirements have been satisfied.

(C) ADDITIONAL TRANSFER PRICING METHODS FOR CONTROLLED SERVICES TRANSACTIONS

For services that cannot qualify for SCM method, The regulations provide five additional specified transfer pricing methods and unspecified methods for determining taxable income in connection with a controlled services transaction. The selection and application of these methods is subject to the general transfer pricing principles described in Reg. § 1.482–1, including the best method rule, comparability analysis, and the arm's-length range, except when modified in the new regulations. The five additional specified methods are as follows.

- *Comparable Uncontrolled Services Price Method (Reg. § 1.482–9(c))*—This method is the analog of the comparable uncontrolled price method for tangible property transactions described in section 1.482–3(b).

- *Gross Services Margin Method (Reg. § 1.482–9(d))*—This method is the analog of the resale price method for tangible property transactions described in section 1.482–3(d).

- *Cost of Services Plus Method (Reg. § 1.482–9(e))*—This method is the analog of the cost plus method for tangible property transactions described in section 1.482–3(c).

- *Comparable Profits Method (Reg. § 1.482–9(f))*—This method incorporates the CPM rules in Reg. § 1.482–5 and adds the net cost plus profit level indicator, which is equal to the ratio of operating profit to total services costs.

- *Profit Split Method (Reg. § 1.482–9(g))*—This method is ordinarily used in controlled services transactions involving a combination of routine and nonroutine contributions by multiple controlled taxpayers and incorporates the profit split method rules in Reg. § 1.482–6.

There is a special rule in Reg. § 1.482–9(m)(2), for services transactions that constitute the transfer of intangible property, or may result in a transfer, in whole or in part, of intangible property. Under this rule, the arm's-length result for the intangibles element of the services transaction must be determined under the transfer pricing rules for transfers of intangible property under Reg. § 1.482–4. This often results in a higher transfer price than might occur under transfer pricing rules applying to services.

The following example from the Regulations illustrates the rule: USCO and Forco are members of a controlled group. Both companies perform research and development activities relating to integrated circuits. In addition, Forco manufactures integrated circuits. In years 1 through 3, USCO engages in substantial research and development activities, gains significant know-how regarding the development of a particular high-temperature resistant integrated circuit, and memorializes that research in a written report. In years 1 through 3, USCO generates overall net operating losses as a result of the expenditures associated with this research and development effort. At the beginning of year 4, USCO enters into a technical assistance agreement with Forco. As part of this agreement, the researchers from USCO responsible for this project meet with the researchers from Forco and provide them with a copy of the written report. Three months later, the researchers from Forco apply for a patent for a high-temperature resistant integrated circuit based in large part upon the know-how obtained from the researchers from USCO.

Under the Regulations, the controlled services transaction between USCO and Forco includes an element that constitutes the transfer of intangible property (such as, knowhow). Because the element relating to the intangible property is material to the arm's length evaluation, the arm's length result for that element must be determined by an analysis under § 1.482–4. See Reg. § 1.482–9(m)(5) Ex. 5.

§ 9.13   THE OECD TRANSFER PRICING GUIDELINES

Outside of the United States most countries with transfer pricing provisions generally follow the Transfer Pricing Guidelines for Multinational Enterprises and Tax Administrations issued by the Organization for Economic Cooperation and Development (the "OECD Guidelines"). As noted in earlier parts of this chapter, the principles applied under the OECD Guidelines are largely consistent with the principles applied under the U.S. transfer pricing guidelines which affords multinational corporations the ability to coordinate more effectively its transfer pricing across the world. The OECD first issued transfer pricing guidelines in 1979 followed by updates in 1995 and most recently in July 2010. The most recent revisions to the OECD Guidelines were made after various rounds of consultation the main changes are focused on the standards of comparability used in the application of the methods including a shift away from the previous "hierarchy of methods" whereby transactional methods were preferred to profits based methods to a "best method" standard similar to that applied in the U.S. whereby the facts and circumstances of the transactions and availability of information will be the bases for the method selection. The 2010 OECD Guidelines added Chapter IX which focuses on the cross border redeployment of a multinational functions, risks or assets (business restructurings) from two angles: (i) whether the restructuring itself is arm's length, and (ii) whether the transaction may require compensation.

In 2013, the OECD began work on their Base Erosion and Profit Shifting ("BEPS") project to address concerns that current principles of national and international taxation were failing to address tax planning strategies that exploit gaps and mismatches in tax rules to make profits 'disappear' for tax purposes or to shift profits to locations where there is little or no real activity but the taxes are low. *See supra*, § 13.06 for an overview of BEPS. Actions 8–10 of the BEPS project relate to transfer pricing.

In relation to Action 8, the OECD released a discussion draft in relation to Action 10 that proposes a simplified transfer pricing approach for low value-adding intragroup services. The aim is to reduce base erosion through excessive management fees and head office expenses, particularly in developing countries. The simplified approach, which a group may elect to adopt, recognizes that the arm's length price is closely related to costs and allocates the costs of providing each category of such services to the group companies that benefit from using the services using consistent group-wide allocation keys with an associated consistent small mark-up. In relation to Action 10, the OECD in 2015 released a discussion draft in relation to developing an approach to price the transfer of "hard-to-value intangibles." Like the "commensurate with income" standard under I.R.C. § 482, the OECD discussion draft, the discussion draft proposes that tax authorities may use actual results ("ex post" outcomes) in years subsequent to the transfer to determine whether a price adjustment is necessary.

CHAPTER 10

CONTROLLED FOREIGN CORPORATIONS AND RELATED PROVISIONS

§ 10.01 OVERVIEW

If a U.S. taxpayer conducts business abroad directly through a branch, there is one U.S. tax on the foreign income earned. (That tax may be reduced by any applicable foreign tax credit.) If instead, the U.S. taxpayer conducts business abroad through a foreign corporation, there is often no U.S. taxation until and unless the earnings of the foreign corporation are distributed to the shareholder. At that time, there may be both a direct tax credit for withholding taxes imposed on the dividend and in some cases an indirect tax credit for taxes imposed on the distributing corporation's income out of which the dividend was distributed. *See supra* § 8.05. In short, generally a foreign corporation is respected for tax purposes as a separate foreign taxpayer not subject to U.S. taxation on its foreign activities.

To the extent that a foreign corporation operates in a low tax jurisdiction, the corporation enjoys deferred U.S. taxation on the foreign income earned. For example, if U.S. Co.'s wholly-owned subsidiary in the Cayman Islands earned income, that income might escape all taxation until the earnings were repatriated to U.S. Co. Concerned that U.S. taxpayers were taking advantage of such deferral, in 1962 Congress enacted subpart F of the Code. In general, the purpose of subpart F is to discourage U.S. taxpayers from using foreign corporations to defer U.S. taxes by accumulating certain types of income in foreign "base" companies located in low-tax jurisdictions. Subpart F is primarily directed at two types of income: passive investment income and income derived from dealings with related corporations (*i.e.*, using a base company to shift income away from related parties in high-tax jurisdictions). Both of these types of income may be easily movable from one taxing jurisdiction to another. Active business operations conducted by a foreign corporation dealing with unrelated parties are not generally affected by the subpart F provisions.

The basic concept underlying the subpart F provisions is straightforward: certain U.S. taxpayers are taxed immediately (*i.e.*, as if the foreign corporation were a flow-through entity) on certain income earned by certain controlled foreign corporations ("CFCs"). However, complexity abounds as this underlying concept has been translated into operational detail by Congress and Treasury.

§ 10.02   DEFINITIONS: CONTROLLED FOREIGN CORPORATION AND UNITED STATES SHAREHOLDER

In order for subpart F to be triggered, there must be a controlled foreign corporation ("CFC"). A foreign corporation is a CFC if "United States shareholders" own more than 50 percent of the total combined voting power of its stock or more than 50 percent of the stock's total value. I.R.C. § 957(a). A "United States shareholder" is defined as a United States person (as defined in I.R.C. § 957(c)) owning at least 10 percent or more of the total combined voting power of the corporate stock. I.R.C. § 951(b). If eleven unrelated U.S. individuals own equal voting interests in a foreign corporation, the corporation is not a controlled foreign corporation because each shareholder owns less than a 10 percent interest. Such a corporation would have no United States shareholders. If the same ten individuals are partners in a U.S. partnership that owns 100 percent of the corporation, the corporation would be a controlled foreign corporation as a U.S. partnership is a U.S. shareholder that owns more that 50 percent of the stock of the corporation.

A foreign corporation with ten equal unrelated U.S. individual shareholders is a controlled foreign corporation. On the other hand if one shareholder owns 50 percent and the other nine own the remaining 50 percent equally, the corporation is not a controlled foreign corporation because U.S. shareholders (*i.e.*, 10 percent shareholders measured by vote) do not own *more* than 50 percent (measured by vote or value) of the corporation's stock. Notice that if a U.S. shareholder and a foreign shareholder enter into a foreign joint venture conducted through foreign corporate entity with each participant owning precisely 50 percent of the vote and value of the entity, the entity will not be a controlled foreign corporation.

In testing whether a foreign corporation is a controlled foreign corporation, the Code looks to direct and indirect ownership and to constructive ownership. I.R.C. §§ 957(a) and 958. Suppose that the voting stock of a foreign corporation is owned equally by six U.S. individuals and six foreign corporations (each corporation's stock being owned by one of the six individuals). Each of the twelve shareholders holds directly an 8 1/3 percent interest in the foreign corporation and so it appears that there are no United States shareholders. However, because the six individuals are deemed to own indirectly the stock owned by their wholly-owned corporations, each individual is deemed to be a 16 2/3 percent shareholder and therefore a United States shareholder. I.R.C. §§ 957 and 958(a)(2). Because the United States shareholders own more than 50 percent of the stock of the foreign corporation (*i.e.*, they own 100 percent), the foreign corporation is a CFC. Similarly, when foreign partnerships or trusts own shares in foreign corporations, it is necessary to attribute the entity's ownership of the shares to the partners or beneficiaries.

Apart from indirect ownership, a U.S. person is deemed constructively to own stock owned by certain related persons. I.R.C. § 958(b). For example, if Parent owns 9 percent of the voting stock of a foreign corporation and Child owns 4 percent, Parent is a U.S. shareholder for purposes of deciding whether the foreign corporation is a CFC. Child is also a U.S. shareholder, but stock cannot be counted twice in determining whether the foreign corporation is a CFC. The constructive ownership rules of I.R.C. § 958(b) employ the constructive ownership rules of I.R.C. § 318 with certain modifications specified in § 958(b)(1) through 4.

To illustrate a couple of constructive ownership situations, consider the following. FP, a foreign corporation owns 100 percent of the stock of FS, a foreign subsidiary and 100 percent of the stock of U.S. Sub. Is FS a CFC? Under I.R.C. § 318(a)(3) U.S. Sub is deemed to own what its shareholder owns. So it first appears that U.S. Sub would own 100 percent of FS. However, § 958(b)(4) clarifies that the constructive ownership rules in § 318(a)(3) should not be used to make a U.S. person (U.S. Sub) the owner of stock owned by a foreign person (FP).

Suppose that U.S. Co. owns 10 percent of the voting stock of FC1 (the other 90 percent is owned by unrelated foreign shareholders). FC1 owns 51 percent of the voting stock of FC2 (the other 49 percent is held by a single unrelated U.S. shareholder). Is FC2 a CFC (FC1 is not)? Starting with the indirect ownership rules in § 958(a)(2), U.S. Co. would appear to own 5.1 percent of FC2 (10 percent × 51 percent). So U.S. Co. would not be a U.S. shareholder (*i.e.,* 10 percent owner) and FC2 would not be a CFC (U.S. shareholders own only 49 percent of FC2). However, the constructive ownership rules also apply, and if those rules provide more ownership than the indirect ownership rules, the constructive ownership rules prevail. Reg. § 1.958–2(f)(2). Under the § 318(a)(2)(C) attribution rules as modified by § 958(b)(3) and (b)(2), U.S. Co. would be deemed to own 10 percent of FC2 (10 percent × 100 percent) as FC1, by owning more than 50 percent, is considered to own 100 percent of FC2 under § 958(b)(2). Consequently, U.S. shareholders would be deemed to own 59 percent of FC2 which would be a CFC.

One could play all day in the indirect and constructive ownership sandbox (*e.g.,* when CFC stock is owned by a partnership, is the general partner deemed to exercise the vote or is it the limited partners that can remove the general partner?), but it is beyond the scope of this book to do so, and mental health experts may not permit it.

§ 10.03 INCOME TAXABLE TO SHAREHOLDERS

If a foreign corporation is a CFC under I.R.C. § 957(a) for an uninterrupted period of 30 days or more during the taxable year, each United States shareholder (who owns stock on the last day of the year) must include in income the sum of two major components: the shareholder's pro rata share of subpart F income plus any earnings of the CFC invested in U.S. property. I.R.C. § 951(a). A taxpayer's pro rata share of subpart F income is based on direct and indirect ownership (but not constructive ownership). In effect, I.R.C. § 951(a) treats United States shareholders as having received a current distribution out of subpart F income plus any non-subpart F foreign earnings invested in U.S. property.

When income is included as subpart F income, the CFC maintains an account of previously taxed income (PTI) so that there is no double inclusion. *See* I.R.C. § 959. After all, a U.S. shareholder includes income for tax purposes even though that income has not been distributed to the taxpayer. Suppose a CFC, wholly-owned by U.S. Co., earns $1,000 of subpart F income in year 1 and makes a $300 distribution to U.S. Co. in the same year or in year 2. U.S. Co. includes $1,000 in income under subpart F but does not include the $300 distribution (even if CFC has earnings and profits that were not previously taxed as subpart F income) because the distribution is out of previously taxed income.

In many cases, a United States shareholder may not actually receive a distribution of income that is deemed to be included under subpart F. But a United States shareholder is treated as if the shareholder has income. Note that subpart F inclusions are not treated as actual dividends for many purposes under the Code (*e.g.*, for purposes of reduced tax on dividends under I.R.C. § 1(h)(11)). Where there is no actual distribution, the United States shareholder is treated essentially as if the shareholder contributed the deemed inclusion amount back to the corporation which in turn results in an increase in the shareholder's stock basis. I.R.C. § 961. On a subsequent distribution of previously taxed income (PTI), there is typically no further taxation, although the stock basis of a United States shareholder must be reduced upon the distribution. I.R.C. §§ 959 and 961. The income that is deemed distributed to United States shareholders as a subpart F inclusion may carry with it an indirect foreign tax credit for any creditable income foreign taxes paid. I.R.C. § 960.

(A) SUBPART F INCOME

As noted previously, subpart F income tends to be income that is easily movable to a low-tax jurisdiction. Subpart F income is composed of several categories of income: income derived from insurance of U.S. risks, foreign base company income, certain income from countries engaged in international boycotts, and certain illegal payments. I.R.C. § 952(a). The most important category is foreign base company income. The term "foreign base company income" itself is composed of four categories. I.R.C. § 954. These categories are directed primarily at a holding structure where a U.S. parent corporation creates a foreign subsidiary (*i.e.*, a base company) in an effort to isolate either passive income or some of the income from the parent's active business in a low-tax jurisdiction. For example, a U.S. manufacturing parent might sell its products to a foreign subsidiary in a low tax jurisdiction which then sells to the product's end-users not located in that jurisdiction. By manipulating prices, some of the income from the manufactured products might be isolated in that low-tax jurisdiction even though there may no business reason to be there. While it is true that I.R.C. § 482 may allow the IRS to reallocate income between parent and subsidiary, the CFC provisions offer a more targeted weapon which can apply, for example, even when the dealings between parent and subsidiary are at arm's length.

(1) Foreign Personal Holding Company Income

The first category of foreign base company income is foreign personal holding company income. I.R.C. §§ 954(a)(1) and (c). This category generally consists of passive income such as interest, dividends, rents, royalties, and net gains from the sale of assets producing these income flows or sales of non-income producing assets or payments that are considered to be dividend or interest substitutes. (Also gains from commodities transactions or foreign currency gains are foreign personal holding company income.) So if a U.S. parent corporation (or a U.S. individual) employs a controlled foreign corporation (CFC) to hold investments in order to isolate the investment income in a low-tax jurisdiction, the income will be in turn: foreign personal holding company income, which is foreign base company income, which is subpart F income, which is subject to U.S. federal taxation of the U.S. shareholders in the United States even if not distributed by the CFC. (Note that some states do not tax subpart F income until the income is repatriated.)

Foreign personal holding company income also includes income that is the equivalent of interest. For example, suppose an accrual basis U.S. parent sells property (with a $0 basis) or performs services for a third party in exchange for an account receivable of $10,000 which it sells (*i.e.*, factors) to a CFC for $7,000. In the absence of a remedial provision, the U.S. parent would report net income of $7,000 ($10,000 accrued income minus the $3,000 loss on the sale of the receivable). The CFC would report $3,000 of income when the receivable was paid. Under I.R.C. § 864(d), the transaction is treated as a $7,000 loan by the CFC to the obligor under the receivable with the $3,000 income received by the CFC treated as interest. The $3,000 income characterized as interest is foreign personal holding company income that will normally be taxable under I.R.C. § 951(a) to the U.S. parent. So the parent corporation reports $7,000 of net income when the receivable is factored and $3,000 of income when the CFC collects on the receivable.

There is a special rule for interest and income derived in the active conduct of a banking or financing business. Qualified banking or financing income of an eligible controlled foreign corporation will not constitute foreign personal holding company income. I.R.C. § 954(h). Generally, an eligible controlled foreign corporation is one that is predominately engaged in the active conduct of banking or financing. A corporation is "predominately engaged" if it is a licensed bank or securities dealer or more than 70 percent of its gross income is from the active and regular conduct of a lending or finance business. To avoid foreign personal holding company income, an eligible controlled foreign corporation must earn qualified banking or financing income which essentially is active banking or financing income derived from customers outside the United States where the activities generating the income are conducted by the corporation in its home country. I.R.C. § 954(h)(3). A qualified business unit (*i.e.*, a branch) of an eligible controlled foreign corporation can satisfy these requirements as well. The banking and financing business exception has been on life support with one year extensions passed by Congress every year. It remains to be seen if the provision will be extended for 2015. Then the nail-biting is likely to continue for 2016, 2017. . . . For a similar exception for active insurance income, *see* I.R.C. § 954(i).

There is a similar "active business" exception for rents and royalties reflecting that these income flows can be generated from an active business. If rents or royalties are derived from an active trade or business conducted by the CFC's employees and are not received from related taxpayers (*e.g.*, a subsidiary of the subsidiary or a brother/sister corporation owned by the common U.S. parent), the receipts do not constitute foreign personal holding company income. I.R.C. § 954(c)(2)(A). For example, rents received by a CFC from a retail car-leasing business involving substantial maintenance, repair and marketing by the CFC-owner's employees would not be foreign personal holding company income. The "active business" exception can be satisfied through either extensive production activities or through marketing and servicing activities. *See e.g.,* Reg. § 1.954–2(d)(1) and Treas. Reg. § 1.954–2(T).

Although rents or royalties from a related party cannot meet the active rents or royalties exception, they are excluded from foreign personal holding company income, if the payments are for use of property located in the country where the CFC is organized. I.R.C. § 954(c)(3). For example, if a CFC incorporated in Ireland leases an Irish factory to Subco, an Irish corporation, which manufactures and sells machine tools, the rent received by the CFC is not subpart F income even though the active business exception does not apply. This "same country exception" for related parties presumably reflects the fact that the CFC receiving rents (or royalties) has a legitimate business purpose if it is organized where the property is located. However, the easing of the related party rule does not apply if the rent payment reduces Subco's subpart F income. I.R.C. § 954(c)(3)(B). For example, if Subco earns $50,000 from passively subleasing the rented property to an unrelated party and pays $40,000 in rent to the CFC, the rental payment it makes to the CFC is foreign personal holding company income. Otherwise only $10,000 of $50,000 of rental income would be foreign personal holding company income.

Dividends and interest which are normally foreign personal holding company income may not be foreign personal holding company income if received from a related person organized and engaged in a trade or business in the same country as the CFC. I.R.C. § 954(c)(3)(A). For example, if a CFC has a subsidiary (organized in the same country) which conducts a trade or business and uses most of its assets (more than 50 percent pursuant to Reg. § 1.954–2(b)(4)(iv)) in that country, dividends or interest paid to the CFC are not foreign personal holding company income. If the CFC had conducted the trade or business, there would have been no subpart F income. The decision to conduct the CFC's trade or business through a subsidiary therefore does not avoid U.S. taxation. As in the case of rental payments from related parties, interest paid by a related party that decreases the payer's subpart F income is treated as foreign personal holding company income to the CFC (*e.g.*, in addition to its active trade or business the subsidiary has passive income to which any interest paid is allocated).

In 2006, Congress enacted a new look-through rule in I.R.C. § 954(c)(6) that is much broader in application than the "same country" exception. Dividends, interest, rents, and royalties from a CFC which is a related person shall not be treated as foreign personal holding company income to the extent attributable to income of the payor which is not subpart F income. The "related person" definition looks to more-than-50 percent common control. Note that the related person does not need to reside in the same country. However, the look-through rule does not apply to payments from a U.S. company. To the extent that the passive payment reduces or is allocable against subpart F income of the payor income received by the payor, subpart F treatment will result to the recipient. *See* Notice 2007–9, 2007–1 C.B. 401, for guidance on how to determine if the payment is allocable against subpart F income of the payor. This "(c)(6)" look-through rule which is a mainstay of international tax planning, is on life-support (like the active financing rule for banks and finance companies in I.R.C. § 954(h)), relying on a year-by-year Congressional extension for oxygen. Will the plug be pulled in 2015, 2016. . . . (and will readers have to continue to endure this tortured metaphor)? We will have to wait and see.

To illustrate how I.R.C. § 954(c)(6) works, suppose that U.S. Co. owns all the stock of two subsidiaries—Lux Co. and French Co. French Co. is engaged in an active trade or business. Assume that Lux Co. is subject to a nominal rate of tax and that French Co. is taxed at a 30 percent rate. If French Co. pays interest or royalties to Lux Co., which functions as the financing and licensing company for the U.S. Co. worldwide group, there may be a deduction in France under its tax system and little or no tax in Luxembourg—thereby reducing the worldwide group's effective tax rate. Historically, prior to enactment of I.R.C. § 954(c)(6), the interest or royalties received by Lux Co. would have been foreign personal holding company income taxable under subpart F in the United States, resulting in a 35 percent U.S. tax. So historically the strategy was not tax efficient. Under I.R.C. § 954(c)(6) the strategy may be tax efficient because we look through the interest/royalty payment to the underlying active trade or business income and treat the payment received by Lux Co. accordingly. So if French Co. generates active income, then the interest/royalty payment should not be subpart F income.

While at first glance this may appear to some to be bad U.S. tax policy, perhaps it is not. If France earned $100 of income from its active trade or business and paid no interest to Lux Co., there would be no subpart F income and no U.S. taxation. So why should the United States be concerned if some of that $100 of "good income" (*e.g.,* a $30 interest or royalty payment) is moved from France to Luxembourg? Viewed in this manner, it is really only France that is affected by giving a deduction. There is no reason for the United States to turn "good income" into subpart F income. (Indeed, this financing structure may reduce overall foreign taxation which means that when there is repatriation in the future, there will be a small foreign tax credit and more residual U.S. tax.)

Now if the payment of interest or royalties from French Co. reduced the subpart F of French Co., the look-through rule would not apply. Suppose that French Co. earned $20 of interest from a loan to an unrelated borrower and $80 of non-subpart F active trade or business income. Under the rules governing how expenses are allocated in CFCs, a $30 interest payment to Lux Co. would first offset the $20 of interest earned by French Co. and then offset $10 of active business income of French Co. I.R.C. § 954(b)(5) and Reg. § 1.954–1(c)(1)(i)(C).

Accordingly, Lux Co. would be deemed to receive $20 of subpart F income (*i.e.,* foreign personal holding company income) and $10 that would qualify as non-subpart F income under the look-through.

One area of historical contention between the IRS and taxpayers arises out of the sale of a foreign business. Suppose that U.S. Co. owns all of the stock of Foreign Holdco the only asset of which is all of the stock of Foreign Opco, a manufacturing corporation. Assume that the stock of Foreign Holdco and the stock of Foreign Opco are highly appreciated. An unrelated Purchaser wants to acquire the foreign operations. If Purchaser buys the stock of Foreign Holdco, U.S. Co. will have a gain for U.S. purposes. If Purchaser buys the stock of Foreign Opco from Foreign Holdco, in some cases there may be no tax in Foreign Holdco's jurisdiction (many countries exempt gain from the sale of stock), but historically some or all of the gain on the sale of stock might be subpart F income (*i.e.,* foreign personal holding company income) which would be taxable to U.S. Co.

Suppose instead that Purchaser buys the assets directly from Foreign Opco. Under this scenario, typically there may be no foreign personal holding company income because Foreign Opco is selling assets used in a trade or business. Reg. § 1.954–2(e)(3). (Note that the taxpayer would also have to determine whether the sale gave rise to a different category of subpart F income—foreign base company sales income discussed below.) But the country in which Foreign Opco is located is likely to impose a tax on the sale of assets. Faced with these alternatives, a taxpayer might seek a transaction which is treated as a nontaxable sale of stock for foreign purposes but a sale of trade or business assets not giving rise to subpart F income for U.S. purposes.

Suppose that U.S. Co. causes Foreign Opco to check-the-box to be treated as a disregarded entity for U.S. tax purposes. A U.S. check-the-box election has no effect on foreign taxation, but in this situation for U.S. tax purposes, the election is treated as if Foreign Opco liquidated into Foreign Holdco. A foreign-to-foreign liquidation typically has no immediate U.S. tax consequences. *See infra* § 13.03. Now Foreign Holdco sells the "stock" of Foreign Opco. The foreign jurisdiction treats the transaction as a sale of stock and does not tax. But for U.S. tax purposes Foreign Opco is not a corporation, and there is no stock. Instead, there is a sale of trade or business assets that does not create subpart F income. *See Dover Corp. v. Commissioner*, 122 T.C. 324 (2004) (rejecting IRS argument that assets were not trade or business assets in the hands of Foreign Holdco).

(2) Foreign Base Company Sales Income

The second category of foreign base company income is foreign base company sales income. I.R.C. §§ 954(a)(2) and (d). This category includes income from property purchased from (or sold to) a related party (defined in I.R.C. § 954(d)(3) using a more than 50 percent ownership test based on value or vote) if the property is manufactured and sold for use outside the CFC's country of incorporation. For example, if a U.S. parent corporation manufactures computers which are sold to its CFC (typically in a low tax jurisdiction) for resale abroad, income received by the CFC is foreign base company sales income to the extent that the computers are sold for use outside the CFC's country of incorporation. Similarly, if the CFC purchases computers from an unrelated foreign manufacturer and sells them to the CFC's U.S. parent for resale in the United States, the CFC's income is foreign base company sales income. If the goods sold by the CFC are intended for use or disposition inside the country of its incorporation, the income is not foreign base company sales income ("destination exception").

In addition to the "destination exception," there are two manufacturing exceptions relating to foreign base company sales income. There is a statutory manufacturing exception where the goods sold are manufactured in the country where the CFC is incorporated. I.R.C. § 954(d)(1)(A). For example, if U.S. Co. owns all of the stock of Foreign Opco1 and Foreign Opco2, both located in Brazil. If Foreign Opco1 manufactures inventory and sells it to Foreign Opco2 for sale outside of Brazil, there is no foreign base company sales income even though there is a purchase from a related person and sale outside the country of incorporation because the inventory is manufactured in Brazil. The outcome would not change if Foreign Opco 2 purchased the inventory from an unrelated Brazilian manufacturer and then sold to a related distributor outside of Brazil. The key point is that in either of these situations that there is a business reason for Foreign Opco 2 to be located in Brazil—that's where the goods are manufactured.

There is a second manufacturing exception that applies wherever manufacturing takes place. If the CFC manufactures or constructs the property sold, the income is not foreign base company sales income—subject to the branch rule discussed below. Reg. § 1.954–3(a)(4)(iii). Often determining whether manufacturing has occurred is not clear, but income from a CFC that merely assembles goods manufactured by its parent may not escape classification as foreign base company sales income. Whether a CFC that hires another corporation (whether related or unrelated) to manufacture on its behalf under strict supervision is considered a manufacturer, is an area of great importance and great uncertainty. This arrangement is often referred to as "contract manufacturing" if the CFC buys from the manufacturer or "toll manufacturing" if the CFC pays the manufacturer a service fee to manufacture where the CFC owns the raw materials, works-in-progress and finished inventory throughout the production process.

Note that in order for a CFC to have foreign base company sales income, the related corporation need not be a U.S. corporation. Suppose that U.S. Co., a U.S. corporation has two subsidiaries—MfgCo in high-tax country M and SalesCo in low-tax country S. MfgCo manufactures thermostats and then sells them at an arm's-length price to SalesCo which sells them throughout Europe. Under I.R.C. § 954(d)(1) the income earned by SalesCo is foreign base company sales income which is subject to U.S. taxation under subpart F because SalesCo purchases personal property manufactured outside of country S from a related party (*see* I.R.C. § 954(d)(3)) and sells the property for use outside of country S. It is odd that subpart F should reach the income of SalesCo when the manufacturing activity that gives rise to such sales income is located abroad. There is no U.S. connection to the SalesCo income. The fact that MfgCo isolates its sales function in SalesCo may be of interest to state M tax authorities but that decision does not decrease U.S. tax revenues. If country S is a low-tax jurisdiction, the United States will ultimately collect more in tax revenue than it would if the sales function was carried out in country M because the indirect foreign tax credit would be smaller on dividends paid by the subsidiaries to U.S. Co.

Furthermore, there may be good business reasons for geographically separating the sales from the manufacturing functions. Locational factors, advanced communications, the availability of credit, availability of a sales force, risk diversification, etc. all may be reasons why Salesco was located in country S rather than country M, the United States or the country of the destination of the manufactured products. But even if the decision is tax motivated (*i.e.*, taxes are lower in country S), it is country M where the productive economic activity occurs not the United States that is disadvantaged.

Suppose that a U.S. corporation has a wholly-owned manufacturing subsidiary in Germany which establishes an unincorporated branch office in Switzerland through which all sales are made to European customers. Assume that the sales income in Switzerland is not subject to tax in Germany. Aside from U.S. tax considerations, this structure might minimize European taxes to the extent that the Swiss tax on sales by the Swiss branch is less than the German tax if the sales were taxable in Germany. At first glance, it appears that there is no subpart F problem because the German corporation is a manufacturing corporation. However, under I.R.C. § 954(d)(2), the branch may be treated as a subsidiary so that the sales income of the branch to customers outside of Switzerland will be treated as foreign base company sales income taxable to the U.S. parent corporation. This treatment will occur where the sales branch income is taxed at an effective rate that is less than 90 percent of, and at least 5 percentage points less than, the effective rate of tax that would have applied if the sales were made by the German corporation in Germany. Reg. § 1.954–3(b)(1).

Notice that the "branch rule" is also odd. If the German corporation were to conduct both the manufacturing and sales activities in Germany, subpart F would not apply. Upon a dividend distribution from the German corporation to its U.S. parent, the United States would assert its tax jurisdiction. However, the dividend would also carry with it an indirect tax credit for foreign income taxes paid by the German company to Germany with respect to the income distributed. The United States would collect fewer tax dollars as a result of this credit.

If the sales activities are conducted through a branch in Switzerland and as a result the total foreign tax burden is lower, on the eventual dividend distribution to the U.S. parent there will be a smaller foreign tax credit, resulting in more tax dollars for the United States. That is, discouraging a foreign corporation from setting up a foreign sales branch may tend towards lowering not raising U.S. tax revenues.

The "branch rule" not only applies to a sales branch, but can apply to a manufacturing branch. Suppose that an Swiss subsidiary handles the sales of goods manufactured by the subsidiary's unincorporated branch in Germany. Although the Swiss subsidiary is engaged in manufacturing (through its German branch), the U.S. corporation may be deemed to have foreign base company sales income nevertheless. Under the manufacturing branch rule, the German manufacturing branch is treated as if it were a separate subsidiary. Accordingly, the Swiss subsidiary is deemed to be purchasing from a related party (*i.e.*, the German branch treated as a corporation) and to the extent that it sells to customers outside of Switzerland, foreign base company sales income is generated by the Swiss subsidiary.

The manufacturing branch rule only applies if the effective tax rate of the sales subsidiary is less than 90 percent of or more than 5 percentage points less than the effective tax rate that would have applied to the sales income had it been earned in the manufacturing country. Reg. § 1.954–3(b)(1). Therefore, in order for the rule to apply in this example, essentially, the income earned by Switzerland must be taxed at an effective tax rate that is less than effective tax rate had the income been earned and taxed in Germany. The regulations do not provide much guidance on how to determine the "effective tax rate." But *see* GLAM2015–002. Whether there is a sales branch or a manufacturing branch, subpart F may apply only where the sales unit (whether a branch or the rest of the corporation) is taxed at a lower rate than the manufacturing unit (whether the rest of the corporation or the branch).

There is no end to branch rule permutations and combinations. For example, a CFC could have a manufacturing branch and a sales branch. In this situation, essentially, the rate disparity test involves a comparison of whether the effective rate of taxation in the sales branch is less than the rate of taxation in the manufacturing branch (manufacturing branch rule). It is not necessary to apply the rate disparity test to the home office if no manufacturing is done there. If a CFC has multiple manufacturing branches with respect to the product being sold, the manufacturing branch with the lowest tax rate (*i.e.*, a pro-taxpayer rule) is used for the rate disparity test. If a CFC has multiple sales branches, the rate disparity test must be performed for each sales branch and the manufacturing branch.

The IRS has tried to expand the application of the branch rule. In *Ashland Oil, Inc. v. Commissioner*, 95 T.C. 348 (1990), the Service argued unsuccessfully that sales income of a CFC in a low tax jurisdiction was subject to subpart F even though the property sold was purchased from an unrelated manufacturer in another country. The manufacturer was a "contract manufacturer" which manufactured good according to the CFC's specifications and received compensation equal to the sum of its costs plus a fixed fee. In *Vetco Inc. v. Commissioner*, 95 T.C. 579 (1990) the IRS tried again to expand the branch rule to cover any perceived abuse involving a sales or manufacturing subsidiary, this time arguing unsuccessfully that a subsidiary could constitute a branch or similar establishment within the meaning of I.R.C. § 954(d)(3).

Having lost both *Ashland* and *Vetco*, the IRS now concedes the position that a contract manufacturer cannot automatically be considered a branch for purposes of I.R.C. § 954(d)(2). Rev. Rul. 97–48, 1997–2 C.B. 89. So, for example, a Hong Kong CFC which sells goods manufactured under its specifications by an unrelated contract manufacturer in Indonesia to customers outside of Hong Kong will not generate subpart F income under the branch rule. However, the IRS also takes the position that a CFC's use of a contract manufacturer does not automatically make the CFC a manufacturer for purposes of I.R.C. § 954(d)(1).

Suppose that the Hong Kong CFC purchases raw materials from a related Chinese corporation and arranges for the Indonesian contract manufacturer to do the manufacturing. (Note that Hong Kong and China are treated as separate countries for U.S. tax purposes.) Sales are then made throughout Asia. Unless the CFC is viewed as manufacturing, the purchase of goods from a related party and the sale to unrelated parties outside the country of the CFC's incorporation leads to foreign base company sales income in the view of the IRS even though the goods purchased from a related party (raw materials) are not the same as the goods sold by the CFC (finished goods).

A CFC can be a manufacturer where another party (related or unrelated) does the physical manufacturing. Reg. § 1.954–3(b) considers whether the CFC makes a "substantial contribution" to the manufacturing looking at the following factors:

1. Oversight and direction of the activities and process pursuant to which the property is physically manufactured;

2. Activities that are considered in, but that are insufficient to qualify as, physical manufacturing;

3. Material selection, vendor selection, or control of the raw materials, work-in-process or finished goods;

4. Management of manufacturing costs or capacities (for example, managing the risk of loss, cost reduction or efficiency

initiatives associated with the manufacturing process, demand planning, production scheduling or hedging raw material costs);

5. Control of manufacturing related logistics (*e.g.*, arranging delivery of raw materials, but would not include post-manufacturing logistical activities such as shipment of finished goods to customers);

6. Quality control (for example, sample testing or establishment of quality control standards); and

7. Developing, or directing the use or development of, product design and design specifications, as well as trade secrets, technology or other intellectual property for the purpose of physically manufacturing the property.

Suppose that U.S. Co. owns all of the stock of CFC, located in Ireland. If CFC buys inventory from U.S. Co. and resells throughout Europe, CFC's income will be foreign base company sales income (*i.e.,* buying from a related party and selling outside the country of CFC's incorporation). Suppose instead of buying and reselling that U.S. Co. sells directly to the customers and CFC earns a sales commission paid by U.S. Co. This rearrangement of the way business is done does not cure the subpart F problem. The sales commission to the extent attributable to sales outside the CFC's country of incorporation is treated as foreign base company sales income in the hands of CFC that is taxed directly to U.S. Co. I.R.C. § 954(d)(1) (parenthetical language).

Suppose that Parentco, a U.S. corporation, has a CFC, Subco, in the Cayman Islands which is a controlling partner in a Cayman Islands partnership. The partnership acts as a purchasing agent for Parentco with respect to footwear manufactured in Brazil and received compensation for its services. The footwear imported by Parentco was sold in the United States. Does Subco have foreign base company sales income with respect to its share of the partnership's commissions? *See* I.R.C. § 954(d) (commissions for the purchase of personal property on behalf of Parentco)?

Following a defeat in *Brown Group, Inc. v. Commissioner*, 77 F.3d 217 (8th Cir. 1996), where the court determined that there was no subpart F income because a partnership cannot have subpart F income under I.R.C. § 952 and because that characterization carries through to Subco, regulations were issued to clarify that under the aggregate theory of partnerships, the income of a partnership will be evaluated as if the partner earned it. Because the sales commission would have been subpart F income in the hands of Subco, Parentco has subpart F income. Reg. § 1.954–1(g)(3), Ex. 1.

As another example, suppose that CFC1, a controlled foreign corporation organized in Country A, is an 80-percent partner in Partnership, a partnership organized in Country B. CFC2, a controlled foreign corporation organized in Country

B, owns the remaining 20 percent interest in Partnership. CFC1 and CFC2 are owned by a common U.S. parent, USP. CFC2 manufactures inventory in Country B. Partnership earns sales income from purchasing the inventory from CFC2 and selling it to third parties located in Country B that are not related persons with respect to CFC1 or CFC2. In this situation, to determine whether CFC1's distributive share of Partnership's sales income is foreign base company sales income, CFC1 is treated as if it purchased the inventory from CFC2 and sold it to third parties in Country B. Under section 954(d)(3), CFC2 is a related person with respect to CFC1. Thus, with respect to CFC1, the sales income is deemed to be derived from the purchase of personal property from a related person. Because the property purchased is both manufactured and sold for use outside of Country A, CFC1's country of organization, CFC1's distributive share of the sales income is foreign base company sales income. Because Product A is both manufactured and sold for use within CFC2's country of organization, CFC2's distributive share of Partnership's sales income is not foreign base company sales income presumably for any one of three reasons: either because CFC2 meets one of the two manufacturing exceptions (*i.e.,* the good are manufactured in CFC2's country of incorporation or CFC2 is the manufacturer) or because CFC2 meets the destination exception by selling to customers in the same country.

(3) Foreign Base Company Services Income

The third category of foreign base company income is foreign base company services income. I.R.C. §§ 954(a)(3) and (e). This category is composed of income derived from the performance of specified services for, or on behalf of, a related person (defined in I.R.C. § 954(d)(3)) outside the country where the CFC is organized. The services covered are: technical, managerial, engineering, architectural, scientific, skilled, industrial, commercial, or like services. For example, suppose the U.S. parent manufactures computers for sale abroad, and a wholly-owned Swiss subsidiary—a CFC—services the installed computers throughout the rest of Europe on behalf of its parent. The income realized by the CFC that is not generated from services performed in Switzerland is foreign base company services income which is foreign base company income which is subpart F income which is directly taxable to the U.S. parent corporation. The purpose of this category is to discourage the parent corporation from isolating services income in a low-tax jurisdiction.

If the services are performed in the country in which the CFC is organized, the income is not foreign base company services income. I.R.C. § 954(e)(1)(B). For example, services income earned by the Swiss corporation from servicing computers in Switzerland is not foreign base company services income. However, suppose that the U.S. parent has a wholly-owned Lux subsidiary that wholly-owns all the "stock" of a French disregarded entity. If the

French disregarded entity performs services in France on behalf of the U.S. parent, the income generated will be foreign base company services income because the services are performed outside of Luxembourg—the CFC that is tested.

Note that if services performed on behalf of the parent corporation are directly related to the sale by the CFC of property it manufactured and are performed before the time of sale, the income is not foreign base company services income. I.R.C. § 954(e)(2). A CFC's services income on its own behalf directly related to property it manufactures is not foreign base company services income whenever performed because the services are not "for or on behalf" of a related person.

A CFC's services are performed on behalf of a related person if the CFC receives compensation from a related person, if the CFC performs services that the related party was obligated to perform, if the services are a material part of a sale by a related person, or if the related party provides "substantial assistance" contributing to the performance of services by a CFC to an unrelated person. Reg. § 1.954–4(b). "Substantial assistance" may include the related party providing meaningful supervision or loaning employees or providing financial assistance. Reg. § 1.954–4(b).

For example, suppose that U.S. Co. has two wholly-owned subsidiaries, Helper Co. and LowTax Co., in two different jurisdictions. LowTax Co. enters into an agreement with unrelated customers for LowTax Co. to perform services. LowTax Co.

then hires Helper Co. to perform those services on its behalf. Customers pay LowTax Co. which pays an arm's length fee to Helper Co. for performing the services. The income earned by Helper Co. may be foreign base company services income if Helper Co. is not a U.S. corporation and if the services are performed outside Helper Co.'s country of incorporation. Even then, Helper Co. may avoid subpart F income under the high tax exception in I.R.C. § 954(b)(4).

Regardless of the treatment of Helper Co., the net income of LowTax Co. (after deducting the fee to Helper Co.) from services performed outside its country of incorporation may be foreign base company services income because LowTax Co. receives substantial assistance from Helper Co. Reg. § 1.954–4(b)(2)(ii). Whether LowTax Co. will or will not have foreign base company services income depends on whether Helper Co. is a U.S. company and the extent to which Helper Co. provides assistance. Notice 2007–13, 2007–1 C.B. 410, provides that "substantial assistance" consists of assistance furnished (directly or indirectly) by a related *United States* person or persons to the CFC if the assistance satisfies an objective cost test. If Helper Co. is a foreign entity providing assistance, LoTax Co. should not have foreign base company services income. If Helper Co. is a related U.S. corporation, then LoTax Co. may have subpart F income to the extent that the cost to LoTax Co of the services furnished by Helper Co. equals or exceeds 80 percent of the total cost to LoTax Co. of performing the services.

(4) Other Foreign Base Company Income

Generally, income from the manufacture and distribution of oil and gas products outside the United States is foreign base company income unless the products were extracted from, or for use in, the country where the CFC was organized. I.R.C. § 954(a)(5) and (g).

(5) Allocation and Apportionment of Deductions

A U.S. shareholder is taxed on net foreign base company income. I.R.C. § 954(a)(5). Consider a situation where a CFC earns both subpart F and non-subpart F income. A taxpayer would prefer to have expenses allocated to reduce the subpart F income rather than to reduce non-subpart F income which won't be taxable to the U.S. shareholder. The Regulations under the source rules and the foreign tax credit rules apply for this purpose. Reg. § 1.954–1(c). *See* Reg. § 1.861–8 et seq., discussed *supra* at § 3.02 and Reg. § 1.904–5. Note though, that interest paid to a related person is allocated first to passive foreign personal holding company income with any remainder allocated to other subpart F or non-subpart F income. I.R.C. § 954(b)(5). Any remaining interest expense at the CFC level would be allocated and apportioned against subpart F and on-subpart F income either by apportioning interest expense pro rata based on the CFC's gross income subject to some modifications ("modified gross income method") or pro rata based on the assets of the CFC ("asset method"). The method selected must be used for all CFCs.

(6) Relief Provisions

Any CFC—even one actively engaged in manufacturing—is likely to have some foreign base company income. For example, a manufacturing CFC typically may have interest from bank accounts or interest from financing sales. In order not to bring the full weight of subpart F crashing down on every foreign corporation, the Code provides a *de minimis* rule. If the **gross** foreign base company income (plus certain insurance income) is less than the lower of 5 percent of the CFC's gross income or $1 million, none of the CFC's income is treated as subpart F income. I.R.C. § 954(b)(3)(A). Conversely, if a CFC has gross foreign base company income (and certain insurance income) in excess of 70 percent of the CFC's gross income, the entire gross income for the taxable year is treated as subpart F income. I.R.C. § 954(b)(3)(B).

Even if a CFC has foreign base company income in excess of the *de minimis* amount, it may be inappropriate to subject the United States shareholder to immediate taxation on the CFC's earnings. After all, the foreign parent may be operating through a CFC only for nontax reasons. Rather than trying to ascertain the subjective motivation behind setting up a CFC, the Code relieves a United States shareholder from taxation under subpart F if the CFC can satisfy an objective standard. Essentially upon the taxpayer's election, no item of income that would otherwise be foreign base company income or insurance income is included in those categories if the income is subject to an effective rate of foreign income tax greater than 90 percent of the maximum U.S. corporate tax rate. I.R.C. § 954(b)(4). This "high tax exception" allows a U.S. shareholder to avoid subpart F treatment for an item of income earned by a CFC that is essentially taxed at the same rate it would have been taxed had it been earned directly by the U.S. shareholder.

In determining whether the high tax exception is met, a pooling concept is used. The item of income is compared to the CFC's earnings and profits and that ratio is multiplied by the CFC's tax pool (*i.e.,* post-1986 taxes paid). Reg. § 1.954–1(d)(3). This multiplication produces the taxes that are considered associated with the item of subpart F income for purposes of applying the high tax exception. So an item of income that itself is not subject to foreign tax could still qualify for the high tax exception if the CFC had a high tax pool compared to the CFC's earnings and profits. Conversely, an item of income that itself is highly taxed may not qualify for the high tax exception if the overall tax pool is quite low compared to the earnings and profits.

To illustrate, suppose that CFC with a U.S. dollar currency earns $10 of subpart F foreign base company sales income that is not taxed. If the E&P pool (including the subpart F income) of CFC is $100 and the tax pool is $100, then $10 of tax is associated with the $10 of subpart F income. Thus the effective rate of tax for that item is 50 percent ($10 of tax on what is deemed to be $20 of pre-tax income) and it could qualify for the high tax exception. Now suppose instead that CFC earns $20 of subpart F income on which a $10 tax is imposed. Suppose that the E&P pool is $100 (including the subpart F income) and the tax pool is $20 (including the tax on the subpart F income). For purposes of applying the high tax exception, the $10 net subpart F inclusion (tax paid is subtracted pursuant to I.R.C. § 954(b)(5)) will be deemed to have associated with it a $2 tax liability (($10 sub F inclusion/$100 E&P) × $20 tax pool). Consequently, the effective tax rate of 16.67 percent ($2 of tax on what is deemed to be $12 of pre-tax income) will not meet the high tax exception.

The amount included as subpart F income cannot exceed the current earnings and profits for the CFC's taxable year. I.R.C. § 952(c)(1)(A). To the extent that the potential subpart F inclusion exceeds the current earnings and profits (*i.e.*, there is a deficit in the non-subpart F earnings and profits), non-subpart F income in future years is "recaptured" as subpart F income. I.R.C. § 952(c)(2). For example, suppose in year 1 a CFC has $10 million of subpart F income and a $6 million loss from non-subpart F activities (*e.g.*, from an active manufacturing business). The subpart F inclusion for the year is limited to $4 million—the net amount of earnings and profits for the year. In year 2, if CFC earns $7 million of non-subpart F income, $6 million of that income ($10 million – $4 million) will be recaptured as subpart F income. I.R.C. § 952(c)(2).

Suppose a CFC has an earnings and profits deficit from subpart F activities for a prior year, a "qualified" deficit can be carried forward and offset any current earnings and profits so that current subpart F income would not be taxable. I.R.C. § 952(c)(1)(B). To be "qualified," an earnings and profits deficit must arise in the same activity as the current subpart F income. For example, foreign base company sales income in a current year cannot be lowered through a deficit arising from passive activities in a prior year. Also, current foreign personal holding company income cannot be offset by an earnings and profits deficit in a prior year even if it arose from passive activities.

Not only can a CFC reduce subpart F income by applying a qualified deficit against the current earnings and profits limitation, it can also reduce subpart F income under the "chain deficit rule" which permits an earnings and profits deficit of certain related corporations to offset current earnings and profits in applying the earnings and profits ceiling rule. I.R.C. § 952(c)(1)(C). For example, suppose that CFC has subpart F income of $100 million and earnings and profits of $100 million. Suppose that CFC owns all the stock of Subco which has an earnings and profits deficit of ($100 million). If the chain deficit rule applies, U.S. shareholders of CFC will have no subpart F income for the year. In order for the chain deficit rule to apply, the two corporations must be incorporated in the same foreign country and there must be 100 percent ownership (constructive ownership rules apply). Also, for subpart F income to be offset, the deficit must arise from the same type of activity and must have occurred while in the chain. If the subpart F income is foreign personal holding company income, the chain deficit rule usually will not apply even if the deficit arose from passive activities.

(7) Insurance Income

Another troublesome category of subpart F income deserves a brief mention. Under I.R.C. § 952(a)(1), certain insurance income—basically the insurance of risks outside the country in which a CFC is organized—is the type of easily moveable income which subpart F addresses. Even with insurance income treated as subpart F income, U.S. shareholders historically sought to avoid taxation by organizing a captive insurance company (*i.e.*, one that insured its U.S. shareholders) which had more than 10 equal U.S. shareholders. If each shareholder held less than 10 percent of the stock, there would be no United States shareholders within the meaning of I.R.C. § 951(b) and therefore no CFC under I.R.C. § 957. However, under I.R.C. § 953(c), if even 25 percent of a captive insurance company is owned by any U.S. persons (*i.e.*, not necessarily 10 percent shareholders) the company is a CFC, and the income is taxed to the U.S. persons regardless of their percentage ownership.

(8) Ordering Rules

In determining the potential subpart F inclusion for a U.S. shareholder, Reg. § 1.954–1(a) prescribes the following order:

1. Determine gross foreign base company income

2. Apply the de minimis and full inclusion rules to arrive at adjusted gross foreign base company income

3. Properly allocable deductions are subtracted to arrive at net foreign base company income

4. Net foreign base company income then becomes adjusted net foreign base company income by making two adjustments: first, the E&P limitation under I.R.C. § 952(c); second, the high tax exception under I.R.C. § 954(b).

5. Insurance income is then taken into consideration

6. Finally, any non-subpart F income that is recaptured as subpart F income under I.R.C. § 952(c)(2) is added to the total

To illustrate how these ordering rules might apply, consider a CFC that under the high tax exception does not appear to have subpart F income. However, if that CFC is subject to I.R.C. § 952(c)(2) recapture, because that step is the last step and comes after the high tax exception, there will be a subpart F inclusion. Moreover, the taxpayer cannot again assert the high tax exception to the I.R.C. § 952(c)(2) recapture amount. Reg. § 1.954–1(a)(7) (last sentence).

(B) INCREASE IN EARNINGS INVESTED IN U.S. PROPERTY

Recall that a United States shareholder is taxable on the shareholder's portion of the CFC's subpart F income (primarily foreign base company income) and the CFC's investment of any non-subpart F earnings in U.S. property. I.R.C. § 951(a). For example, suppose that a CFC is a manufacturing corporation that has no subpart F income. The CFC earns $5 million of non-subpart F income and makes a loan of $3 million to its U.S. parent. Unless the parent corporation is taxed, it has the current use of $3 million on which U.S. taxes have been deferred. Section 956 was enacted to deter U.S. taxpayers from repatriating non-subpart F earnings of a CFC through loans and other investments in U.S. property in a tax-free manner where the earnings have not been subject to U.S. tax.

Under I.R.C. §§ 951(a)(1)(B) and 956, a United States shareholder is taxed on the shareholder's pro rata share of any increase in the earnings of the CFC invested in U.S. property. In the example above, the parent corporation is taxed on the $3 million invested in the U.S. debt instrument in the current year. The increase in earnings invested in U.S. property is measured essentially by comparing the average adjusted basis of such U.S. property (minus allocable liabilities) for the tax year (using the close of each quarter as a measuring date) with the adjusted basis at the end of the previous year. Regulations and rulings attempt to ensure that taxpayers cannot manipulate the amount invested in U.S. property right before year end.

Suppose that a calendar-year CFC with no prior investments in U.S. property makes a $1 million loan to its U.S. parent on January 1 of Year 2 which remains outstanding all year. Because the loan was outstanding all year, there would be an increase (*i.e.,* $0 investment in U.S. property in Year 1) of $1 million invested in U.S. property (($1m + $1m + $1m +$1m)/4). If, instead the loan were made in April and remained outstanding for the remainder of the year, the investment in U.S. property would be $750,000 (($1m + $1m + $1m)/4). If there is no change throughout the following year, Year 3, there would be a $250,000 increase in the investment in U.S. property (*i.e.,* $750,000 at the beginning of Year 3 and $1 million at the end of Year 3), and therefore a potential I.R.C. § 956 inclusion of $250,000 (if there are at least $250,000 of "applicable earnings" (*i.e.,* earnings and profits with a few adjustments)).

In effect, the amount invested in U.S. property is treated as if distributed to the U.S. parent as a dividend where the CFC has non-subpart F earnings and profits. Foreign taxes associated with any inclusion under § 956 can be credited by the U.S. recipient. *See* I.R.C. § 960(a)(1) discussed *infra* in § 10.05. Because the § 956 amount is treated as a distribution, § 956 will result in an inclusion only to the extent of the CFC's earnings and profits.

Note that if a CFC has subpart F income and uses that income to invest in U.S. property, there is a potential double tax to the United States shareholder—once when the subpart F income is earned and once when invested in U.S. assets. However, I.R.C. § 959(a) protects a United States shareholder against a double tax when previously taxed income ("PTI") is invested in U.S. property. Furthermore, I.R.C. § 959(c) provides that investment in United States property is deemed first to come out of previously taxed subpart F income. Only when the investment in United States property exceeds that amount is I.R.C. § 956 triggered if there is non-PTI E&P.

The term "United States property" refers to any property which is tangible property located in the United States, any security issued by a U.S. payor (*i.e.*, stock issued by a domestic corporation or an obligation issued by a U.S. borrower), or the right to use in the United States certain intangible property such as patents, copyrights, secret formulae, designs or other similar property. I.R.C. § 956(c)(1). For example, if a CFC acquires the right to produce a patented computer chip in the United States, the amount paid for that right (whether a lump sum or periodic royalties) is considered an investment in U.S. property. Similarly, if a CFC invests in stock of the U.S. parent or of a related U.S. corporation, the U.S. parent may be taxed on the fair market value of the investment. A CFC that is a partner in either a U.S. or foreign partnership is considered to own a pro rata share of U.S. property owned by the partnership. Treas. Reg. § 1.956–2(a)(3).

Suppose a CFC makes a loan to a foreign partnership with a U.S. shareholder as a partner. The partnership then makes a distribution of the loan proceeds to its partners. If the loan is not viewed as a § 956 investment by the CFC, then the CFC has found a way to get cash home without any U.S. tax consequences. (Note that a loan to a U.S. partnership is a § 956 investment.)

Temporary Regulations provide a new anti-abuse rule (Treas. Reg. § 1.956–1T(b)(5)) that treats a CFC-owned obligation of a foreign partnership in some cases as an obligation of the partnership's partner (*e.g.*, a partner that is a United States person). A foreign partnership's obligation is treated as an obligation of a partner when: (1) the foreign partnership makes a distribution to the partner; (2) "[t]he foreign partnership would not have made the distribution but for a funding of the partnership through the obligation;" and (3) the partner is related to the CFC.

There are several notable exceptions to the definition of United States property where the investment does not directly benefit a related U.S. person. For example, while a CFC that invests in a debt obligation of the parent corporation has invested in United States property thereby subjecting the U.S. parent to taxation on the invested funds, a CFC that invests in obligations of the U.S. government (*e.g.*, U.S. Treasury notes) is not treated as having invested in United States property. I.R.C. § 956(c)(2)(A). A similar exception is provided for deposits by a CFC in a U.S. bank. There is also an exception for an investment in a debt obligation of the parent corporation where the investment over any quarter is of very short duration (30 days or less) and the total duration of such parent corporation debt for the year does not equal or exceed 60 days. Notice 88–108, 1988–2 C.B. 445.

If the CFC invests in the stock of an unrelated U.S. corporation, the stock is not considered U.S. property. I.R.C. § 956(c)(2)(F). For this purpose, stock in a U.S. corporation less than 25 percent of the voting power of which is owned by United States shareholders of the U.S. parent is not U.S. property. In addition, exceptions are provided for investment in U.S. property relating to foreign activities such as property for export abroad or relating to export property (*e.g.*, transportation facilities). I.R.C. § 956(c)(2)(B), (D), (G), and (I). Finally, a CFC may make a loan to a U.S. affiliated person without the resulting debt instrument constituting United States property to the extent the loan is made in connection with the sale or processing of property under normal arm's-length business relations. I.R.C. § 956(c)(2)(C), Reg. §§ 1.956–2(b)(5) and 1.956–2T(d)(2) (similar rule for services performed by CFC for U.S. person).

Suppose a U.S. parent corporation with a manufacturing CFC is aware that any investment of the CFC's funds in United States property may trigger a tax to the parent under I.R.C. §§ 951(a)(1)(B) and 956. Can the parent avoid taxation by borrowing money from a bank where repayment is guaranteed by the CFC? If so, the U.S. parent has found a way to indirectly repatriate its foreign earnings by borrowing in the United States using the strength of those earnings as collateral. However, under I.R.C. § 956(d) if the CFC guarantees the loan or pledges property for security, the guarantee (or pledge) is treated as an investment in U.S. property. However, if the parent corporation borrows money pledging the stock of the CFC, I.R.C. § 956(d) does not apply, and there would be no adverse tax consequences to the parent corporation unless 2/3 of the voting stock is pledged and there are negative covenants preventing the disposition of assets by the CFC. Reg. § 1.956–2(c)(2). Consequently, to help facilitate loan agreements, many U.S. lenders will insist on a U.S. borrower pledging 65 percent of the stock of its CFCs, thereby not triggering I.R.C. § 956.

While I.R.C. § 956 was originally enacted as an "anti-taxpayer" provision (*i.e.,* to prevent tax-free repatriation through loans), as is often the case, taxpayers have found affirmative uses for I.R.C. § 956. There is nothing that prevents a taxpayer from invoking I.R.C. § 956. Suppose that a CFC with earnings and profits has cash that is needed by its U.S. shareholders. In many cases, if that cash is distributed as a dividend, the country of the CFC may impose a withholding tax on the dividend and the dividend will be taxable to the recipient. Or perhaps the CFC has insufficient "distributable reserves" under local country corporate law to make a distribution or faces a local country withholding tax on a distribution. However, by lending the cash to the U.S. shareholder, the CFC may avoid the local country withholding tax while under I.R.C. § 956 the U.S. shareholder will still be taxable (and can still take a foreign tax credit under I.R.C. § 960 which would be calculated in the same manner as the indirect foreign tax credit under I.R.C. § 902). *See* § 10.05.

Suppose ProfitCo, a CFC with ample cash makes a loan to its U.S. parent. Assuming that the ProfitCo has E&P, the loan would likely be taxable under I.R.C. § 956. While the U.S. tax on the inclusion may be offset by available foreign tax credits associated with the inclusion (or excess credits available to the U.S. parent), assume that no such credits are available. Now suppose that instead of lending directly back to the U.S. parent that ProfitCo lends to related DeficitCo, a CFC that has a deficit in E&P and which ProfitCo is deemed to control under constructive ownership rules. DeficitCo then lends to the U.S. parent. Can the U.S. parent avoid an inclusion because there are no "applicable earnings?" Tax planners have to work harder than that to achieve tax-efficient results, as an anti-abuse rule would treat the loan as if it came from ProfitCo and I.R.C. § 956 would apply. Reg. § 1.956–1T(b)(4). In 2015, this anti-abuse rule was expanded in several respects to include any indirect funding (not just through capital contributions or debt) of the controlled lender to the U.S. shareholder and to make clear that even if the controlled lender has E&P (so it might look like avoiding § 956 is not the motivation), the anti-abuse rule could apply if the controlled lender has tax attributes (*e.g.*, foreign tax credits) that would mitigate any inclusion under § 956.

Suppose that U.S. parent owns LowTaxCo, a CFC, which in turn owns HighTaxCo, a CFC. Historically, U.S. parent may have repatriated earnings by arranging for HighTaxCo to make a loan to U.S. parent. If HighTaxCo has a high-taxed E&P pool and U.S. parent can use foreign tax credits, there may have been little or no residual U.S. tax on the inclusion under I.R.C. § 956. Note that had HighTaxCo simply made a distribution to LowTaxCo which then distributed to U.S. parent, aside from any additional local taxes that might be imposed on the distribution, the high-tax pool at HighTaxCo would become a diluted tax pool at LowTaxCo and more residual U.S. tax would result upon a distribution to U.S. parent. This is exactly the approach that I.R.C. § 960(c) now takes to prevent the "hopscotching" of high-taxed income over the low-taxed income directly to the U.S. This anti-hopscotch rule only applies where it would result in a smaller foreign tax credit to the taxpayer so it would not apply if HighTaxCo owned LowTaxCo and the loan came from LowTaxCo back to U.S. parent. Moreover, the rule only applies for the purpose of determining the amount of foreign taxes that are deemed associated with the I.R.C. § 956 inclusion—not for purposes of determining the amount of the inclusion itself.

§ 10.04   ADJUSTMENTS TO STOCK BASIS

Suppose a U.S. parent incorporates a CFC by exchanging $10 million for the corporation's stock. In the first year of operation, the CFC has subpart F income (*e.g.*, foreign base company sales income) of $2 million that is taxed to the U.S. parent. Or suppose that the CFC earns $2 million of non-subpart F income but on the first day of the taxable year makes a $2 million 1-year loan to the U.S. parent that is taxable under § 956. When the parent is taxed on the CFC's subpart F income or § 956 inclusion, the basis of the CFC's stock is increased from $10 million to $12 million as if the CFC had made a distribution to the parent which had then reinvested the proceeds in the CFC. I.R.C. § 961. In the next year, assume the CFC has no further earnings but distributes $2 million to the U.S. parent corporation. Under I.R.C. § 959(a), the parent is not taxed on the distribution of previously taxed subpart F or § 956 income, but the parent must reduce its stock basis in the CFC by $2 million to $1 million. I.R.C. § 961(b)(1). If basis has been reduced to $0, any excess distribution is taxed as a capital gain. Reg. § 1.961–2(c).

If a U.S. parent owns a lower-tier CFC through a series of upper-tier CFCs, any subpart F inclusion leads to a basis step-up that ripples down the chain. I.R.C. § 961(c). If an upper-tier CFC disposes of stock of a lower-tier CFC, the basis step-up resulting from a subpart F inclusion by the lower-tier entity may decrease or eliminate any gain on the sale of the stock for subpart F purposes (*i.e.,* foreign personal holding company income), but the basis step-up is only for that purpose. There is no basis step-up for purposes of determining the earnings and profits of the upper-tier foreign entity resulting from the sale.

§ 10.05   FOREIGN TAX CREDIT

When a U.S. parent corporation is taxed on a CFC's subpart F income or under § 956, it is taxed on what is usually foreign source income on which there is normally a foreign income tax. Code section 960 provides a foreign tax credit for income taxed to a U.S. shareholder under subpart F or under § 956. As in the case of a dividend paid by any subsidiary to its parent corporation, a dividend deemed paid under subpart F or under § 956 includes the grossed-up foreign income taxes on the deemed distribution. I.R.C. § 78. Recall that the indirect foreign tax credit under I.R.C. § 902 is not available for individual shareholders. However, individual U.S. shareholders can get the benefit of the I.R.C. § 960 tax credit (but lose the benefit of PTI distributions) by electing to be taxed at U.S. corporate rates on their income taxable under subpart F. I.R.C. § 962.

When a U.S. parent is taxable under subpart F and claims a foreign tax credit under I.R.C. § 960, the treatment of the taxable income under subpart F is important for tax limitation purposes under I.R.C. § 904. Generally, income that is includible in a United States shareholder's income under subpart F is placed in baskets corresponding to the CFC's underlying income. I.R.C. § 904(d)(3)(B). If a CFC makes an interest, royalty, or rental payment to a United States shareholder, the recipient generally "looks through" the payment to the income earned by the CFC that is used to make the distribution. I.R.C. § 904(d)(3)(C). For example, if a CFC which earns only manufacturing income pays rent to its U.S. parent, the rent is placed in the general basket. However, interest paid to a United States shareholder is deemed first to be fully allocable to any passive income received by the CFC before being allocated to other income received by the CFC. I.R.C. § 954(b)(5). If the CFC makes a dividend distribution (or invests in United States property), there is a similar look-through rule. I.R.C. § 904(d)(3)(B). For example, if a U.S. parent corporation receives a $200 dividend from a CFC whose $1,000 of earnings and profits consists of manufacturing income the dividend is placed in the general basket for purposes of the foreign tax credit.

If the CFC has no foreign base company income or insurance income because of the *de minimis* rule of I.R.C. § 954(b)(3), distributions made by the CFC to United States shareholders are treated as general basket income. I.R.C. § 904(d)(3)(E). Even if the CFC does have subpart F income so that a distribution would be subject to the look-through rules, the distribution is treated as general basket income if the subpart F income is passive income and is subject to an effective foreign tax rate of greater than 90 percent of the maximum U.S. tax rate. I.R.C. § 904(d)(3)(E).

The previous discussion focuses on how any subpart F inclusion or § 956 inclusion is treated for foreign tax credit purposes, but what are the foreign tax credit implications of a subsequent distribution of previously taxed income? Because a distribution of previously taxed income is not taxable to the U.S. recipient under I.R.C. § 959, it cannot generate foreign source income. Consequently, if a foreign withholding tax is imposed on the amount distributed, the foreign tax credit limitation under I.R.C. § 904 may pose a problem. Fortunately, I.R.C. § 960(b) provides relief by increasing the I.R.C. § 904 limitation enough so that, in many cases, any withholding tax imposed may be creditable.

For a discussion of a special foreign tax credit rule for inclusions under I.R.C. § 956, *see* the discussion above at the end of § 10.03.

§ 10.06   SALE OF CFC STOCK

The U.S. international tax system is constructed to ensure that foreign earnings of a foreign subsidiary will at some point be subject to U.S. tax at ordinary tax rates (*i.e.,* not treated as a capital gain). Suppose that U.S. Co. wholly owns CFC. If CFC earns subpart F income, that income is immediately subject to tax in the hands of U.S. Co. as ordinary income. If CFC earns non-subpart F income, there is no immediate tax to U.S. Co. as long as the earnings remain outside the United States. If CFC distributes a dividend, U.S. Co. will be taxed at ordinary income rates. If CFC makes a loan to U.S. Co., U.S. Co. will be taxed under § 956 as if a dividend were received. If CFC liquidates into U.S. Co. in what would otherwise be a tax-free parent-subsidiary liquidation under I.R.C. § 332, I.R.C. § 367(b) will cause U.S. Co. to be taxed at ordinary income rates on CFC's earnings and profits. *See* § 12.03. All roads lead to eventual taxation of U.S. Co. on the foreign earnings at ordinary income rates.

Now consider what happens if CFC earns non-subpart F income and instead of making a distribution, U.S. Co. sells the appreciated stock of CFC. In the absence of a remedial provision, a U.S. shareholder could avoid ordinary income treatment that would occur on a distribution. If the stock were sold to foreign shareholders, there may be no further U.S. tax to the shareholders upon any subsequent nonliquidating or liquidating distribution of CFC's earnings.

In order to ensure that the non-subpart F income of a CFC is taxed at ordinary income rates whenever and however a U.S. shareholder cashes in on the earnings, I.R.C. § 1248 requires that gain on a disposition of stock in a CFC that would otherwise be treated as capital gain be reported as a dividend to the extent of the CFC's earnings and profits other than those previously included in the U.S. taxpayer's income under subpart F. I.R.C. § 1248(d)(1). The earnings and profits inclusion also picks up an earnings and profits in lower-tier CFCs. The provision generally applies to a sale by any U.S. person owning at least a 10 percent interest in the CFC. For I.R.C. § 1248 to apply, the corporation whose stock is sold need not be a CFC at the time of sale, if it was a CFC at any time during the preceding five years. If the selling shareholder is a U.S. corporation, the shareholder can take an indirect foreign tax credit for the taxes paid by the CFC associated with the ordinary income reported. Reg. § 1.1248–1(d).

Suppose U.S. Co. owns stock of CFC1 with a basis of $3 million and a FMV of $10 million. CFC1 has earnings and profits of $2 million. CFC1 holds stock of CFC2 which has earnings and profits of $1 million. U.S. Co. has held the CFC1/CFC2 chain since its formation. If U.S. Co. sells all the stock of CFC1 the $7 million gain will consist of a dividend to the extent of the $3 million of earnings and profits and $4 million of capital gain. The taxes associated with the dividend portion of the gain will be available to U.S. Co. as an indirect tax credit (and must be grossed-up as income under I.R.C. § 78). Under the look-through rule of I.R.C. § 904(d)(3), often the I.R.C. § 1248 inclusion will go into the general foreign tax credit basket. So, for example, if the foreign tax associated with the $3 million dividend fully offsets the inclusion, only the $4 million capital gain will draw additional U.S. tax. (Any § 1248 E&P that is included in income by a U.S. shareholder is treated as previously taxed income (PTI) under I.R.C. § 959(e).)

For this reason—availability of foreign tax credit—(and for the reason that a corporate taxpayer is taxed on both capital gain and ordinary income at a 35 percent rate), I.R.C. § 1248 is often a taxpayer-friendly provision. Indeed, tax planning often involves creating foreign earnings and profits (particularly if it can be done in a manner that does not trigger any additional foreign tax and the U.S. shareholder has excess foreign tax credits which can be used to offset the potential U.S. tax on the enhanced § 1248 inclusion) prior to a sale of stock in a CFC. For example, if CFC2 could generate an additional $4 million of earnings and profits in a manner that does not generate any additional foreign tax, and U.S. Co. has excess foreign tax credits, then instead of having a $4 million capital gain, U.S. Co. would have no capital gain, and the potential $2.45 million U.S. tax on the $7 million I.R.C. § 1248 inclusion may be fully offset by available foreign tax credits.

The principle of I.R.C. § 1248 has been extended to sales of lower-tier foreign subsidiaries by upper-tier foreign subsidiaries. If a controlled foreign corporation sells or exchanges stock in a lower-tier foreign corporation, any gain on the sale or exchange is treated as a dividend to the same extent that it would have been so treated under I.R.C. § 1248 if the controlled foreign corporation were a U.S. person. For example, if a U.S. corporation owns 100 percent of the stock of a foreign corporation (FC1) which owns 100 percent of stock of a second corporation (FC2), gain on any sale or exchange by FC1 of stock of FC2 is treated as a dividend to the extent of the earnings and profits of FC2 for purposes of subpart F income inclusion by the U.S. shareholder. I.R.C. § 964(e). Under the look-through rule in I.R.C. § 954(c)(6), the dividend portion of the gain on FC1's sale of stock will not be subpart income if FC2 generates only active business income. But should the look-through rule of I.R.C. § 954(c)(6) not be extended, then the dividend portion of FC1's gain (along with the non-dividend portion) will be subpart F income. *See* I.R.C. § 964(e)(2).

§ 10.07 PASSIVE FOREIGN INVESTMENT COMPANIES (PFICS)

You may recall that subpart F is an anti-deferral provision that applies to "U.S. shareholders"—those U.S. person who own at least 10 percent of the voting power of the CFC. However, the subpart F anti-deferral provision does not apply to U.S. persons who own less than 10 percent of the voting power of the a CFC or to any U.S. persons who own stock of a foreign entity that is not a CFC. Yet, these U.S. taxpayers potentially may be able to defer U.S. taxation on passive income. To address this issue, Congress has enacted a set of rules for passive foreign investment companies ("PFICs"). A PFIC is defined as a foreign corporation which meets either an income or an asset test. Under the income test, at least 75 percent of the corporation's income must be passive income for the PFIC rules to apply. I.R.C. § 1297(a)(1). Passive income includes dividends, interest, passive rents and other income treated as foreign personal holding company income for purposes of subpart F. I.R.C. § 1297(b).

The passive income test is based on gross income. For example, if a foreign corporation earns interest income, the fact that deductions exceed the interest income does not change the fact that the foreign corporation would be a PFIC with respect to a U.S. owner. In applying the passive income test, under I.R.C. § 1297(c) described below the income of 25 percent owned subsidiaries can be taken into account. There is also another look-through rule under I.R.C. § 1297(b)(7) for certain foreign corporations that own at least 25 percent (by value) of the stock of a U.S. corporation. If the conditions of this rule are met, the stock itself is not treated as a passive asset and any dividends with respect to that stock are not treated as items of passive income.

Under the asset test, a foreign corporation is a PFIC if at least 50 percent of the corporation's assets (by value) are held for the production of passive income. I.R.C. § 1297(a)(2). Such a corporation would be a PFIC even if it did carry on an active business such as manufacturing. A non-publicly traded foreign corporation can elect to use adjusted basis rather than fair market value as a measuring rod, but once the election is made it cannot be revoked without IRS consent. I.R.C. § 1297(e)(2).

Under § 1297(c), where a foreign corporation owns, directly or indirectly, at least 25 percent by value of the stock of another corporation (a "subsidiary"), the subsidiary look-through rule generally applies. Where the subsidiary look-through rule applies, the foreign corporation being tested for PFIC status is treated as if it held directly its proportionate share of the subsidiary's assets (both passive and active), and directly earned its proportionate share of the subsidiary's income (both passive and active). Second and more remote tiers of foreign corporations are also subject to this treatment if they are 25 percent or more indirectly owned by the foreign corporation being evaluated for PFIC status.

In Rev. Rul. 87–90, 1987–2 C.B. 216, the IRS mapped out how the PFIC provisions could be applied to a typical controlled foreign corporation engaged in manufacturing via the application of the subsidiary look-through rule. In the ruling, a first-tier controlled foreign corporation held directly $1100x worth of assets, plus all the stock of a second-tier controlled foreign corporation. Of the directly held assets, $1000x were active and $100 were passive. The manufacturing controlled foreign corporation had contributed its active profits to the second-tier corporation, which had invested them in assets valued at $1000x that produced only passive income. Applying the asset test (the income test was not discussed), the IRS held that the parent manufacturing controlled foreign corporation was a PFIC. The lower tier entity was also a PFIC. This was the result because, under the subsidiary look-through rule, the parent was treated as holding directly $1100x worth of passive assets (its own plus the subsidiary's) and only $1000x of non-passive assets, and thus 50 percent or more of its total assets was passive.

In applying the income test for testing PFIC status, interest, dividends, rents or royalties which are received from a related party (under I.R.C. § 954(d)(3), more than 50 percent voting power applying constructive ownership rules) receive look-through treatment. I.R.C. § 1297(b)(2)(C). For example, if an entity that is being tested for PIFC status receives interest from a related brother/sister corporation (*i.e.,* a common parent owns both the lender and the borrower) that conducts an active business, the interest income, while normally passive income, will be treated as non-PFIC income for purposes of I.R.C. § 1297(a). If the lender was a wholly-owned subsidiary, presumably the interest income would be disregarded for PFIC testing as the borrower would be deemed to own all of the lender's assets and to receive all of the lender's income. I.R.C. § 1297(c).

Three alternative methods may apply with respect to a U.S. owner of a PFIC. For a qualified electing fund (QEF) under I.R.C. § 1295 that provides information necessary to determine the income and identity of its shareholders, electing U.S. owners are taxed currently on their pro rata portions of the company's actual income under I.R.C. § 1293, subject to an election to defer payment of tax (plus an interest charge) until a distribution is made or a disposition of stock occurs. I.R.C. § 1294.

The QEF election can be made by any U.S. person holding PFIC stock. If a QEF shareholder is a domestic corporation which owns at least 10 percent of the QEF's stock, the shareholder may be permitted an indirect tax credit. I.R.C. § 1293(f). A

U.S. partnership must make the election for its partners. If a QEF election is in place, any qualifying U.S. shareholders can get the beneficial tax capital gains tax rate under I.R.C. § 1(h)(11) for any capital gains at the PFIC level. Because a QEF shareholder is generally taxed as income is earned by the PFIC, there is no additional PFIC taxation upon distribution or if a QEF shareholder disposes of the PFIC stock where the QEF election is made in the first year the U.S. owner becomes an owner. I.R.C. § 1291(d)(1). A U.S. owner that reports income as a result of a QEF election increases basis in the stock of the PFIC. I.R.C. § 1293(d).

Note that a taxpayer with a QEF election only picks up the income of the foreign corporation in years that the entity is a PFIC under the asset or income tests in I.R.C. § 1297(a). So if a QEF election is made in Year 1, the electing shareholder would include all of the entity's income in Year 1. If the entity is not a PFIC in Year 2, then the electing shareholder does not include the PFIC's income. If the entity again becomes a PFIC in Year 3, the electing shareholder includes the income. *See* Reg. § 1.1295–1(c)(2)(ii).

A second method, the deferred interest charge method, allows a U.S. owner ex post to compute an annual inclusion based on reasonable assumptions and to defer payment of the taxes (plus an interest charge) until an "excess distribution" from the PFIC or a disposition of stock occurs. I.R.C. § 1291. Under this method, gain recognized on the disposition of stock is considered to be earned pro rata over the shareholder's holding period of the investment. The U.S. tax due on disposition equals the yearly taxes due plus interest running from each year's due date. The tax rate applied is the highest statutory rate for the owner during the time the stock was held. Notice that under this method, no gain on a sale will qualify for capital gains treatment. Note also that the definition of a disposition is quite broad. For example, if a U.S. owner pledges PFIC stock, that pledge is a disposition for PFIC purpose. I.R.C. § 1298(b)(6). Even a nonrecognition event may trigger taxation. I.R.C. § 1291(f).

The portion of the total actual distributions for the taxable year of the U.S. investor that constitutes an excess distribution is determined by comparing the total distributions received to the average amount of distributions received during the preceding three years, or, if shorter, during the taxpayer's holding period prior to the current year (the "base period"). The amount of the excess distribution is the amount by which total distributions for a taxable year exceeds 125 percent of the base period.

If a shareholder has made a timely QEF election (a "pedigreed QEF") to be taxed as if the PFIC were a pass-thru entity, the deferred interest charge method will not apply. For example, if a U.S. owner with a timely QEF election in effect has gain on the sale of PFIC stock, the gain may qualify for capital gain treatment. For this reason, taxpayers who own stock of a PFIC generally try to make timely QEF elections. But if the shareholder has made an untimely QEF election after the first year it is a PFIC with respect to that owner, the deferred interest charge method may apply even though the QEF election is in effect. For example, a shareholder selling stock of a PFIC at a gain will be subject to a deferred interest charge with respect to that gain. In some cases, a shareholder who fails to make a timely pedigreed QEF election can do so retroactively. Reg. § 1.1295–3.

To illustrate how the deferred interest charge method functions, suppose that a PFIC shareholder has shares of stock in a PFIC with a basis of $100 and fair market value of $600. Suppose that the shareholder has held that stock for five years and that the corporation was a PFIC for each of those five years. Upon the sale, the gain will be spread out over the holding period so that $100 is attributable to each of the five years. With respect to the $100 deemed to have been earned in Year 1, the shareholder will owe tax at the highest marginal tax rate for that year, plus an interest charge equal to the tax that would have been paid if the taxpayer did not defer payment multiplied by an applicable interest rate multiplied by the four years between the end of year 1 and the end of year 5 when the sale takes place. The same analysis applies for the $100 deemed to have paid in year 2, except the interest runs for only three years, and so on. I.R.C. § 1291. Essentially, the interest charge is for the "loan" from the IRS for the tax that should have been paid each year but was not paid. However, note that if there is no gain on the sale of the stock, there is no PFIC interest charge.

This method can be quite punitive. For example, capital gain on the sale of stock may not be due to earnings of the PFIC but may be due to asset appreciation. Also gain on a sale may not have accrued in a pro rata manner but may have occurred shortly before the sale. For these and other reasons, QEF elections are often made where possible.

A third method for reporting PFIC income is the mark-to-market election. I.R.C. § 1296. A U.S. shareholder holding marketable stock in a PFIC (*e.g.*, stock listed on a recognized stock exchange) may elect to recognize either gain or loss annually on the difference between the shareholder's basis at the beginning of the year and the fair market value of the stock at the end of the year. PFIC inclusions are not eligible for the lower tax rate on qualified dividends available to individuals. I.R.C. § 1(h)(11)(C)(iii).

As noted above, essentially a U.S. owner can make a QEF election or if no QEF election is made PFIC liability occurs under the deferred interest charge method. Steps can be taken under either method to minimize potential PFIC liability. Consider first a U.S. owner not making a QEF election.

Once a foreign corporation qualifies as a PFIC with respect to a U.S. owner, it remains a PFIC—the "once a PFIC, always a PFIC" rule—which can lead to some surprising results. For example, suppose that a U.S. shareholder of a PFIC is subject to tax under the deferred interest charge method discussed above. Even if the foreign corporation in a subsequent year no longer meets the PFIC requirements (*i.e.,* when the active business produces profits), any excess distribution or sale of the stock will give rise to a deferred interest charge applied to the shareholder's entire holding period, including that portion when the corporation was not a PFIC.

However, a shareholder can purge the PFIC taint by electing to treat the stock as having been sold on the last day of the last year the foreign corporation met the PFIC qualifications. I.R.C. § 1298(b)(1). This deemed sale is subject to the deferred interest charge but any subsequent gain in the value of the stock or distribution from the foreign corporation will not be subject to the deferred interest charge as long as the foreign corporation does not again become a PFIC. If the deemed sale would not result in any gain, then the purge election is essentially costless. There is also a deemed dividend purge election (instead of the deemed sale purge) for U.S. investors owning stock in a PFIC that is also a CFC. For example, a 7 percent U.S. investor could make the deemed dividend purge as long as the U.S. investor simultaneously elects QEF treatment. I.R.C. § 1291(d)(2)(B).

Recall that a U.S. owner making a QEF election after the first year the owner becomes an owner, remains subject to the QEF regime and the deferred interest charge regime. However, there is another purge provision that allows a shareholder of an unpedigreed QEF (*i.e.,* where the QEF election is not timely made in the first year of PFIC status) to avoid the deferred interest charge method on any subsequent sale of stock or excess distribution if the shareholder agrees to treat the stock as sold immediately before the QEF election takes effect in a transaction subject to the deferred interest charge. That purge would mean that any subsequent appreciation in the stock or any subsequent distributions would not be subject to the deferred interest charge method. Reg. § 1.1291–10.

To prevent the application of the subpart F rules and the PFIC rules, Congress has enacted an "overlap" rule that essentially provides that any shareholder that is a U.S. shareholder with respect to a CFC will not be subject to the PFIC rules. However, the PFIC rules could apply to any U.S. persons who are not shareholders of that entity. For example, suppose that U.S. Co. owns 95 percent of the stock of FC, a foreign corporation and a U.S. individual owns the remaining 5 percent of the stock. The PFIC rules do apply to the U.S. individual even though the subpart F rules apply to U.S. Co.

Under I.R.C. § 1298(f) and Temp. Reg. § 1.1298–1T, a U.S. person that is a shareholder of a PFIC must file a Form 8621 annually. The Regulations eliminate some duplicative reporting. For example, A partner in a U.S. partnership that owns stock of a PFIC where a QEF election is in place (or where the mark-to-market rules apply) does not have to file a Form 8621 if the U.S. partnership files the form.

CHAPTER 11
FOREIGN CURRENCY

§ 11.01 OVERVIEW

Foreign exchange markets work very much like markets in general. When demand is great, the price of a particular currency rises; if supplies of a currency are increased, each unit of currency is worth less when compared to other currencies. For example, suppose that the demand for Dutch tulips in the United States increases. Other things being equal, the demand for the euro (€) needed to pay for the tulips will increase, and the price of the euro relative to other currencies will rise. The exchange rate may move from, say, $1.00 = 1€ to $1.00 = .8€.

Notice that this process has a stabilizing element in that once the price of the euro rises to meet increased demand for tulips, the demand for tulips will decrease because their cost to American customers whose functional currency is the U.S. dollar has increased. In addition, if the euro becomes more expensive for Americans, the dollar becomes cheaper for the Dutch, thereby making U.S. goods more attractive. As the Dutch buy more U.S. dollars needed to purchase the U.S. goods, the price of the dollar will tend to increase relative to the euro.

U.S. tax liability is determined in U.S. dollars. With foreign exchange rates constantly fluctuating, the tax issue that arises is how and when a taxpayer's foreign exchange gains and losses are converted to dollars? For example, if a U.S. taxpayer purchases Japanese yen (with U.S. dollars) as an investment and following a shift in exchange rates sells the yen (for U.S. dollars), how is any gain (or loss) to be treated? Or suppose a French branch of a U.S. business conducts its activities using the euro, how and when should the gains (or losses) of the branch be converted from Euros to dollars?

Tax issues involving foreign currency usually arise in one of the following contexts: (1) isolated business or investment transactions of a U.S. business involving foreign currency; (2) the translation from foreign currency into dollars of the income or loss from continuous activities of a foreign branch or foreign subsidiary of a U.S. business; (3) isolated transactions not connected with the conduct of business or investment (*e.g.*, currency conversion on a vacation). These topics are considered below after an introduction to some of the basic definitional elements of the foreign currency provisions. Even before looking at the statutory apparatus, consider the following three principles that guide the U.S. tax treatment of currency transactions.

First, foreign currency is generally considered to be property the purchase and sale of which are treated in the same manner as the purchase and sale of any other type of property. This general principle has more application to isolated transactions involving the acquisition and disposition of foreign currency rather than the translation from foreign currency into U.S. dollars for the operation of a foreign branch or foreign subsidiary of a U.S. business. For example, a foreign branch or foreign subsidiary of a U.S. corporation does not have to compute gain and loss every time the branch or subsidiary acquires and then exchanges foreign currency for office supplies. Instead, the translation into dollars typically occurs at the end of the taxable year using the average exchange rate for the year.

Second, gain (or loss) from currency transactions is generally treated as ordinary income (or loss) rather than capital gain (or loss). This treatment stems from the fact that Congress views currency fluctuation, in effect, as an interest substitute. To illustrate, suppose that a taxpayer purchases 130,000 Japanese yen (¥) for $1,000 at an exchange rate of $1.00 = 130¥. At the same time the taxpayer lends the yen for three months at a nominal interest rate of 2 percent per year. Suppose, that the interest rate is low relative to interest rates in the United States because the Japanese yen is a strong currency that is expected to get stronger relative to the dollar. In fact, the taxpayer upon purchasing the yen also agrees in the forward market to sell the yen in three months at a rate of $1.00 = 128. The $15.63 gain ($1,015.63 at a conversion rate of $1.00 = 128 minus the $1,000 original cost of the yen) that the taxpayer experiences at the end of three months when the loan is repaid and the yen are sold for dollars is really an interest substitute to supplement the low rate of interest on the yen-denominated loan.

Conversely, suppose that a taxpayer purchases foreign currency of a country experiencing high rates of inflation (so that the currency is weak relative to the dollar), and at the same time enters into a forward contract to sell the currency in three months at a specified rate which is less favorable than the exchange rate on the day of the purchase. If the taxpayer then lends the purchased currency, the nominal interest rate in the loan agreement would be high relative to U.S. interest rates. At the end of three months when the taxpayer sells the foreign currency pursuant to the forward contract, the sales price (in dollars) would be less than the purchase price (in dollars). In effect, the taxpayer would have to "give back" some of the high nominal interest earned on the loan.

Both the gain in the first example and the loss in the second example resulting from the forward contracts are treated, respectively, as ordinary income and loss under the currency exchange rules. While this treatment may be appropriate where the taxpayer locks in the gain or loss by hedging in the forward market, not all currency fluctuations result from changes in interest rates. Issues such as trade and capital flows, the political climate and the credit worthiness of the sovereign all influence currency fluctuation.

Moreover, even where interest rates influence currency fluctuation, treating exchange gains (or loss) as ordinary income (or loss) transactions may be unwarranted. To treat the gain (or loss) from foreign currency transactions as ordinary income (or loss) is inconsistent with the treatment of gain (or loss) from dispositions of other types of property. For example, suppose that the rental value of real property increases because a new road is built nearby. If a taxpayer sits back and collects the rents, the income will be ordinary income. However, if the taxpayer sells the real estate at a profit representing the expected increased rental value, the gain will nevertheless be a capital gain. It is not clear why gain (or loss) from foreign currency dispositions should assume the character of the periodic payments (*i.e.*, interest) generated by the property.

As a third general principle governing currency transactions, currency gains and losses are treated separately from related transactions. For example, suppose that a taxpayer borrows Euros which the taxpayer uses to purchase Italian real property. Any gain or loss on the sale of the real property is determined separately from any gain or loss on the ultimate purchase of Euros to repay the loan. The gain or loss on the sale of the real property may be a capital gain or loss while the currency exchange transaction will produce ordinary income or loss. However, in some cases a taxpayer is permitted to integrate currency gain/loss with gain or loss on the underlying property if ahead of time a taxpayer designates the currency transaction as a qualified hedge. Reg. § 1.988–5(b).

§ 11.02 FUNCTIONAL CURRENCY

Under I.R.C. § 985(b), a U.S. taxpayer's functional currency is typically the U.S. dollar in which case a taxpayer must measure income or loss from dealings in foreign currency in U.S. dollars on a transaction-by-transaction basis. In some circumstances, a taxpayer may use a foreign currency as its functional currency. For example, if a U.S. taxpayer has a self-contained, unincorporated foreign branch in England which conducts all of its business in pounds sterling (£), then the pound sterling may be the functional currency of the branch of the U.S. taxpayer. *See infra* § 11.04(A). Generally, the use of a foreign currency as a functional currency results in deferral of exchange gain or loss, compared with a transaction-by-transaction approach.

The use of a foreign currency as a taxpayer's functional currency is appropriate for a "qualified business unit" (QBU) if the selection is the currency of the "economic environment" in which the QBU's operations are conducted, and the QBU maintains its books and records in such currency. I.R.C. § 985(b)(1)(B). A QBU is defined as any separate and clearly identified unit of a trade or business of the taxpayer which maintains separate books and records. I.R.C. § 989(a). A taxpayer can have several QBUs. Every foreign corporation is a QBU, and the activities of a foreign branch may constitute a QBU if they include every operation that forms a part of the process of earning income. For example, suppose that a U.S. corporation that manufactures and sells product X in the United States has a French sales office with one salesperson whose only function is to solicit orders for product X in France. The French office may not constitute a QBU and would likely use the U.S. dollar as its functional currency because it is not a clearly identified, self-sustaining unit.

Even if the activities a foreign branch or subsidiary constitute a QBU, if the economic environment of the QBU is deemed to be the United States, the dollar will be the functional currency. Determining the economic environment depends on the facts and circumstances surrounding the QBU. The Regulations list several factors which may be considered in making this determination, but they all basically turn on what currency the QBU uses in its day-to-day activities. *See* Reg. § 1.985–1(c)(2). For example, suppose that a U.S. taxpayer has a wholly-owned subsidiary in Belgium that sells its parent's exports throughout Europe with transactions denominated for the most part in U.S. dollars while maintaining its euro-based books. Under these circumstances the dollar may be the functional currency.

In some cases, a U.S. taxpayer with business activities in a foreign branch or subsidiary that is a QBU might nevertheless like to use the dollar as its functional currency and can elect to do so under I.R.C. § 985(b)(3). For example, suppose that U.S. Co. has a foreign branch that conducts activities that constitute a QBU in a foreign country that uses the "h" as its currency. Suppose that the branch purchases goods for 100,000h at a time when the conversion rate is $1.00 = 4h. Because of inflation, the "h" currency becomes worth 1/100 of its previous value so that $1.00 = 400h. If the branch sells the goods for 10,000,000h (*i.e.*, 100 times the purchase price) there is no real gain; the nominal gain of 9,900,000h is due solely to inflation. Nevertheless, the taxpayer faces a $24,750 gain (9,900,000h/400h) for U.S. income tax purposes if $1.00 = 400h is the weighted average exchange rate under I.R.C. § 989(b)(4).

A taxpayer is required to use the U.S. dollar as its functional currency for any QBU whose functional currency would be a "hyperinflationary currency" absent a U.S. dollar election. Reg. § 1.985–2(d). A hyperinflationary currency is defined as the currency of a country in which there is cumulative inflation of at least 100 percent during the 36 calendar months immediately preceding the last day of such taxable year. Under I.R.C. § 985(b)(3), the QBU is required to keep its books and records in U.S. dollars and the taxpayer is required to use a method of accounting that approximates a separate transactions method (*i.e.*, converting the gain or loss from each transaction into dollars when the transaction occurs), referred to as the "U.S. **D**ollar **A**pproximate **S**eparate **T**ransactions" **M**ethod (DASTM, pronounced "dastum").

In the example above, the application of I.R.C. § 985(b)(3) allows the taxpayer to avoid any gain recognition due to the hyperinflation. The goods would have a $25,000 dollar basis (100,000h/4h) at the conversion rate ($1.00 = 4h) existing when the goods were purchased. The amount realized would be $25,000 (10,000,000h/400h) at the $1.00 = 400h conversion rate existing at the time of sale.

When DASTM is required, the taxpayer prepares an income or loss statement in the hyperinflationary currency from the books of the QBU. Then that account is conformed to U.S. financial and tax principles and translated into U.S. dollars (usually on a monthly or shorter basis). Reg. § 1.985–3(b). To that income or loss, the taxpayer adds DASTM gain or loss. The DASTM gain or loss that the taxpayer must recognize is equal to the dollar value of the sum of: the QBU's net worth at the end of the year plus any dividends or remittances to the home office minus the sum of the net worth at the end of the preceding year and the QBU's income or loss for the current year and any capital contributions to the QBU. Reg. § 1.985–3(d)(1). Net worth is translated into dollars on a monthly or shorter basis. Dividends and net remittances are translated into dollars using the spot rate. To study DASTM in action, *see* Reg. § 1.985–3(d)(9) Example.

§ 11.03   FOREIGN CURRENCY TRANSACTIONS

Once the functional currency is established, the Code provides a comprehensive set of rules for nonfunctional currency transactions. A nonfunctional currency is treated as property so that its disposition is a taxable event. For example, if the U.S. dollar is the functional currency, a disposition of Mexican pesos (*e.g.*, the exchange of pesos for Mexican goods or U.S. dollars) can be a taxable event. If the Mexican peso is a taxpayer's functional currency, then the purchase and disposition of Euros (or U.S. dollars) can be a taxable event, but the disposition of pesos (*e.g.*, in exchange for Mexican goods) would not be a taxable event.

Statutorily, I.R.C. § 988(a) provides that any foreign currency gain or loss attributable to a "section 988 transaction" constitutes ordinary income (or loss). A "section 988 transaction" includes: (1) the acquisition of a debt instrument or becoming the obligor under a debt instrument; (2) accruing any item of expense or gross income which is to be paid or received after the date of accrual; (3) entering into certain forward contracts; (4) disposing of any nonfunctional currency. I.R.C. § 988(c). Gain or loss realized is generally sourced by reference to the residence of the taxpayer. I.R.C. § 988(a)(3). However in the case of a QBU, the source of gain or loss will be where the principal place of business of the QBU is located.

The best way to understand how I.R.C. § 988 operates is to consider a range of transactions involving foreign currency. In the examples that follow, assume that the taxpayer's functional currency is the U.S. dollar (USD) and that the transactions described are business or investment (*i.e.*, not personal) transactions.

(A) ACQUISITION AND DISPOSITION OF FOREIGN CURRENCY

Because foreign currency is treated as property for U.S. tax purposes, the acquisition and disposition of such property follows normal U.S. domestic tax rules. I.R.C. § 988(c)(1)(C). To illustrate, if a U.S. taxpayer buys 1.2 million Hong Kong dollars (HKD) and the conversion rate is $1.00 = 6 HKD, the taxpayer's basis in the is $200,000. When the HKDs are "sold" (*i.e.*, exchanged for U.S. dollars), there is a gain or loss if the conversion rate has changed. I.R.C. § 988(c)(1)(C). For example, if the conversion rate changes to $1.00 = 5 HKD, a taxpayer has a $40,000 gain (treated as ordinary income) on the sale of the HKDs ($240,000 amount realized on the conversion to dollars minus the $200,000 basis in the HKDs). The gain is treated as U.S. source income. I.R.C. § 988(a)(3).

If instead of converting HKDs to U.S. dollars, the taxpayer disposes of the nonfunctional currency by purchasing Hong Kong goods for 1.2 million HKDs when the conversion rate is $1.00 = 5 HKDs, the result is again recognition of $40,000 of U.S. source, ordinary income. The taxpayer will have an adjusted basis in the purchased Hong Kong goods of $240,000 (the original basis of $200,000 plus the recognized gain of $40,000 or the value of 1.2 million HKDs (at $1.00 = 5 HKD) at the time of the purchase). *See* Reg. § 1.988–2(a)(2)(iii)(A).

If instead of purchasing property, the taxpayer lends the HKDs to a borrower, the exchange of the HKDs for a debt instrument issued by the borrower again constitutes a taxable disposition. However, depositing a foreign currency in a bank or other financial institution does not cause recognition of gain or loss until there is a disposition of the currency. I.R.C. § 988(c)(1)(C)(ii). Note that if a taxpayer acquires HKDs and immediately lends to a borrower, there may be no gain or loss on the disposition of the nonfunctional currency.

(B) LENDING AND BORROWING FOREIGN CURRENCY

Both acquiring a debt instrument (*i.e.*, lending) denominated in a nonfunctional currency or becoming an obligor under such a debt instrument (*i.e.*, borrowing) are section 988 transactions that may have U.S. tax consequences. I.R.C. § 988(c)(1)(B)(i). Suppose that a U.S. taxpayer purchases a Brazilian bond paying 7 percent interest at a cost of 1,800,000 Brazilian Real (BRL) at a time when the conversion rate is $1.00 = 1.8 BRL. Under these circumstances there may be two times when gain or loss is recognized. As discussed above, if the exchange rate fluctuates between the time the taxpayer purchases BRLs for dollars and the time the BRLs are exchanged for the bond, gain or loss must be recognized. There may be additional gain or loss recognized if there is a currency fluctuation between the time the taxpayer purchases the bond and when the taxpayer disposes of the bond.

Suppose the bond is redeemed after more than a year at face value (1,800,000 BRL) at a time when the exchange rate is $1.00 = 1.7 BRL. The taxpayer's gain on the section 988 transaction is equal to an amount realized of $1,058,824 (the bond was redeemed for 1,800,000 BRL when $1.00 = 1.7 BRL) minus an adjusted basis of $1,000,000 (the bond was purchased for 1,800,000 BRL when $1.00 = 1.8 BRL) or $58,824. In addition, the taxpayer typically would accrue any interest payable by the borrower and convert that interest to dollars at the average spot rate of interest for the year in question, or if the taxpayer was a cash basis taxpayer, interest would be translated into dollars at the spot rate of exchange on the day of payment.

Now consider a situation where a cash-basis taxpayer with a USD functional currency borrows foreign currency rather than lends it. Suppose a taxpayer borrows £100 when £1 = $1, promising to repay the lender £100 plus 10 percent due in one year. Suppose that the taxpayer uses the £100 to purchase office equipment. A month before repayment is due, the taxpayer purchases on the open market £110 when £1 = $.70, and deposits it in a bank. A month later when £1 = $.60, the taxpayer pays off the loan.

This series of events results in the following section 988 transactions:

(a) the initial borrowing and repayment (I.R.C. § 988(c)(1)(B)(i));

(b) the disposition of the borrowed currency in exchange for the office equipment (I.R.C. § 988(c)(1)(C)(i));

(c) the acquisition of currency in the open market and its subsequent disposition (I.R.C. § 988(c)(1)(C)(i)).

The £100 borrowing by the taxpayer constitutes a section 988 transaction so that a $40 gain (*i.e.*, the taxpayer borrowed the equivalent of $100 and repaid the equivalent of $60) is recognized resulting from currency fluctuations between the booking date (*i.e.*, the date of the loan) and the payment date (*i.e.*, the day the loan is paid off). I.R.C. §§ 988(c)(1)(B)(i) and 988(b). If there is no currency fluctuation between the date the currency is borrowed and the date it is used to purchase the machinery, the disposition of the borrowed funds does not produce a currency gain or loss. The purchased machinery has a basis equal to the dollar purchase price on the date of purchase at the spot exchange rate of the dollar and the pound sterling.

When the taxpayer purchases £110 in the open market, the basis in the currency is $77. When that currency is transferred to the lender to repay the loan (with interest) at a time when the £110 has a value of $66, the taxpayer suffers an $11 foreign currency loss. The deposit of pounds sterling in the bank is not a section 988 transaction. I.R.C. § 988(c)(1)(C)(ii). Finally, although not a section 988 transaction, the payment of interest generally generates a deduction. For a cash basis taxpayer, the deduction is the dollar equivalent of the £10 payment, or $6 at the spot exchange rate on the date of repayment.

Suppose a U.K. controlled foreign corporation wholly-owned by U.S. Co. uses the £ as its functional currency. If the CFC generates a currency gain (*e.g.,* a dollar-denominated loan made by the CFC was settled at a time when the dollar strengthened relative to the £), is that currency gain subpart F income (*i.e.,* foreign personal holding company income) for U.S. tax purposes? Under I.R.C. § 954(c)(1)(D), foreign currency gains generally are considered subpart F income unless the gains are directly related to the business needs of the controlled foreign corporation (*e.g.*, loans to customers to encourage inventory purchases).

(C) ACQUISITION AND DISPOSITION OF ASSETS DENOMINATED IN FOREIGN CURRENCY

Generally, fluctuations in exchange rates producing gains and losses upon the purchase and disposition of non-debt assets are not treated as section 988 gains or losses. Instead, the amount of gain or loss, the character, the timing and the source are determined under general tax principles. For example, suppose a U.S. taxpayer purchases 1,000 shares of Toyota stock on the Tokyo stock exchange at ¥13,000 per share at a time when $1.00 = ¥130. More than one year later, the shares are sold for ¥15,000 per share at a time when the conversion rate is $1.00 = ¥125. The taxpayer's gain is $20 per share ((¥15,000/¥125) minus (¥13,000/¥130)), or an overall gain of $20,000. The gain consists of a market gain of $16 per share (¥15,000/¥125 minus ¥13,000/¥125) and a $4 currency gain per share

(¥13,000/¥125 minus ¥13,000/¥130). But because section 988 does not apply to the transaction, the entire gain of $20 per share, or $20,000 overall is treated as long-term capital gain. Similarly if a taxpayer purchased business plant or equipment any gain or loss attributable to currency fluctuation would probably be a capital gain or ordinary loss under I.R.C. § 1231; gain or loss from the disposition of inventory would produce ordinary income or loss.

(D) ACCOUNTS RECEIVABLE AND PAYABLE

While gain or loss on the sale of goods due to currency fluctuation is not normally subject to tax as a section 988 transaction, currency gain or loss resulting from deferred payments for the sale or purchase of goods or services is taxable as a section 988 transaction. If an accrual basis U.S. taxpayer sells goods (or performs services) in exchange for an account receivable denominated in a nonfunctional currency, any gain or loss due to currency fluctuation while the taxpayer holds the receivable will be U.S. source, ordinary income when the receivable is paid. I.R.C. § 988(c)(1)(B)(ii).

For example, suppose an accrual basis U.S. taxpayer sells inventory in Spain in exchange for an account receivable calling for payment of 122,000 euro (€) at a time when the conversion rate is $1.00 = 122€. At the time of the sale, the accrual basis taxpayer accrues any gain on the sale of the inventory itself. If the conversion rate is $1.00 = 100€ when the purchaser pays the receivable, the seller must account for any gain or loss resulting from fluctuations in the value of the receivable. Under these circumstances, the taxpayer would report U.S. source, ordinary income of $220 ($1,220 amount realized minus $1,000 adjusted basis in the receivable). If the receivable was received by a QBU in Spain that was using the dollar as a functional currency, the gain would be foreign source income. I.R.C. § 988(a)(3)(B).

The same principles govern accounts payable. A change in exchange rates between the time the taxpayer accrues an account payable and the time of payment will also result in ordinary income or loss for the taxpayer. I.R.C. § 988(c)(1)(B)(ii). For example, suppose an accrual basis U.S. taxpayer for business purposes hires the architectural services of a Spanish architect for 122,000 euro (€) at a time when the conversion rate is $1.00 = 122€. Between the time the U.S. taxpayer accrues the liability and the time payment is made, the conversion rate changes to $1.00 = 100€. Under these circumstances, the taxpayer would report an ordinary loss of $220 ($1,220 cost of acquiring the 122,000 euros minus the $1,000 deduction previously accrued).

(E) FORWARD, FUTURES AND OPTION CONTRACTS

A section 988 transaction includes entering into or acquiring any forward, futures or option contract or any similar financial instrument if the contract is not subject to the annual accrual (*i.e.*, marked to market) rules of I.R.C. § 1256. I.R.C.

§ 988(c)(1)(B)(iii). These contracts generally obligate the taxpayer either to sell or purchase foreign currency at some point in the future for a price designated in the present upon entering the contract. For example, suppose a U.S. taxpayer enters into a forward contract to sell 30,000 Taiwan dollars (TWD) in six months at a conversion rate of $1.00 = 30 TWD. At the end of six months when the conversion rate is $1.00 = 40 TWD, the purchaser pays the taxpayer $250 (*i.e.,* the difference between the $1,000 contract price and the $750 cost of 30,000 TWD on the spot market) to cancel the contract, or the taxpayer sells the contract for $250, producing a foreign currency gain. I.R.C. § 988(c)(1)(B)(iii).

In general, I.R.C. § 988 will not apply (and the marked to market rules will apply) to a contract to purchase or sell currency if the contract is of a type traded on the interbank market. I.R.C. § 1256. Under the marked to market rules, a forward contract is subject to tax at the end of the year as if it had been sold and then repurchased. If I.R.C. § 1256 applied to the example above, the taxpayer would recognize $250 of foreign currency gain if the conversion rate was $1.00 = 40 TWD on the last day of the year even if the payment date was in the following year. No further gain would be recognized upon payment of the TWD under the contract if there were no subsequent change in the exchange rate.

(F) HEDGING

A section 988 hedging transaction is typically a mechanism to reduce the effect of currency fluctuation on taxable income. Under I.R.C. § 988(d)(1), if a section 988 transaction is part of a section 988 hedging transaction, all transactions should be integrated and treated consistently. There are three requirements of a 988 hedging transaction: (1) a "qualified debt instrument" and (2) a "hedge" that is part of (3) an "integrated economic transaction." Reg. § 1.988–5(a)(1). Any debt instrument will qualify as a "qualified debt instrument" unless it is an account receivable or payable. Reg. § 1.988–5(a)(3). A "hedge" is any instrument or series of instruments that when combined with the qualified debt instrument will allow the calculation of yield to maturity in a currency other than that of the qualified debt instrument. Reg. § 1.988–5(a)(4)(i). A qualified debt instrument and a hedge will constitute an "integrated economic transaction" basically if the hedge fully covers the payments under the qualified debt instrument, the parties to the hedge are unrelated, and the transaction is identified by the taxpayer as a 988 hedging transaction no later than then close of business on the day the hedge is acquired. Reg. § 1.988–5(a)(5). If all these requirements are met the qualified debt instrument and the hedge will be treated as a single "synthetic debt instrument" denominated in the currency received under the hedge.

For example, assume a taxpayer borrows 1,000 units of a weak foreign currency ("F") for 2 years at 30 percent interest—the market interest rate. Interest payments are F300 in each of the next 2 years, plus a principal payment of F1,000 in 2 years. The high interest rate reflects the anticipated devaluation of the foreign currency relative to the dollar.

If the spot market for the F currency is $1.00 = F2, the loan would be the equivalent of $500 (F1,000/F2). Suppose the F foreign currency can be purchased one year ahead in the forward market at $1.00 = F2.5 and 2 years ahead at $1.00 = F2.75. Under these facts, the taxpayer can protect against any unexpected exchange rate fluctuation (*e.g.*, a stronger F currency relative to the dollar) by purchasing F300 1 year ahead for $120 (F300/F2.5) and F1300 2 years ahead for $473 (F1300/F2.75). These transactions will lock in the F300 interest payments in Years 1 and 2 plus the repayment of F1,000 principal at the end of Year 2. With this full hedge, the foreign currency borrowing is converted into a dollar borrowing of $500 with a payment of $120 in Year 1 and $473 in Year 2, resulting approximately in a 10 percent yield to maturity, rather than the nominal 30 percent.

Instead of deducting $120 of interest in Year 1 (F300/F2.5) and reporting a $27 gain in Year 2—$136 of currency income ($500 minus F1,000/F2.75) minus a $109 interest deduction (F300/F2.75)—the taxpayer would have a $50 deduction ($500 × 10 percent) under the OID rules of I.R.C. § 1271 et seq.

The remaining $70 paid in Year 1 is considered a repayment of principal, leaving $430 of principal to be repaid at the end of Year 2. In Year 2, the taxpayer would deduct $43 of interest ($430 principal outstanding × 10 percent). Over the 2 year period, the application of the hedging rules does not change the amount of the overall deduction (*i.e.*, $93), but the effect is to prevent an acceleration of the deduction into year 1 (with a recognition of gain in year 2).

Similar rules apply to hedged executory contracts to purchase or sell goods or services or stock. For example, suppose that a U.S. taxpayer makes a contract to purchase engineering services in six months for a price denominated in a foreign currency. To protect against exchange rate fluctuation (taxpayer wants to be in the engineering business not the currency fluctuation business), the taxpayer might immediately enter into a forward contract to purchase the foreign currency needed to pay for the engineering services at a fixed price. Under these circumstances, the purchase of the engineering services and the forward contract hedge are integrated with the cost of the services being the locked-in dollar price of the foreign currency.

Suppose that a U.S. corporation enters into an agreement to sell stock in a German corporation for €80 million. If the seller is worried about fluctuating rates between the date the sales agreement is signed and the day the transaction closes, the U.S. corporation might enter into a forward contract to sell the €80 million. By locking in the exchange rate when the agreement is signed, the seller can eliminate currency risk. If the euro strengthens relative to the dollar, then the amount received at closing will buy more dollars, but there will be a corresponding loss on the forward contract. Conversely, if the euro weakens relative to the dollar, the amount received at closing would buy fewer dollars, but the forward contract would have increased in value. In either case, the dollar value of the sale is locked in.

In this situation, the taxpayer may not want to risk capital loss on the sale and ordinary income on the forward contract. For the corporate seller, capital loss cannot offset ordinary gain. Fortunately, the seller can integrate the forward with sales contract as a hedged executory contract. Reg. § 1.988–5(b)(2). To create a hedged executory contract, the following requirements must be met:

1. The executory contract and the hedge are identified as a hedged executory contract. The Regulations do not detail exactly how the identification is achieved other than to say: a taxpayer must establish a record **before the close of the date the hedge is entered into** which contains a clear description of: (a) the executory contract; (b) the hedge; and (c) that the hedge is entered into in accordance with Reg. § 1.988–5(b)(3).

2. The hedge itself is entered into after **on or after** the date the executory contract is entered into.

3. The hedge continues and ends **on or after** the accrual date.

4. The hedge is not with a related party.

5. The hedge and the executory contract are entered into by the same person (*e.g.*, parent hedging a subsidiary's contract cannot be a hedged executory contract).

As noted, Reg. § 1.988–5 provides for the integration of a section 988 transaction in two limited circumstances. First, Reg. § 1.988–5(a) provides for the integration of a nonfunctional currency debt instrument and a § 1.988–5(a) hedge. Second, Treas. Reg. § 1.988–5(b) provides rules for the integration of a hedged executory contract.

Even if a hedging transaction cannot be integrated with an underlying transaction under Reg. § 1.988–5, it still may be considered in some circumstances a hedging transaction under I.R.C. § 1221(b)(2)(A) and Reg. § 1.1221–2(b). If the definitional requirements were satisfied and the identification requirements are satisfied, then the gain or loss under the forward contracts would be subject to the hedge timing rules under Treas. Reg. § 1.446–4 which essentially provides that while the underlying transaction and the hedge are not integrated, the timing of gain or loss with respect to both are taken into account in the same year.

A hedging transaction is defined under § 1221(b)(2)(A) to include any transaction entered into by the taxpayer in the normal course of its trade or business primarily (i) to manage risk of price changes or currency fluctuations with respect to ordinary property which is held or to be held by the taxpayer, and (ii) to manage risk of interest rate, price changes or currency fluctuations with respect to borrowings made or to be made, or ordinary obligations incurred or to be incurred, by the taxpayer. Property is ordinary property of the taxpayer only if a sale or exchange of the property by the taxpayer could not produce capital gain or loss under any circumstances.

§ 11.04   FOREIGN CURRENCY TRANSLATION

If a U.S. taxpayer operates abroad through either an unincorporated branch or a foreign subsidiary and the activities are conducted in a foreign currency (*i.e.*, is a QBU) it is necessary to convert the operating results of the foreign business into U.S. dollars at some point in order to determine U.S. taxes. For a branch (and this treatment would include a hybrid entity that is treated as disregarded for U.S. tax purposes but as a corporation for local country purposes), the converted profit or loss is included currently in the taxable income of the U.S. taxpayer. For a foreign subsidiary, any actual or deemed distributions (*e.g.*, subpart F income) must be translated into U.S. dollars in order to determine the taxable income of the U.S. parent. In addition, foreign taxes paid must be converted to dollars for purposes of computing the foreign tax credit.

(A)   FOREIGN BRANCHES

Under I.R.C. § 987, a taxpayer with a "qualified business unit" (QBU) must account for currency gain/loss from both operations and remittances back to the home office. I.R.C. § 989 and Reg. § 1.989(a)–1(b) treats a corporation or a partnership as a QBU. Moreover, activities of a corporation, partnership, trust, estate, or individual also rise to the level of a QBU if the activities constitute a trade or business, and a separate set of books and records are maintained. Reg. § 1.989(a)–1(c) defines a trade or business as a "specific unified group of activities that constitutes (or could constitute) an independent economic enterprise carried on for profit . . ." Currently, there are no Temporary or Final Regulations that detail how I.R.C. § 987 actually works. However proposed regulations were issued in 2006. Even though the regulations were issued in proposed form, the preamble to the regulations indicates that the proposed regulations are a reasonable interpretation of existing law under I.R.C. § 987. As a result and in the absence of any other guidance, the proposed regulations may take on importance even in their proposed form. However, because of the complexity of the 2006 proposed regulations, many taxpayers—probably most taxpayers—continue to rely on the withdrawn 1991 proposed regulations (still deemed a reasonable method by the IRS) until final regulations are issued.

(1) 2006 Proposed Regulations

In 2006, proposed Regulations were issued that explain how I.R.C. § 987 applies. The rules are complicated, but the general approach of the regulations is fairly straightforward. For purposes of the discussion that follows, assume that the proposed regulations are in effect and assume the following: USCO owns DE, a disregarded entity for U.S. purposes and a corporation for foreign purposes. DE conducts a foreign trade or business in a non-dollar functional currency. The rules that follow could also apply where instead of DE, there is a true foreign branch (*i.e.,* branch for U.S. and foreign purposes) engaged in the same activities. Similarly, if USCO were a partner in a partnership that carried on the same activities, the activities would constitute a section 987 QBU. Finally, suppose USCO owned all the stock of CFC, a controlled foreign corporation. If CFC operates a trade or business through a branch, disregarded entity or partnership that uses a functional currency that differs from the functional currency of the CFC, § 987 gain/loss may occur on a remittance to the CFC. In some cases, § 987 gain could be subpart F income, taxable to a U.S. shareholder.

The proposed 2006 Regulations were issued at the same time as proposed changes to the I.R.C. § 989 regulations. The proposed 2006 Regulations require recognition of currency gain/loss with respect to a will be subject to foreign currency gain/loss with respect to a "section 987 QBU." A section 987 QBU (*i.e.,* qualified business unit) is defined in Prop. Reg.

§ 1.987–1(b)(2) as an eligible QBU that has a functional currency different from its owner. An "eligible QBU" is defined in Prop. Reg. § 1.987–1(b)(3) as an activity of an individual, corporation, partnership or DE that is a trade or business; maintains separate books and records and assets and liabilities used in conducting such activities are reflected on such books and records; and the activities are not subject to special rules in Reg. § 1.985–3 relating to hyperinflationary currencies.

Under the 2006 proposed Regulations, there are some basic principles that apply. First, the rules apply to activities not to entities. For example, a foreign disregarded entity (*i.e.,* corporation for foreign purposes but disregarded for U.S. tax purposes) that merely holds stock in a foreign corporation does not carry on an activity that is a section 987 QBU. Second, currency gain/loss with respect to day-to-day operations of a section 987 QBU (*i.e.,* income and deductions) will flow through to the owner, reflected in the income or loss related to the operations themselves. Third, there may be unrecognized foreign currency gains/losses relating to assets and liabilities held in connection with the section 987 QBU. The mechanism for keeping track of the net unrecognized section 987 gain or loss is referred to as the "foreign exchange exposure pool." These net unrecognized currency gains/losses will be recognized upon a remittance from the section 987 QBU to the owner. For example, if a section 987 QBU owns foreign currency or a note receivable or a note payable denominated in a foreign currency, as that foreign currency fluctuates there may be unrecognized § 987 gain/loss. Assets and liabilities that give rise to potential unrecognized § 987 gain/loss are referred to as "marked" assets. These assets and liabilities are valued in dollars at the year-end exchange rate. All other assets/liabilities are referred to as "historic" assets/liabilities. These would include property, plant, equipment, and inventory. The assets and liabilities are valued at the historic exchange rates when they are acquired by the section 987 QBU. Changes in currency rates are not deemed to affect these historical assets/liabilities and therefore no § 987 unrecognized gain/loss arises with respect to them.

Fourth, the unrecognized § 987 gain/loss is computed by comparing the balance sheet (with appropriate adjustments to reverse out any additions to, or subtractions from, the section 987 QBU) of the section 987 QBU at the beginning of the year and the end of the year. Any change is deemed to be a net unrecognized section 987 gain/loss. Fifth, on any remittance from the section 987 QBU, a proportionate amount of the net unrecognized section 987 gain/loss is recognized. To see these rules in operation consider the following example.

USCO forms a Japanese branch on 7/1/Year 1 with the following attributes:

- $1,000 of cash (immediately converted to ¥100,000)

- a building with an adjusted basis of $500 (depreciation ignored)

- Branch borrows ¥10,000 on 7/1/Year 1
- Branch earns ¥10,000

Exchange rates:

- Average Exchange rate for Year 1 from 7/1/Year 1 to 12/31/Year 1 = $1: ¥110.01 (¥1: $0.009090)
- Spot rate on 7/1/Year 1 = $1.00 : ¥100
- Spot rate on 12/31/Year 1 = $1.00 : ¥120 (¥1 : $0.00833)

Year 1	Beginning Yen	Beginning Dollars	Ending Yen	Ending Dollar	Comments
Cash	0	0	120,000	1,000.00	Marked item $1.00 : ¥120
Building	0	0	50,000	500.00	Historic item $1.00 : ¥100
Liabilities	0	0	(10,000)	(83.33)	Marked item $1.00 : ¥120
Net Value	0	0	160,000	1,416.67	
Increase				1,416.67	
Adjustments:					
Transfers In				(1,500.00)	
Taxable income				(90.90)	Yearly Average Exchange Rate
Net Unrecognized section 987 G/(L)				(174.23)	

What I.R.C. § 987 requires is a comparison of the balance sheet (in dollars) at the beginning of the year and the end of the year with certain adjustments. In the first year of this section 987 QBU, the beginning balance sheet is $0. At the end of the year, the balance sheet reflects "marked items" (essentially, financial assets and liabilities) at the year-end conversion rate (*i.e.*, the items are marked-to-market) while historic assets (*e.g.*, building) reflect their historical dollar conversion rate. Then adjustments are made to the balance sheet. Items contributed during the year (*i.e.*, dollar basis in cash and building) are subtracted and income during the year is also subtracted as the currency gain with respect to that income is already taken into account by USCO. The net unrecognized section 987 loss that results therefore reflects the following.

Components	Yen	Value Before Dollars	Value After Dollars	Change Dollars
Cash Contributed	100,000	1,000 $1.00 : ¥100	833.33 $1.00 : ¥120	(166.67)
Cash Earned	10,000	90.90	83.33 $1.00 : ¥120	(7.56)
Cash Borrowed	10,000	(100.00) $1.00 : ¥100	83.33 $1.00 : ¥120	(16.67)
Liability	−10,000	(100.00) $1.00 : ¥100	(83.33) $1.00 : ¥120	16.67
Total				(174.23)

There is no unrecognized section 987 gain or loss attributable to the historic assets (*e.g.*, the building). The net unrecognized section 987 loss is not taken into account by USCO until there is a remittance. Now let's follow the same example into Year 2 where the following occurs.

- Branch borrows another ¥10,000 on 5/31/Year 2 and purchases equipment (depreciation ignored)
- Branch earns ¥25,000 during Year 2

- Branch transfers ¥70,000 to owner on 12/31/Year 2

Exchange rates:

- Average Spot rate for Year 2 = $1.00 : ¥131.58
- Spot rate on 5/31/11 = $1.00 : ¥130
- Spot rate on 12/31/11 = $1.00 : ¥140

The balance sheet of the section 987 QBU is as follows at the end of Year 2.

Year 2	Beginning Yen	Beginning Dollars	Ending Yen	Ending Dollar	Comments
Cash	120,000	1,000	75,000	537.71	Marked item $1.00 : ¥140
Building	50,000	500.00	50,000	500.00	Historic item $1.00 : ¥100
Equipment			10,000	76.92	Historic item $1.00 : ¥130
Liabilities	(10,000)	(83.33)	(20,000)	(142.86)	Marked item $1.00 : ¥140
Net Value	160,000	1,416.67	115,000	969.77	
Decrease				(446.90)	
Adjustments:					
Transfers Out				500.00	Spot rate
Taxable income				(190.00)	Average rate
Net Unrecognized section 987 G/(L)		(174.23)		(136.90)	Total = (311.13)

Notice that the ending value of the section 987 QBU (in dollars) has decreased by $446.90 but adjustments must be made to reflect section 987 inflows and outflows. To get a true picture of how currency fluctuation affected the section 987 QBU, any distributions out must be added back (*i.e.,* ¥70,000 distribution = $500). Next, the income of the section 987 QBU must be subtracted in computing net unrecognized section 987 gain or loss because any currency gain or loss in connection with the income event is already recognized by USCO when it reports the $190 of income. That leaves an additional net unrecognized section 987 loss of $136.90. The following table illustrates what accounts for the additional unrecognized loss.

Components	Yen	Value Before Dollars	Value After Dollars	Change Dollars
Beginning Cash	120,000	1,000 $1.00 : ¥120	857.14 $1.00 : ¥140	(142.86)
Cash Earned	25,000	190.90	178.57 $1.00 : ¥140	(11.43)
Cash Borrowed	10,000	(100.00) $1.00 : ¥100	83.33 $1.00 : ¥120	(16.67)
Beginning Liability	–10,000	(83.33) $1.00 : ¥120	(71.43) $1.00 : ¥140	11.90
New Liability	–10,000	(76.92) $1.00 : ¥130	(71.43) $1.00 : ¥140	5.49
Total				(136.90)

In Year 2, there was a remittance of ¥70,000. To determine whether a remittance has taken place, all of the contributions to the branch and distributions from the branch for the year are netted. In this example, there is only one transfer—the ¥70,000 distribution. That remittance results in USCO recognizing a portion of the $311.13 total net unrecognized section 987 loss. Notice that while the ¥70,000 remittance is a remittance of a marked asset, even if an historical asset (*e.g.,* the building) were remitted, § 987 gain/loss might occur. The portion of the loss that is recognized is equal to the "remittance proportion" multiplied by the net unrecognized section 987 gain/loss ($311.13 loss). The remittance proportion is the $500 remittance in dollars (¥70,000/¥140 spot rate at year-end) divided by the dollar basis of the gross assets in the section 987 QBU at year-end increased by the amount of the remittance (*i.e.,* $969.77 plus $500), or 34.02%. Accordingly, the section 987 loss that is recognized on the otherwise tax-free remittance from the branch is $105.84 ($311.13 × 34.02%) which can be deducted against other income USCO may generate. The gain or loss is ordinary and its character is based on the type of income that the assets in the section 987 QBU generate. Going into Year 3, the net unrecognized section 987 loss would be $205.29 ($311.13–$105.84).

Branch remittances that can trigger gain or loss under I.R.C. § 987 include ongoing remittances as well as branch terminations. Remittances can be obvious such as the direct remittance in the example above, but remittances can also arise in less obvious situations. For example, the incorporation of a branch (*i.e.,* transfer of the branch to a controlled foreign corporation in a transaction governed by I.R.C. § 351) is treated as a complete termination of the section 987 QBU that would result in taxation to the owner of the QBU of all the net unrecognized section 987 gain or loss. Suppose that USCO owns a disregarded entity that conducts a trade or business using a non-dollar functional currency. If P, a purchaser, buys 50 percent of the disregarded entity from USCO, the disregarded entity is converted to a partnership. Under the proposed regulations, 50 percent of the assets of the section 987 QBU are deemed to be distributed to USCO, resulting in a recognition of 50 percent of the net unrecognized currency gain or loss.

(2) 1991 Proposed Regulations

Under the now-withdrawn 1991 proposed regulations, section 987 gain/loss is determined by calculating an "equity pool" and a "basis pool." Essentially, the equity pool is the taxpayer's investment in the branch stated in the branch's functional currency. The basis pool is the investment in the branch in the taxpayer's overall currency which for a U.S. taxpayer is probably the dollar. A remittance from a QBU is taxable to the extent that the dollar value on the date of remittance exceeds that portion of the basis pool allocable to the remittance. Note that a remittance would also include any payment of principal or interest on a disregarded "loan" from the home office to the branch.

For example, suppose a U.S. corporation with a U.S. dollar functional currency organizes a branch in country X that uses the "u" as its functional currency. During Year 1, the taxpayer transfers 1000u to the branch when 1u = $1 and transfers $1,000 to the branch when 1u = $2. At this point, the equity pool is 1,500u and the basis pool is $2,000. In the same year, the branch has profits of 1,000u which is translated into dollars at the weighted average rate for the year of 1u = $2. The equity pool is increased by 1,000u to 2,500u; the basis pool is increased by $2,000 to $4,000. Finally, in Year 1 the branch remits 1,000u to the taxpayer's home office when 1u = $2. The taxable portion of the remittance is equal to the excess of the dollar value of the remittance at the spot rate ($2,000) minus the portion of the basis pool that is attributable to the distribution. That portion is determined by the following formula:

$$\frac{1{,}000\text{u remittance}}{2{,}500\text{u equity pool}} \times \ \$4{,}000 \text{ basis pool} = \$1{,}600$$

Accordingly, the § 987 gain is $400, and the 1,000u remitted is given a basis of $2,000. The equity pool at the end of year 2 is 1,500u (2,500u minus the 1,000u remittance) and the basis pool is $2,400 ($4,000 minus the $1,600 charge to that pool on the remittance).

(B) FOREIGN CORPORATIONS

Unless a foreign corporation is a controlled foreign corporation with subpart F income, or a passive foreign investment company, the income or loss of a foreign corporation normally has no immediate U.S. tax consequences. However, a distribution or a deemed distribution from a foreign corporation to its U.S. shareholders is a taxable event for U.S. tax purposes. When a distribution is made (or is deemed to be made), it is necessary to translate into dollars the amount of the distribution, the amount of the earnings and profits from which the dividend is paid and the amount of the foreign tax associated with the dividend if the shareholder is entitled to the indirect foreign tax credit under I.R.C. § 902. For a foreign corporation that that does not generate subpart F income, E&P pools of the corporation are maintained in the functional currency. I.R.C. §§ 986(a) and 989 require that both the distribution itself and the earnings and profits out of which it is paid are translated into dollars at the spot rate on the date the distribution is included in income. Foreign taxes paid by the subsidiary are generally translated into dollars using the average exchange rate for the year the taxes were accrued. I.R.C. § 986(a)(1). For distributions of previously taxed income that was included under I.R.C. § 951 as subpart F income or a I.R.C. § 956 inclusion, section 986(c) requires currency gain or loss.

These rules are illustrated by the examples below:

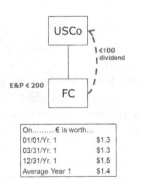

- FC has a euro (€) functional currency
- FC has never incurred any foreign taxes
- FC pays €100 dividend on 3/31/Year 1

On..........€ is worth...	
01/01/Yr. 1	$1.3
03/31/Yr. 1	$1.3
12/31/Yr. 1	$1.5
Average Year 1	$1.4

USCo would include a $130 dividend, translated at the spot rate on date of distribution under I.R.C. § 989(b)(1).

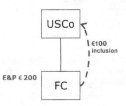

- FC has a euro (€) functional currency
- FC has never incurred any foreign taxes
- FC has a subpart F inclusion of €100 for Year 1 under §951(a)(1)(A)

On..........€ is worth...	
01/01/Yr. 1	$1.3
03/31/Yr. 1	$1.3
12/31/Yr. 1	$1.5
Average Year 1	$1.4

USCo would include a $140 inclusion, translated at the average exchange rate for Year 1 under I.R.C. § 989(b)(3).

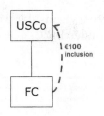

- FC has a euro (€) functional currency
- FC has never incurred any foreign taxes
- FC has a calendar tax year
- FC has a §956 inclusion of €100 for Year 1

On..........€ is worth...	
01/01/Yr. 1	$1.3
03/31/Yr. 1	$1.3
12/31/Yr. 1	$1.5
Average Year 1	$1.4

USCo would include a $150 inclusion, translated at the exchange rate on the last day of Year 1 under I.R.C. § 989(b).

- USCo owns stock in an unrelated foreign corporation
- USCo is an accrual basis taxpayer
- USCo receives a €100 dividend on 3/31/Yr. 1
- The dividend is subject to a 10% withholding tax (i.e., €10)

On.........€ is worth...	
01/01/Yr. 1	$1.3
03/31/Yr. 1	$1.3
12/31/Yr. 1	$1.5
Average Year 1	$1.4

USCo would have a dividend of $130 under I.R.C. § 989(b)(1) and would be deemed to pay a foreign withholding tax of $14 under I.R.C. § 986(a)(1), assuming no election was made under I.R.C. § 986(a)(1)(D).

Now consider the foreign currency considerations of an indirect foreign tax credit under I.R.C. § 902.

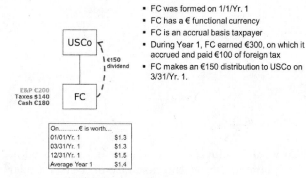

- FC was formed on 1/1/Yr. 1
- FC has a € functional currency
- FC is an accrual basis taxpayer
- During Year 1, FC earned €300, on which it accrued and paid €100 of foreign tax
- FC makes an €150 distribution to USCo on 3/31/Yr. 1.

The foreign tax credit resulting from the distribution is determined as follows.

$$\frac{\text{Dividend (in local currency)}}{\text{Undistributed Earnings (in local currency)}} \times \begin{array}{c}\text{Taxes Incurred}\\\text{by FC}\\\text{(in USD)}\end{array}$$

Accordingly, the gross-up under I.R.C. § 78 and the foreign tax credit would be $105 as follows:

$$\frac{€150}{€200} \times \$140 = \$105$$

For the last example, consider the implications under I.R.C. § 986(c) of a distribution of previously taxed income (PTI) that arose from an inclusion under subpart F. In this situation, any currency gain/loss between the time of subpart F inclusion and the date of distribution must be taken into account.

The subpart F income is translated into $65, the average exchange rate for Yr 1, under I.R.C. § 989(b)(3). U.S. has a $65 subpart F inclusion for

Yr 1. The distribution is translated at the spot exchange rate on 12/31/Yr. 1 of €1 = $1, under § 989(b)(1). U.S. has a $65 basis in its PTI for Yr 1 U.S. receives the equivalent of $100 on 12/31/Yr. 1. Accordingly, U.S. has $35 of foreign currency gain under § 986(c). The source of § 986(c) gain (or loss) is the same as the underlying subpart F—typically foreign source. Under Notice 88–71, 1988–2 C.B. 374, the basket of the gain/loss is also the same as the underlying subpart F inclusion.

§ 11.05 TREATMENT OF INDIVIDUALS

Code section 988 does not apply to "personal transactions" entered into by an individual. Personal transactions are any transactions except to the extent that expenses attributable to such transactions would be deductible under I.R.C. § 162 as a trade or business expense or I.R.C. § 212 as an expense of producing income. I.R.C. § 988(e)(3). For personal transactions entered into by individuals, general tax principles apply. Suppose that a U.S. taxpayer goes to Europe on vacation, purchasing 2,000 Euros when the conversion rate was $1.00 = 1€. There are no tax consequences as the taxpayer spends the Euros on vacation even if there is currency fluctuation. At the end of the vacation suppose the taxpayer converts 600 Euros into $900 at a time when the conversion rate is $1.00 = .67€. Under general tax principles, the taxpayer recognizes a $300 capital gain for tax purposes. Had the gain been less than $200 the de minimis rule of I.R.C. § 988(e)(2) would have applied and the taxpayer would have recognized no gain. If the taxpayer received $450 dollars on reconversion because the exchange rate was $1.00 = 1.33€, the taxpayer would have a $150 capital loss for tax purposes. *See* Rev. Rul. 74–7, 1974–1 C.B. 198. However, a loss resulting from a foreign currency transaction by an individual in a non-profit-seeking context is normally not deductible.

Suppose a U.S. citizen purchases a personal residence in country U for 95,000u, paying 10,000u in cash and borrowing 85,000u. At the time of the purchase the conversion rate is $1 = 1u. Later, at a time when the conversion rate is $1 = .95u, the taxpayer sells the residence for 142,500u, of which 85,000u is used to repay the mortgage. The taxpayer must recognize gain of $150,000 (142,500u/.95u) minus $95,000 (95,000u/1u) on the sale of the residence. The taxpayer also has a loss on the repayment of the mortgage equal to the $89,474 value of the amount paid in satisfaction of the mortgage (85,000u/.95u) minus the $85,000 value of the amount borrowed (85,000u/1u). However, the loss is nondeductible because it is not incurred in a trade or business or a transaction entered into for profit. *See* Rev. Rul. 90–79, 1990–2 C.B. 187.

CHAPTER 12

INTERNATIONAL TAX-FREE TRANSACTIONS

§ 12.01 OVERVIEW

Transfers of property across international boundaries—particularly transfers from taxpayers within the United States to taxpayers outside the United States—create the possibility of tax avoidance in circumstances where nonrecognition provisions would normally render the transaction tax-free. For example, suppose a U.S. corporation holds an appreciated asset with a basis of $8 million and a fair market value of $30 million that it intends to sell. If it sells the asset, it must recognize the $22 million gain for U.S. tax purposes. Suppose instead that the corporation transfers the asset in a nonrecognition transaction governed by I.R.C. § 351 to a foreign subsidiary which (which without negating § 351 treatment) then sells the asset. If the foreign subsidiary is not engaged in a trade or business in the United States, the gain from the sale of the asset may not be subject to U.S. taxation even though the appreciation occurred while the asset was held by the U.S. entity. Gain may not be taxable under subpart F if the asset transferred is going to be used in the foreign subsidiary's trade or business. Reg. § 1.954–2(e)(3). Moreover, the taxpayer might have taken deductions, such as depreciation, in connection with the asset that decreased U.S. tax liability and should be recaptured on the sale, but the taxpayer is now attempting entirely to avoid U.S. taxation on the gain from a disposition of the asset.

I.R.C. § 367 was enacted to impose a "toll charge" on the transfer of assets across international boundaries in transactions which might otherwise be tax-free. While I.R.C. § 367 addresses a variety of nonrecognition transactions, there are essentially three categories of transactions governed by I.R.C. § 367: (a) "outbound" transactions where assets used in the United States are transferred to a foreign taxpayer; (b) "inbound" transactions where assets used by a foreign taxpayer are transferred to a U.S. taxpayer; (c) foreign-to-foreign transactions in which assets used by a foreign taxpayer are transferred to another foreign taxpayer. Generally, I.R.C. §§ 367(a) and (d) (focusing on intangibles) address outbound transactions; I.R.C. § 367(b) addresses the other two categories. I.R.C. § 367(e) contains a rule that specifically addresses outbound liquidations and outbound divisive reorganizations.

In order effectively to apply this toll charge, I.R.C. § 367 denies U.S. taxpayers the benefits of several corporate nonrecognition rules. Within the three categories of nonrecognition transactions outlined above, the most important kinds of transactions are: (1) transactions that implicate I.R.C. § 351 or otherwise constitute contributions to the capital of foreign corporations; (2) transactions where a U.S. subsidiary of a foreign parent or a foreign subsidiary of a U.S. parent is liquidated in accordance with

I.R.C. §§ 337 and 332; and (3) transactions involving corporate reorganizations governed by I.R.C. § 368 and related provisions. Without attempting to plumb the inner recesses of these provisions, a basic understanding is helpful in explaining the operation of I.R.C. § 367.

First, under I.R.C. § 351, a transferor of property does not recognize gain or loss when property is transferred in exchange for stock of a corporation if the transferors receive stock of the transferee corporation, and if immediately after the exchange, the transferors of property own at least 80 percent of each class of stock of the transferee corporation. I.R.C. § 368(c). Nonrecognition under I.R.C. § 351 can apply both to the formation of a new corporation and to transfers to an existing corporation. Under I.R.C. § 367(c)(2), a contribution to capital (*e.g.*, where the transferor contributes property but does not receive stock in return) is essentially treated as a transaction under I.R.C. § 351.

Second, amounts distributed in complete liquidation of a corporation are generally treated as received by the shareholders in exchange for their stock, thereby triggering gain or loss equal to the difference between a shareholder's stock basis and the fair market value of the distributed assets. I.R.C. § 331. Moreover, the liquidating corporation also recognizes gain to the extent that it distributes appreciated assets. I.R.C. § 336. But under I.R.C. §§ 337 and 332, when a parent corporation satisfying an 80 percent ownership test liquidates a subsidiary corporation, the parent corporation does not normally recognize gain on the difference between the parent's basis in the subsidiary's stock and the fair market value of the property distributed. Instead, the parent corporation takes a basis in the distributed assets equal to the basis of those assets in the hands of the subsidiary. In a parent/subsidiary liquidation, the subsidiary can avoid the recognition of gain inherent in any appreciated assets which are distributed. I.R.C. § 337.

Third, there are a variety of forms that a corporate reorganization can take. Consider this common form: suppose X Corp. merges into, or transfers its assets to, Y Corp. before ending its corporate existence with the shareholders of X Corp. becoming shareholders of Y Corp. (This commonly occurs when the shareholders of X transfer their X Corp. stock to Y Corp. and then "check-the box" on X Corp. to make it disregarded—stepped together this "drop and check" is simply an asset transfer from X Corp. to Y. Corp.) Sometimes the former shareholders of X Corp. will end up with stock of Y Corp.'s parent corporation. These transactions are generally "asset reorganizations."

Or alternatively, the X Corp. shareholders may transfer their X Corp. stock to Y Corp. in exchange for Y Corp. stock (or stock of Y Corp.'s parent). These reorganization are sometimes referred to as "stock reorganizations."

Where two corporations reorganize as a single corporate entity (or an acquired corporation becomes a subsidiary of an acquired corporation) and no cash is involved, normally there are no tax consequences to the transferor-corporation, the transferee-corporation or the shareholders. *See* I.R.C. §§ 368, 361, 354. The surviving corporation in such an acquisitive reorganization (*e.g.,* a merger) takes a carryover basis in the assets that it receives, while the shareholders of the transferring corporation substitute their stock bases in the transferring corporation's stock as the bases of their new stock in the surviving corporation.

These types of acquisitive reorganization can be contrasted with a divisive reorganization where a single corporation divides into multiple corporate entities. Suppose X Corp. is owned by A and B who want to go their separate ways. It is possible for X Corp. to transfer one of its businesses to newly-formed Y Corp., distributing the Y Corp. stock to B in exchange for B's X Corp. stock in a tax-free reorganization where X Corp. is not taxed on its transfer and B is not taxed on the exchange of stock. Similarly, A and B may want to remain as investors together but separate two businesses. It may be possible for X Corp. to contribute one of the businesses to Y Corp. and then distribute the Y Corp stock pro rata to A and B. Of course, these simplified reorganization patterns do not capture the complexity of the reorganization provisions but perhaps give enough of a flavor to make I.R.C. § 367 somewhat intelligible.

When it applies, I.R.C. § 367 overrides the nonrecognition patterns outlined above by denying corporate status to the foreign corporation involved in the transaction. For example, if a U.S. taxpayer transfers appreciated property to a foreign corporation in a transaction that would otherwise be tax-free under I.R.C. § 351, the application of I.R.C. § 367 will deny the transferee-corporation corporate status for purposes of calculating gain (although § 351 applies to other aspects of the transaction), thereby resulting in taxation of the built-in gain to the transferor under I.R.C. § 1001. As indicated below, the denial of corporate status would also override nonrecognition in the context of subsidiary liquidations and reorganizations. Similarly if the assets of a U.S. corporation are merged into, or otherwise acquired by, a foreign corporation in an asset reorganization, nonrecognition under section 361 may not be available.

§ 12.02 OUTBOUND TRANSACTIONS

(A) GENERAL RULE

The general rule of I.R.C. § 367(a) is that, in certain transactions, gain (but not loss) must be recognized when a U.S. person transfers property to a foreign entity. In order to effectuate this outcome, I.R.C. § 367(a) denies a transferee-corporation its corporate status for purposes of determining the recognition of gain on the transfer. In the case of a transaction apparently governed by I.R.C. § 351, the transferor must recognize gain on the exchange of appreciated property for stock, because the transferee is not considered to be a corporation. I.R.C. § 367(a). As a result, I.R.C. §§ 351 and 1001(c) do not provide nonrecognition, but rather I.R.C.

§ 1001(a) requires recognition of any gain. Similarly, on a contribution to the capital of a foreign corporation, the transfer will be treated as a sale or exchange of the contributed property for an amount equal to its fair market value, thereby forcing the transferor to recognize gain on the transfer. I.R.C. § 367(f). Where I.R.C. § 367(a) requires recognition of a built-in gain, the character and source of the gain is determined as if the property had been disposed of in a taxable exchange with the transferee foreign corporation. Reg. § 1.367(a)–1T(b)(4).

Suppose that a U.S. person transfers loss property to a corporation in a transaction meeting the requirements of I.R.C. § 351. If the transferee is a U.S. corporation, then the transferor would be denied recognition of the loss by I.R.C. § 351. On the other hand, where loss property is transferred to a foreign corporation which is denied corporate status by I.R.C. § 367, the logical inference would be that I.R.C. § 351 does not apply to the transfer and the transferor might be able to recognize the loss (subject to the loss disallowance rules in I.R.C. § 267). Congress recognized the potential for selective transfers (*e.g.,* only loss property) in this type of transaction. Therefore, I.R.C. § 367(a) only applies to gain—loss recognition is not permitted. Reg. § 1.367(a)–1T(b)(3)(ii). Furthermore, when multiple items of property are transferred simultaneously, the provision is applied to each item separately, so that it denies nonrecognition treatment to the transfer of appreciated property and forces nonrecognition where loss property is transferred, thereby maximizing the taxable income of the U.S. transferor. *See* Reg. §§ 1.367(a)–1T(b)(1) and (b)(3)(ii).

If a U.S. subsidiary liquidates into its foreign corporate parent, I.R.C. § 367(e) will preclude the liquidating U.S. corporation from relying on I.R.C. § 337 to avoid taxation. Normally, I.R.C. § 337 provides nonrecognition of gain for a subsidiary on a distribution of appreciated property to its parent corporation, but rather the application of I.R.C. § 367(e)(2) causes the U.S. subsidiary to be taxed on the distribution of appreciated property to its foreign parent. There are exceptions if the foreign parent continues to operate a U.S. business distributed by the U.S. subsidiary for ten years (but any appreciated intangibles that are liquidated out of the United States cannot qualify for this exception even if used in a U.S. trade or business) or if the distributed property is a United States Real Property Interest or if the U.S. subsidiary distributes stock of its own U.S. subsidiary in which there is at least 80 percent ownership of the voting power.

If a U.S. corporation transfers its assets to, or merges into, a foreign corporation in exchange for stock of the foreign corporation and that stock is distributed to the former shareholders of the U.S. corporation, normally the U.S. corporation would not be required to recognize gain on the transfer. I.R.C. § 361. However, if I.R.C. § 367 denies the foreign entity corporate status in determining the recognition of gain, the U.S. corporation-transferor will be forced to recognize gain on the transfer of its appreciated assets to the foreign corporation.

In some cases, as discussed below, if a U.S. shareholder transfers stock of a U.S. corporation in exchange for stock of a foreign corporation in what would otherwise be a tax-free reorganization, the U.S. shareholder will have to recognize gain in accordance with § 367. Reg. § 1.367(a)–3(c). In some cases a U.S. transferor will be deemed to transfer stock of a U.S. corporation to a foreign corporation even though no actual transfer has taken place.

Notwithstanding the general recognition rule of I.R.C. § 367 with respect to outbound transfers of appreciated assets, there are some important exceptions discussed below which, when available, prevent the disqualification of the otherwise applicable nonrecognition provisions. The exceptions provide a way to avoid the "toll charge" created by I.R.C. § 367 and lead to the same outcome as that which would result had I.R.C. § 367 not been enacted.

(B) THE ACTIVE TRADE OR BUSINESS EXCEPTION

The principal exception to the automatic toll charge rule of I.R.C. § 367(a) provides that there is no denial of the transferee's corporate status (and so there is no toll charge) where the property transferred to the foreign corporation is intended for use in the active conduct of a trade or business outside the United States. I.R.C. § 367(a)(3). This exception stems from the original purpose of I.R.C.

§ 367—to prevent transfers for tax avoidance motives. Where the transfer has a business purpose, the appropriate nonrecognition provision applies even though the asset may be beyond U.S. taxing jurisdiction when, and if, the asset is ultimately sold by the foreign transferee.

This exception to taxation under I.R.C. § 367(a) applies if four tests are satisfied. Reg. § 1.367(a)–2T(b). First, the transferee must have a trade or business defined as a "specific unified group of activities that constitutes (or could constitute) an independent economic enterprise carried on for profit." Second, the activities of the transferee must constitute the active conduct of the trade or business. This test is satisfied only if "substantial managerial and operation activities" are carried out by officers and employees of the transferee or of a related entity (if supervised and directly or indirectly paid for by the transferee), disregarding for this purpose the activities of independent contractors.

The third test requires that the transferee's trade or business be conducted outside the United States. This test is satisfied if the primary managerial and operational activities of the trade or business are conducted outside the United States and immediately after the transfer, substantially all of the transferred assets are located outside the United States. For example, if a U.S. parent transfers appreciated business assets to a foreign subsidiary but the assets remain in the United States as a branch operation, the exception to I.R.C.

§ 367(a) recognition for the parent corporation does not apply. It is not clear why gain should be recognized in this case but not if the assets are used in a trade or business outside the United States. Indeed, there appears to be more reason to tax any inherent gain when the assets leave the U.S. jurisdiction.

Under the fourth test, the transferred property must itself be used or held for use in the trade or business of the foreign corporation. The test is met if the transferred property is: (1) held for the principal purpose of promoting the present conduct of the business; (2) held in the ordinary course of the business; or (3) held to meet the present needs of the business and not anticipated future needs, such as diversification or expansion. The active business exception is presumed to be satisfied where the property was previously used in the transferee's country of organization and the transfer is legally required as a condition of doing business there (or is compelled by genuine threat of immediate expropriation). Reg. § 1.367(a)–4T(f).

Even where the requirements of the active trade or business exception of I.R.C. § 367(a)(3) are met, the exception will not apply to the transfer of certain types of assets. The assets which do not qualify for the active business exception include: inventory and other property held for sale to customers in the ordinary course of business; installment obligations and accounts receivable; foreign currency and obligations denominated in foreign currencies; and copyrights, patents and similar intangibles. I.R.C. § 367(a)(3)(B). If business property (*e.g.*, machinery, equipment, real estate) would otherwise qualify for the active business exception but is subject to depreciation recapture, the recapture is subject to U.S. tax liability. Reg. § 1.367(a)–4T(b)(1). An even more significant asset transfer cannot qualify for the active trade or business exception—the transfer of intangibles (including foreign goodwill/going concern value). The transfer of certain intangible assets is addressed below in § 12.02(D).

Prior to September 14, 2015, it was possible for a U.S. parent corporation operating a foreign branch to transfer foreign goodwill to a foreign corporation as part of the active trade or business exception. Treasury has issued proposed regulations under §§ 367(a) and (d) (focusing on intangibles) address outbound transactions; that would eliminate the ability of taxpayers to transfer foreign goodwill or going concern value outbound on a tax-free basis. Once finalized, the regulations would apply with retroactive effect to transfers occurring on or after September 14, 2015. The proposed regulations allow taxpayers to choose to have the foreign goodwill:

- Subject to immediate tax under § 367(a) and the regulations thereunder; or

- At the election of the taxpayer, subject to tax over its useful life under § 367(d).

This significant change largely guts the active trade or business exception for any successful business where the value is not in the tangible assets but resides in foreign goodwill.

The active trade or business exception is not available if the transferor corporation is owned by individual shareholders or is not controlled (*i.e.,* 80%) by five or fewer U.S. corporations. I.R.C. § 367(a)(5) and Reg. § 1.367(a)–7. Suppose that U.S. individual residents own USCO which transfers all of its assets to Forco, a foreign corporation, in exchange for Forco stock which is then distributed to the shareholders in cancellation of the USCO stock. This transaction depending on exactly how it was done would constitute an acquisitive tax-free reorganization, under I.R.C. § 368(a)(1)(A), (C), (D) or (F). In the absence of I.R.C. § 367(a)(5), there would be no corporate-level gain on the appreciation in the USCO assets if the transfer of those assets satisfied that active trade or business test of I.R.C. § 367(a)(3). *See* I.R.C. § 361. However because of I.R.C. § 367(a)(5), gain would be recognized on the appreciation in the assets transferred.

The purpose of I.R.C. § 367(a)(5) is to ensure that there is a U.S. corporate-level gain on the appreciation in the assets held by a U.S. corporation. If no gain were recognized on the reorganization then Forco could sell the appreciated assets free of U.S. corporate-level gain and distribute the proceeds to the shareholders in a liquidation where there would only be shareholder-level gain. Indeed, if instead of U.S. individuals, the stock of USCO was owned by foreign corporations, there would not even be shareholder level gain. Note that I.R.C. § 367(a)(5) would not apply if USCO's shareholder was a U.S. parent corporation. In that case, the reorganization would be tax-free in the United States. The U.S. parent corporation would receive the appreciated stock of Forco which would be subject to U.S. corporate-level taxation on its sale or if Forco sold the assets and then liquidated into the U.S. parent (*i.e.*, under I.R.C. § 367(b)) or on the liquidation of the parent where it would recognize the gain on the distribution of Forco stock. I.R.C. § 367(e)(2). Adjustments are required under I.R.C. § 367(a)(5) and Reg. § 1.367(a)–5 to ensure that the U.S. parent's stock basis in Forco preserves the gain in the appreciated assets that were transferred.

(C) BRANCH LOSS RECAPTURE RULE

The active business exception under I.R.C. § 367(a)(3) (*see supra* § 12.02(B)) to the general recognition rule of I.R.C. § 367(a) does not apply to the transfer of the assets of a foreign branch of a U.S. corporation to a foreign subsidiary to the extent that the branch sustained net losses before the transfer. I.R.C. § 367(a)(3)(C). Under this "exception to the exception," the transferor—the domestic parent corporation—must recognize gain equal to the lesser of the gain on the transfer or the previously deducted branch losses. The gain will have the same character as the branch losses, but the gain will always be deemed foreign source income.

The branch loss rule is prompted by the fact that often there may be losses during the start-up period of a branch of a U.S. corporation which are deducted by the taxpayer against non-branch income (*e.g.*, foreign source income generated by the home office). If the assets of the branch are then transferred to a foreign corporation at the point when the branch starts to show a profit, the United States in effect has permitted deductions without taking into account the income generated by expenses deducted. The solution is to require the recognition of gain on the incorporation transfer to the extent of the losses of the branch that were previously deducted.

Note that if a branch has suffered losses, those losses may have offset other foreign source income of the U.S. corporation that operates the branch in which case there will be branch loss recapture. Alternatively, those losses may have offset U.S. source income of the U.S. corporation that operates the branch in which case there will be overall foreign loss (OFL) account recapture. *See supra* § 8.04(C). In both cases the recapture is triggered by the incorporation of a branch in a I.R.C. § 351 transaction or a reorganization. If there is potential OFL and branch loss recapture, OFL recapture occurs first (*i.e.*, if there is not enough built-in gain in the transferred assets to permit both OFL and branch loss recapture). I.R.C. § 367(a)(3)(C)(ii)(II).

For example, suppose X Corp., a U.S. corporation, has operated a foreign branch, B1, that produced a loss of $300,000 three years ago and no income or loss for the last two years. The loss offset income X Corp. had from other foreign sources. In the current year, X Corp. transfers the assets of B1—which have a basis of $200,000 and a fair market value of $700,000—to Y Corp., a newly formed foreign subsidiary of X Corp. Under I.R.C. § 367(a)(3), X Corp. must recognize a gain of $300,000 on the transfer of the branch's assets. The gain is treated as foreign source income. Reg. §§ 1.367(a)–6T(c). If the branch losses, had been used to offset U.S. income (rather than other foreign source income), I.R.C. § 904(f)(3) would characterize any gain on the transfer of the branch assets as U.S. source income. *See supra* § 8.04(C) and Reg. § 1.367(a)–6T(e)(3). If X Corp. had both $300,000 of potential OFL recapture and $300,000 of potential branch loss recapture, then X Corp. would recognize $500,000 of gain on the I.R.C. § 351 transaction, consisting of $300,000 of OFL recapture and $200,000 of branch loss recapture.

On the incorporation of a foreign branch, there may also be recapture of dual consolidated losses (*see infra* § 13.04).

(D) INTANGIBLE ASSETS

Concerned that U.S. taxpayers would offset U.S. source income with the costs of producing certain intangible assets and then transfer the intangibles beyond the U.S. taxing jurisdiction when they become income producing assets, Congress enacted I.R.C. § 367(d) specifically to address the transfer of intangibles to a foreign corporation. When marketing and manufacturing intangibles are transferred to a foreign corporation in a transaction that falls under I.R.C. §§ 351 or 361, the transferor is treated as having sold the intangibles in exchange for royalty payments (*i.e.*, ordinary income) over the life of the property. I.R.C. § 367(d). The transferor must continue to recognize the deemed royalties for the property's entire "useful life," (no longer limited to 20 years). Deemed royalty payments under I.R.C. § 367(d) are treated as foreign source income to the same extent that an actual royalty payment would be considered to be foreign source income.

For example, suppose X Corp., a U.S. corporation, incurs various research expenses deductible under I.R.C. §§ 162 or 174 (thereby reducing X Corp.'s taxable income) in developing a patented pharmaceutical product. When the product is commercially feasible, X Corp. transfers the foreign rights to the patent to Y Corp., a wholly-owned foreign subsidiary in a transaction normally accorded nonrecognition under I.R.C. § 351 or as a contribution to capital. Y Corp. uses the patent to manufacture and sell the product. Under I.R.C. § 367(d), X Corp. has to report foreign source ordinary income each year equal to an arm's-length royalty for the deemed contingent sale of the patent.

Deciding whether a foreign corporation ought to pay an actual royalty on the acquisition of an intangible from a shareholder or be deemed to pay a royalty under I.R.C. § 367(d) may be affected by foreign tax rules as the U.S. tax treatment will be the same in either case. A deemed royalty payment may not attract a foreign withholding tax although an actual royalty might. On the other hand, an actual royalty payment may be deductible for foreign tax purposes whereas a deemed royalty payment may not.

"Intangible property" includes manufacturing intangibles such as patents, formulas, processes, designs, patterns, and know-how; marketing intangibles such as franchises, trademarks, trade names and brand names; and operating intangibles such as long-term purchase and supply contracts, surveys, studies, customer lists, and similar property not ordinarily licensed to unrelated parties. Reg. § 1.367(d)–1T(d). Gain with respect to foreign goodwill or going concern value of a business conducted outside of the United States is taxable at the taxpayer's choice under §§ 367(a) or (d). Copyrights or literary, musical or artistic compositions may fall under I.R.C. 367(d) if the transferor created the property by its own personal efforts or has a basis in the property determined with reference to the creator's basis.

The amount of gain that a transferor must recognize on the transfer of intangibles to a foreign transferee is accelerated if the transferor severs its relationship to the intangibles either by the transferee disposing of the intangibles or the transferor disposing of the stock of the transferee. I.R.C. § 367(d)(2)(A)(ii)(II) and Reg. § 1.367(d)–1T. Essentially, the re-transfer rules subject a U.S. transferor to a one-time recognition in lieu of future royalties equal to the difference between the amount realized on the sale and the adjusted basis of the intangibles on the original transfer date. If the re-transfer is a sale of stock by the transferor, gain recognized on the sale of stock is decreased by gain recognized under I.R.C. § 367(d). If the re-transfer of intangibles is to a related party, the original U.S. transferor continues to report annual royalty payments. If the stock of the original transferor is transferred to a related foreign person, the transferor continues to report the annual royalty payments. If the transferor goes out of existence (*e.g.*, on an outbound reorganization), then unless the shareholder of the transferor is essentially a U.S. corporation, the transferor must recognize gain on the § 367(d) intangibles. Notice 2012–39, 2012 C.B. 95. If the transferor of the foreign acquiring corporation's stock transfers it to a U.S. related corporation, the U.S. corporation must continue to report the annual payments. Reg. § 1.367(d)–1T(e).

In some situations, a U.S. person transferring intangibles in an outbound transaction would prefer to have the transaction treated as an immediate sale (assuming that nonrecognition treatment is unavailable) rather than as a licensing agreement producing annual deemed royalties that for tax purposes may increase under the "super royalty" provision (*see supra* § 9.07(F)). I.R.C. § 367(d)(2)(A). The Regulations permit a deemed sale election in three limited circumstances: (1) if operating intangibles (*e.g.*, a customer list) are transferred outbound (because operating intangibles are not likely to be sold or licensed by the transferee); (2) where there is a compulsory transfer of any intangible required by the government of the transferee-corporation; or (3) if intangibles are transferred to a foreign corporation pursuant to a joint venture as specified in the Regulations. Reg. § 1.367(d)–1T(g)(2). For purposes of the deemed sale election, an operating intangible is an intangible of a type not ordinarily licensed for consideration contingent upon the licensee's use. For example, customer lists and supply contracts might be considered operating intangibles.

Finally, suppose that I.R.C. § 367(d) does create a deemed royalty, but in fact no payment is made from the foreign transferee to the U.S. transferor. Because the deemed royalty is already taxed in the U.S. each year, Reg. § 1.367(d)–1(g) creates an account receivable each year. If a royalty is actually paid, it will not be taxable again but will instead be a return of basis. If no royalty is paid (perhaps more likely as there was no actual license), then after three years, the receivable is deemed to be contributed to capital so that the transferor at least gets additional stock basis for the deemed inclusion.

Historically, one way of avoiding I.R.C. § 367(d)'s application and still move valuable intellectual property (IP) offshore was to use a partnership freeze structure in which the U.S. owner of IP would typically set up a partnership with a related foreign corporation. The U.S. partner would transfer appreciated IP to the partnership in exchange for a preferred partnership interest that paid a fixed return but essentially shifted the IP's upside to the related foreign corporation. By its terms, I.R.C. § 367(d) does not apply to transfer to a partnership.

However, Notice 2015–54, regulates many of these structures by limiting the U.S. taxpayer's ability through special allocations or other means from shifting income from the IP to related foreign entities that may not be subject to U.S. taxation. In some cases, the very transfer of IP itself to a partnership might be taxable event. Nevertheless, moving future appreciation in the value of IP to a foreign entity outside the U.S. tax net in order to minimize taxation of royalties or eventual IP disposition remains an essential part of U.S. international tax planning.

(E) THE STOCK OR SECURITIES EXCEPTION— FOREIGN CORPORATION

In general, if a U.S. person transfers appreciated stock of a foreign corporation to a foreign corporation in what would otherwise be a tax-free transaction (*e.g.,* a § 351 transaction or a reorganization), nonrecognition is nevertheless permitted if the U.S. transferor owns less than five percent—measured by voting power or value—of the stock of the transferee foreign corporation, or if a U.S. transferor which owns five percent or more of the stock of the transferee enters into a five-year gain recognition agreement. I.R.C. § 367(a)(2).

For example, suppose that USCO owns all of the stock of ForSub1 and ForSub2, both foreign corporations. If USCO transfers the appreciated stock of ForSub2 to ForSub1 in exchange for additional ForSub1 voting stock, the transaction qualifies as a B reorganization. I.R.C. § 368(a)(1)(B) and as an I.R.C. § 351 transaction. After the transaction USCO owns all of the stock of ForSub1 which now owns all of the stock of ForSub2. Under the reorganization provisions (or I.R.C. § 351), USCO is not taxed on the exchange of appreciated stock in ForSub2 for stock in ForSub1. I.R.C. § 354. Code section 367(a) does not overrule this nonrecognition if USCO meets the conditions outlined above, including entering into a gain recognition agreement.

Suppose instead that instead of transferring the ForSub2 stock in exchange for ForSub1 stock, USCO sells the stock of ForSub2 to ForSub1for cash or a note. This would be a transaction described in I.R.C. § 304. Basically, § 304 treats the transfer as if USCO first received stock of ForSub1 which is then redeemed for cash or a note in a transaction that is treated as a § 301 distribution under § 302(d). Note that the deemed stock for stock exchange also requires a GRA (on which gain is triggered on the deemed redemption unless USCO enters into a new GRA). *See* Notice 2012–15, 2012–1 C.B. 424.

A gain recognition agreement (GRA) obligates the transferor to recognize any gain that was not recognized on the transfer to the foreign transferee if the transferee disposes of the transferred stock or securities (or the underlying assets are disposed of) during the gain recognition period. Reg. § 1.367(a)– 8. The purpose of the gain recognition agreement is to prevent U.S. taxpayers from transferring stock or securities to a foreign transferee corporation in a manner that does not require recognition under I.R.C. § 367(a), where the foreign transferee subsequently disposes of the transferred property often beyond U.S. tax jurisdiction.

If a transferee disposes of the transferred property during the period that the gain recognition agreement is in effect, the transferor must not only recognize any previously unrecognized gain but also an appropriate interest charge for the deferral of that recognition. In the example above, such an agreement would require USCO to amend its earlier tax return and report the unrecognized gain on its original transfer of the ForSub2 stock to ForSub1 (plus an appropriate interest charge for the tax deferral) if ForSub1 disposes of the ForSub2 stock or if ForSub2 disposes of substantially all of its assets. Reg. § 1.367(a)–8(c) and –8(j). Alternatively, USCO with proper identification can elect to have the gain, plus interest, reported on its current return.

The need for a GRA can also apply is situations where there is deemed to be an indirect stock transfer. Reg. § 1.367(a)–3(d). For example, suppose that USCO owns all of the stock of ForSub1 and all the stock of ForSub2. In a transaction described in I.R.C. § 368(a)(1)(D), all of the assets of ForSub1 are transferred to ForSub2 and ForSub1 liquidates. This is not considered a stock transfer even though pursuant to I.R.C. § 354, stock of ForSub1 is exchanged for stock of ForSub2. Reg. § 1.367(a)–3(d), Ex. 16. However, if ForSub2 were to drop the newly-acquired assets of ForSub1 into ForSub3 pursuant to I.R.C. § 368(a)(2)(C), the transaction does involve an indirect stock transfer and a GRA is necessary in order for USCO to avoid recognition on the deemed transfer of ForSub1 stock.

The indirect stock transfer rules in Reg. § 1.367(a)–3(d) can apply to a variety of triangular reorganizations. For example, suppose that USCO owns the stock of USSub. An unrelated Forco owns all of the stock of ForSub. Suppose that ForSub acquires all the assets of USSub in exchange for 30 percent of the stock of Forco. USSub then liquidates so that USCO ends up owning 30 percent of Forco which owns 100 percent of ForSub which owns the former assets of USCO. This can be structured as a nontaxable triangular I.R.C. § 368(a)(1)(C) transaction (*i.e.,* a C reorganization using stock of ForSub's parent). Even though there is no direct transfer of stock of a foreign corporation by USCO, it does end up holding stock of a foreign entity that in turn owns stock of another foreign entity. Accordingly, this will be treated as an indirect transfer of foreign stock and a GRA is necessary if USCO wants to avoid recognizing any gain inherent in the stock of USSub. Reg. § 1.367(a)–3(d)(3), Ex. 8. Note in this transaction that the indirect stock transfer rules will apply only to the extent that the active trade or business exception in I.R.C. § 367(a)(3) applies when USSub transfers its assets to ForSub so that gain is not recognized.

(F)   THE STOCK OR SECURITIES EXCEPTION— U.S. CORPORATION

Now instead of transferring foreign stock, suppose a U.S. person transfers the appreciated stock or securities of a domestic corporation (the U.S. target company) to a foreign corporation. In this situation, the transferor may be forced to recognize the built-in gain under I.R.C. § 367(a). Reg. § 1.367(a)–3(a) without the opportunity to enter into a GRA. However, there is a narrow exception that allows this transfer to be exempt from recognition under I.R.C. § 367(a) if the U.S. target company complies with certain reporting requirements and the following four conditions are met. Reg. § 1.367(a)–3(c). First, the transferors must not receive more than 50 percent of both the total voting power and the total value of the foreign transferee corporation's outstanding stock after the transaction. Reg. § 1.367(a)–3(c)(1)(i). Second, immediately after the transfer, U.S. persons who are officers or directors of the U.S. target or who own by vote or by value at least 5 percent of the U.S. target company must not own more than 50 percent—both by vote and by value—of the transferee's outstanding stock. Reg. § 1.367(a)–3(c)(1)(ii). Third, the transferor either must not own 5 percent or more of the stock of the foreign transferee corporation by vote or value immediately after the transfer or must enter into a "gain recognition agreement" with the IRS. Reg. § 1.367(a)–3(c)(1)(iii). Finally, the foreign transferee corporation or a qualified subsidiary must have been engaged in an active trade or business outside the United States for at least 36 months before the transfer transaction and the fair market value of the foreign transferee is at least equal to the fair

market value of the U.S. target company. Reg.
§ 1.367(a)–3(c)(1)(iv).

Both the "more than 50 percent" and the "active
trade or business" requirement are intended to
prevent manipulation by the U.S. person who may
seek to move the appreciated assets of the U.S.
target company beyond U.S. tax jurisdiction. This
type of manipulation is sometimes referred to as a
corporate "inversion" or corporate "expatriation"
(*i.e.*, a U.S. corporation (often with foreign
subsidiaries) owned by a U.S. shareholder becomes
a U.S. subsidiary of a foreign corporation). The
concern here is that by interposing a foreign
corporation between the U.S. shareholders and the
U.S. target company, the opportunity for those U.S.
shareholders to avoid U.S. taxation may be
enhanced.

For example, suppose that individual
shareholders of USCO (*e.g.*, 100 shareholders each
owning 1 percent) transfer their stock in USCO in
exchange for 100 percent of the stock of Forco. This
is both a transaction under I.R.C. § 351 and a B
reorganization. The governmental concern is that
this inversion may allow tax to escape the U.S. tax
net. For example, if USCO were able to transfer
stock of a controlled foreign corporation (CFC) that
it owned to Forco in a tax free manner (or to "freeze"
current foreign operations in the CFC and put new
operations in a new foreign corporation owned by
Forco), then the transferred CFC would no longer be
a CFC because there are no U.S. shareholders (*i.e.*,
10 percent owners). Consequently, no subpart F

income would be taxable in the United States. Furthermore, inverting a U.S. corporation may facilitate "earnings stripping" where a USCO erodes the U.S. tax base by paying interest to its foreign parent. *See* I.R.C. § 163(j) discussed at § 404[a][5]. To prevent these perceived abuses, if the shareholders receive back more than 50 percent of the stock of Forco, they will be taxed on the exchange of stock in USCO for the stock in Forco, and no GRA is available to avoid this gain.

(G) INVERSION—U.S. CORPORATION

But now suppose that because of a depressed stock market, for many shareholders the fair market value of the USCO stock does not exceed the basis of the stock. In this situation I.R.C. § 367(a) treating an otherwise tax-free transaction as a taxable transaction is not likely to prevent the transaction from taking place. Accordingly, Congress has enacted another provision aimed at making inversions less appealing. Section 7874 provides rules for expatriated entities and their surrogate foreign corporations. An "expatriated entity" is defined essentially as a domestic corporation or partnership with respect to which a foreign corporation is a surrogate foreign corporation.

A foreign corporation is treated as a "surrogate foreign corporation" if, pursuant to a plan or a series of related transactions: (i) the foreign corporation directly or indirectly acquires "substantially all" (a still-undefined term) of the properties held directly or indirectly by a domestic corporation, or substantially all the properties constituting a trade or business of a domestic partnership; (ii) after the acquisition at least 60 percent of the ownership interest of the foreign entity is held by former owners of the domestic entity; and (iii) the expanded affiliated group (EAG—essentially, 50 percent related corporations) that includes the foreign corporation does not have business activities in the foreign country in which the foreign corporation was created or organized that are substantial when compared to the total business activities of the EAG.

The tax treatment of expatriated entities and surrogate foreign corporations varies depending on the level of owner continuity. If the percentage of stock (by vote or value) in the surrogate foreign corporation held by former owners of the domestic entity, by reason of holding an interest in the domestic entity, is 80 percent or more, the surrogate foreign corporation is treated as a domestic corporation for all purposes of the Code. That is, the inversion will not be respected for U.S. tax purposes. If such ownership percentage is 60 percent or more (but less than 80 percent), the surrogate foreign corporation is treated as a foreign corporation but certain income or gain required to be recognized by the expatriated entity on the inversion itself or for a 10-year period cannot be offset by net operating losses or credits (other than credits allowed under I.R.C. § 901).

In determining the level of stock ownership, stock owned by the EAG is disregarded (statutory EAG rule). To illustrate, assume a domestic corporation (DC) is wholly owned by a U.S. parent corporation (USP), and that USP transfers all the DC stock to a newly formed foreign corporation (FA) in exchange for all of the stock of FA. Absent the statutory EAG rule, the ownership fraction would be 100 percent and the foreign acquiring corporation would be treated as a domestic corporation (assuming the EAG does not have substantial business activities in the relevant foreign country). However, under the statutory EAG rule, the stock of FA held by USP is excluded from the numerator and the denominator of the ownership fraction, so that the numerator and the denominator of the ownership fraction are zero and FA is respected as a foreign corporation.

However, application of the statutory EAG rule does not always lead to the appropriate result, for example, when a domestic entity has minority shareholders. To illustrate, assume that DC is owned 90 percent by USP and 10 percent by individual A, and that USP and individual A transfer all of their DC stock to newly formed FA in exchange for 90 percent and 10 percent, respectively, of the stock of FA. Absent an exception to the statutory EAG rule, the stock of FA held by USP would be excluded from the numerator and the denominator of the ownership fraction, such that the ownership fraction would be 100 percent (10/10) and FA would be treated as a domestic corporation.

To address this and other inappropriate results, Reg. § 1.7874–1 provides two exceptions to the statutory EAG rule: the internal group restructuring exception and the loss of control exception. When either of these exceptions applies, stock of the foreign acquiring corporation held by members of the EAG is excluded from the numerator but not the denominator of the ownership fraction. Thus, both exceptions have the potential to decrease the ownership fraction. In general, the internal group restructuring exception applies when the domestic entity and the foreign acquiring corporation are members of an affiliated group (membership generally being based on an 80 percent vote and value requirement) with the same common parent both before and after the acquisition. The loss of control exception applies when the former owners of the domestic entity do not hold more than 50 percent of the stock of any member of the EAG after the acquisition. In the example, the internal group restructuring rule would apply and the fraction would be 10/100 so that FA would not be treated as a domestic corporation.

In determining ownership under the 60 or 80 percent tests, certain stock—"disqualified stock"—is not taken into account. Reg. § 1.7874–4T. The type of transaction giving rise to the "disqualified stock" rules can be illustrated as follows. Suppose shareholders of a domestic corporation (DC) transfer all their DC stock to a newly-formed foreign corporation (New FCo) in exchange for 79 percent of the stock of New FCo and, in a related transaction, an investor (perhaps a private equity fund) transfers cash to New FCo in exchange for the remaining 21 percent of the New FCo stock. The shareholders of DC have inverted—DC is now owned by FCo—but because ownership by shareholders of DC in FCo is less than 80 percent, absent a special rule I.R.C. § 7874 would not apply to deem FCo to be a domestic corporation.

Treasury thought that this fact pattern did not present a legitimate case for allowing inversion—no real combination of U.S. and foreign businesses. To prevent this result, stock issued for "nonqualified property"—cash or cash equivalents, marketable securities, certain notes, etc. is considered disqualified and would not be taken into account. So in the example above, the former owners of DC would be deemed to own 100 percent of FCo and § 7874 would apply to treaty FCo as a domestic corporation. There is a de minimis rule that turns off the disqualified stock rule where shareholders of the domestic corporation end up with less than 5 percent of the foreign acquirer (*e.g.,* if the investor had transferred enough cash to constitute 96 percent of the value of FCo and shareholders of DC ended up with 4 percent of the stock of FCo). This rule with respect to disregarded stock also would apply to stock of a foreign acquiror where more than 50 percent of the foreign acquiror's EAG constitutes of nonqualified property. Notice 2014–52, 2014–2 C.B. 712.

Note that I.R.C. § 7874 will not apply (and the foreign parent will not be treated as a U.S. corporation) where the "substantial business activities" test is met (*i.e.,* where the new foreign parent and/or related entities have a business reason to invert). Unfortunately for taxpayers, Reg. § 1.7874–3 takes a hard line approach based on a very hard-to-meet objective test. An expanded affiliated group will have substantial business activities in the relevant foreign country only when the number of group employees, the employee compensation and the group assets is at least 25 percent of those in the EAG as a whole throughout the world. Note that each of these three metrics must be satisfied. It is not sufficient if the average of the three metrics is at least 25 percent if any one metric is less than 25 percent. There are no exceptions to this objective test.

There is little doubt that both Congress and Treasury regard inversions as pernicious. Apparently, the same American open border ethos that has caused us to look with horror at the former Berlin Wall, or emigration restrictions in the former Soviet Union or Cuba, does not apply to corporations that want to leave the United States. In Notice 2014–52, 2014–2 C.B. 712, Treasury has announced a rash of future Regulations that would: ignore attempts by domestic companies to "skinny down" their assets prior to an inversion through non-ordinary distributions in an effort to bring ownership of a foreign acquiror below 80 percent (or in some cases 60 percent), avoid I.R.C. 956 after an inversion by making loans to certain related foreign corporations that are not CFCs (*e.g.*, a loan from a CFC to the foreign parent of an inverted U.S. corporation), discourage nontaxable ways of converting CFCs to non-CFCs after an inversion, and more.

(H) INTERPLAY OF I.R.C. §§ 367(a) AND 7874

Of course, if the transferors end up with 50 percent or less of the transferee corporation and file a gain recognition agreement, then neither I.R.C. § 7874 nor § 367(a) should apply. To illustrate, suppose that USCO owns DomSub, a U.S. corporation. Suppose that Forco, a foreign corporation not owned by USCO acquires all of the stock of DomSub from USCO in exchange for Forco stock in a transaction that qualifies as a B reorganization. If after the transaction USCO owns 50 percent or less of Forco stock, I.R.C. § 367(a) would not force USCO to recognize any gain inherent in the DomSub stock if USCO enters into a 5-year gain recognition agreement and the "active trade or business" requirements are satisfied. Section 7874 should not apply in this situation where ownership in Forco by U.S. shareholders is less than 60 percent.

Other reorganizations that indirectly resemble a stock transfer also can trigger I.R.C. § 367(a) and § 7874. For example, suppose USCO owns all of the stock of USSub, and unrelated Forco owns all of the stock of Newco, a newly-formed U.S. corporation. Suppose that in a reorganization described in I.R.C. § 368(a)(1)(C), USSub transfers all of its assets to Newco in exchange for stock of Newco's parent, Forco. USSub then liquidates with USCO receiving the Forco stock. In this situation for purposes of I.R.C. § 367(a), USCO is treated as if it had transferred the stock of USSub to Forco in exchange for Forco stock even though USCO did not exchange the stock directly with Forco. If USCO receives 50 percent or less of the Forco stock, meets the active trade or business test and enters into a 5-year gain recognition agreement, there will be no immediate tax resulting from I.R.C. § 367(a). If USCO receives more than 50 percent of the Forco stock, USCO must recognize any gain on the transfer of the USSub stock. The same analysis would apply if USSub merges into Newco or if Newco merges into USSub where USCO receives Forco stock. *See* I.R.C. §§ 368(a)(2)(D) and (E). Furthermore, I.R.C. § 7874 may apply to an indirect transfer if the U.S. shareholders acquire 60 percent or more of the Forco stock. In such a case, Forco may be treated as a U.S. corporation for U.S. tax purposes (if ownership is 80 percent or more) or certain tax attributes may be unavailable if U.S. ownership is between 60 and less than 80 percent.

(I)   OUTBOUND SPIN-OFFS

Suppose that USCO owns USSub that has long conducted both U.S. and foreign businesses. USSub transfers the foreign businesses to a new subsidiary—ForSub—and then distributes the stock of ForSub to USCO. In a domestic context, this would generally qualify as tax-free divisive reorganization under I.R.C. § 355. In a foreign context, if the distribution is to qualified U.S. shareholders, there may be no § 367 consequences on the distribution. The transfer of assets to a ForSub, a foreign corporation, may satisfy the active trade or business exception of I.R.C. § 367(a)(3). There is no tax on USSub when it distributes any appreciated ForSub stock because the appreciated stock will be held by a U.S. shareholder and is subject to U.S. tax when, and if, the shareholder sells the stock. I.R.C. § 367(e)(1) and Reg. § 1.367(e)–1. But *see* the discussion of Reg. § 1.367(b)–5 *infra* in § 12.03.

But suppose that instead of USCO, the owner of USSub is Forco, a foreign shareholder. Now if Forco sells the ForSub stock, there would generally be no U.S. tax on the gain. Accordingly on the distribution of stock to foreign shareholders, the distributing U.S. transferor must recognize gain on the distribution of the appreciated stock of ForSub. Note that there would be no tax imposed on USSub if stock of a U.S. rather than a foreign subsidiary were distributed regardless of whether the recipient is a U.S. or foreign distributee. Reg. § 1.367(e)–1(c).

(J) OUTBOUND LIQUIDATIONS

The focus of I.R.C. § 367(e)(2) is to force recognition when appreciated assets are removed from U.S. tax jurisdiction through a liquidating distribution. When a U.S. subsidiary liquidates into its foreign parent in what would be a tax-free liquidation under I.R.C. §§ 332 and 337 had the transaction occurred in a domestic context, I.R.C. § 367(e)(2) provides for taxation of the U.S. subsidiary on the distribution of appreciated property in the liquidation. However, no recognition under I.R.C. § 367(e)(2) is required if the foreign parent uses the distributed property in the conduct of a trade or business in the United States for at least 10 years after the liquidation. Reg. § 1.367(e)–2(b)(2). The logic for this exception from immediate recognition by a liquidating subsidiary on the distribution of appreciated assets to a foreign parent is that the foreign parent would be taxed on the effectively connected income of its U.S. branch under I.R.C. § 882, on any repatriation of those earnings under the branch profits tax of I.R.C. § 884, and on any sale of the branch's assets under I.R.C. § 882. The exception will not apply to the extent that an intangible is distributed by the U.S. subsidiary as part of the liquidating distribution even if the intangible remains in the U.S. as part of a U.S. trade or business.

Similar logic excepts a liquidating U.S. subsidiary from recognizing gain on an outbound liquidation to the extent that the liquidating corporation (if it is not a United States Real Property Holding Company distributing stock of a U.S. corporation that is not a United States Real Property Holding Company) distributes stock of a U.S. subsidiary (at least 80 percent ownership) to its foreign parent, Reg. § 1.367(e)–2(b)(2). Also, nonrecognition is permitted on a liquidating distribution of a United States real property interest (*e.g.,* U.S. real property or stock in a United States real property holding company) because the foreign shareholder of the liquidating U.S. subsidiary would be subject to U.S. tax on any sale of the United States real property interest.

(K) TRANSFERS TO ESTATES, TRUSTS AND PARTNERSHIPS

On transfers of property to a U.S. or foreign partnership, Treasury has been authorized to promulgate Regulations (but has not done so) denying the normal nonrecognition provided by I.R.C. § 721, a provision in the partnership context that is parallel to I.R.C. § 351 in the corporate context. I.R.C. § 721(d). The Regulations will address transfers by a U.S. partner to a partnership where any gain inherent in the contributed property ultimately will be recognized by a foreign person. In effect, the Regulations will look through the partnership to determine if the gain will be recognized by a foreign person. Because there is great flexibility under partnership agreements for allocating gain, the Regulations will have to look closely at what a partnership agreement provides. Congress has also authorized Treasury to promulgate Regulations to provide similar treatment in the case of a transfer of an intangible asset to a foreign partnership as the I.R.C. § 367(d) deemed royalty provision for transfers of an intangible asset to a foreign corporation. Notice 2015–54, 2015–34 I.R.B. 210, can override I.R.C. § 721 nonrecognition in some circumstances where intellectual property is transferred to a partnership which fails to allocate or report allocations in accordance with IRS requirements.

When a U.S. person transfers appreciated property to a foreign trust or estate, the transferor must recognize gain. Therefore, a transfer of property by a U.S. person to a foreign trust or estate is treated as a sale or exchange of the property for its fair market value. If a U.S. trust becomes a foreign trust, all trust assets are treated as having been sold to the foreign trust.

§ 12.03 NON-OUTBOUND TRANSACTIONS

Without a full explanation of the tax law of corporate reorganizations, it is difficult at best to understand the operation of I.R.C. § 367 to non-outbound transactions. What follows is a skeletal summary of I.R.C. § 367(b), the provision that governs the treatment of such transfers.

While I.R.C. § 367(a) is concerned with U.S. taxpayers transferring appreciated assets beyond U.S. tax jurisdiction without recognizing the gain inherent in the appreciation, I.R.C. § 367(b) is concerned with another matter altogether. If a U.S. corporation runs a business through a foreign subsidiary, the income is not normally taxable in the United States unless it is subpart F income. *See supra* Chapter 10. However, those foreign earnings are subject to a U.S. corporate-level tax at ordinary income rates when a dividend is paid from the foreign subsidiary to its U.S. parent. Of course if the income is subpart F income, it is subject to a U.S. tax at ordinary income rates when earned by the foreign corporation. To prevent a U.S. shareholder from converting what would be ordinary income if earned directly by the shareholder into a capital gain, I.R.C. § 1248 treats gain on a sale or other disposition of the stock of such a foreign subsidiary as ordinary income to the extent of the foreign subsidiary's earnings and profits which have not been taken into U.S. income. *See supra* § 10.06(A). In sum, the U.S. tax system is designed to ensure that foreign earnings are subject to a U.S. corporate-level tax at ordinary income rates at some point in time.

The purpose of I.R.C. § 367(b) is ensure that foreign earnings and profits are subject to a U.S. corporate-level tax at ordinary income tax rates when certain otherwise tax-free transactions result in the repatriation or deemed repatriation of those earnings to the United States. Code section 367(b) is itself quite general, providing essentially that in most reorganizations (or subsidiary liquidations) to which the outbound rules of I.R.C. § 367(a) do not apply, a foreign corporation is accorded treatment as a corporation, thereby paving the way for appropriate nonrecognition under I.R.C. §§ 332, 351, 354, 355, 356 or 361, except to the extent that the Regulations provide otherwise. *See* Reg. § 1.367(b)–1(b).

The following types of transactions are governed by I.R.C. § 367(b): (1) the repatriation of foreign assets in an inbound liquidation or inbound reorganization; (2) certain foreign-to-foreign reorganizations; and (3) certain divisive reorganizations involving a foreign corporation. In these transactions, the primary tax policies reflected in the Regulations are: (a) to provide immediate taxation when untaxed (by the United States) earnings of a foreign corporation are repatriated to

U.S. corporate shareholders; and (b) to prevent the U.S. transferor from avoiding any potential ordinary income taxation under I.R.C. § 1248.

Applying these policies to the transactions outlined above yields the following results under I.R.C. § 367(b) and the Regulations. In a complete liquidation of a foreign subsidiary into its U.S. parent corporation that would otherwise be tax-free under I.R.C. §§ 332 and 337, the parent is taxed on the "all earnings and profits amount"—essentially the E&P of the liquidating corporation attributable to the U.S. shareholder's ownership. Reg. § 1.367(b)–3. This ensures that any foreign earnings and profits will be potentially taxable at the U.S. corporate level.

Similarly, if a foreign subsidiary of a U.S. parent corporation reorganizes into a U.S. subsidiary, the U.S. parent must include in income the earnings and profits of the foreign subsidiary attributable to the parent's stock in the foreign subsidiary. For example, suppose that USCO owns all of the stock of ForSub, a foreign subsidiary with earnings and profits. ForSub transfers all of its assets to USSub, a U.S. subsidiary, in exchange for the stock of USSub. ForSub then liquidates distributing the USSub stock to USCO. This asset reorganization (probably a D reorganization under I.R.C. § 368(a)(1)(D)) would normally be tax-free to all parties. However, note that the foreign earnings and profits have been repatriated to the United States. In the absence of § 367(b) those earnings would not be taxed in the United States at the corporate level.

However, I.R.C. § 367(b) will force USCO to be taxed on those foreign earnings.

In these transactions, the amount that must be recognized as ordinary income by the U.S. parent corporation is "the all earnings and profits amount." Reg. § 1.367(b)–2(d). Essentially, the "all earnings and profits amount" (or "all E&P amount") consists of the foreign earnings and profits of the subsidiary involved in the inbound liquidation or reorganization which accrued while the U.S. taxpayer held the stock. The earnings and profits of any lower tier subsidiaries are not counted as that E&P remains potentially taxable if repatriated to the ultimate U.S. parent. The all earnings and profits amount includes earnings of a foreign corporation attributable to a U.S. shareholder's stock, even if that corporation was not a controlled foreign corporation at the time the earnings accrued.

A U.S. taxpayer which has to recognize the all earnings and profits amount under I.R.C. § 367(b) as a deemed dividend is entitled to credit foreign income tax attributable to those earnings and profits in accordance with I.R.C. § 902. In some cases, the inclusion of the all earnings and profits amount might exceed the actual gain the U.S. shareholder has on the transaction. For example, suppose that USCO has a basis of $5 million in the stock of its wholly-owned foreign subsidiary, ForSub which has a fair market value of $6 million and an "all earnings and profits amount" of $3 million. If ForSub liquidates, I.R.C. § 367(b) requires that

USCO recognize a $3 million dividend. The regulations under I.R.C. § 367(b) will not permit the taxpayer to limit income to the gain in the shareholder's stock; instead, the USCO must recognize the all earnings and profits amount.

Generally, a foreign-to-foreign reorganization does not result in recognition under I.R.C. § 367(b). For example, if USCO is a shareholder in FC1, a foreign corporation, whose assets are acquired by FC2, another foreign corporation, in a reorganization with the U.S. shareholder receiving FC2 stock, the shareholder will not recognize any gain or loss on the transaction under I.R.C. § 354. Reg. § 1.367(b)–1(b). However, if FC1 is a controlled foreign corporation and FC2 is not (or the shareholder is not a 10 percent shareholder of FC2), then the potential I.R.C. § 1248 recognition on a sale or exchange of FC2 stock (which should reflect the potential § 1248 amount of the FC1 stock) is eliminated, because I.R.C. § 1248 does not apply to the stock of FC2 if it is not a controlled foreign corporation. Similarly, even if FC2 is a controlled foreign corporation, I.R.C. § 1248 does not apply if the U.S. shareholder does not own at least a 10 percent stock interest. In these and similar situations, I.R.C. § 367(b) generally requires the U.S. shareholder to recognize the earnings and profits of FC1 that are allocable to the stock held by the U.S. shareholder in order for the rest of the transaction to be tax-free. Reg. § 1.367(b)–4.

Note that in this foreign-to-foreign context the amount that is recognized by USCO is "the § 1248 amount" rather than "the all E&P amount." The § 1248 amount consists of foreign earnings and profits and, unlike the all earnings and profits amount, may include the earnings and profits of subsidiaries. To understand why the all earnings and profits amount is limited to the E&P of the top tier company while the § 1248 amount includes E&P of lower tier entities, consider the following. USCO owns all the stock of ForSub1 which in turn owns all the stock of ForSub2. If ForSub1 liquidates, there is no need for the E&P of ForSub2 to be taxable to USCO because later distributions or a later liquidation would result in U.S. corporate level taxation. But suppose USCO transfers the stock of ForSub1 to ForSub3 in a reorganization under I.R.C. § 368(a)(1)(B) where USCO receives only 20 percent of the stock of ForSub3 and assume that unrelated foreign shareholders hold the remainder of the stock. Now ForSub1 and ForSub2 are no longer CFCs. If USCO is not taxed on all of the E&P in both ForSub1 and ForSub2 on the transaction, that E&P may never be subject to U.S. corporate level taxation.

Suppose that USP owns all the stock USS, a U.S. subsidiary the only asset of which is all of stock of CFC1. Suppose further that USP owns stock of CFC2. In a reorganization under I.R.C. § 368(a)(1)(D), USS transfers all of its assets (*i.e.,* the stock of CFC1) to CFC2 and liquidates. It would not appear that I.R.C. § 367(b) should pose a problem as CFC1 remains a CFC. The new U.S. shareholder (under the indirect ownership rules of I.R.C. § 958(a)(2)) is USP rather than USS which liquidated as part of the I.R.C. § 368(a)(1)(D) reorganization. Even though the former U.S. shareholder no longer exists, USP is not taxed on the earnings and profits (*i.e.,* the § 1248 amount) of CFC1. Reg. § 1.367(b)–4(b). Note that USS faces potential tax under I.R.C. § 367(a) on any gain with respect to its transfer of CFC1 stock, but if a GRA is filed, there should be no gain recognized. Reg. § 1.367(a)–3T(e)(3). If USP fails to enter into a gain recognition agreement, USP would have to recognize all of the built-in gain on the stock transferred and a portion of that gain equal to the § 1248 amount determined under I.R.C. § 367(b) would be treated as a dividend.

The third general type of transaction governed by I.R.C. § 367(b) (the first two being liquidations/reorganizations into the United States and certain foreign-to-foreign reorganizations) is the non-outbound divisive reorganization. In a divisive reorganization, essentially a corporation makes a distribution to one or more of its shareholders, consisting of stock of a controlled corporation where both the distributing and distributed corporations conduct active trades or businesses. I.R.C. §§ 368(a)(1)(D) and 355. If all of the statutory requirements are met, the parties are not taxed in a divisive reorganization. Section 367(b) alters this nonrecognition treatment where either the distributing or controlled corporation is foreign.

If a domestic corporation distributes stock of a CFC to a U.S. corporation, the CFC is deemed to be a corporation and the reorganization is generally tax-free as long as basis adjustments in the stock of the CFC preserve the § 1248 gain. *See* Reg. § 1.1248(f)–2(b)(2) and (3). If the distributee is a U.S. individual, the distributing corporation recognizes gain on the distribution. Reg. § 1.367(b)–5(b).

If the distributing corporation is a CFC, the level of complexity escalates. But essentially if the divisive reorganization distribution is pro rata to the shareholders, the bases in the stock of both the distributing corporation and the corporation whose stock was distributed (the controlled corporation) are adjusted downwards to ensure that any pre-reorganization potential § 1248 gain is preserved in the hands of the shareholders if they dispose of the stock of either the distributing or the controlled corporation. That is, there is no immediate income to the shareholders, but they face the same § 1248 gain potential that they faced before the divisive reorganization. If the distribution is not pro rata, but instead a shareholder gives up the stock in the distributing corporation in exchange for the stock in the distributed corporation, then the shareholder has a deemed distribution equal to the shareholder's pro rata share of the earnings and profits of the stock surrendered in the reorganization. Reg. § 1.367(b)–5(d)(2). For those readers with problems getting to sleep, there is a numerical illustration of the rules in this paragraph, *see* Reg. § 1.367(b)–5(g) Ex. 1.

§ 12.04 CARRYOVER OF TAX ATTRIBUTES IN FOREIGN-TO-FOREIGN NONRECOGNITION EVENTS

Suppose that USCO owns all of the stock of CFC1 and CFC2 (for ease of computation, assume all entities use the USD as functional currency). CFC2 owns all of the stock of CFC3. In year 2 CFC1 merges into CFC2 in a transaction described in I.R.C. § 368(a)(1)(A). What happens to the E&P and tax pools in CFC1? In accordance with I.R.C. § 381 and Reg. § 1.367(b)–7, in an asset reorganization essentially the E&P and tax pools of CFC1 combine with those of CFC2. Similar treatment would result if CFC3 were to liquidate into CFC2 in year 4 in a tax-free liquidation under I.R.C. §§ 332 and 337.

Now suppose that CFC1 has a $100 deficit of accumulated E&P at the end of year 1 and CFC2 has $100 of positive accumulated E&P (and $100 of cash). Neither corporation has any E&P in year 2. In the absence of the merger, had CFC2 distributed $100 to USCO in year 2, it would have been a dividend under I.R.C. § 301(c)(1). However, following the merger CFC2 has $0 accumulated E&P (including CFC1's deficit). If CFC2 now makes a distribution, it may be a nontaxable return of basis under I.R.C. § 301(c)(2)—tax-free foreign repatriation. To prevent this perceived abuse, following a reorganization or a liquidation of a subsidiary into a parent under I.R.C. § 332, if one (or both) of the parties has an E&P deficit, it "hovers"—sort of like a drone. Reg. § 1.367(b)–

7(d)(2). In addition, any foreign tax pool associated with the hovering deficit also hovers.

A hovering deficit is not immediately available to offset E&P. So in the example above, CFC1's hovering deficit cannot offset CFC2's positive E&P. When CFC2 distributes $100 to USCO in year 2, it will still be a dividend in the same way as if the merger had never occurred. Now suppose that in year 3 CFC2 earns $200 and pays $60 of local country tax. CFC2's current E&P would be $140 and its tax pool would be $60. If CFC2 distributes $140 in year 3, it will be a dividend. Indeed, with the gross-up under I.R.C. § 78, the dividend will be $200 and USCO can take a $60 tax credit against the $70 U.S. tax on that dividend. Notice that the hovering deficit continues to hover.

Now suppose that CFC2 makes no distribution in year 3 but accumulates the E&P until year 4—a year when no new E&P is generated by CFC2. As soon as the year 3 E&P accumulates over a year-end, all or a portion of the hovering deficit (and the associated hovering tax pool) is released and no longer hovers. The amount released does not exceed the newly accumulated E&P. As a result, if CFC2 makes a distribution in year 4, the E&P is $40 rather than $140. With the $60 gross-up, USCO will report a dividend of $100. The $60 indirect foreign tax credit will not only offset the potential $35 tax on the dividend but is available to offset U.S. tax on other foreign source income in the same basket that USCO might have. So one lesson here is that hovering deficits are not always unwelcome. Sometimes they can facilitate tax planning.

CHAPTER 13

TAX ARBITRAGE AND ECONOMIC SUBSTANCE

§ 13.01 INTRODUCTION

Double taxation may occur when two competing jurisdictions claim to have the primary authority to tax the same income with neither providing any relief for taxes imposed by the other jurisdiction. For example, suppose that U.S. Co. renders services, training Indian computer programmers in the United States. The Indian programmers use their newly-acquired skills in India. Under U.S. law, the services were rendered in the United States and U.S. Co.'s compensation for those services is U.S. source income. If India treats the services as having been performed in India (*i.e.*, where the services are used), India may impose a tax on the compensation paid. Because the United States will not generally give a tax credit for foreign taxes imposed on what the United States regards as U.S. source income, the result may be double taxation (although in some cases the credits may be available to offset U.S. tax on other foreign source income in the same income basket, or Indian taxes may be creditable under the U.S.-India tax treaty).

One job of the international tax advisor in serving clients is to avoid double taxation. The intersection of different tax systems can produce double taxation, as outlined above, but it can also provide opportunities to minimize and, at times, eliminate tax liability. When two countries classify the same transaction differently or even within a country when tax treatment is inconsistent, the opportunity for tax arbitrage arises. Tax arbitrage is simply the process of exploiting the differences between two different tax results for the same transaction. Tax arbitrage essentially is the other side of the double taxation coin. Through tax arbitrage, taxpayers can often receive the same tax benefit in more than one jurisdiction.

Suppose A, a U.S. resident who has worked in country X for many years and is now retired, receives a distribution from a country X payor which the United States considers to be similar to a social security payment but that country X considers to be a pension distribution. If a treaty based on the 2006 U.S. Model treaty is applicable, the United States would refrain from taxing the distribution because Article 17(2) cedes exclusive taxing authority to country X over payments similar to social security, while country X would refrain from taxing the distribution because Article 17(1) grants exclusive taxing authority to the United States over pensions. The result would be double nontaxation—often the holy grail for international tax advisors and their clients. This result arises because of differing views of the transaction by both the United States and country X. Those differing views which can sometimes lead to double taxation can also sometimes lead to double nontaxation.

Suppose X Corp. is incorporated in country X but is managed and controlled in country Y (*e.g.*, important corporate decisions are made in country Y). X Corp. earns business income in country X but does not have a permanent establishment there. If country X uses a "place of effective management" test to determine residence while country Y uses a "place of incorporation" test, the result may be that the income of X Corp. escapes taxation. Country X may not exercise source state taxing authority because X Corp.'s presence there does not rise to the level of a permanent establishment. Country X may not exercise residence-based taxing authority because, it considers X Corp. to be a country Y resident, while country Y may not exercise residence-based or source-based taxation because it considers X Corp. to be a country X resident that earns income in country X.

The ability to arbitrage differences between tax systems can arise in a variety of circumstances where two countries characterize transactions inconsistently. Differing rules with respect to source, residence, transfer pricing, etc. offer openings for taxpayers to avoid or minimize overall taxation from cross-border transactions. What follows is a mere sampling of how tax arbitrage opportunities can shape cross-border transactions. Often tax arbitrage advantages arise because of conflicting characterizations of who the taxpayer is.

Suppose U.S. Co. is a domestic corporation and the sole shareholder of Forco, a foreign corporation doing business in country X. Forco earns non-subpart F income and therefore is not subject to current U.S. taxation. Forco has net profits of $1 million that are subject to a foreign tax of 45 percent, or $450,000. Suppose that U.S. Co. sets up another entity, Reverse Hybrid, in country X that is treated as a corporation for U.S. purposes but as a partnership for country X purposes (the second owner of Reverse Hybrid is another member of the U.S. Co. consolidated group). Reverse Hybrid makes a loan to Forco and receives interest from Forco in the amount of $250,000. The United States does not tax the interest received by Reverse Hybrid as subpart F income. Either the look-through rule of I.R.C. § 954(c)(6) or if that provision expires then the same country exception in § 954(c)(3) may apply. But country X thinks the interest payment is made to a partnership with U.S. partners. If under the applicable treaty, there is no country X withholding tax (*e.g.,* 2006 U.S. Model Treaty Art. 11), then Forco may be able to deduct the $250,000 in interest income it pays out to Reverse Hybrid. Forco would be left with taxable income of $750,000 that will be subject to a 45 percent rate, or $330,750, and there is no further tax imposed. The total foreign tax liability of $330,750 represents a reduction of $119,250 from the tax liability Forco would incur in the absence of the loan by Reverse Hybrid.

The tax arbitrage here is that Forco is able to reduce its overall foreign tax liability through an "interest" payment that under U.S. law is treated as received by a foreign corporation, Reverse Hybrid, as non-subpart F income, but is treated as received by the U.S. consolidated group by country X. If the

United States followed the characterization of country X, the interest received by Reverse Hybrid would have been taxable to U.S. Co. and the other U.S. owner of Reverse Hybrid. This transaction capitalizes on the inconsistent classifications countries have for business entities. When an entity is inconsistently categorized it is sometimes known as a "hybrid" or "reverse hybrid" entity. Hybrid and reverse hybrid entities are fundamental to many tax arbitrage transactions.

§ 13.02   THE CHECK-THE-BOX REGULATIONS

The use of hybrid entities such as the one above grew exponentially when the Treasury released the check-the-box regulations. Reg. §§ 301.7701–1 through –4. The check-the-box regulations greatly simplified entity classification by allowing a many entities to simply choose (*i.e.*, check-the-box) if it wanted to be treated as a corporation or transparent entity for U.S. tax purposes. This simplification also brought with it certainty where little existed before.

The regulations permit "eligible entities" to choose among various business classifications. Both domestic and foreign businesses may be "eligible entities" if they meet the requirements of the regulations. Generally, once a change in classification is made, a subsequent change in classification cannot be made for five years. However, an election by a newly formed eligible entity is not considered a change. Reg. § 301.7701–3(c)(1)(iv). For example, if an eligible entity elects on creation to be treated as a corporation, it can change that election in year 3 and be treated as a flow-through entity. An "eligible entity" may be classified as a corporation, partnership or a single member entity. A single member entity (sometimes informally referred to as a "tax nothing" or "disregarded entity") provides flow-through taxation and resembles a partnership but with only one member. This creates an "entity" that will be ignored for tax purposes in the United States. When an entity is transparent for U.S. tax purposes but is recognized as a corporation in the country of operation, it is a "hybrid entity." When an entity is recognized as a corporation in the United States but is treated as a transparent entity in a foreign country, it is sometimes referred to as a "reverse hybrid entity."

The check-the-box regulations have a number of requirements. The first requirement is that a separate entity must exist for federal tax purposes. Reg. § 301.7701–1(a). A mere contractual relationship (*e.g.,* joint tenancy) does not qualify as an entity. Once an organization is deemed to be an entity separate from its owners, the next step is to determine if it is a business entity. A business entity is any entity that is not classified as a trust or subject to special treatment under the Internal Revenue Code. Reg. § 301.7701–4. A business entity with two or more members is classified as either a corporation or a partnership for federal tax purposes. A business entity with only one owner is classified as either a corporation or a single member entity. Once a business entity exists, a determination of eligibility must be made.

A business entity will be ineligible to choose its classification as a transparent or corporate entity if the business form chosen appears on a "per se" list. There is one list for domestic business entities and another for foreign business entities. For example, an entity incorporated in any U.S. state cannot elect to be treated as a transparent entity. Similarly, a United Kingdom Public Limited Company (PLC) or a Brazilian Sociadade Anonima (SA) cannot choose to be treated as a transparent entity. Reg. § 301.7701–2.

Eligible entities failing to make an election will be classified under default rules in the regulations. Reg. § 301.7701–3(b). The regulations attempt to classify entities as they would most likely classify themselves if an election had been made. If two or more members create an unincorporated domestic entity (*e.g.*, a U.S. partnership or a U.S. limited liability company (LLC)) it will be given transparency treatment and be classified as a partnership. If only one member creates an unincorporated domestic entity (*e.g.*, a U.S. LLC), it will be treated as a single member entity and be disregarded (*i.e.*, treated as transparent).

Foreign eligible entities will be classified depending on whether there is unlimited liability or not. A foreign eligible entity consisting of more than one member, when all members have limited liability (*e.g.*, a limited liability company), will be deemed a corporation under the default rules. A single member foreign entity with limited liability will also be a corporation. On the other hand, a foreign eligible entity with more than one member will be a partnership if any member has unlimited liability (*e.g.*, a limited partnership where the general partner has unlimited liability). A single member foreign eligible entity with unlimited liability will be disregarded (*i.e.*, treated as transparent).

A check-the-box election can be made retroactively effective up to 75 days before the election is made. In some cases, in the initial year it is possible to make the election retroactive more than 75 days. *See* Rev. Proc. 2002–59, 2002–2 C.B. 615.

§ 13.03   A TAX ARBITRAGE SAMPLER

Arbitraging differences in tax systems is an important aspect of international tax practice. It is not possible to detail fully all the circumstances where arbitrage opportunities occur. What follows are some illustrations of tax arbitrage transactions—some involving hybrid entities. While some of these transactions have been addressed by U.S. tax authorities, others have not. Tax arbitrage can occur with respect to: (a) entities; (b) character of income; (c) source of income; (d) tax base.

What follows is a brief, non-exclusive sampler of various tax arbitrage transactions and some of the U.S. tax authority actions that have been taken in response to perceived taxpayer excesses.

(A) ENTITIES

(1) Check-the-Box Elections

Assume U.S. Co. owns all of the shares of Forco, a foreign corporation. Forco operates in county X and is on the per se list. Because Forco is on the per se list, it may not choose its classification for U.S. tax purposes and will be deemed a corporation for both U.S. and country X tax purposes. Suppose that Country X has a 45 percent corporate tax rate. Forco wholly owns two other entities, ForcoSub and SME Co. ForcoSub is a country X operating entity and, because it too is on the per se list, it cannot elect its classification. However, SME Co., a country Y entity, is not on the per se list and can therefore elect its classification for U.S. tax purposes. Country Y has a 10 percent corporate tax rate. If SME Co. elects to be a single member entity, it will be disregarded for U.S. tax purposes and all tax items will flow through to Forco, its owner.

Although the United States will treat SME Co. and Forco as one entity, assume that countries X and Y treat them as separate taxable entities. SME Co. makes a loan to ForcoSub when both ForcoSub and Forco have net profits of $1 million. SME Co. receives a $250,000 interest payment from ForcoSub. ForcoSub will be able to take an interest deduction under the laws of country X. The deduction will reduce net profits to $750,000, and with a tax rate of 45 percent, will result in a tax liability of $333,500. SME Co. will realize $250,000 of interest income and at a 10 percent rate owe tax of $25,000 on that amount. This will result in an overall foreign tax savings of $87,500. The United States will characterize this transaction as a loan from Forco to ForcoSub because Forco and SME Co. are treated as a single entity. Forco will be treated as having $250,000 of interest income, which because it is made by a related party located in the same country may not be subpart F income and therefore immediately subject to U.S. tax. I.R.C. § 954(c)(3). Indeed, the interest payment may also be entitled to look-through treatment under the less restrictive look-through provision of I.R.C. § 954(c)(6), if that provision continues to be extended. In sum, the use of a hybrid entity may lower overall foreign tax liability in this example without causing any immediate increase in U.S. tax liability.

As another variation on this theme, suppose that U.S. Co. owns all the stock of Foreign Opco in country X which is a high tax jurisdiction. U.S. Co. "sells" all of the stock of Foreign Opco to a newly-formed, wholly-owned country X hybrid entity, Foreign Hybrid, in exchange for a note. Foreign Hybrid is disregarded for U.S. purposes and treated as a corporation for country X purposes. When U.S. Co. "sells" the stock of Foreign Opco to Foreign Hybrid, the transaction is disregarded for U.S. tax purposes (U.S. Co. is basically selling to itself because a sale to a branch is disregarded). However, for country X purposes, now there is a note in place and interest expense runs from Foreign Hybrid to U.S. Co. If country X permits Foreign Hybrid to file a consolidated return with Foreign Opco (or to merge), then an accrued interest deduction can offset the income from operations, lowering the country X tax rate. At the same time, the accrual of "interest" from what the U.S. sees as a branch of U.S. Co. to the U.S. Co. home office would be ignored for U.S. tax purposes. The result is a deduction with no income inclusion.

A deduction with no income inclusion is sometimes referred to as a "double dip" transaction. A "double dip" is best thought of us a situation where there is one more deduction than there is an inclusion. For example, a situation where there are two deductions and only one inclusion would also be a double dip. If in the example above U.S. Co. borrowed from a bank and "loaned" money to Foreign Hybrid, now there would be two interest deductions (one by U.S. Co. for interest paid to the bank and one by Foreign Hybrid) and only one inclusion (the bank would report interest income).

There is no end to how resourcefully taxpayers utilize the check-the-box election which is explicitly permitted by the regulations. For instance, under I.R.C. § 902 only U.S. corporations that own at least 10 percent of the voting stock of a foreign corporation can receive a foreign tax credit for the income taxes paid by the foreign corporation. The use of a transparent entity can eliminate this difficulty. Suppose U.S. Co. owns 8 percent of Forco, a foreign corporation. Under I.R.C. § 902, U.S. Co. would not be able to claim a foreign tax credit for any of the taxes paid by Forco because U.S. Co. does not satisfy the 10 percent voting stock threshold.

However, if Forco elects to be treated as a transparent entity, any taxes paid by Forco will be treated for U.S. purposes as if the owners had paid them. This will allow U.S. Co. to claim 8 percent of the taxes paid as a foreign tax credit under I.R.C. § 901. At the same time, the U.S. election does not affect how Forco will be treated for foreign tax purposes. Accordingly, Forco may be treated as a corporation for foreign tax purposes, thereby providing limited liability protection for its owners, including U.S. Co. The downside to this sort of transaction is the loss of deferral for U.S. tax purposes. That is, if Forco is disregarded for U.S. tax purposes, any income (as well as the taxes imposed on that income) will flow through to U.S. Co. This may not be a problem if a credit for the foreign taxes paid will completely shelter the income that U.S. Co. must report.

The reverse hybrid structure—an entity is considered to be a corporation for U.S. tax purposes but transparent for foreign tax purposes—may also provide some arbitrage opportunities. Suppose that a country X partnership with country X partners is engaged in a trade or business in the United States. All of the partners would be required to file U.S. tax returns because the U.S. trade or business would be attributable to them. I.R.C. § 875(1). This prospect is burdensome and the partners may regard it as intrusive as well. If the partnership checks the box to be treated as a corporation for U.S. tax purposes, only the corporation and not the "shareholders" would be required to file a U.S. tax return (there would be U.S. corporate-level taxation instead of taxation of ECI earned by foreign investors). At the same time for country X tax purposes, the income earned would be taxable directly to the "partners." There would not be any country X corporate tax imposed.

Reverse hybrids are also commonly used as financing mechanisms to create "nowhere income"—income that is not currently subject to tax in any jurisdiction. Suppose that U.S. Co. owns all the stock of Foreign Opco, a country X corporation with a high rate of tax. U.S. Co. forms (by exchanging cash for stock) Foreign Reverse Hybrid, a country X corporation for U.S. tax purposes but a flow-through entity for country X Corp. tax purposes. Foreign Reverse Hybrid makes a loan to Foreign Opco. What happens when interest is accrued or paid by Foreign Opco? From the country X perspective, there is an interest deduction for Opco (which lowers its tax liability). The interest payment flows through Foreign Reverse Hybrid to the United States. If country X concludes that the applicable treaty provides for 0 percent withholding on interest paid by a country X resident to a U.S. recipient, then country X Corp. will not tax the interest received. At the same time, the U.S. may not tax the interest received. From the U.S. perspective, the interest is received by Foreign Reverse Hybrid which is a foreign corporation. While interest is potentially foreign personal holding company income, the "same country" exception in I.R.C. § 954(c)(3) provides an exception. The look-through rule of I.R.C. § 954(c)(6) also would prevent a subpart F inclusion and would permit the Reverse Hybrid to be set up outside of country X, if the statutory provision continues to be extended by Congress. To sum up, there is a deduction in country X and no tax on the inclusion for either U.S. or country X tax purposes.

Although considerable international tax planning arises as a result of the ability through check-the-box elections to create entity arbitrage, it is difficult for U.S. taxing authorities to get the toothpaste back in the tube. Rather than wholesale repeal of the ability to check-the-box, the U.S. taxing authorities have instead begun to pare back some of the advantages through targeted changes.

For example, suppose a U.S. individual taxpayer or less than 10 percent corporate shareholder checks the box on a foreign corporation in an attempt under the technical taxpayer rule to convert would otherwise be a noncreditable indirect income tax imposed on a foreign corporation into a creditable direct tax imposed on the shareholder. *See supra* § 8.03(F). Under the "anti-splitter" provision in I.R.C. § 909, now the tax imposed on the owner will not be creditable until the underlying income is taxable in the hands of the taxpayer (*i.e.,* when a distribution is made). Note that the changes do not undermine the check-the-box election itself but do impact the time of benefits achieved through the check-the-box election.

In other situations, U.S. domestic law and tax treaties attempt to harmonize U.S. tax treatment of an entity with foreign tax treatment. For example, suppose that a U.S. corporation pays interest to a U.K. reverse hybrid entity owned by Singapore shareholders. In determining whether the U.S.-U.K. tax treaty applies which would reduce the withholding tax from 30 percent under U.S. domestic law to 0 percent under the treaty, the U.S. will extend benefits only if the U.K. sees the interest payment as taxable in the hands of a U.K. resident (and resident meets the limitation on benefits requirements). Because that is not the case where the entity is a flow-through for U.K. purposes, no treaty benefits would be available under I.R.C. 894 and under Article 1(8) of the treaty itself.

Still, the ability to create hybrid and reverse hybrid entities remains as a mainstay in international tax planning.

(2) Dual Resident Corporations

A dual resident corporation is an entity that is considered to be a resident in two jurisdictions. For example, suppose that X Corp., a country X corporation owns all of the stock of DRC. DRC is managed and controlled in country X and is therefore a country X resident under the country X residence rules. However, DRC is incorporated in the United States and is a U.S. resident for U.S. tax purposes. DRC owns all of the stock of U.S. Co., a U.S. corporation. During the taxable year, suppose that X Corp. earns $100 and that U.S. Co. earns $100. DRC's only activity is the payment of $100 of interest on a bank loan. In the absence of special rules and assuming consolidated tax treatment both in country X and the United States, in country X DRC and X Corp. would file a consolidated return showing $0 net income. In the United States, DRC and U.S. Co. would file a return showing $0 net income. Yet, in the aggregate, these affiliated entities earn $100 of net income. The disconnect arises because the DRC deduction for interest paid to the bank is deducted twice (*i.e.,* a double dip)— once in country X and once in the United States.

The use of dual resident corporations is not limited to inbound transactions nor is it limited to true corporations. For example, suppose that U.S. Co. owns 100 percent of XDE, a country X entity that is disregarded for U.S. tax purposes but is treated as a corporation for country X tax purposes. Suppose further that XDE owns all the stock of X Corp. Assume that X Corp. and U.S. Co. each earns $100 and that XDE's only activity is $100 interest expense on a bank loan. Again, notwithstanding $100 of overall income, there may be no income for tax purposes in the United States and country X. In the United States in the absence of remedial legislation, XDE's interest expense flows through and can be used by U.S. Co. to offset its income. In country X, if XDE and X Corp. can consolidate, the interest expense would offset X Corp.'s interest income. Even though XDE is not a corporation for U.S. tax purposes, it can generate a dual consolidated loss.

A dual consolidated loss transaction capitalizes on inconsistent characterization by multiple tax jurisdictions to permit a double deduction for losses. The transaction usually involves a corporation (or hybrid entity) that has connections to both a foreign country and the United States and, because of inconsistent tax residence requirements, is a resident of both countries—a dual resident corporation (DRC). Typically, the DRC is also part of a consolidated group in both countries. When the DRC experiences a loss, it takes a current deduction for the amount of the loss, offsetting consolidated income in both countries. The loss suffered by the corporation may be an operating loss or it may arise as a result of a deduction for interest payments on funds used to finance other members of the consolidated groups. In any case, the DRC may, in the absence of remedial legislation or regulations, be able to make use of the same deduction in two jurisdictions because the dual resident corporation (or hybrid entity) is treated inconsistently by the two jurisdictions involved.

Congress has enacted a variety of "anti-abuse" provisions to put out perceived abuse fires as they arise. For example, the problem of dual consolidated losses is addressed in I.R.C. § 1503(d)—the dual consolidated loss provision. Section 1503(d) generally prohibits domestic corporations or disregarded entities or branches from using "dual consolidated losses" to offset the income of other members of the corporation's affiliated group. A "dual consolidated loss" is a net operating loss of a U.S. corporation that is also subject to residence-based taxation in a foreign country because the corporation is considered to be a resident. Such a corporation is a "dual resident corporation." Furthermore, loses incurred by branches of, or interests held by, the corporation may also be considered dual consolidated loses and therefore will not be available for use by the corporation to reduce its income for U.S. tax purposes. This will include interests in hybrid entities treated as corporations by the foreign country. In the examples *supra* in § 13.03(A)(2), DRC and XDE would each be a "dual resident corporation" and any net operating loss it incurs would be a "dual consolidated loss" (DCL) that may not (subject to an election discussed below) be used by U.S. Co. to offset the group's consolidated U.S. income tax.

The detailed operation of the DCL rules is explained in the regulations and is beyond the scope of this book. But some of the key concepts are discussed in general terms below.

First, what is a "dual resident corporation"? In general, a dual resident corporation (DRC) is an entity that is subject to residence based tax both in the United States and in a foreign country. A DRC can include a hybrid entity. For example, if U.S. Co. owns Foreign Hybrid which owns Foreign Opco, Foreign Hybrid can be a DRC because its income is included in the U.S. group and it is a corporation taxed as a resident in a foreign country.

Second, what constitutes a DCL? In general, the U.S. rules govern this determination. If there is a loss determined under U.S. tax principles incurred by a DRC, then there is a DCL regardless of whether the items that give rise to that loss are deductible under the tax laws of the foreign country. Conversely, even if a payment is deductible for foreign tax purposes, it will not give rise to a DCL if there is no deduction for U.S. tax purposes. Suppose that U.S. Co. owns 100 percent of a foreign disregarded entity (FDE) that owns 100 percent of the stock of Foreign Opco. Suppose U.S. Co. borrows from a bank and in turn FDE "borrows" from U.S. Co. If FDE accrues an interest deduction on the loan, the loan and the interest deduction are ignored for U.S. tax purposes. So if FDE's only activity is to generate a deduction, that deduction is not a DCL because there is no loss from a U.S. perspective (*i.e.,* the "interest payment" on a "loan" from U.S. Co. to FDE is disregarded for U.S. tax purposes). So while the DCL rules eliminate some types of double deductions, they do not eliminate all of them. In this case, U.S. Co. receives a deduction for interest paid to the bank and FDE has a deduction which may be usable to offset income of Foreign Opco but which is not includible in income by U.S. Co. However, there is a "booking rule" that allows the IRS to treat the bank loan as borrowed by the FDE, thereby creating a DCL where a principal purpose of the arrangement is to avoid booking the bank loan directly to the FDE.

Third, if there is DCL, what are tax consequences? Generally, a U.S. taxpayer with a DCL cannot use the loss generated by the DRC to offset income of another member of the U.S. group. That is, if U.S. Co. owns DRC which owns Foreign Opco, a loss incurred by DRC (*e.g.,* the only activity is an interest expense on a bank loan) cannot be used to offset income of U.S. Co. Note that the DCL rules do not prohibit DRC from using its own deductions to offset its own income. For example, if the $100 interest expense on a bank loan were used to offset $100 of DRC's own income, there would be no DCL. In this case, the $100 could be deducted in the United States and in the foreign jurisdiction. But that is because the $100 of income is also taken into account twice—once in the United States and once in the foreign jurisdiction. But if DRC generates no income, DRC cannot use the $100 deduction on a consolidated return to offset income of U.S. Co. where the deduction also is used to offset income in a foreign jurisdiction.

Fourth, under specified circumstances, DRC can make an election not to use the loss to offset income of another foreign taxpayer (a "domestic use election" or DUE under Reg. § 1.1503(d)–6(d)). If a domestic use election is made, the loss of the dual resident corporation then can be used to offset income of another member of the U.S. group. That election can only be made if the taxpayer can certify that under no circumstances that loss can be used to offset income of another foreign entity over a five-year period. In sum, a DCL can either be taken to offset income of another U.S. taxpayer or to offset income of another foreign taxpayer—but not both.

Fifth, if a domestic use election is made to use a DCL to offset income of another member of the U.S. group (upon the promise not to use the loss to offset income of another foreign taxpayer), then when the DRC is sold or moves outside the control of the taxpayer that made the election, the potential for that loss to be used by another foreign taxpayer arises. In this situation, one of two things happens depending on the nature of the disposition. If the IRS can be sure that that acquiring entity will not or cannot under applicable foreign law use the DCL to offset income of another person, then from a DCL perspective the transaction is insignificant. But if there is no way to ensure that the DCL won't ever be used to offset income of another person, then the U.S. group must give up the benefits it enjoyed (*i.e.,* the use of a deduction to offset income of another member of the U.S. group) by recapturing the losses deducted plus interest upon the disposition (basically interest on the taxes that would have been paid if the domestic loss had not been taken). There is an opportunity to mitigate the DCL recapture to the extent that the DRC itself earned income subsequent to the use of the DCL losses to offset income of another member of the U.S. group, or if the domestic use election resulted in the foreign losses merely becoming part of a U.S. net operating loss rather than actually offsetting income.

(3) Tax-Exempt Entities

Suppose an entity that is not taxable under U.S. law (*e.g.,* a tax-exempt pension fund or a foreign entity not subject to U.S. tax) has a tax attribute that has no value to the entity (because it is tax-exempt) but has value to other tax-paying entities. In this scenario, one can expect a market to exist that would allow the taxpaying entity to "purchase" the tax attribute in a way that benefits both the buyer and the seller at the expense of the U.S. government because the tax attribute has gone to the highest and best use.

For example, suppose that a tax-exempt entity owns $100 million worth of foreign stock on which a $20 million dollar dividend is about to be paid. The dividend is subject to a $3 million foreign withholding tax which is not creditable by the tax-exempt organization. So the tax-exempt entity sells the stock to U.S. Co. for $100 million. Assume that U.S. Co. has a large capital gain from some other transaction. U.S. Co. receives the dividend and then sells the stock back to the tax-exempt entity for $82 million.

The tax-exempt entity ends up with an $18 million profit (more than the $17 million net dividend it would have received). U.S. Co. reports a $20 million dividend and takes a $3 million foreign tax credit. With the credit, U.S. Co. has a $4 million net U.S. tax liability on the $20 million dividend (assuming a 35 percent U.S. tax rate). On the sale back to the tax-exempt entity, U.S. Co. takes an $18 million loss deduction which saves $6.3 million in U.S. taxes (assuming a 35 percent rate). In total, U.S. Co. receives a $17 million net dividend and suffers an $18 million real loss on the stock sale. But the $6.3 million tax saving on the loss deduction not only covers the $4 million net U.S. tax on the dividend (after the foreign tax credit) but also covers the $1 million economic loss and produces a $1.3 million profit for U.S. Co. This transaction appears to be a win-win situation for the tax-exempt entity and U.S. Co.

However, Congress enacted I.R.C. § 901(k) which denies a foreign tax credit to U.S. Co. if it has not held the stock for a specified number of days. Stated differently, I.R.C. 901(k) seeks to prevent taxpayers from buying tax benefits without undertaking the risk that comes with true ownership of property. A similar provision applies to payments other than dividends (*e.g.,* royalties). I.R.C. § 901(*l*). Treasury has acted on a variety of fronts to deter taxpayers from entering into transactions that are perceived to take undue advantage of arbitrage possibilities or are motivated by tax considerations.

For example, suppose that U.S. Co. purchases for $75 all rights to a copyright that is about to expire. The expected income from the copyright is a $100 royalty subject to a 30 percent country X withholding tax. Economically, U.S. Co. has paid $75 to receive $70 (*i.e.,* $100 royalty minus the $30 country X withholding tax). U.S. Co. might engage in this transaction because the $30 tax credit not only will offset any U.S. tax on the royalty income but will also save more than $5 of U.S. tax on other foreign source income U.S. Co. might have. For example, U.S. Co. might have $100 of gross income from the royalty and $40 of expenses associated with the royalty. On the $60 of net income, the United States would impose a tax of $21 (assuming a 35 percent rate) which will fully be offset by the $30 withholding tax on the royalty. In many cases, U.S. Co. will be able to use the $9 of withholding tax that did not offset U.S. tax on the royalty to offset potential U.S. tax on other foreign source income. Taking taxes into account, the $75 investment will produce more than $75 of cash flow (*i.e.,* the $70 net royalty and $9 of U.S. tax savings). But unless U.S.

Co. meets the holding period requirement of I.R.C.
§ 901(*l*) (more than 15 days), no foreign tax credit is
available.

(B) CHARACTER OF INCOME

While a hybrid entity is an organization that is
characterized as a corporation by one jurisdiction
and a transparent entity by another jurisdiction, a
hybrid instrument is an obligation that is classified
as equity by one jurisdiction and as debt by another
jurisdiction. For example, suppose that U.S. Co.
transfers cash to Forco in exchange for a financial
instrument. Under the terms of the instrument,
Forco is obligated to make an annual payment equal
to 6 percent of the amount it received. U.S. Co. is
obligated upon repayment of the instrument to use
the proceeds to purchase additional Forco stock (*i.e.,*
U.S. Co. has entered into a forward contract). For
foreign tax purposes, the instrument might be
classified as debt and each periodic payment as
interest which is deductible when accrued by an
accrual basis taxpayer in country X and can
therefore reduce the tax on Forco's income from
operations. Moreover, under an applicable treaty
country X may not impose a withholding tax on
interest payments actually paid to a U.S. resident.

For U.S. tax purposes, the "loan" coupled with a
forward contract to buy stock may be treated as an
equity investment so that periodic payments would
be dividends rather than interest and would only be
taxable when paid and not on accrual. AM 2006–
001. If the indirect tax credit under I.R.C. § 902

associated with the dividend is sufficient to offset the U.S. tax liability on the dividend, the overall result may be a deduction in country X and no additional tax on the recipient by either country X or the United States. *See e.g.,* FSA 200206010. In many cases, country X may allow X Corp. to accrue an interest deduction thereby generating a deduction while for U.S. tax purposes a dividend is not taxable unless and until it is actually paid. Reg. § 1.301–1(b).

To illustrate the use of a hybrid instrument in an inbound context, suppose that Forco, a country X taxpayer, owns all the stock of U.S. Co. which owns stock of USSub. Suppose that U.S. Co. "sells" the stock of USSub to Forco for cash with an obligation to repurchase in three years. When USSub pays a dividend, the cash ends up in the hands of Forco. What is the tax treatment?

From a country X tax perspective, Forco has purchased the stock of USSub and if dividends are exempt from country X taxation or if there is a tax credit for underlying taxes that USSub might have paid on its earnings, there may be no country X liability. For U.S. tax purposes, this sale with an obligation to repurchase—commonly referred to as a "repo" (as in—**repo**ssession of the underlying stock)—may be treated as a loan. That is, Forco loaned cash to U.S. Co. (*i.e.,* the so-called purchase price is treated as a loan) which is secured by the stock of USSub, when it comes time for repayment, U.S. Co. will repay the loan (*i.e.,* payment to

"repurchase" the stock) and receive back the stock of
USSub.

Viewed in this manner, when a dividend is paid
on the USSub stock, that dividend is received by
U.S. Co., the owner, rather than by Forco, which
holds the stock merely as a security interest. But
then how does the cash end up in Forco's hands?
U.S. Co. is deemed to pay interest equal in amount
to the dividend. The result would be a nontaxable
dividend between members of a U.S. consolidated
group followed by a deduction in the United States
for a deemed interest payment to Forco. Under
many U.S. treaties no withholding on the interest
payment to Forco.

Sometimes hybrid instruments can be used to
duplicate foreign tax credits. Assume that U.S. Co.
forms X Entity, a country X entity, by contributing
$100,000 and receiving in return a 100 percent
ownership interest. X Entity in turn approaches
Forco, a country X corporation, to set up a loan from
Forco to X Entity in the amount of $900,000 with an
8 percent interest rate. Forco and X Entity are
unrelated. X Entity subsequently purchases
$1,000,000 in preferred stock of Y Corp., an
unrelated country Y corporation. Y Corp. pays
dividends at an annual rate of 10 percent. Assume
that the dividends received from Y Corp. will be
subject to a withholding tax of 20 percent in country
Y.

Suppose that under the laws of country X the loan
from Forco to X Entity is treated as an equity
investment in X Entity, which country X treats as a

partnership. When the "partnership" pays the 20 percent tax to country Y (withheld by Y Corp. on paying the dividend), Forco will claim 90 percent of the $20,000 tax expense as its foreign tax credit in country X. However, under U.S. law the loan is respected and treated as debt. Furthermore, let us assume that under the check-the-box regulations, X Entity will be disregarded as a separate entity because U.S. Co. elected to have it treated as a single member entity. Because the loan is respected for U.S. tax purposes, U.S. Co. is regarded as the sole owner of X Entity for U.S. purposes and is therefore entitled to claim a foreign tax credit for the full amount of the withholding taxes paid to country Y. Because of the inconsistent treatment of this instrument by country X and the United States, Forco and U.S. Co. are able to duplicate the benefit of the foreign tax credit.

While the use of hybrid instruments remains a useful tax-planning technique, other character mismatches have been addressed by U.S. taxing authorities. For example, if a nonresident sells U.S. real estate at a gain, section 897 may allow the U.S. to tax the gain. But rather than buy the real estate directly and be subject to tax on an eventual sale, suppose instead that the nonresident enters into a notional principal contract ("NPC") with a U.S. counterparty which agrees to buy the property. Under the NPC the nonresident profits if the real estate appreciates (that is, to the extent the underlying United States real property appreciates in value) over certain levels. Conversely, the nonresident suffers a loss if the real estate depreciates (or fails to appreciate more than at a specified rate). Has the nonresident successfully converted the character of real estate gain into gain under the NPC that would not be subject to U.S. taxation under section 897? Presumably, the I.R.S. would treat the nonresident as the beneficial owner of the property and apply section 897. *See* Revenue Ruling 2008–31, 2008–1 C.B. 1180 (which reaches the opposite result where the benefit to the nonresident is based on an index of real estate, rather than one particular parcel of real estate).

(C) SOURCE OF INCOME

Suppose that U.S. Co. manufactures product in the United States and sells to both U.S. and Canadian purchasers. Suppose further that U.S. Co. has a $35 excess foreign tax credit (*i.e.,* foreign taxes that have not yet been used to offset potential U.S. tax on foreign source income). If U.S. Co. can shift $100 of U.S. source income to foreign source income, then the excess foreign tax credit could be used to save $35 of U.S. tax, assuming that all income generated in these transactions is in the same (*e.g.,* active) basket. The problem is that if U.S. Co. manages to shift $100 of U.S. source income to foreign source income, the foreign jurisdiction (*e.g.,* Canada) may tax the income. This would result in additional cash tax and would not limit the ability to use excess foreign tax credits.

But suppose that income could be treated as Canadian source income for U.S. tax purposes but Canada would not see the income as Canadian source income subject to tax in Canada? In that case, there may be no additional Canadian tax but $100 of additional foreign source income the U.S. tax on which could be offset by the excess foreign tax credit. To illustrate, suppose that U.S. Co. sells $200 of product to a Canadian purchaser with title passing in the United States. The income would all be U.S. source income. But if U.S. Co. passes title (and all the benefits and burdens of ownership) in Canada, then under I.R.C. § 863(b), 50 percent of the income is sourced in the United States where the manufacturing takes place and the other 50 percent of the income is sourced for U.S. purposes by where title passes. So $100 of income would be foreign source income but there may be no additional Canadian tax because Canada does not use mere title passage to determine whether income is taxable in Canada.

As is the case with income character, the source of income has the potential to be changed through the use of a derivative instrument. For example, a nonresident seeking returns from the U.S. equity markets could purchase stock in U.S. companies. Dividends paid on this stock generally would be considered U.S.-source and therefore would be subject to withholding tax at a 30-percent (or reduced treaty) rate. Instead of actually owning the stock, however, the non-U.S. investor could create synthetic ownership by entering into a "total return swap." Under a typical "total return swap," the investor would enter into an agreement with a counterparty under which returns to each party would be based on the returns generated by a notional investment in a specified dollar amount of stock. The investor would agree for a specified period to pay to the counterparty interest on the notional amount of stock and any depreciation in the value of the stock, and the counterparty would agree for the specified period to pay the investor any dividends paid on the stock and any appreciation in the value of the stock. Typically, amounts owed by each party under a total return swap typically are netted so that only one party makes an actual payment

This swap would be economically equivalent to a transaction in which the foreign investor actually purchased the stock from the counterparty, using funds borrowed from the counterparty, and at the end of the period sold the stock back to the counterparty and repaid the borrowing. Although the equity swap resembles a leveraged purchase of stock, the tax treatment of the foreign investor would be different. Because the source of income from an equity swap (in tax terms, a notional principal contract) is determined by reference to the residence of the recipient of the income, amounts representing dividends in this example would be foreign source and therefore would not be subject to U.S. withholding tax. Reg. § 1.863–7(b).

In response to this perceived type of source rule manipulation, I.R.C. § 871(m) now treats certain dividend equivalent payments as U.S. source payments.

(D) TAX BASE

(1) Timing Differences

Different countries may have different rules to determine for tax purposes when a deduction can be taken or when income must be reported. For example, suppose that U.S. Co. makes an investment in a Luxembourg company that is treated as equity for U.S. tax purposes but as debt for Lux tax purposes (this might be a Convertible Preferred Equity Certificate or CPEC). This type of hybrid instrument was discussed above as an example of an income characterization mismatch. That is, accruals on the instrument would be ignored for U.S. tax purposes (dividends are not taxable until received) but interest for Lux purposes. But this instrument also illustrates a timing mismatch that arises out of the characterization mismatch. For Lux purposes, an interest deduction can be accrued without actual payment. If payment were made, there would be a dividend inclusion for U.S. tax purposes. But with an accrued payment, there is a deduction in Luxembourg and no dividend inclusion until payment. Reg. § 1.301–1(b).

Suppose USCO wholly owns a foreign reverse hybrid (FRH) treated as a corporation for U.S. but a flow-through for foreign purposes. When FRH earns income, the local country imposes the tax on USCO, but for U.S. tax purposes the E&P is "split" from the taxes and resides at FRH. Historically, the resulting foreign tax credit was available to offset U.S. taxes on other foreign source income. This result is essentially a timing issue as the taxes have historically been available in the U.S. before the E&P was distributed to USCO by FRH.

On some occasions, the timing arbitrage is not based on different U.S. and foreign treatment but rather based on inconsistent treatment within the U.S. tax system. For example, suppose that Forco wholly-owns stock of USCO. When USCO earns gross income, some of the tax base may be eroded by accrued interest or other deductions resulting from payments to Forco. However, any U.S. withholding tax that might be imposed on the U.S. source FDAP income is normally only imposed upon payment rather than accrual. In the absence of a remedial provision, the result is tax base erosion in the U.S. without an offsetting collection of a withholding tax which may arise later upon actual payment of the interest or other payment.

The timing issues that result in a mismatch of foreign taxes paid and the underlying E&P were highlighted in Notice 2004–19, 2004–1 C.B. 606. That Notice, in part, refers to the Administration's revenue proposal calling for a broad grant of regulatory authority to address "inappropriate" separation of foreign taxes from related foreign income in cases "where foreign taxes are imposed on any person with respect to income of an entity." The Notice indicates that such regulations "may provide for the disallowance of a credit for all or a portion of the foreign taxes or for the allocation of the foreign taxes among the participants in the transaction in a manner that is more consistent with the underlying economics of the transaction."

Pursuant to Notice 2004–19, new regulations have been issued to address the use of partnerships to separate taxes paid from the underlying income. For example, suppose that U.S. Co. owns two controlled foreign corporations, CFC1 and CFC2. Those two entities form a partnership. Under the partnership agreement, 90 percent of the partnership income net of expenses other than foreign tax is allocated to CFC2 and 10 percent is allocated to CFC1. The tax expense is allocated 90 percent to CFC1 and 10 percent to CFC2. Assume that capital accounts will be adjusted to reflect this special allocation. If in year 1 the partnership earns $100 net of all expenses and foreign income tax of $40. CFC1 is allocated $10 of income and $36 of tax expense paid. If CFC1 now distributes a dividend of $10, U.S. Co. reports a dividend of $46 (*i.e.,* there is a deemed distribution of the $36 of taxes paid under I.R.C. §§ 902 and 78). If U.S. Co. has $54 of untaxed foreign source income from other sources that is potentially subject to a U.S. tax, the "super-charged" dividend ($10 actual dividend associated with $36 of foreign tax) will not only offset the potential U.S. tax on the dividend itself but also offset the potential U.S. tax on the other $54 of foreign source income (*i.e.,* $100 of total foreign source income and a $36 credit, leaving a $1 excess foreign tax credit).

Generally, new partnership regulations under I.R.C. § 704 will uphold a special allocation of tax expense (*i.e.,* tax expense allocated to one partner and underlying income to another partner) only if the partnership agreement allocates the foreign tax in proportion to the partners' distributive shares of income to which the creditable foreign tax relates.

More recently, the concerns underlying Notice 2004–19 led to the enactment of section 909—the "anti-splitter" legislation. *See* the discussion of section 909 *supra* in § 8.03(F). That provision essentially suspends the ability of a U.S. taxpayer to utilize foreign tax credit from specified splitter transactions until the underlying E&P is distributed to the U.S. For example, it would impact the reverse hybrid structure described above. It also impacts the timing of foreign tax utilization under certain foreign consolidation regimes.

For example, in Germany an *Organschaft* is the German equivalent of a consolidated group. Under German law, the parent company in the Organschaft is liable for the taxes on the earnings of the entire corporate group. Some taxpayers have taken the position that the foreign tax pool resides in the parent of the Organschaft while the underlying earnings reside in each member of the group that earned them. PLR 200225032. This splitting of taxes from earnings would allow U.S. taxpayers, to bring home the foreign taxes (*i.e.,* the German parent would make a small dividend distribution that would bring with it a large amount of foreign tax) which could be used to offset a potential U.S. tax on other foreign source income of the U.S. taxpayer.

In *Guardian Industries Corp. v. United States*, 2005 WL 741755 (Fed.Cl.2005), Guardian, through foreign subsidiaries, had large operations in Luxembourg. The subsidiaries filed consolidated returns in Luxembourg. The first-tier Luxembourg entity was a disregarded entity for U.S. tax purposes. The tax paid by the first-tier entity, therefore, was a creditable tax on the U.S. parent's return, while most of the income was earned by the foreign corporations in the Luxembourg consolidated group. Guardian was successful in court in showing that there was no joint and several liability for the Luxembourg tax among members of the Luxembourg consolidated group. That is, only the first-tier Luxembourg entity was liable for the tax. Thus, Guardian was entitled to claim the foreign tax credit on its U.S. return.

Section 909 and changes to the technical taxpayer rule in Reg. § 1.910–2(f)(4) now prevent taxpayers from utilizing foreign tax credits under these and similar consolidation regimes prior to picking up the underlying E&P. Essentially, in the case of foreign consolidation taxes are aligned with income. Regulations issued under I.R.C. § 909 have begun to address some of the difficult issues of determining when any suspended foreign tax credits are released (*i.e.,* how are foreign taxes matched with foreign E&P).

Suppose Forco wholly owns USCO and has capitalized USCO in part with a loan. If USCO can accrue an interest deduction, but FORCO is not subject to U.S. withholding tax until payment is made, this U.S. internal timing difference can result in a reduction of the U.S. tax base. Congress by enacting I.R.C. § 267(a)(3) essentially puts USCO on the cash basis method for purposes of the interest expense deduction to match up with the cash basis orientation of Reg. §§ 1.1441–1(a) (requiring "payment") and 1.1441–2(e) (defining "payment"). (Recall also that I.R.C. § 163(j) may also defer a deduction for any payment that is actually made. *See* § 4.04(A)(5).)

(2) Permanent Differences

Differences in the measurement of income by the United States and another country can also lead to tax arbitrage opportunities. For example, suppose USCO purchases all of the stock of Forco and makes an election under I.R.C. § 338(g). The effect of the election is for U.S. tax purposes to treat Forco as if immediately prior to USCO's purchase it had sold its assets to a new Forco—unrelated to old Forco. Often that deemed sale does not give rise to any U.S. taxation, but if the assets of Forco are appreciated, the effect of the election is to step up the basis of the assets for U.S. tax purposes. Often this basis-step up results in foreign goodwill with a stepped-up basis. The stepped-up basis in the goodwill or other assets can be amortized or depreciated for U.S. tax purposes (*e.g.*, goodwill can be amortized over a 15-year period under I.R.C. § 197). This § 338(g) election has no impact for local country tax purposes. The result can be an amortization or depreciation deduction for U.S. tax purposes that results in lower earnings and profits for U.S. purposes than for foreign tax purposes—a permanent difference in the amount of income.

To illustrate, suppose that following the § 338(g) election Forco earns $100 of net income for local country purposes on which $35 of foreign tax is paid. However, assume that because of the amortization of goodwill for U.S. tax purposes the net income is $50 (and the earnings and profits (net income minus taxes paid) is only $15). When Forco makes a distribution of all of its cash earnings ($65) to USCO, historically USCO would have reported a dividend of $15, plus a $35 gross-up under I.R.C. § 78, for a total inclusion of $50 (with the remaining distribution constituting a return of capital or capital gain pursuant to I.R.C. § 301(c)(2) or (3)). The $35 indirect tax credit under I.R.C. § 902 would not only have offset the potential U.S. tax of $17.50 on the $50 but would have been available to offset $17.50 of U.S. tax on $50 of other foreign source income in the same tax basket. Moreover, any distribution in excess of the $15 distribution (*e.g.*, the other $50 of cash available after foreign tax) may be received tax-free as a return of basis under I.R.C. § 301(c)(2). The result is that even though the local country taxes at the same rate as the United States, because of differences in the way that the local country and the United States determine the amount of income, there is a potential to save $17.50 of potential U.S. tax on USCO's other foreign source income.

The same outcome has historically been available where USCO wholly-owns the stock of a controlled

foreign corporation (CFC). CFC buys all of the
outstanding "stock" of Foreign Target Co., an entity
that is treated as a disregarded entity for U.S. tax
purposes but a corporation for local country tax
purposes. From a U.S. perspective, CFC has bought
assets which if appreciated now produce a high tax
basis for U.S. purposes. However, from a local
country tax perspective, CFC has bought stock with
no asset basis step-up.

These and other transactions that have the
impact of producing amortization or depreciation for
U.S. federal tax purposes but not for local country
purposes gave rise to the enactment of I.R.C.
§ 901(m)—the "covered acquisition transaction"
provision. *See* the discussion of I.R.C. § 901(m)
supra in § 8.03(G). The purpose of the provision is to
prevent the "hyping" of foreign tax credits. The term
"hyping" sometimes refers to the practice of
associating relatively high levels of foreign taxes
paid with low levels of U.S. E&P—often as a result
of amortization or depreciation for U.S. tax purposes
that is not available for local country tax purposes.
This essentially can be a permanent tax base
difference because that extra U.S. deduction
resulting from amortization or depreciation
deductions may never be available for foreign tax
purposes.

Essentially, I.R.C. § 901(m) disallows credits for
any foreign taxes paid that are associated with the
slice of income for foreign purposes that does not
exist for U.S. tax purposes because of the extra
deductions resulting from the basis step-up of a

section 338(g) election or the purchase of "stock" of a
hybrid entity. In the § 338(g) election example
above, under I.R.C. § 901(m) the disqualified portion
of potential federal tax credit equals the excess
basis for U.S. tax purposes (50) divided by the
foreign source income (100). So for U.S. federal tax
purposes the E&P remains $15 but the tax pool is
reduced to $17.50—rather than $35. Notice that
I.R.C. § 901(m) does not work perfectly as written
because the effective rate of the tax pool which was
70% prior to the change ($35 tax pool/($15 E&P +
$35 tax pool)) is still 54% ($17.50 tax pool/($15 E&P
+ $17.50 tax pool)). The failure to bring the effective
rate to 35% stems from the fact that the full $35 tax
liability (*i.e.,* even the disqualified portion) reduces
E&P. If E&P were reduced only by the allowed
portion of foreign taxes paid then the effective rate
of the pool would be 35% ($17.50 tax pool/($32.50
E&P + $17.50 tax pool)).

§ 13.04 ECONOMIC SUBSTANCE AND OTHER DOCTRINES

In recent years, tax authorities have had some
success convincing courts or have issued rulings
that transactions that may carefully navigate
detailed statutory or regulatory provisions should
nevertheless be recharacterized to reflect their
substance. *See e.g., CCA 201515020; Salem Fin. Inc.
v. United States,* 786 F.3d 932 (3d Cir. 2015)*; Bank
of N.Y. Melon Corp. v. Commissioner,* 140 T.C. 15
(2013)*; Klamath Strategic Inv. Fund v. United
States,* 568 F.3d 537 (5th Cir. 2009); *H.J. Heinz Co.
v. United States*, 76 Fed Cl 570 (2007); *Coltec*

Industries, Inc. v. United States, 454 F.3d 1340 (Fed. Cir. 2006); *Compaq Computer Corp. v. Commissioner*, 277 F.3d 778 (5th Cir. 2001).

The courts have used a variety of common law doctrines to invalidate the positions taken by taxpayers. Before considering those doctrines, note that each of these cases typically features the following: large-dollar transactions where either no or little economic analysis took place, non-existent or poor documentation of the economic benefit to be derived from the transaction, witnesses and/or documents that were harmful to the taxpayer's position.

The courts have relied on several overlapping doctrines to reject the taxpayer's position. Terms such as "sham transaction," "economic substance," "business purpose," "step transaction," "form over substance" pepper these opinions. The thrust of all of these opinions is that the taxpayer was unable to justify the reported tax results by showing objectively that there were economic factors, aside from tax factors, that made the transaction worthwhile or in the absence of objective economic substance, there was at least a subjective business purpose, even if misplaced.

Under the economic substance doctrine, the IRS requires the taxpayer to prove that the transaction has a pre-tax profit potential. In applying this test, the IRS has put taxpayers on notice that foreign tax should be treated as an expense rather than a creditable item. *See* Notice 2010–62, 2010–2 C.B. 411.

Every case that focuses on economic substance also examines whether the taxpayer has a "business purpose" in engaging in the transaction in question. The business purpose doctrine arises out of a domestic tax case *Helvering v. Gregory*, 69 F.2d 809 (2d Cir.1934), affirmed 293 U.S. 465 (1935), where the taxpayer carefully followed the divisive reorganization statute, but the transaction had no business purpose. The Court ruled for the government in disallowing the favorable tax treatment taxpayer had sought. Among the factors that would establish a positive business purpose are the following: the transaction originated in a nontax function of the taxpayer; even though the transaction originated in the tax function of the taxpayer, structure was adopted and supported by nontax function and management; the transaction addressed business concerns raised by a nontax function; the ultimate decision whether to undertake the transaction was based primarily on nontax factors; the transaction involved restructuring the exiting business or the formation of a genuine business; the transaction is expected to generate returns in excess of capital cost but also has a corresponding risk of loss. Negative business purpose factors would include: the transaction was planned and executed without regard to pre-tax economic consequences; internal memoranda prior to the transaction focused on tax benefits; the transaction was structured in a manner to preclude generating pre-tax profit; the plan was marketed to taxpayer by a promoter as a tax-driven instrument; the business purpose was the effect of tax savings on financial statements; taxpayer's investigation and due diligence with respect to the transaction was not business-like.

The "business purpose" test appears to have a low threshold. As the court in *Compaq* stated: "To treat a transaction as a sham, the court must find that the taxpayer was motivated by no business purposes other than obtaining tax benefits . . . and that the transaction has no economic substance." *See* generally *Wells Fargo & Co. v. United States*, 2014 WL 4070782 (D. Minn. 2014).

In general, the federal courts have incorporated the business purpose requirement into a broader "sham transaction" or "economic substance" doctrine. Under this doctrine, a transaction will be respected if: (1) the transaction has objective economic substance; and/or (2) the taxpayer has a subjective non-tax business purpose. Some courts apply a disjunctive test (*i.e.,* taxpayer must satisfy either economic substance or business purpose). *See e.g., IES Industries v. United States*, 253 F.3d 350 (8th Cir. 2001); *Rice's Toyota World v. Commissioner*, 752 F.2d 89 (4th Cir. 1985). Other courts apply a conjunctive test (*i.e.,* the taxpayer must show both economic substance and business purpose). *See e.g., United Parcel Service, Inc. v. Commissioner,* 254 F.3d 1014 (11th Cir. 2001). Still other courts seem to combine the two tests rather than applying a rigid two-part test. *See e.g., ACM Partnership v. Commissioner*, 157 F.3d 231 (3d Cir. 1998).

In *Coltec Industries Inc. v. United States*, 454 F.3d 1340 (Fed. Cir. 2006), Coltec had recognized a

1996 capital gain of $240.9 million but through one of its subsidiaries faced substantial asbestos-related litigation claims. As part of same plan, the Coltec consolidated group made transfers to a formerly dormant Coltec subsidiary, in exchange for stock, assumption of the asbestos liabilities and managerial responsibility of litigation claims. Coltec then sold its newly-acquired stock, and under the applicable basis rules of I.R.C. § 358, Coltec properly reported a capital loss which was used to offset its capital gain.

The court determined that the assumption of liabilities did not effect any real change in the flow of economic benefits, provide any real opportunity to make a profit, or appreciably affect Coltec's interest aside from creating a tax advantage; it served no purpose other than to artificially inflate stock basis. The decision identified five principles of economic substance:

- The law does not permit the taxpayer to reap tax benefits from a transaction that lacks economic reality,

- Taxpayer has the burden of proving economic substance,

- The economic substance of a transaction must be viewed objectively rather than subjectively,

- The transaction to be analyzed is not the overall transaction but rather the step that gave rise to the alleged tax benefit, and

- Arrangements with subsidiaries that do not
  affect the economic interest of independent
  third parties deserve particular close
  scrutiny.

The focus on the particular step that gave rise to the
tax benefit marked a shift in the longstanding
approach to viewing the transaction in its entirety.

In an effort to get to the substance of a
transaction, courts will often "step" together
purportedly independent transactions in order to
view the steps as a whole. The courts have generally
developed three methods of testing whether to
invoke the step transaction doctrine: (1) the end
result test; (2) the interdependence test; and (3) the
binding commitment test. The end result test is the
broadest of the three articulations. The end result
test examines whether it is apparent that each of a
series of steps are undertaken for the purpose of
achieving the ultimate result. The interdependence
test attempts to prove that each of the steps were so
interdependent that the completion of an individual
step would have been meaningless without the
completion of the remaining steps. The binding
commitment test is the narrowest of the three
articulations and looks to whether, at the time the
first step is entered into, there is a legally binding
commitment to complete the remaining steps.

As an example of the step-transaction doctrine in
the international tax context, consider *Del
Commercial Properties, Inc. v. Commissioner*, 251
F.3d 210 (D.C. Cir. 2001). In *Del Commercial*, the
court ruled that an interest payment from a U.S.

borrower to a purported Dutch lender which then paid interest to a Canadian lender was really a loan directly from the Canadian lender to the U.S. borrower which was subject to a 15 percent withholding rate under the U.S.-Canada treaty rather than 0 percent rate under the U.S.-Netherlands treaty. Under modern treaties (including the current treaty with the Netherlands), limitation-on-benefits provisions (*see supra* § 5.05(F)) might prevent unintended treaty benefits. The conduit financing regulations under Reg. § 1.881–3 have the same effect under U.S. domestic law (*see supra* § 4.04(A)(2)). Nevertheless, the judicially-created step-transaction doctrine remains a potent weapon to put together interdependent steps. *See e.g.*, CCA 201334037 (circular cash flow prevented taxpayer from deducting interest because of lack of payment under I.R.C. § 267(a)(3)); *Barnes Group v. Commissioner*, 593 Fed Appx. 7 (2d Cir. 2014) (taxpayer obtained the funds of its Singaporean subsidiary, by channeling the funds through a foreign financing subsidiary and a domestic financing subsidiary, both created solely to facilitate the transfer and avoid dividend treatment).

In 2010, Congress enacted new I.R.C. § 7701(*o*), codifying the common law "economic substance" doctrine ("ESD"). I.R.C. § 7701(*o*)(5)(C) provides that "[t]he determination of whether the economic substance doctrine is relevant to a transaction shall be made in the same manner as if this subsection had never been enacted." Congress also enacted I.R.C. § 6662(b)(6), a strict liability penalty set at

40% (reduced to 20% in the case of disclosure on the return) of any underpayment attributable to any disallowance of claimed tax benefits by reason of a transaction lacking economic substance.

Under I.R.C. § 7701(*o*), in the case of any transaction to which the economic substance doctrine is relevant, a transaction is treated as having economic substance only if:

- It changes in a meaningful way (apart from federal income tax effects) the taxpayer's economic position, and
- The taxpayer has a substantial purpose (apart from federal income tax effects) for entering into the transaction.

A taxpayer may rely on profit potential to satisfy both prongs of the conjunctive analysis required by the economic substance doctrine. There is no minimum return required to satisfy the profit potential test. Profit potential will be taken into account only if the present value of the reasonably expected pre-tax profit from the transaction is substantial in relation to the present value of the expected net tax benefits that would be allowed if the transaction were respected. The legislative history states that a taxpayer may rely on factors other than profit potential to demonstrate that a transaction results in a meaningful change in the taxpayer's economic position or that the taxpayer has a substantial non-federal-income-tax purpose.

Notice 2014–58, 2014–2 C.B. 746 (the "Notice") provides additional guidance regarding the

codification of the economic substance doctrine and
the related penalty amendments. With respect to
what "transaction" must meet the economic
substance doctrine, the Notice takes a broad view.
Facts and circumstances determine whether a plan's
steps are aggregated or disaggregated when
defining a transaction. Generally, when a plan that
generated a tax benefit involves a series of
interconnected steps with a common objective, the
"transaction" includes all of the steps taken
together—an aggregation approach. This means
that every step in the series will be considered when
analyzing whether the "transaction" as a whole
lacks economic substance. However, when a series of
steps includes a tax-motivated step that is not
necessary to achieve a non-tax objective, an
aggregation approach may not be appropriate. In
that case, the "transaction" may include only the
tax-motivated steps that are not necessary to
accomplish the non-tax goals—a disaggregation
approach.

The legislative history also makes clear that
I.R.C. § 7701(o) is not intended to alter the tax
treatment of certain basic business transactions
that, under longstanding judicial and
administrative practice are respected, merely
because the choice between meaningful economic
alternatives is largely or entirely based on
comparative tax advantages. It provides four non-
exclusive examples of such basic business
transactions:

- The choice between capitalizing a business enterprise with debt or equity;
- A U.S. person's choice between utilizing a foreign corporation or a domestic corporation to make a foreign investment;
- The choice to enter into a transaction or series of transactions that constitute a corporate organization or reorganization under subchapter C; and
- The choice to utilize a related-party entity in a transaction, provided that the arm's length standard of I.R.C. § 482 and other applicable concepts are satisfied.

§ 13.05 TAX GOVERNANCE AND TRANSPARENCY

(A) REPORTABLE TRANSACTIONS AND LISTED TRANSACTIONS

When previously lionized Enron Corporation imploded in 2001, the regulatory tsunami that resulted significantly impacted tax governance. For example, the Sarbanes-Oxley Act of 2002 (SOX) introduced chief executive officer (CEO) and chief financial officer (CFO) certification of financial statements to ensure that they do not contain any misstatements of material fact or omit any material facts that would make the statements misleading.

In 2002, the IRS addressed "listed transactions" and other "reportable transactions" by requesting tax accrual workpapers when it audited returns that claimed benefits from those transactions and from certain other reportable transactions. Under the tax shelter regulations (Reg. § 1.6011–4), a transaction is a reportable transaction and must be specially disclosed on a taxpayer's return if, subject to some specified exceptions, it falls within any one of the following six categories:

- Listed transactions;
- Confidential transactions;
- Transactions with contractual protections;
- Transactions generating tax losses exceeding certain stated amounts;
- Transactions resulting in a "significant" book-tax difference; and
- Transactions generating a tax credit if the underlying asset is held for less than 45 days.

A "listed transaction" is a transaction that is the same as or substantially similar to a transaction type that the IRS has determined to be a tax avoidance transaction and has, therefore, designated in published guidance (*e.g.,* Notice 2009–59, 2009–2 C.B. 170) as a listed transaction. Confidential transactions are those offered under conditions to a client of confidentiality for the benefit of "any person who makes or provides a statement, oral or written, (or for whose benefit a statement is made or provided) as to the potential tax consequences that may result from the transaction."

A transaction will be deemed to have contractual protections if the taxpayer has obtained or been provided with contractual protection against the possibility that part or all of the intended tax consequences will not be sustained. For example, a fee contingent on achieving certain tax consequences would constitute a contractual protection to a client.

A transaction is a "loss transaction" for this purpose if it results in, or is reasonably expected to result in, a specified level of loss under I.R.C. § 165 (*e.g.*, for corporations—$10 million in a single year/$20 million in a combination of years). The "significant book-tax difference" category applies only to taxpayers that are either: (1) reporting companies under the Securities Exchange Act of 1934 (and related business entities); or (2) business entities with gross assets greater than or equal to $100 million (including assets of related business entities). A book-tax difference for a transaction will be considered "significant" only if it is, or is reasonably expected to be, more than $10 million on a gross basis in any taxable year. A transaction falls within the less than 45 day holding requirement category if it results in, or is reasonably expected to result in, a tax credit in excess of $250,000 and the asset giving rise to the credit is held by the taxpayer for less than 45 days.

Every "organizer and seller" (including a material advisor receiving a specified fee) of a "potentially abusive tax shelter" is required to maintain a list under section 6112. For this purpose, a "potentially abusive tax shelter" is:

1. any transaction required to be registered as a tax shelter under section 6111; and

2. "any transaction that a potential material advisor knows or has reason to know, at the time the transaction is entered into or an interest is acquired, meets one of the categories of a reportable transaction"—*i.e.*, a transaction for which disclosure is required based on the above-mentioned six categories of transactions.

The lists must be furnished to the IRS when and if requested.

(B) UNCERTAIN TAX POSITIONS (UTP)

In 2006, the Financial Accounting Standards Board (FASB) issued FASB Interpretation No. 48, *Accounting for Uncertainty in Income Taxes—an interpretation of FASB Statement No. 109* (FIN 48 which is now codified as Topic 740 of the Accounting Standards Codification), which clarifies the accounting for uncertainty in tax positions. This Interpretation requires that a taxpayer in its financial statements, recognizes the impact of a tax position, if that position is more likely than not of being sustained on audit, based on the technical merits of the position.

However, taxpayers may have taken a position for tax purposes that it cannot "book" for financial purposes (*i.e.,* it creates a reserve for financial statement purposes). The difference between tax positions taken for financial statement purposes and for tax purposes—often referred to as "book-tax" differences—are reflected on Schedule M–3 of the corporate tax return (Form 1120) to provide the IRS with more efficient reporting and transparency between book and tax reporting.

The IRS issued a new Schedule UTP that requires certain large business taxpayers to report their uncertain tax positions (UTPs) on their annual tax returns. It is the view of the IRS that preparation of Schedule UTP should flow naturally from the preparation of financial statements, listing out U.S. income tax positions for which a reserve has been established in audited financial statements, or those for which a decision not to reserve was made because of an expectation to litigate. The Schedule UTP essentially provides a roadmap for IRS examiners to positions taken by the taxpayer for tax purposes for which their auditors cannot get to "more likely than not" that the position is correct for financial statement purposes. By having taxpayers highlight their own uncertain tax positions, IRS examiners do not have to divine these positions from the rest of the return and can adjust audit activity accordingly.

§ 13.06 BASE EROSION AND PROFIT SHIFTING (BEPS) INITIATIVE

The OECD published its Action Plan on Base Erosion and Profit Shifting ("BEPS") in 2013. It was motivated in part by a concern that national tax laws have not kept pace with the globalization of corporations and the digital economy, leaving gaps that can be exploited by multi-national corporations to artificially reduce their taxes. One key point underlying the OECD's BEPS initiative is that until national tax laws and treaties are amended to reflect what comes out of the initiative, BEPS has no legal significance. However, it should be noted that several nations—including Australia, the United Kingdom, France and Mexico—have already enacted domestic legislation that is consistent with some of proposed BEPS initiatives.

What follows is a brief overview of the various BEPS initiatives and what kinds of transaction are in the OECD's sights.

Action 1— Digital Economy	• Virtual PE • The attribution of value from the generation of marketable location-relevant data • Characterisation of income and source rules
Action 2— Hybrid Mismatches	• Hybrid entities • Hybrid instruments that result in deductions without inclusions in income
Action 3— CFC Rules	• Creating affiliated non-resident taxpayers and routing income of a resident enterprise through the non-resident affiliate

Action 4— Base Erosion via Interest Deductions	• Design rules to prevent base erosion through the use of related and non-related party debt to achieve excessive deductions or generate exempt income
Action 5— Harmful Tax Practices	• The OECD will revamp the work on harmful tax practices with a priority on improving transparency, including compulsory exchange on rulings related to preferential regimes and on requiring substantial activity for any preferential regime
Action 6— Treaty Abuse	• Clarify that treaties are not intended to create double non-taxation • Identify tax policy issues that countries should consider before entering into a tax treaty
Action 7— Permanent Establishment	• Broaden the definition of PE to include commissionaire relationships and limit specific exemptions such as the exemption for preparatory and auxiliary activities
Actions 8, 9 and 10— Transfer Pricing	• Develop rules with respect to IP • Develop rules that to not inure benefits solely to contractually assumed risks or provided capital. • Restrict benefits of transactions that would not occur between third parties

Action 11— Collect and Analyze Data on BEPS	• Identify whether BEPS is occurring and if so, to what extent is it occurring
Action 12— Disclosure of "Aggressive" Tax Planning	• Design mandatory disclosure rules for aggressive or abusive transactions, arrangements or structures. • Create models for sharing of tax schemes between authorities
Action 13— Transfer Pricing Documentation	• Design rules that require multinational entities to provide all relevant governments with information on their global allocation of income, economic activity and taxes paid among countries
Action 14— Dispute Resolution	• Develop solutions that enable countries to solve treaty related disputes under Mutual Agreement Procedures • Include arbitration provisions in treaties
Action 15— Develop a Multilateral Instrument	• Analyze tax and international law issues related to the development of a multilateral instrument to enable jurisdiction to implement the measures developed in the course of the work on BEPS and amend tax treaties • Interested parties will then develop the instrument

All of these actions are aimed at making sure there is no double non-taxation—where in a transaction between taxpayers in two countries neither country taxes the transaction or the transaction is essentially untaxed. So if a disregarded entity were to make an interest payment to its U.S. owner—USCo, under potential BEPS implementation the country where the DRE is located might deny a deduction with respect to accrued interest and/or deny treaty benefits upon payment. As another illustration, BEPS once implemented might allow greater local country taxation where a principal operating company, operating in a low-tax jurisdiction, operates globally in local countries through local affiliates with limited functions (*e.g.*, through a limited-risk distributor, or through an R & D or logistic center). The anticipated end-game for BEPS would be action along several fronts, including:

- Recommendations for national legislation
- Amendments to the OECD's Model Tax Convention and Commentary
- Amendments to the OECD's *Transfer Pricing Guidelines*
- Development of a Multilateral tax treaty

In October of 2015 the Organization for Economic Cooperation and Development (OECD) released the 2015 Final Reports on the G20/OECD Base Erosion and Profit Shifting (BEPS) project. The 2015 Final Reports recommend changes to domestic laws, the OECD Model Tax Convention (the "OECD Model"), and the OECD Transfer Pricing Guidelines (TPG). In addition, they propose to accelerate the incorporation of recommended treaty changes into existing bilateral treaties through a multilateral convention to be entered into by interested countries.

The practical difficulties of achieving consensus among the countries that participated in the BEPS project are reflected in the fact that almost every recommendation generally reflects only one of three possible levels of endorsement; they are indicated by, in descending order, the terms "minimum standards," "common approaches," and "best practices." (One of the 2015 Final Reports (Action 7, regarding changes to the OECD Model definition of a permanent establishment ("PE")) lacks even one of these levels of consensus.) "Minimum standards" reflect commitments to consistent implementation of standards laid out in final reports, and agreements to be subject to monitoring by the OECD during and after implementation. "Common approaches" reflect agreement as to "general tax policy direction," with the aspiration that they will become "minimum standards" over time. "Best practices" are offered where the negotiators failed to reach a consensus that countries must adopt legislation on the particular topic in question.

So whether, how and when BEPS will be implemented by the participating countries remains uncertain. The European Council may intend to implement these minimum standards and best practices across all of the EU's 28 member states in conjunction with the implementation plan outlined in the 2015 Final Reports. The U.S. Congress has not been directly involved in the BEPS project, and to this point has shown little interest in implementing it. However, the 2015 Final Reports, and subsequent actions by other nations, may motivate Congressional action of some sort on international tax issues in the future.

While BEPS is not currently implemented globally, it nevertheless casts a pall over all international tax planning. Taxpayers are not eager to build structures on the railroad tracks when they think they hear the train a-coming.

CHAPTER 14

INTERNATIONAL BOYCOTT AND FOREIGN BRIBERY PROVISIONS

§ 14.01 OVERVIEW OF INTERNATIONAL BOYCOTT PROVISIONS

Since 1976, I.R.C. § 999 has penalized U.S. taxpayers for participation in certain international boycotts. While the provisions are broadly written, they were enacted in response to the Arab boycott of Israel. Where the boycott provisions are applicable to a specific operation, a U.S. taxpayer is not entitled to any otherwise applicable foreign tax credit for foreign income taxes imposed on income from the operation. In addition, if the participating entity is a controlled foreign corporation, income earned from the operation is taxed directly to the U.S. shareholders even if the subpart F provisions would not otherwise apply.

The operation of I.R.C. § 999 is set forth in Guidelines published by the IRS in question and answer form. They were first issued in 1976 and have been revised several times since then, although the last major revision was in 1978. 1978–1 C.B. 521. The citations that follow refer to questions in the Guidelines.

Not all boycotts trigger the tax penalties of I.R.C. § 999. Boycotts sanctioned by U.S. law or an Executive Order—such as the sanctions against

Iran—are not penalized. I.R.C. § 999(b)(4)(A). Furthermore, not all or even most unsanctioned boycotts are subject to I.R.C. § 999. Restrictions on the import or export of goods from a specific country—a primary boycott—are not addressed by I.R.C. § 999. I.R.C. § 999(b)(4). The principle of national sovereignty permits any country the right to decide who its trading partners will be. So for example, the fact that Syria does not permit Israeli products to be imported or that Kuwait requires that its exported oil not be resold to Israel does not trigger I.R.C. § 999 for a U.S. seller or buyer. Or a U.S. bank's conditioning the payment of a letter of credit on providing a certificate that the goods did not come from a boycotted nation is not boycott cooperation. Guidelines H–31. However, capital is treated differently from goods and services so that an agreement not to use capital originating in a boycotted nation in the production of goods is boycott cooperation. Guidelines I–6.

It is secondary and tertiary boycotts that are addressed by I.R.C. § 999. A secondary boycott is where a country refuses to deal with a company because that company (or a related corporation) deals with a boycotted nation in other transactions even though no products of the boycotted nation are involved in the transaction at hand. A tertiary boycott is where a country refuses to deal with a U.S. company that does no business with the boycotted country but which has dealings with other companies that deal with the boycotted country.

Specifically, I.R.C. § 999(b)(3) provides that a taxpayer cooperates with an international boycott if the taxpayer agrees to refrain from: (a) doing business with a boycotted nation; (b) doing business with anyone who does business with a boycotted nation; (c) doing business with any company whose management consists of people of a particular nationality, race, or religion; (d) hiring people of a particular nationality, race, or religion; (e) shipping or insuring products bound for the boycotting nation if the shipper or insurer does not cooperate with the boycott. I.R.C. § 999(b)(3).

Even if a taxpayer does not participate in an international boycott, the taxpayer may have a reporting obligation under I.R.C. § 999(a). There is a duty to report to the IRS any request for participation in an international boycott if a taxpayer or any related person had "operations" related to a boycotting country, its companies, or nationals. A request to participate in a primary boycott need not be reported. The Secretary of the Treasury maintains a list of boycotting countries. As of July 1, 2015, the list includes: Iraq, Kuwait, Lebanon, Libya, Qatar, Saudi Arabia, Syria, United Arab Emirates, and Yemen.

§ 14.02   BOYCOTT PARTICIPATION

In order for there to be participation in a boycott, a taxpayer must "agree" to certain prescribed conduct as a condition of doing business with a boycotting country. I.R.C. § 999(b)(3). An agreement not connected with business in a boycotting country is not addressed by I.R.C. § 999. For example, if a company doing business in Greece agrees with a vessel charterer to avoid Israeli ports, there is no boycott participation because the agreement was not made as a condition of doing business in an Arab country. Guidelines H–27.

If a taxpayer is doing business with an Arab country, an agreement (either oral or written) can be specific or can be inferred from a general course of conduct. If there is no agreement but a company in fact complies with the Arab boycott by refusing to hire Jewish workers, such actual compliance is not by itself an agreement. However, such compliance when combined with other factors might present a course of conduct that constitutes an agreement. The other factors might include the termination or lessening of business relationships with blacklisted firms in the absence of compelling non-boycott reasons or the refusal to enter into such relationships when there are compelling reasons to do so. Guidelines H–3. Conversely, if the company enters into an agreement to boycott which the company regularly ignores, tax penalties nevertheless apply. Guidelines H–18.

Perhaps the most transparent distinction in the Guidelines is the difference between "apply" and "comply." A contract term providing that an Arab country's boycott laws "apply" does not make the contract an agreement to boycott, but a term that says a company will "comply" with the same laws does. Guidelines H–3 and H–4. It is true that an "apply" provision can be one factor in an overall course of conduct from which an agreement to boycott may be inferred although repeated use of the "apply" provision does not give rise to the inference.

§ 14.03 EXAMPLES OF PENALIZED CONDUCT

(A) DISCRIMINATORY REFUSALS TO DO BUSINESS

As indicated above, a taxpayer is penalized if there is an agreement to refrain from doing business: (a) with a boycotted country (or in a boycotted country), its nationals, or companies; (b) with a U.S. company doing business with a boycotted country (or in a boycotted country), its nationals, or companies; (c) with companies whose ownership is comprised of individuals of a specified nationality, race, or religion.

With respect to the first category (*i.e.,* secondary boycotts), an agreement to refrain from doing some types of business in a boycotted country but not others is cooperation with the boycott. Guidelines H–21. An agreement not to supply a boycotting country with goods produced or manufactured with capital originating in a boycotted country is also prohibited conduct. Guidelines I–6.

The tertiary boycotts that trigger I.R.C. § 999 are refusals to do business with U.S. persons that conduct business with a boycotted nation. Consequently, a refusal to do business with a foreign company because it conducts business with a boycotted country is not penalized. Guidelines J–2B and J–11. However, an agreement not to deal with blacklisted companies constitutes boycott cooperation if no U.S. companies are presently on the list because they could be added to the list in the future. Guidelines J–4. An agreement to subcontract only with named subcontractors gives rise to a boycott inference unless the excluded companies were specified for reasons having nothing to do with the boycott. Guidelines H–3. Similarly, an agreement by a U.S. company to purchase goods from a specific supplier named by the boycotting country is boycott cooperation if the U.S. company must certify that the supplier is not on the blacklist. Guidelines H–1B. On the other hand, a U.S. company's conditioning the hiring of subcontractors on a delivered-in-country basis when the laws of the boycotting country blacklist certain companies from importing into that country does not constitute cooperation because the inability of the blacklisted companies to meet the company's conditions is due to the boycotting country's laws not the company's conditions. Guidelines J–7.

The third refusal-to-do-business category applies if in order to do business in a boycotting country, the ownership or management of a company cannot consist of individuals of a specified nationality, race or religion. For example, compliance with a country's request that the leader of an underwriting syndicate exclude from the syndicate a particular company because of the religion of its directors would trigger I.R.C. § 999. Guidelines K–3. Similarly, a condition that an exporter obtain goods from a supplier designated by a boycotting country and certified not to be on the blacklist by the exporter is boycott cooperation if the exporter should know that it cannot obtain the certificate because of the nationality, race, or religion of the supplier's ownership or management. Guidelines H–1B. On the other hand, an agreement by an exporter of goods that the goods will not bear any mark symbolizing a particular religion or a particular boycotted country does not constitute boycott cooperation. Guidelines K–1.

(B) DISCRIMINATORY HIRING PRACTICES

The manner in which a restriction is drafted often determines if a provision amounts to boycott participation or not. For example, a contract provision precluding employment within the boycotting country or abroad of individuals who are members of a particular religion or nationals of a boycotted nation is boycott cooperation. Guidelines L–1 and L–5. On the other hand, if the U.S. company conditions employment upon an individual's obtaining a visa from a boycotting country which is categorically unavailable, there is no boycott cooperation. Guidelines H–10 through 12. Similarly, an agreement to employ only nationals of the United States or of the boycotting nation is not boycott cooperation because it excludes nationals of friendly and unfriendly nations in an even-handed manner. Guidelines L–2.

(C) DISCRIMINATORY SHIPPING AND INSURANCE ARRANGEMENTS

An agreement not to use a blacklisted shipper or insurer is boycott cooperation. Guidelines M–1 and M–7. But if a sale is made on f.a.s. terms making the boycotting country purchaser responsible for shipping and insurance, there is no boycott cooperation even if the U.S. seller knows that the purchaser will arrange shipping or insurance with carriers or insurers that participate in the boycott and even if the shipping terms were changed from c.i.f. to f.a.s. so that the seller could avoid the selection. Guidelines M–2 and M–3. Furthermore, to protect goods from damage or loss, a seller is permitted to agree not to ship goods to or from a boycotting country on a ship registered in a boycotted country or owned or operated by nationals or companies from such country or on a ship that during the voyage calls at the boycotted country enroute to or from the boycotting country. Guidelines M–5.

§ 14.04 TAX EFFECT OF BOYCOTT PARTICIPATION

Once it has been determined that a U.S. person has cooperated with an international boycott, a presumption arises that all operations in the boycotting country involve cooperation with the boycott. In ascertaining what activities are affected, the term "operations" takes on great importance. I.R.C. § 999(b)(1). The term "operations" has been interpreted to include all forms of business activities including purchasing, leasing, licensing, banking, extracting, manufacturing, transporting, and services of any kind. Guidelines B–1. Because the presumption relates to operations "in" a boycotting country, operations outside the boycotting country even with the boycotting country itself (or nationals or companies thereof) are not presumed to involve cooperation with the boycott, although cooperation can be found from the presence of independent factors. Guidelines D–1.

Not only is there a presumption that if boycott cooperation is found, all activities in the boycotting country are tainted, but I.R.C. § 999(b)(1) also presumes that the operations of all related persons involve boycott cooperation. Generally, related corporations are those with more than a 50 percent common ownership link, including brother-sister corporations controlled by a common parent as well as parent-subsidiary corporations. I.R.C. § 993(a)(3). The application of the related persons rules is more complicated than indicated but the thrust of the rules is to prevent U.S. taxpayers from isolating the boycott cooperation activities in one corporation without contaminating other business activities carried on through other related corporations with the boycotting nation.

The presumptions that contaminate all dealings with the boycotting country by a boycott-cooperating U.S. person and its related parties can be overcome by showing that some of the operations in the boycotting countries are clearly separate and identifiable from the boycott operations in which the taxpayer cooperated. I.R.C. § 999(b)(2). Among the factors which may be considered in determining whether an operation is clearly separable and identifiable from the tainted operation are the presence of: (a) different entities; (b) operations supervised by different management personnel; (c) distinctly different products or services; (d) separate and distinct contracts; (e) separate negotiation and performance if the operations are not continuous over time. Guidelines D–3.

Once the extent of the boycott cooperation has been determined, there are two alternative methods for computing the loss of tax benefits: the international boycott factor method or ascertaining the taxes and income specifically attributable to the tainted income. Method election is annual.

The "international boycott factor" is defined as a fraction, the numerator of which reflects the foreign operations of a person (and related persons) in or related to the boycotting country with which that person (or related persons) cooperates during the taxable year. The denominator represents the entire foreign operations of the person (or related persons). I.R.C. § 999(c). More specifically, the numerator is the sum of: (a) purchases made from all boycotting countries associated in carrying out a particular international boycott; (b) sales made to or from all boycotting countries associated in carrying out a particular international boycott, and; (c) payroll paid or accrued for services performed in all boycotting countries associated in carrying out a particular international boycott. Reg. § 7.999–1(c)(2).

Recall that the presumption of cooperation extended to all operations *in* a boycotting country while the international boycott factor formula is more sweeping. Consequently, the I.R.C. § 999(b)(1) presumption is more important using the method that determines specifically attributable taxes and income.

When the international boycott factor has been determined, it is used in computing tax penalties. Under I.R.C. § 908, the foreign tax credit that would otherwise be allowed under I.R.C. § 901 is reduced by the product of that amount and the international boycott factor. For example, suppose the numerator of the international boycott factor fraction (*i.e.*, purchases, sales, and payroll in the boycotting country) is $200,000 and the denominator (*i.e.*, total foreign purchases, sales, and payroll) is $1 million. Assume further that X Corp. would normally have a foreign tax credit computed under I.R.C. § 901 of $30,000. Under I.R.C. § 908, the foreign tax credit is reduced by $6,000 ($200,000/$1 million × $30,000) to $24,000. Oddly, foreign taxes which are not creditable because of I.R.C. § 908 may be deductible under I.R.C. § 164 or as a business expense under I.R.C. § 162. I.R.C. § 908(b).

To the extent that a controlled foreign corporation cooperates in an international boycott, income which would not otherwise be treated as subpart F income (*e.g.*, income from active business operations such as construction) is treated as subpart F income. I.R.C. § 952(a)(3). As a result, the income from the boycotting country will be treated as if it were distributed to the U.S. shareholders as a dividend. The amount of the constructive dividend is equal to the product of the international boycott factor and the income of the controlled foreign corporation which would not otherwise be treated as a constructive distribution.

Under some circumstances, the application of the international boycott factor method results in a loss of substantial tax benefits even when most of the benefits are not related to boycott operation. This arises because the international boycott factor is multiplied by, in the case of the foreign tax credit, the worldwide foreign tax credit of the taxpayer, and in the case of a controlled foreign corporation, the worldwide income which would otherwise be deferred.

To avoid this broad reach, a taxpayer can elect to determine the boycott penalty by identifying the specific taxes or income attributable to the boycott operations. Under this method, a taxpayer loses the tax benefits specifically attributable to operations tainted by cooperation with the boycott. This "specifically attributable" method is particularly attractive where the boycott-related operations produce little income and insignificant foreign taxes but would produce a large international boycott factor because of heavy purchases, sales, or payroll activities.

§ 14.05   FOREIGN BRIBERY PROVISIONS

Deterring cooperation with an international boycott is not the only ethical engineering in which the Code engages. The Code also discourages the payment of certain bribes and kickbacks to a foreign government in a number of ways. First, such payments are not deductible under I.R.C. § 162(c)(1) to the extent the payments violate the Foreign Corrupt Practices Act of 1977. Second, earnings attributable to bribes and kickbacks paid by a controlled foreign corporation are treated as subpart F income which is directly taxed to U.S. shareholders. Furthermore, the payments do not decrease the earnings and profits of the controlled foreign corporation. I.R.C. §§ 952(a)(4) and 964(a).

These restrictions apply only to certain types of bribes and kickbacks. On one hand, a free market philosophy suggests that the United States should be indifferent to bribes paid to foreign government officials. After all, such payments are business expenses paid for business reasons. Indeed, the line between a bribe and a commission can be quite fuzzy. Moreover, because other companies from other nations may have less compunction about paying bribes or kickbacks, U.S. companies need to make such payments to compete in a global economy. On the other hand, there is a notion that the U.S. government should not subsidize corrupt conduct by providing tax benefits to offending companies even if payments are made abroad. The payment of a bribe or kickback is corrupt under U.S. standards even if the recipients are not offended by the payments and such payments are standard operating procedure elsewhere.

The uneasy compromise arising out of these conflicting goals perhaps lacks a theoretical basis. The Foreign Corrupt Practices Act makes it illegal to make payments to foreign government officials with the intent of influencing official action to obtain business. However, payments to foreign government employees to expedite ministerial action in the course of business—"grease payments" or more euphemistically "facilitating payments"— are not prohibited. Facilitating payments might include: payments for expediting shipments through customs, securing adequate police protection, obtaining required permits, or payment to keep an oil rig from being destroyed.

One could be cynical and view the distinction between illegal bribes and kickbacks and grease payments as a U.S. attempt to benefit low-level foreign government officials rather than high-level officials that decide with whom to do business. One would suspect that profit-maximizing high-level foreign officials use low level officials as conduits to funnel grease payments to the high level officials. It seems doubtful that the Foreign Corrupt Practices Act has been much of a deterrent in eliminating the payments of bribes and kickbacks. Indeed, over the years, Congress has weakened the Foreign Corrupt Practices Act by: lessening criminal penalties; creating a good faith defense for reasonable expenses incurred for product promotion or to ensure contract performance; clarifying that payments which are legal in the recipient's country do not violate U.S. law, and; clarifying that payments made to expedite ministerial government actions (grease payments) are not violations.

INDEX

References are to Pages

DETERMINATION DATE

DEVELOPING COUNTRIES

FOREIGN BASE COMPANY RULES

FOREIGN BRANCHES

FOREIGN CORRUPT PRACTICES ACT

FOREIGN CURRENCY